CU00646165

Burglars and Bobbies

Burglars and Bobbies:
Crime and Policing in Victorian London

By

Gregory J. Durston

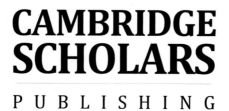

CAMBRIDGE
SCHOLARS
PUBLISHING

Burglars and Bobbies:
Crime and Policing in Victorian London,
by Gregory J. Durston

This book first published 2012

Cambridge Scholars Publishing

12 Back Chapman Street, Newcastle upon Tyne, NE6 2XX, UK

British Library Cataloguing in Publication Data
A catalogue record for this book is available from the British Library

Copyright © 2012 by Gregory J. Durston

All rights for this book reserved. No part of this book may be reproduced, stored in a retrieval system,
or transmitted, in any form or by any means, electronic, mechanical, photocopying, recording or
otherwise, without the prior permission of the copyright owner.

ISBN (10): 1-4438-4006-8, ISBN (13): 978-1-4438-4006-4

CONTENTS

ACKNOWLEDGEMENTS

I would like to acknowledge the invaluable assistance provided by the staff of the British Library, the British Newspaper Library, the Bancroft Library in Tower Hamlets, and the libraries of Kingston University, the L.S.E., New Scotland Yard and Lincoln's Inn. Additionally, I am grateful to the National Archives in Kew, the old Metropolitan Police History Museum and the current Metropolitan Police Historical Collection for their assistance. My interest in this subject stems from aspects of a Ph.D thesis written in the 1990s, and I thank my supervisors of that time, Professors Paul Rock and Robert Reiner, for their encouragement. I am also very grateful for the helpful comments of Clive Emsley and Judge Nicholas Philpot on the manuscript.

Gregory J. Durston

London, 24th December 2011

PREFACE

In the early 1800s, many 'respectable' Londoners were frightened of crime and prone to demonizing their city's criminals, often attributing sophistication and organisation to their activities. In reality, 'conventional' Metropolitan crime was largely the product of acute social disorganisation, much of it committed by a marginalised stratum of the working class. Change in policing in the years after 1829 was oriented towards dealing with the unsophisticated, opportunistic, offences that emanated from this section of society and, at the same time, promoting new standards of public decorum. The 'new' police of this period appear to have made an important, if sometimes exaggerated, contribution to the major reduction in conventional crime and improvement in public order that occurred in the capital during the second half of the nineteenth century.

However, too much significance has been placed on a simple police presence on the streets. The Metropolitan force was effective largely because it promoted social discipline, and so indirectly discouraged offending, in a manner that accords with the modern 'broken windows' theory of crime control. It was much less successful in *directly* combating conventional crime. As this became increasingly apparent, many came to believe that the institutional result achieved in 1829, and characterised by the triumph of the Peelite school of preventative policing, was inherently flawed. This prompted a major reassessment of the value of detective work.

Victorian policing in the Metropolis also had a darker side. The imposition of new standards of public order impinged on many traditional aspects of urban working-class life, often exciting bitter antipathy amongst the policed. It threatened long accepted civil liberties, several of which became increasingly attenuated during the period, and sometimes impinged on rights to 'due process'. Urban policing that was focused on dealing with incivilities was also a breeding ground for police corruption, perjury, and brutality, though this was limited by the relatively strict disciplinary regime that characterized the nineteenth-century Metropolitan force. This was, in part, the price paid for the radically improved personal and public security of the late Victorian period.

CHAPTER ONE

INTRODUCTION

The nineteenth century opened amid an apparent, though certainly not novel, 'law and order' crisis in the Metropolitan area, with burgeoning recorded crime rates eliciting widespread anxiety.[1] This concern lasted until the late 1850s. It then declined steadily if unevenly until, by the end of the century, crime *generally*, rather than some of its more eye-catching manifestations, had ceased to be viewed as a major Metropolitan problem. Recorded crime-rates were falling and optimism about offending levels, ending almost 200 years of public pessimism, was common, especially amongst well-informed and educated people.

Unlike their predecessors, nineteenth-century Londoners had an unprecedented faith in 'progress' and the potential for government intervention, based on rational study, to improve their personal security, and this grew steadily stronger as the era advanced. They would have been shocked by their forebears' relative indifference to the capital's crime problems, and strongly believed that the State could act as both 'moral tutor' and controller of their city's criminal elements.[2] Even the Reverend Francis Close, writing on the threat posed by the 'dangerous classes', thought that their crimes were: "...more or less remediable by public measures".[3] Forty years later, the early criminologist, Havelock Ellis, observed that the crime problem, far from being hopeless, was largely a social fact, and so "most under our control".[4] As a result of this confidence, the era witnessed major innovations and reform in all areas of criminal law enforcement. One of the most important of these was the advent of the 'new' Metropolitan Police Force in 1829.

Because the peak of the apparent law and order crisis of the early nineteenth century (roughly) coincided with the emergence of this body, it was inevitable that the former's remarkable decline and the latter's

---

1. On much earlier crises see, Shoemaker, Robert, 1991, at p.15.
2. Gatrell, V.A.C., 1990, at p.48.
3. Close, Francis, 1850, at pp.4-5.
4. Ellis, Havelock, 1890, at p.297.

development should be linked, both then and now. Even modern academics of a radical stamp have claimed that the fall in crime between 1860 and 1914 reflected a "transient-advantage" that the new police had over criminals, and a rare triumph for the 'policeman-state'.[5] One of the aims of this book is to assess the validity of such a connection, in a London context. However, it also aims to chart the development of nineteenth-century urban policing and the complicated and sometimes competing mixture of political concerns, operational priorities, public and 'expert' opinion that it reflected.

Sources of Information

The two main sources for the study of nineteenth-century crime are 'literary' accounts, whether found in newspapers, memoirs, journals, Royal Commission reports, or recorded trial testimony, and criminal statistics. Both are inherently flawed. Although the growth of the latter makes the nineteenth century the first for which a detailed analysis using crime figures is at all practical, statistics suffer from major problems involving changing offence definition, levels of public sensitivity, policing priority and enforcement, ease and cost of prosecution, interpretation and collation.

Illustrative of this, in the late 1870s, the Metropolitan Police drew up a memorandum for the Home Office complaining of the distorting effect that the then recent re-classification of offences had had on their crime statistics. It claimed that three quarters of all additional burglaries reported over previous months could be attributed to this change alone.[6] Similarly, in the mid-nineteenth century, although the police actively prosecuted many indictable felonies, such as murder, rape, and burglary, they were often much less interested in pursuing summary matters, frequently leaving this to the injured parties. However, by the 1880s, they regularly prosecuted a range of lesser offences in magistrates' courts, including drunkenness, assaults, and disorderly conduct, for the state, themselves, or on behalf of victims who otherwise could not (or would not) prosecute matters personally.[7] This process inevitably had an impact on the statistics for minor crimes.

More generally, and as in the modern era, many frequently victimized Victorian Londoners felt that reporting crimes to the police was pointless,

---

5. Gatrell, V.A.C., 1990, at p.291.
6. Emsley, Clive, 1988, at p.41.
7. Godfrey, Barry, 2008, at p.173.

while senior officers massaged figures using mechanisms such as the 'suspected stolen' book to avoid formally recording offences. Some individual offences were also heavily affected by specific social developments. For example, a gradual move to tighter clothes, with less obvious pockets, eventually affected the incidence of pick-pocketing. Similarly, the supply of corpses for medical dissection occasioned by the Anatomy Act of 1832 slowly brought an end to grave robbing.[8]

Nevertheless, statistics continue to be of *some* value. For example, if recorded crime rates for mainstream offences decrease markedly over a period during which police efficiency and willingness to prosecute is known to have improved, as appears to have been the case for the later 1800s, it can *probably* be concluded that the trend reflects a real reduction in the incidence of crime, rather than the effect of purely administrative factors, at least to some degree.[9] Statistics can reflect changes in both the reality of crime *and* attitudes towards it.[10]

Of course, some statistics are more useful than others, those for public drunkenness being amongst the least valuable, and those for homicide the most significant, although, even here, it seems that many homicides went unrecognized in early nineteenth-century London. In the absence of witnesses, obvious suspects and overt signs of violence, coroners were likely to return verdicts of accidental death, especially if the deceased was poor or a stranger, even if the surrounding circumstances were inherently rather suspicious.[11] In the late nineteenth century, many potentially violent deaths were still not subject to proper investigation, although such limitations, if consistent over time, would affect incidence rather than trends in crime rates.[12]

However, the position of those who completely reject statistical evidence in favour of literary sources ignores the parochial and socially determined nature of many of the latter, and their frequent dependence on untypical and anecdotal evidence.[13] Literary evidence usually has an upper or middle class provenance; these are social groups that might be expected to portray offenders as members of a distinct criminal class.[14] Its authors also tend to be male and significantly older than the average for the general population. Additionally, it must be remembered that many

---

8. White, Jerry, 1980, at p.342 and p.355.
9. Gatrell, V.A.C. & Haddon, T.B., 1972, at p.374 .
10. Beattie, J.M., 1986, at p.200.
11. Emmerichs, Mary Beth, 2001, pp.93-100.
12. King, Peter, 2010, pp.671-698.
13. Graff, H.J., 1992, at p.152.
14. See on this, Jones, David, 1982, at p.3.

commentators of the period based their literary opinions on contemporary statistics, for which, at times, there was a near mania. Thus, they are merely providing statistical evidence at one remove, refracted through the prism of 'opinion'.[15]

Some of these problems are slightly modified by the availability of 'alternative' sources for the period. These include a tiny number of works of oral history for the late Victorian era, these usually being recorded between the 1950s and early 1970s. When it comes to the 'criminal classes' of this time, evidence is not always limited to the accounts of policemen, courts or paternalistic social workers.[16] The Victorian period also saw the first real attempts at ethnography. These include, very notably, Augustus Miles' work in 1830s' London and that of Henry Mayhew and John Binney in the capital during the 1850s. To these can be added, *inter alia*, Clarence Rook's detailed study of a Lambeth 'hooligan' in 1899. They provide a useful alternative (though not a replacement) to the more 'establishment-oriented' sources.[17]

Ironically, despite this literary/statistical debate, for much of the nineteenth century, especially the period after about 1850, there is considerable agreement between statistics and what might pass for 'received' opinion in the more informed and serious literature as to the direction of Metropolitan crime trends.

Nineteenth-Century Crime Rates

Most of the available evidence suggests a society that was becoming steadily less prone to serious violence throughout the era, especially in London, and markedly less prone to instrumental crime from the mid-century onwards, having seen a modest increase, from an already high incidence until the late 1840s (albeit to nothing like the degree suggested by official statistics).[18]

Nevertheless, real or not, the apparently rapid rise in crime during the early century prompted acute alarm, especially in London, which appeared to be its epicentre. Thus, the Duke of Wellington informed the House of Lords, with almost no dissent, that the defective nature of policing in the capital was "clearly proved" by the increase in offending levels. Committals for the City of London and urban Middlesex had gone up from

---

15. See on this, Philips, David, 1977, at p.19.
16. Thompson, E. P., 1973, at p.59.
17. Hammersley, M., and Atkinson, P., 1995, at p.23.
18. Gatrell, V.A.C., 1990, at p.250.

2,539 cases in 1822 to 3,516 in 1828. Lord Durham felt that the growth in crime was so "perfectly notorious" that the Duke did not even need to discuss it, or support his assertions with statistics.[19] In the Lower House, Sir Robert Peel cited similar figures, and pointed out that they represented an increase in crime of 41%, despite a population growth of just 15 1/2% during the same period. He, too, believed that such major increases were largely a Metropolitan phenomenon, those for the rest of the country being very modest, and some counties even registering a decline. When introducing his Police Bill on April 15th 1829, he declared that there was one criminal charge in London for each 383 people, compared to only one in 822 elsewhere.[20]

Although the State's figures seemed to suggest a rapidly expanding crime level during the early decades of the nineteenth century, especially in London, whether this really occurred is questionable. A sharp increase *may* have taken place over short periods. For example, the statistics appear to show a particularly major expansion between 1815 and 1819, and this is entirely plausible. The end of the Napoleonic wars in 1815 released 200,000 servicemen on to a contracting labour market.[21] Traditionally, times were difficult during such mass demobilisations, especially in London, where many paid-off soldiers and sailors ended up. A short-term crime wave was predictable, if only because there was not enough work initially available to employ disbanded men.[22] Some also blamed the brutalization attendant on 20 years of armed conflict and the presence of numerous battle-scarred veterans for the problem.[23] As will be seen, as a more *general* trend, a major sustained increase in crime levels in the early nineteenth century is much more doubtful.

By the 1840s, the huge rise in the gathering of statistics, accompanied by an attendant lack of sophistication in their use, was encouraging widespread feelings of imminent social dissolution. They moved one journal to declare that it was difficult to predict the fate of a country, such as England, in which the "astonishing" progress of "human depravity" was so much more rapid than the increase of its people. This was evidenced by the 700% growth in crime rates since 1805, despite the country's

---

19. *Hansard's Parliamentary Debates*, 1929, Vol. XXI, New Series, 31 March-24 June, at pp.1750-1752 and pp.869-870.
20. 'Proceedings in Parliament', *The Gentleman's Magazine*, Vol.99, 1829, at p.360.
21. Emsley, Clive, 1988, at p.40.
22. *The Gentleman's Magazine*, Vol. 115, 1814, at p.229.
23. Anon, 1822, Thoughts on Prison Discipline, at p.17.

population increasing by just 65%.[24] At about the same time, Friedrich Engels accepted the official figures unquestioningly, and also felt that they reflected an "extraordinarily rapid" sevenfold growth in crime. Assorted amateur criminologists, whether prison officials, clerics, or J.P.s, shared such beliefs. Most dramatically, Samuel Phillips Day suggested that the incarcerated population had increased tenfold from the turn of the century. Slightly more realistically, the Reverend Henry Worsley, a London prison chaplain, thought that crime had increased fivefold during that period. Although these were alarmist estimates, it was received opinion, in the words of the Reverend Alexander Thomson, that: "...our criminals are steadily increasing, not only in absolute numbers, but in relative proportion to the rest of the population".[25]

Far from believing that the figures might suggest enhanced levels of detection, reporting and government funding for prosecutors, some observers were becoming increasingly aware of the degree of under-reporting of London crime, fearing (rightly) that it concealed a much larger 'dark figure' of hidden offences. Thus, in 1825, it was suggested that not only was the number of offenders increasing at a frenetic rate, but: "...by far the greatest number of robberies never reaches the public ear".[26] As late as the 1880s, it was noted that many robbery victims in Rotherhithe did not even bother to report crimes to the police.[27] Official figures could not be relied upon for this reason, although usually assumed to be "correct indications of the state of crime".[28]

However, by the second half of the century, reservations were growing about the value of criminal statistics. Even as concern about the 'crisis' in urban law and order reached its zenith in the 1840s, there were a few observers who were openly sceptical about whether much of the apparent increase in offending over the previous few decades was not simply made up of offences that were being brought: "...to light through the superior organisation of the police, and the more rigid enforcement of the law".[29]

---

24. 'Causes of the increase of crime', *Blackwoods Edinburgh Magazine*, Vol. LV1, No. CCCXLV, July 1844, at p.1.
25. Pearson, Geoffrey, 1983, at p.163, & Wiener, Martin J., 1994, at p.15.
26. Memoir forwarded to Sir Robert Peel in 1825, reproduced in Cobin, J., 1832, at p.8. Many of the reasons advanced for such under-reporting have been closely replicated in the modern British Crime Survey. In particular, that it would involve too much trouble for no real prospect of gain, as the case would never be solved, or the stolen items recovered.
27. Fuller, Robert, 1912, at p.23 & p.24.
28. pp.12.b.1839, at p.2.
29. Worsley, Henry, 1849, at p.27.

Among them was the judge John Mirehouse, who felt that the causes and incidence of crime were much the same as they had always been. The presence of the Metropolitan Police meant that offences were identified more frequently and criminals' chances of escape reduced by this "excellently conducted force".[30] The crime historian Luke Owen Pike was also confident that the increase from 4,605 felonies recorded in 1805 to 29,359 in 1854 was largely caused by a steady improvement in the nation's policing.[31]

Doubts about the value of statistics gradually became more widespread. Thus, in 1856, the *National Review* noted that crime and detected crime were not synonymous: "Government statistics, therefore present us with a part of the case only".[32] Thomas Beggs feared that the fashionable surveys of the era could easily produce mistaken conclusions, leading those: "...unaccustomed to the use of statistics, [into] making calculations founded on some isolated or exceptional fact".[33] This gradually filtered into popular consciousness. In 1856, even John Glyde, a Suffolk artisan with Chartist sympathies, appreciated that those comparing the number of prisoners at different periods were prone to ignoring the impact of changes in law, policing, and the financial assistance available for prosecutors.[34] By 1877, when the industrialist William Hoyle, a mainspring in the temperance movement, gave evidence to a Select Committee using impressive statistics to show that increased drunkenness also led to a large increase in crime, the Earl of Onslow swiftly replied that anything could be 'proved' by "judiciously manipulating statistics".[35]

Of course, statistics were not the sole cause of this early nineteenth-century anxiety about crime. It was also linked to the problems engendered by industrialization, rapid urbanization, and the rise to political power of a middle class possessed of a new set of values and concerns. In this last respect, the four decades between the end of the eighteenth century and the accession of Queen Victoria appear to have been crucial to the development of modern notions of public manners. During this period, restraint, thrift and sobriety in public behaviour came to dominate the values (if not always the activities) of most social strata, from the ambitious sections of the working class to the bulk of the aristocracy.[36]

---

30. Mirehouse, John, 1840 at p.11 & p.12.
31. Pike, L. O., 1876, Vol.2 at p. 478 & p.481.
32. Anon, 1856, 'Crime in England and its Treatment', at p.290.
33. Beggs, Thomas, 1849, at pp.16-18.
34. Glyde, John, 1856, at p.116.
35. Emsley, Clive, 1988, at p.41.
36. Simpson, Anthony, 1988, at p.100.

Indeed, it has been argued that this cultural trend provides unity to the period after 1850 for Europe generally. A new cultural model for personal conduct became dominant. It was reinforced and reproduced through social institutions like schools, unions, and churches that placed an emphasis on self-control, domesticity in private life, and public respectability. It also emphasized hard work, order and, cleanliness.[37]

A central theme of the radical Francis Place's autobiography was the change in London manners, for the better, from his youth in the 1780s to the 1830s.[38] By 1856, *The National Review* could observe, albeit with a little exaggeration, that: "Words and allusions which sixty years ago were common in the mouths of 'persons of quality' would now be deemed unclean in the mouth of any respectful scavenger".[39]

More generally, there was a 'gentling' in society during the period. Thus, duelling had become one of the "infamies of a past generation" by the middle of the century.[40] Cruel sports also began a gradual decline; regulated and gloved boxing slowly replaced prize-fighting; bear-baiting and cock-fighting were abolished or hidden; societies devoted to the prevention of cruelty to children and animals were formed. Arguably, a rising tide of order reduced a previous tolerance for disorder.[41]

There were practical, as well as cultural, reasons for greater 'bourgeois' concern about crime. It was small urban tradesmen, not gentlemen, who suffered most from theft.[42] As Edward Gibbon Wakefield noted in 1832, the middling orders, unlike the very rich in Grosvenor Square, could not keep country establishments to secure their wealth, or abandon their London businesses at short notice.[43] With the vantage of hindsight, a change on the part of perceiver is often readily apparent. At the time, however, it was frequently attributed to the behaviour of the perceived.

Decline in Violence

Irrespective of the figures for property offences (see below), observers who concentrated on crimes of violence (actual or threatened) were unlikely to feel that Metropolitan security was bad, or deteriorating, even in the early nineteenth century. Indeed, Patrick Colquhoun's own figures

---

37. Eisner, Manuel, 2008, at p.303.
38. Place, Francis, 1972 (1835), at pp.14-15 & p.70.
39. Greg, W.R., 1856, at p.291.
40. Ballantine, William, 1890, at p.41.
41. Paley, Ruth, 1989, at pp.95-97.
42. Gatrell, V.A.C., 1990, at p.248.
43. Wakefield, Edward Gibbon, 1832, at p.2.

suggested that the most violent crimes, such as armed robbery and murder, were on the wane.[44] There was also a body of police committee evidence suggesting such a fall.

During the nineteenth century, the homicide rate in both England and London continued a decline that had been underway for at least 200 years. By the end of the century, it was at the very low rate of 1 per 100 000 a year (lower even than modern levels). There was a fall in reported homicides of 53% from the late 1860s to the late Edwardian period.[45] This process was especially marked in the capital, which by the 1890s produced an average of only about 60 homicides (20 murders and 40 manslaughters) a year, in a population of about six million people, despite having very inferior medical resources when compared to the modern era.[46] Perhaps understandably, by the start of the twentieth century, Sir Robert Anderson, a former head of Metropolitan C.I.D., could describe this high level of physical security in the Metropolis as a "standing miracle".[47]

Other forms of violent (or potentially violent) crime also appear to have diminished as the century advanced. In 1822, the magistrate Sir Richard Birnie opined that street robberies in London had "very much" declined in recent times, especially at night, and that robberies in the environs of the city had also fallen.[48] John Townsend, a famous Bow Street runner, and his experienced colleague John Vickery, admitted astonishment at the falling away of highway robbery. He recalled that at the start of his long career, in the 1790s, there would frequently be several reports a day. By 1816, there were very few such crimes. Even armed footpads had declined greatly, being replaced by pickpockets and snatch-thieves.[49] Two years later, another observer was almost embarrassed to discuss highwaymen in the capital because their rarity made it pointless: "...so seldom are they now heard of compared to what they were formerly".[50]

Similarly, by 1839, one commentator was able to note that burglary with violence had so far declined that few slept with pistols ready to hand, or deemed it: "... necessary to spend a mortal half hour every night in bolting, barring and chaining doors and windows".[51] It has even been

---

44. Rudé, George, 1985, at p.123.
45. Gatrell, V.A.C., 1980, at pp.286-287.
46. Dilnot, George, 1915, at p.28.
47. Anderson, Robert, 1910, at p.142.
48. pp.9.1822, at p.19.
49. Evidence contained in pp.5.1816, at p.144 & p.173.
50. Anon, 1818, *The London Guide,* at p.47.
51. Taylor, W.C., 1839, at p.481.

estimated that the number of aggravated assaults against women heard in London Police courts dropped from 800 in 1853, to about 200 in 1889, despite a population increase and more vigorous prosecution and magisterial attitudes towards the crime, though these figures require a very considerable degree of caution.[52]

Non-lethal assaults generally were viewed more seriously than had been the case in earlier periods, both by the courts and the legislature, this being indicative of a wider change in popular and judicial attitudes towards violence.[53] Throughout the Victorian period, the importance of crimes of violence within the criminal canon, when compared to property offences, increased steadily. Brawls were much more likely to result in formal prosecution and serious sanctions than they had been during the eighteenth century, especially if deemed to have been conducted on unfair terms.[54]

Moral Panics

The optimism that was generated by this process was always subject to short-term media-driven 'scares' and moral panics about violent offenders. These could produce temporary despondency. They were aided by an unprecedented degree of media interest in non-lethal violence after the mid-century, itself a reflection of changing social mores. Prior to this period, few newspapers had specialist crime correspondents (as opposed to court reporters). They were common by the 1870s.[55] In their turn, such scares influenced attitudes towards non-violent crime.

For example, there was acute alarm in London about 'garrotting' in 1856 and, even more so, late 1862.[56] This prompted exaggerated stories about the "reign of terror" which had grown up in the Metropolis, though the same commentator accepted that, generally, crime was "undoubtedly on the decrease".[57] A foreign observer noted that newspapers at this time were filled with accounts of nocturnal outrages, and wondered about what had become of: "…that London police which was said to be the best organized in the world".[58] Similarly, an influx of cheap, foreign, revolvers

---

52. Tomes, Nancy, 1978, at p.330.
53. See generally, King, Peter, 1996, 'Punishing Assault: The Transformation of Attitudes in the English Courts', at pp.43-74.
54. Wiener, Martin, 2004, at p.61.
55. Sindall, Robert, 1990, at p.6.
56. *The Illustrated London News*, 6th December, 1862.
57. Pare, W., 1862, at p.3 & p.15.
58. Blanc, Louis, 1862, vol. 2, at p.236.

in the early 1880s raised fresh concerns about armed burglars, after a small number of incidents involving the shooting of bystanders and policemen.[59] There was to be another major panic, at the end of the century, over 'hooligans'. Such moral panics could influence those in high office. According to Assistant Commissioner James Monro, the introduction of new provisions for the control of 'habitual' criminals occurred the year after the garrotting panic because the public mind was: "...very much exercised owing to the vast increase of crime in the kingdom".[60]

However, even at the time, there were many thoughtful individuals who appreciated that such sensationalised reports bore little relationship to the real level of physical security. In 1867, the writer Anthony Trollope could not find a single one of his acquaintances that had been garrotted or who even knew of someone that had been.[61] Similarly, several observers appreciated that end-of-century hooligans were not an unprecedented phenomenon. Thomas Holmes, a police court missionary looking back on 25 years of experience from the vantage-point of 1908, felt that at the close of the 1800s every assault committed by a labouring man, and every bit of disorder in the streets caused by the poor, prompted the cry: "'The hooligans again!' Rubbish! But the people believed it and ... magistrates caught the spirit of the thing, and proceeded to impose heavier sentences on boys charged with disorderly conduct in the streets".[62] In reality, such behaviour was not new. P.C. John Sweeney was to note that in 1879, almost 20 years before the advent of the 'hooligans', numerous gangs of roughs had plagued Hammersmith on Sunday evenings. They would commit petty thefts, engage in violent faction-fights, pursue and abuse passersby, as well as smashing windows and kicking in doors: "Nowadays we should call them hooligans".[63]

Nevertheless, for most of the later nineteenth century, considerable optimism about levels of violence prevailed. By 1901, the Criminal Registrar thought that there had been a: "...great change in manners: the substitution of words without blows for blows with or without words; an approximation in the manners of the different classes; a decline in the spirit of lawlessness".[64]

---

59. Emsley, Clive, 1985, at pp.137-139.
60. PR.14.1886, at pp.3-5.
61. Trollope, Anthony, 1867, at pp.419-424.
62. Holmes, Thomas, 1908, at p.167. Holmes was well aware that other factors were at work; for example, that "allowances" were not made for the poor that were made for the rich and even for soldiers and sailors on leave.
63. Sweeney, John, 1905, at p.13.
64. Quoted in Gatrell, V.A.C. & Haddon, T.B., 1972, at p.241.

Property Crime

Even if decreasing steadily, prosecuted crimes involving violence were always in a small minority. In London, as elsewhere, the great bulk of serious criminal activity was made up of property offences (or 'instrumental crime'). Indeed, Robert Peel described theft as the "paramount" London crime in 1826. Thirty years later, the *National Review* noted that: "Offences against property without violence form at present the staple crime of England". In 1849, the barrister Jelinger Symons opined that crime was "largely composed of thefts alone".[65]

A selection of statistics, from a variety of sources, makes this apparent. For example, until late in the century, about 80% of all committals for trial on indictment were for offences against property that did not involve violence or its threat.[66] From 1820 to 1850, crimes of violence averaged only about 10% of the Old Bailey (i.e. serious indictable Metropolitan) offences that went to trial.[67] In 1859, of 2,853 indictable offences for which a suspect was prosecuted in the Metropolitan area, only 367 were for offences against the person, such as robbery (103 cases) or assault with intent to rob (7 cases).[68] On a smaller scale, of 72 prisoners tried at the Old Bailey Sessions commencing on 11th April 1833, and taken from the City of London, 16 were accused of theft from the person and 34 of larceny.[69]

Nineteenth-century patterns of instrumental crime differed somewhat from the modern era. Larceny from the person appears to have been much more common than residential burglary (unlike today), though commercial burglary may have been just as frequent as in the modern era, in a city that was both a major port and crammed with warehouses. Reported housebreaking was heavily oriented towards wealthier homes, partly, perhaps, because of a lack of 'stealable' goods in poorer residences.

There was very little public optimism about ordinary property crime in the early 1800s. A tiny number were willing to extend the analysis for violence to crime generally. Thus, in 1838, a judge at the Middlesex Sessions noted (with a selective use of figures) that over the previous seven years, the number of trials on indictment had declined significantly, despite an increase in population.[70] Nevertheless, such confidence was highly unusual. A marked decline in property crime during this period

---

65. Symons, Jelinger C., 1849, at pp.19-23.
66. Gatrell, V.A.C. & Haddon, T.B., 1972, at p.367.
67. Rudé, George, 1985, at p.29.
68. See Table No.5, PR.6.1859.
69. PR.4.1833.
70. Adams, John, 1838, at p.9.

would appear very unlikely, and there is some support for the notion of a small increase.[71]

Improvement in Property Crime Rates

However, from the middle of the century, an apparent change in rates of property crime set in. As a result, there was a growing feeling that security was improving in England generally and the Metropolis in particular. Inevitably, not everyone who gave serious thought to the subject accepted that this was a true reflection of reality. To the former Clerkenwell prison chaplain, Canon Robert Gregory, writing in 1885, it was clear that there had been no major decrease in the number of offences committed during the previous fourteen years. He believed that the falling prison population had more to do with decreased detection rates and lenient sentencing than a lower incidence of offending This was, he felt, reflected in the apparent increase of committals to the nation's prisons, up from 157,223 in 1870, to 176,467 in 1884.[72] Similarly, long after the situation was felt by most observers to be improving, Havelock Ellis was still gloomily discussing the "rising flood of criminality".[73] As late as 1892, a lengthy debate between two thoughtful and well-informed men, W. D. Morrison (a Wandsworth prison chaplain) and Edmund Du Cane (an influential penologist and prison administrator) could be conducted in the pages of the *Nineteenth Century* as to whether crime was increasing or decreasing.

Nevertheless, by then, pessimists held a clearly minority view. Even those who feared that there was still a "distressing" amount of crime normally acknowledged that the situation compared favourably with former times.[74] This was particularly noteworthy as there had been a huge increase in the city's population and policing. As Anthony Trollope observed in 1867, the published figures for annual Metropolitan crime, such as the 4,738 pocket-handkerchiefs and 598 watches and other articles reported stolen that year in the capital's streets, though superficially impressive, had to be seen in the light of London's immense population (by then over three million people), when they would appear quite modest. None of his friends or acquaintances knew anyone who had had their pockets picked.[75]

---

71. Gatrell, V.A.C. & Haddon, T.B., 1972, at p.239.
72. Gregory, Robert, 1886, at pp.774-776.
73. Ellis, Havelock, 1890, at p.297.
74. Smith, Henry, 1910 at p.267.
75. Trollope, Anthony, 1867, at pp.419-424.

A selection of statistics is suggestive. Between the early 1860s and late 1890s the number of indictable offences in England and Wales as a whole declined by 43%, most of the reduction being made up of cases of theft.[76] Composite rates for male committals and summary trials for larceny declined from a high point of 459 per 100,000 in 1857 to 329 in 1891. Given the improvements in policing standards, the figures probably reflect a real and major decline in criminal activity, properly deserving of Gatrell's epithet of 'extraordinary'.

The national figure was more than reflected in London, as judged by the Metropolitan Police Crime Returns (M.P.C.R.). These appear to evidence a real change in criminal behaviour.[77] In the capital, it seems that the decline began (very gently at first) between the late 1840s and early 1850s. However, by 1872, the Metropolitan Police Commissioner could opine in his annual report that: "The more serious offences against person and property show a continuous decrease".[78] This was especially the case with regard to burglary and larceny in a dwelling house, with burglary falling from 433 cases in 1871 to 344 in 1872. Additionally, and less reliably, the number of known thieves and suspected persons at large had decreased from 4,336 in 1869 to 3,115 in 1872, and the number of houses of 'bad character' from 1,740 to 1,148 over the same period. Such a report was typical of the generally optimistic assessments found throughout the 1870s. Thus, in 1875, the Commissioner noted (again) that the more serious property offences, such as burglary, robbery, larceny, and receiving stolen goods, had continued to fall over the previous year, which itself had had the smallest number of serious crimes in the decade. In 1868, there had been 14,316 such crimes; by 1875, these had fallen by 4,373 (a fall of just over 30%) despite an increase in population.[79]

This general sense of optimism continued throughout the economically straitened 1880s and into ensuing years. The Commissioner, Charles Warren, noted in 1888 that: "Heavy crimes have been diminishing in the Metropolis year by year, so that even within the official lives of many police officers a marked improvement has taken place".[80] Three years later, a newspaper noted that the almost annual decline in Metropolitan

---

76. Gatrell, V.A.C. et al (Eds.) 1980, at p.240.
77. Jones, David, 1982, at p.143.
78. PR.9.1869-6, at p.1. Although there had been a large increase in the numbers taken into custody in 1872: "Nearly the whole of this large increase is accounted for by the arrest of persons for being drunk, disorderly or both".
79. PR.12.1869-76, at p.3.
80. Warren, Charles, 1888, at p.580.

crime rates disclosed a "most satisfactory record".[81] In 1887, reported loss from theft in the London area stood at only £97,000 for the whole year.[82] During the period from 1879 to 1883, there were 4,856 reported crimes against property per 1,000,000 people in the Metropolis, while in the years 1894 to 1898 there were only 2,755.[83]

Inevitably, there was a lag between improving statistics and signs of optimism becoming widespread amongst the general public. Nevertheless, these were also apparent by the 1870s. By then, many felt it was unquestionable that although the population of the Metropolis had: "…increased there has been a marked diminution of crime".[84] As a result, Luke Owen Pike was confident that there had never been a nation in history in which: "…life and property were so secure as they are at present in England". In most areas of London, it was thought that a man of average stature and strength could wander alone, at any hour of the day or night, without undue concern. This was in marked contrast to the sense of insecurity that had prevailed at the beginning of the century.[85] One observer even went so far as to declare (somewhat implausibly) that, in many respects, when compared to the provinces, the Metropolis was "one of the most innocent places in the kingdom".[86]

There were other indications that, by then, London was not a particularly 'high crime' environment. These included the frequently casual attitudes manifest by traders and shopkeepers towards their own security. For example, of the minor larcenies committed in 1880, 2,806 were a result of the "indefensible practice" of exposing goods for sale without having anyone watching over them, presenting juveniles, in particular, with acute temptation.[87] In 1897, Sir Francis Powell was able to tell Parliament that a reduction in prison sentences had occurred not because of increased public sympathy for offenders, but because of a widespread belief that crime had diminished, reducing the need for harsh deterrence.[88] This confidence sometimes threatened to become exaggerated; in 1899, a leader in *The Times* even suggested that the thief was a disappearing breed![89]

---

81. *The Morning Post*, August 5th, 1891, p.5.
82. Warren, Charles, 1888, at p.588.
83. Anderson, Robert, 1910, at p.141.
84. Anon, 1871, *Our Police System*, at p.693.
85. Pike, L.O., 1876, Vol. 2, at pp.480-481, and p.484.
86. 'Police Criterion of the Criminality of Districts', *The Pall Mall Gazette*, December 23rd, 1875.
87. *The Standard,* August 10th, 1881, p.2.
88. Reproduced in McWilliams, W., 1983, at pp.129-147.
89. *The Times*, February 6th, 1899.

This trend was not confined to the Metropolis. To varying degrees, it was found in most urban areas in England. For example, the crime rate in Middlesbrough almost halved during the 1870s, and continued to decline thereafter, although there is no evidence to suggest this was due to any reluctance to prosecute on the part of the local police force.[90] Indeed, it is a pattern that appears to extend, if less markedly so, to a number of other western cities, whether Sydney or Stockholm, which also experienced a generally sharp fall in crime between the 1850s and the 1870s, and a more gradual reduction thereafter.[91] Nevertheless, the fall was particularly apparent in London.

As a result, it can be said that the second half of the nineteenth century, especially the years after 1860, witnessed both a national and a more specifically Metropolitan decline in the number of offences committed against people and property, this decline continuing until the end of the era and beyond. The academic debate has largely been limited to the rate at which this was happening and, most importantly, *why* it occurred. Many, then and now, linked this decline to changes in nineteenth-century policing, especially in London. Others have stressed the important socio-economic developments of the period.

---

90. Taylor, David, 2004, at p.759.
91. Gurr, Ted, 1981, at p.111.

CHAPTER TWO

THE CRIMINAL 'THREAT' IN NINETEENTH-CENTURY LONDON

Introduction

The perpetrators of 'conventional' (non-white-collar) Metropolitan crime during the nineteenth century can (very roughly) be divided into two main groups. At their apex was a small band of skilled professionals, one that had existed in the capital for almost 200 years. Below them, was a very much larger group of opportunistic offenders; these were largely drawn from the capital's working class. As the Reverend Francis Close (a prominent evangelical of the time) observed, although upper and middle class criminals existed, they were 'rogue' elements within their social groups, individual 'abominations' rather than typical representatives of a wider culture steeped in crime. By contrast, it was a brutal reality that of the criminal offenders who came: "…within the clutches of the law, ninety-nine out of a hundred are taken from the working-classes".[1]

However, by the early 1800s, this class was itself highly fragmented. Much of its crime was the work of those in its lowest reaches, rather than its skilled or 'respectable' elements, and this phenomenon became steadily more marked as the century advanced. This bottom group was termed, at various times, and *inter alia*, the 'residuum', the 'casual poor', and the 'criminal', 'predatory' or 'dangerous' classes.[2] As the Reverend Close noted, the words were usually synonymous.

When the Victorians referred to the 'dangerous classes' they were certainly not alluding to the labouring population as a whole. Whatever may have been the situation in earlier periods, crime was not perceived as being randomly distributed throughout the working class. Thus, if rather implausibly, the social reformer Mary Carpenter had no doubt that juvenile

---

1. Close, Francis, 1850, at pp. 4-5.
2. Emsley, Clive, 1988, at p.36.

crime arose entirely from the "lowest class" within that broader grouping.[3] Henry Mayhew, too, was anxious that the public should not confuse: "...honest, independent working men with the vagrant beggars and pilferers of the country".[4] Such people were quite distinct from the average Londoner, coming from: "below the class from which we usually obtain our domestic servants".[5] They were: "...decidedly lower in the social scale than the labourer".[6]

The Metropolis, with its huge numbers of unskilled casual workers, unregimented by factory 'discipline' (however unattractive that may have been), was thought to be the epicentre of this residuum. In some respects, the identification of this group with offending was the conclusion of a centuries-old process whereby conventional property crime ceased to be something that 'everyman' could have recourse to, even upper-class medieval 'robber-barons', and became heavily associated with a distinct social group.

Of course, this process was confined to conventional (especially property) crime. The very rudimentary development of notions of white-collar crime, and a corresponding failure to police it, meant that levels of middle and upper class deviance were hugely underestimated throughout the century.[7] The Victorians were plagued by white-collar crime like no other people, before or since, with the joint-stock company being an especially common vehicle for fraud. The modern image of the upright Victorian businessman is largely a myth.[8] By the late nineteenth century, 'long-firm' frauds were common in London, with mock businesses being established, acquiring goods on credit, selling them, and then disappearing into the night.[9]

Additionally, many normally 'respectable' working-class men succumbed to temptation or adversity by having recourse to crime. They included poor but "naturally honest" individuals who stole out of desperation to support their families, during cyclical hard times.[10] Nevertheless, contemporary observers were right in thinking that conventional (especially street) crime

---

3. Evidence to Select Committee on Juveniles by Mary Carpenter. Response to Question 799. Reproduced in Tobias, J.J., 1972, *Nineteenth Century Crime,* at p.46.
4. Wiener, Martin J., 1990, at p.23.
5. Bayly, Mary, 1860, at p.11.
6. Ellis, Havelock, 1890, at p.297.
7. Sindall, Robert, 1983, at pp.23-40.
8. Robb, George, 2002, at p.3.
9. Thor, Fredur, 1879, at p.178.
10. Anon, *Convict Life, or Revelations,* 1879, at pp.3-4.

in the London area was disproportionately the work of what might be termed an urban underclass, usually operating on a casual, unsophisticated, and impulsive basis.[11] Professional criminals might originate in this milieu, but they were never typical of it. As a result, educated prison inmates in the 1870s carefully delineated London "roughs" from other Metropolitan criminals.[12]

In recent decades, the identification of such an underclass has become controversial. It is sometimes alleged to be a social construct, rather than a reflection of reality. This is partly because the 'robustness' of many Victorian portrayals, particularly those influenced by social Darwinism, is acutely distasteful to modern eyes. The observers who made them usually came from the middle or upper classes, and often failed to empathize in any meaningful way with their subjects or their very limited life choices.[13] Nevertheless, this does not mean that such elite representations were entirely unfounded.

Then as now, there was also a debate as to the origins of this social group. Was it a response to an economic predicament that was the result of structural inequalities in society, or the result of a cultural commitment by that group to dysfunctional values?[14] This also meant that there was uncertainty as to whether the best method of: "...treating these unfortunate persons were that of sending them to the gaol, or of taking care of them in the eating-house".[15]

However, as the nineteenth century advanced, there was increasing agreement, amongst observers from both left and right, that such an underclass existed in the capital. Thus, Octavia Hill (another active social reformer) drew a sharp distinction between the "tidy and quiet poor" and the rough elements that made the lives of their respectable neighbours a misery by pelting them with dirt, if they went out cleanly attired, and shouting obscenities in their vicinity.[16] Similarly, a newspaper correspondent, although himself from the rough Minories area near the Tower, complained of the: "...class who set all moral decency in open defiance".[17]

---

11. Smith, P.F., 1985, at p.27.

12. Anon, *Five Years' Penal Servitude*, 1877, at p.178.

13. Shore, Heather, 1999, at p.153.

14. Greenstone, J. David, 1991, at p.399.

15. Holland, E.W., 1870, at p.162.

16. Hill, Octavia, in the *Nineteenth Century* for September 1889, reproduced by Monro, James, 1889, at p.9.

17. 'The Social Evil', *East London Observer*, October 29th, 1859.

Unsurprisingly, in these circumstances, street-crime was thought to be heavily concentrated amongst certain families.[18] Indeed, a middle-class prisoner in the 1870s believed that stealing was: "...to a very great extent hereditary in England".[19] Some statistical evidence supports his analysis. Of a selection of 175 boys committed to the Westminster House of Correction in the early 1850s, 99 had uncles, siblings or parents who were in prison or who had been transported, while 53 had a brother in prison.[20] Similarly, in the 1850s and 1860s, crime amongst the residents of the infamous Jennings' Buildings in Kensington appears to have been concentrated amongst about 200 of the location's 900-plus occupants, many coming from the same five extended families.[21]

Definitions

Clearly, the residuum was a group whose style of life seemed a defiance of respectable society.[22] Unfortunately, producing more precise definitions is (and was) inherently difficult. Edward Gibbon Wakefield made an early attempt, based on personal experience acquired in Newgate while serving time for abducting an heiress. He felt that its members lived amid extreme poverty, followed brutalizing pursuits, and were often either out of work or employed as costermongers, chimneysweeps, and scavengers.[23] More generally, Hugh Edward Hoare, of the Charity Organisation Society, felt it was made up of casual labourers who lived "on the brink of starvation and crime".[24]

Vagrants were considered to be a particularly important part of this group.[25] Although not confined to the capital, most were thought to originate from the "great reservoir of crime in London".[26] Vagrancy, like the crime that often accompanied it, was a disproportionately male activity. At least 85% of those who had recourse to the 'casual' (as opposed to residential) wards of workhouses were adult men under the age of 65.[27] Of course, not *all* were criminal. However, some observers thought that

---

18. Beggs, Thomas, 1849, at p.49.
19. Anon, *Convict Life, or Revelations*, 1879, at p.10.
20. Antrobus, Edmund, 1853, at p.19.
21. Davis, Jennifer, 1989, at pp.15-21.
22. Chesney, Kellow, 1970, at p.76.
23. Wakefield, Edward Gibbon, 1832, at p.7.
24. Bailey, Victor, 1981, at p.97.
25. Guy, W.A., 1848, at p.395 & p.400.
26. Miles, W.A., 1836, at p.5.
27. Vorspan, Rachel, 1977, at p.60.

three quarters of those in casual wards would subsist by "begging or thieving" during the day.[28] This pattern also applied to many of the people who lived in cheap, private, 'casual' accommodation, such as the capital's many common lodging-houses, which were seen as the: "…general resort of the dishonest, the vagrant, and the utterly impoverished".[29] (See below). In 1835, the occupant of one such establishment in the East End could note that its residents would regularly ask for companions to go thieving with them.[30]

Contrast with Professional Crime

The casual crime of this underclass was always very different to that of London's small number of professional criminals, who adapted themselves to modern conditions and followed a: "…profession which requires great skill".[31] The imprisoned Irish Nationalist, Michael Davitt, noted that forgers, professional burglars, and high-class swindlers looked with contempt on 'low' thieves.[32] Professional crimes were aimed at producing high-value returns, characterised by careful planning and execution, and frequently involved the effective use of commercial fences. Their perpetrators were also able to exploit the intricacies of the legal system.[33] They included members of London's 'swell mob', criminals able to infiltrate upper-class environments, such as society balls.[34] Burglaries of upper-class homes by specialist "cracksmen" were also largely the province of professionals, as the attendant risks and difficulties were considerable.[35] It was claimed that top-class men could break all but Chubb and Hannah locks in less than three minutes, and knock a man-sized hole in a brick wall in less than two hours.[36] However, this type of burglar was so rare that most of those who worked in the Metropolitan area could be identified by name.[37]

---

28. Holland, E.W., 1870, at p.171.
29. *The Standard*, October 4th, 1893, at p.6.
30. Quoted in Shore, Heather, 1997, at p.196.
31. Ellis, Havelock, 1890, at p.22.
32. Davitt, Michael, 1886, at p.26 & p.32.
33. Mirehouse, John, 1840, at p.28.
34. Wills, W.H., 1850, at p.370.
35. Ryan, Michael, 1839, at p.271.
36. Mayhew, Henry et al, 1862, at p.355.
37. pp.15.1878, at p.24.

Professionals also dominated the commercial handling of stolen goods.[38] The largest receivers owned warehouses well away from their own residences and had furnaces to melt down stolen plate.[39] In many establishments, precious metals could be turned into bullion within minutes of being delivered. There were huge profits to be made, as far less than a quarter of the 'market' value of stolen goods (as opposed to silver) would normally be given to the thief.[40]

The Typical Metropolitan Criminal

Nevertheless, the 'typical' London criminal of the nineteenth century was *not* a sophisticated professional. As a prison missionary noted, much confusion was occasioned by the common inability of the general public to distinguish the mass of the criminal underclass from such high profile offenders.[41] According to Michael Davitt, over two thirds of prison inmates were the grossly ignorant products of a squalid upbringing.[42] Towards the end of the century, Sir Robert Anderson reiterated that the element of professional crime in London was very small and had to be distinguished from a much larger class of opportunistic offenders and habitual, but incompetent, thieves.[43] According to one estimate, of the 6,000 people who made some sort of living from theft in London during the early 1850s, less than 200 were "first-class thieves". Most were habitual petty criminals.[44] Similarly, although Charles Booth could describe Hoxton in the 1890s as the leading criminal area of London, he also noted that its: "…number of first-class burglars is said to be very small".[45] It was a commonplace that the vast majority of Metropolitan pickpockets were drawn from the "dregs of society".[46]

Confusion was partly engendered by sensationalist literature that encouraged people to believe that criminal specialism was typical in the London area.[47] In practice, most criminals varied their *modus operandi* as

---

38. Pike, L.O., 1876, Vol. 4, at p.273.
39. Mainwaring, George B., 1821, at pp.89-93.
40. Mayhew, Henry et al, 1862, Vol. 4, at p.374.
41. Meredith, Susanna, 1881, at p.89.
42. Davitt, Michael, 1886, at p.26 & p.32.
43. Anderson, Robert, 1910, at p.234.
44. Wills, W.H., 1850, at p.371.
45. Quoted in Evans, Alan 1988, at p.15.
46. Mayhew, Henry et al, 1862, at p.188.
47. Mayhew, Henry et al, 1862, Vol. 4, at p.353.

opportunity presented.[48] It also encouraged its readers to attribute sophistication to the crimes emanating from the bottom of society. In reality, the (modern) observation that crime amongst the lower working class tends to be frequent, minor, unsophisticated, and the result of acute social disorganization was especially true of Victorian London.[49] Criminals from this stratum rarely progressed very far in their 'careers', or went on to become members of the 'swell mob'.[50]

However, this part of the working class seems to have declined both proportionately and in absolute numbers during the second half of the nineteenth century. This also made it increasingly distinct from other poor but 'respectable' Londoners. Crime ceased to be a 'normal' part of everyday life for large sections of the working population in the way that it often had been during the 1700s. Information gleaned from the prison and police returns, relating to age, literacy, occupations, and the previous sentences of offenders suggest that, by the late 1800s, they were much less representative of the wider working population than earlier in the century. By then, those who stole were often the most depressed and least literate members of society, while an increase in average age, and number of previous convictions, suggest that many who came before the courts were 'hardcore' criminals in a new sense. Previously respectable workingmen were increasingly absent from their number, except when times were exceptionally hard.[51]

For example, in 1845, 31.8% of male and 44.2% of female offenders were totally illiterate, a figure that was not enormously different from the general working class profile. In 1885, however, it was *still* 26.2% and 36.2% respectively, despite the huge improvement in literacy rates occasioned by educational reform.[52] At the start of the twentieth century, Charles Goring estimated that between 10% and 20% of those in prison were mentally defective, compared to only 0.45% for the national population.[53] The percentage of inmates who had been jailed on a previous occasion increased from 26.1% in 1860, to 45.6% in 1890, spawning the late-Victorian concern with recidivism.[54]

---

48. pp.15.1878, at p.24.
49. Young, Jock, 1994, at p.88.
50. Greenwood, James, 1869, at p.71.
51. Gatrell, V.A.C. & Haddon, T., 1972, at p.379.
52. Jones, David, 1982, at pp.4-6.
53. Goring, Charles, 1972 (1913), at pp.254-255.
54. Jones, David, 1982, at p.6.

Age and Gender

As well as being from the lowest strata of society, the 'typical' Metropolitan criminal was male, this latter generalisation becoming progressively truer over time. In the middle of the century, women were still a significant component in most forms of instrumental crime, other than those attended by violence. In 1847, they formed 27% of defendants tried before a jury. However, by the 1890s, the proportion had declined to only 19%.[55]

He was also young, though he may have aged as the century advanced. Historically, crime has always been a disproportionately youthful occupation, and this was certainly the case in early Victorian London. The 15 to 20 year age group produced more offenders than any other.[56] William Augustus Miles's study of youth crime in London in the 1830s, based on interviews with several dozen thieves on the juvenile prison hulk *Euryalus,* portrays boys from close knit, localized, subcultures (in this case Soho and parts of the East End).[57] Many were unemployable because of their criminal pasts.[58] Several were personally sceptical about any possibility of being reformed. Their views seemed to confirm the opinion of George Chesterton, the Governor of Coldbath Fields House of Correction, who felt that: "Boys brought up in a low neighbourhood have no chance of being honest, because on leaving a gaol they return to their old haunts and follow the example of their parents or associates".[59]

Ralph Ricardo, writing in 1850, felt that no one who walked London's streets could fail to be shocked at the huge number of semi-criminal children loitering about. Until the institution of the Ragged Schools, there was: "...no effort of any kind made to reclaim some 30,000 or 40,000 little vagabonds, who daily support themselves in the streets of London by picking pockets, and by stealing anything within reach".[60] In the absence of legitimate employment, many stole, if only to avoid starving.[61]

Various explanations have been advanced for the change in attitude towards juvenile crime that occurred at the start of the period.[62] In part, it

---

55. Zedner, Lucia, 1991, at p.247.
56. Worsley, Henry, 1849, at p.6 & p.25.
57. Shore, Heather, 1997, at pp.202-203. Miles was later to give evidence to Chadwick's 1839 Royal Commission on Constabulary.
58. Ricardo, Ralph, 1850, at p.4.
59. Shore, Heather, 1997, at p.205.
60. Close, Francis, 1850, at p.23 & p.25.
61. Ricardo, Ralph, 1850, at pp.4-5.
62. See generally, King, Peter, 1998, at pp.116-166.

was probably founded on demographic developments. Rapid population growth had produced a falling average age, especially in London, where the city's many immigrants also tended to be young. Patrick Colquhoun, giving evidence to the 1816 Police Committee, opined, with characteristic bluntness, that many of the capital's juvenile problems had been exacerbated by the advent of vaccination and other medical advances which had, indirectly, produced an unprecedented mass of "infantile delinquency".[63] Previously, many of them would have perished in early childhood.

The disruption occasioned by urbanisation and industrialisation also had a particularly heavy impact on young town dwellers; they may have found a solution to the transition by adopting criminal habits.[64] Another common explanation for increased juvenile crime stressed the reduction in traditional urban youth control mechanisms, such as supervised apprenticeships, during the nineteenth century.[65] Another factor, and one affecting perception rather than reality, may have been the growth of summary jurisdiction in the capital, something that was inherently suited to the prosecution of juveniles. It probably engendered a reduction in the use of informal methods of social control against youths.[66]

However, then as now, most juveniles did not graduate to serious crimes, and their initial offending profiles were not normally very grave. Towards the end of the century, crimes like burglary, housebreaking, and shop breaking were four times more frequent amongst youths over 16 than in those of 15 and under. By contrast, petty larceny and pick-pocketing were proportionately twice as high amongst under-16 year olds as for those in the 16 to 21 year bracket. (It was the frequent criminality of such youths compared to adults that intimated that alcohol was not necessarily a primary cause of crime).[67] Unfortunately, from the numerous ranks of youthful criminals emerged the smaller numbers of hard-core adult felons who moved from misdemeanours to become burglars and robbers.[68] Nevertheless, such hard-core offenders appear to have become older towards the end of the century.

---

63. At p.35 of the Report.
64. Tobias, J.J., 1972, *Urban Crime in Victorian England*, at p.42.
65. See generally, King, Peter, 1998, at pp.116-166.
66. Stack, John, 1992, at p.132.
67. Morrison, William Douglas, 1896, at p.69 & pp.70-71.
68. Worsley, Henry, 1849, at p.2.

Size of the 'Criminal Class'

The size of this criminogenic underclass at any one time was and is impossible to quantify because it lacked any precise definition. Estimates fluctuated wildly, though with a *general* tendency to become smaller as the nineteenth century progressed. In the 1790s, Patrick Colquhoun placed it at 115,000 people or one eighth of the Metropolitan population.[69] According to Wakefield, writing in 1832, there were more than 50,000 members of the criminal class within five miles of St. Paul's Cathedral alone.[70] As late as 1857, Ewing Ritchie suggested that in London: "...one man in every nine belongs to the Criminal class".[71] However, by the early 1860s, Henry Mayhew was much more modest in his estimate, and felt that this group was made up of a little over 12,000 people.[72] In the same decade, Edwin Chadwick came to a similar figure when he argued that the primary targets of the Metropolitan police should be the capital's 14,000 habitual criminals.[73]

These figures differ enormously, depending on time, definition and, most importantly, whether they include dependants and prostitutes. However, one thing is apparent: to contemporary observers the perceived criminal stratum of London society was in no way synonymous with the wider working class. Even allowing for dependants, it is evident that at its peak, observers never estimated this group at more than 20% of the total population, and usually it was seen as being very much smaller. Although Henry Mayhew's mid-century study of London's 'Street Folk', whether beggars, watermen, prostitutes, pickpockets, cabmen or street performers (many of them not criminals by any definition), was taken by some ill-informed contemporary observers, as well as many modern readers, to be an 'authentic' portrayal of a large section of London's mid-century poor, they probably made up little more than 10% to 15% of the urban population. What was (and frequently still is) seen as the 'culture of poverty' was, in reality, the culture of a relatively small subgroup of poor Londoners. Given this, it is not surprising that, in 1843, Robert Vaughan thought that it was the: "...exception rather than the norm which is thus putrid".[74]

---

69. Colquhoun, Patrick, 1796, at p.230.
70. Wakefield, Edward Gibbon, 1832, at p.7.
71. Ewing Ritchie, J., 1857, at p.137.
72. Mayhew, Henry et al, 1862, at p.353.
73. Chadwick, Edwin, 1868, at p.14.
74. Quoted in Himmelfarb, Gertrude, 1984, at p.310.

Despite these qualifications, it is apparent that the 'residuum' still constituted a significant minority in London during the early part of the century. However, nearly all observers agreed that it declined steadily throughout the last forty years of the Victorian era. Even by the late 1850s, a change in attitude was manifest; a more optimistic period had set in.[75] Thus, in 1870 it was claimed that there were only 53,000 known thieves, compared to 77,500 a decade before.[76] Despite occasional setbacks, informed observers in the 1880s, such as Charles Booth, were aware that the number of those belonging to the 'criminal classes', essentially his class A supplemented by elements from the larger class B above it, were small, and declining: "There are barbarians, but they are a handful, a small and decreasing percentage: a disgrace but not a danger". By then, only 1 1/4% of East Enders fell within his Class A.[77] Even in impoverished Tower Hamlets, it was thought that only 71,000 of its 456,000 inhabitants belonged to the: "...class of unskilled labour from which, as a rule, in East London the Criminal classes are recruited".[78] Each year, state intervention, the persistent pressure of the School Board and other agencies, appeared to be confining this group within narrower limits, something that led the socialist Henrietta Barnett to believe that its values would be transmitted across the generations with ever less frequency.[79] By the end of the century, Booth was sure he was examining a phenomenon whose decline was well advanced from an earlier: "...golden age in the days when whole districts of London were in their undisputed possession".[80] In 1900, the battle against the residuum was seemingly being won across most of London. In the words of Gertrude Himmelfarb, their numbers had so shrunk as "no longer to constitute a 'race' or even a major social problem".[81]

At times, the increase in public confidence was so great that it may have outstripped reality, prompting E.W. Holland to warn that the "vagrant class" was still more extensive in London than many believed.[82] In the East End, there remained criminal quarters where crime and vice was the staple trade and drunkenness the common pleasure.[83] At the turn of the

---

75. Bailey, Victor, 1981, at p.150.
76. Radzinowicz, Leon ad Hood, Roger, 1976, Vol. 5, at p.115.
77. Booth, Charles, 1889, Vol. I, pp.33-36.
78. Barnett, Henrietta, 1888, at pp.433-6 and p.340.
79. Barnett, Henrietta, 1888, at pp.33-36.
80. Booth, William, 1890, Vol. i, at p.174.
81. Himmelfarb, Gertrude, 1995, at p. 37.
82. Holland, E.W., 1870, at p.161.
83. Barnett, Henrietta, 1888, at pp.433-6, and p.340.

century, Arthur Harding's Brick Lane was still a "hotbed of villainy".[84] However, by then, such areas were highly localised and could be ignored by respectable Londoners in the absence of dramatic crimes, such as the 1888 Ripper murders. For much of London, the huge demoralised 'residuum' of the 1830s and 1840s, had been reduced to small pockets, with slightly larger ones located in the East and South of the city.

Characteristics

The Victorian underclass appeared to be a Janus-like body to contemporary observers. In one aspect, it was the embodiment of menace: vigorous, dangerous, cunning, coherent and almost structured in its organization.[85] In another guise, it was a community of helpless and pathetic inadequates. Both features were identified throughout the century. What changed was the proportion of observers who stressed one or other typology.

Even in the 1830s, many believed that the term 'desperate', which was commonly applied to the underclass, should not be taken to mean bold or daring, as they were all: "…without exception, pusillanimous and rank cowards".[86] By the mid-century, social investigators were increasingly defining members of this social strata as much by their "incompetence" and general helplessness as by their rebelliousness and menace.[87] In the last quarter of the era, most educated people saw its members as 'social wreckage' rather than the willful enemies of society, aided perhaps in this assessment by the growing eugenics movement. Typically, Thomas Holmes felt that his era's criminals had less strength of character than their predecessors: "…weakness, not wickedness, is their great characteristic".[88]

This change in perception appears to have been linked to their obviously declining numbers and increasingly evident distinction from the mass of working class people, something that made them appear inherently less threatening. Thus, in 1886, when an M.P. referred to the growing threat and audacity of the capital's criminal classes, the Home Secretary, Hugh Childers, was adamant that he was mistaken: "On the contrary, they are, I am glad to say, from year to year diminishing in

---

84. Samuel, Raphael, 1981, at p.111.
85. Adolphus, John, 1824, at p.55.
86. Walls, Charles, 1832, at pp.521-533.
87. Bailey, Victor, 1981, at p.97.
88. Holmes, Thomas, 1908, at p.11.

number, and are becoming much less formidable".[89]

However 'potent' members of the residuum were believed to be, their conduct was virtually the antithesis of the accepted qualities of 'respectability'. Poverty was supplemented by ignorance and the absence of almost all "moral and religious sense".[90] Their lack of any contact with organised worship was almost universal, especially in London, where the: "...vicious classes are generally untouched by the pulpits and other Christianising influences".[91] They were also considered to be improvident, promiscuous, drunken, slovenly, lazy, dishonest, and violent people. Order and cleanliness were "foreign to their ordinary habits".[92] They were notorious for their irregular personal relationships. Marriage was of little significance, many living 'in sin', and fathering children, with nobody knowing or caring about the regularity of their bonds.[93]

The underclass lived for the moment, its members being thought to be unable to defer gratification.[94] Those in London were believed to be particularly prone to a hand to mouth existence, grasping pleasure "at any cost or risk".[95] This meant that they were also fatalistic in their attitude towards prison, viewing the risk of a custodial sentence as something that was beyond their control.[96] They were not suited to work, lacking technical skill, physical strength, and any desire for honest labour, so that there was often no place for them in modern industrial society.[97] Charles Booth doubted whether many would work full time for very long even if they had the opportunity to do so, as most were characterised by "helplessness, idleness, or drink".[98]

Unlike the 'ordinary' poor, who demonstrated impressive levels of charity towards each other when in adversity, they were also devoid of social solidarity, preying on each other as much as on outsiders.[99] They did not belong to working men's institutes, or take an interest in politics, even

---

89. HANSARD 1803-2005, HC Deb 01 March 1886 vol 302 c1532. At www.parliament.uk. Last Accessed 15th October 2011. References to Hansard in other forms are to manuscript sources.
90. Anon, 1853, 'The Dens of London', at p.175.
91. Symons, Jelinger C., 1849, at p.41; See also Kingsmill, J., 1854 at p.52.
92. Anon, 1887, 'Hospital Life in East London', at p.9.
93. Mearns, Andrew, 1883, at p.12, Holmes, Thomas, 1908, at p.109 and p.166.
94. Beggs, Thomas, 1849, at pp.28-29.
95. Meredith, Susanna, 1881, at p.8.
96. Miles, W.A., 1836, at p.4.
97. Holmes, Thomas, 1908, at p.109.
98. See Booth, Charles, 1889, Vol I, at pp.33-36.
99. Malvery, Olive, 1906, at p.228 and p.270.

of the revolutionary sort.[100] They were also notable for their transitory accommodation arrangements, regularly moving between the casual wards of workhouses, private common lodging-houses, multi-occupancy slum rooms, or living rough, as occasion demanded (albeit often within a surprisingly small area of London).[101] Some even appeared to "take a delight" in their nomadic lives.[102]

The Metropolitan underclass was often seen as actively hostile towards the wider society. Clarence Rook's end-of-century examination of the "philosophy of life" of Lambeth hooligans anticipates some twentieth-century sub-cultural paradigms. Rook felt that many hooligans started with a: "...grievance against society, and are determined to get their own back".[103] Such views were already old in the 1890s. Mary Carpenter had produced a similar analysis for the Select Committee on Juveniles of 1851, when she identified the role of social hostility in the commission of crimes by some London 'Ragged School' boys: "...when they are out of school they are in a state of antagonism with society, and consider everything is lawful prey to them if they can but get it".[104]

Most were seen as incorrigible.[105] Many would reject any form of 'healthy' recreation, being interested only in becoming intoxicated. In a brutally outspoken attack, one contributor to *All the Year Round* condemned the amount of attention being given to the "abject" rather than the "respectable" poor for this reason. He termed it "petting the denizens of the slums".[106] Despite the extremism of his views, he was not unique. Even Mary Carpenter feared that the newly established Ragged Schools, of which she was a prime mover, attracted too few children from the "directly vicious class".[107]

To many observers, members of the residuum were as discernible by their physical appearance as by their conduct. According to John Binney, the 'typical' juvenile found in a London criminal location appeared "almost

---

100. Hoare, H.E., 1883, at p.224.

101. Stevenson, S. J., 1986, at pp.42-43.

102. Anon., 1882, *Metropolitan Police Court Jottings*, at p.31.

103. Rook, Clarence, 1899, at p.17.

104. Evidence to Select Committee on Juveniles, Answer to Question 816, by Mary Carpenter; reproduced Tobias, J.J., 1972, *Nineteenth Century Crime*, at p.46.

105. Preface to Hollingshead, John, 1861.

106. Rowsell, E.P., 1864, at p.126 and p.149.

107. Evidence to Select Committee on Juveniles, Answer to Question 815, by Mary Carpenter, reproduced in Tobias, J.J., *Nineteenth Century Crime*, 1972 at p.46.

to belong to a separate race".[108] The Victorian preoccupation with phrenology and atavism meant that bodily differences were frequently attributed to inheritance rather than an exceptionally harsh physical environment, especially during childhood. Even a radical like Annie Besant believed that the type of skull termed 'criminal' was well known, with its retreating forehead and the: "...brutal mouth and jaw, the sloping occiput, characteristic of the class".[109] In general, and much more plausibly, they were smaller, more wiry, sickly and pale-faced than other Londoners.[110]

The Irish Presence

Impoverished Irishmen were always an important part of this marginal group.[111] Even when considerable prejudice is taken into account (and it was always present), there appears to have been a genuine, if often exaggerated, correlation between their presence and higher offending rates in London.[112] Even before the Famine, Thomas Carlyle had been concerned about their criminogenic potential.[113] After the potato blight struck, things became more serious. Jelinger Symons believed that there was "little doubt" that post-Famine Irish immigration was a major cause of the apparently rapid growth of crime in Middlesex during the late 1840s.[114] Their offspring, the English born or raised 'Cockney Irish' were often thought to be even worse than their parents. When discussing the pickpockets of one crime prone London locality in the 1850s, Mayhew's collaborators thought that the great mass were Irish cockneys.[115] Even the imprisoned Fenian, Jeremiah O'Donovan Rossa, reluctantly noted of his English prison companions: "Nearly half these men were of Irish parents, and their crimes were traceable to poverty and whisky".[116]

A comparison of Irish-born commitments to prison and Reform School, compared to non-Irish, gives a possible imprisonment rate in the years from 1861 to 1871 of 3,200 per 100, 000 Irish-born compared to 551 non-Irish-born. When reformatories are taken into account, Irish-born

108. Beggs, Thomas, 1849, at p.49.
109. Besant, Annie, 1885, at p.16.
110. Ewing Ritchie, J., 1857, at p.27.
111. Swift, Roger, 1987, at p.268.
112. Emsley, Clive, 1991, at p.70.
113. Carlyle, Thomas, 1839, at p.32.
114. Symons, Jelinger C., 1849, at p.43.
115. Mayhew, Henry et al, 1862, Vol. 4, at p.197.
116. Priestley, Philip, 1985, at p.58.

children appear to have been four times more likely than English ones to end up in a custodial institution.[117] Irish women were thought to be especially prone to offending when compared to their English counterparts.[118]

Initially, many immigrant Irishmen would stick together in the 'nests of Irish' found in places such as the Commercial Road and Rosemary Lane.[119] According to Kensington's medical officer, the notorious Jennings' Buildings were also inhabited by the: "...lowest sort of persons consisting principally of Irish".[120] In such areas they preserved many of their rural traditions, including faction-fights.[121] However, they swiftly settled in all of the capital's poorer areas, so that in the roughest part of Holborn it could be noted that: "Here as in most Rookeries, are colonies of Irish".[122] Friedrich Engels believed that there were 120,000 poor Irishmen in London by the early 1850s, forming the lowest stratum of the community.[123]

If, as appears likely, Irishmen were disproportionately involved in Metropolitan crime, it is fairly easy to explain why. They were isolated on the basis of their class, nationality, and religion in a way that was not to be exceeded until the arrival of large numbers of East European Jews in the 1880s.[124] They were also very poor. Higher levels of crime are partly explained by their greater levels of material desperation and social alienation.

Abuse of Charity

In the modern period, the underclass has been linked to a widespread withdrawal from the labour market, their members coming to prefer crime, 'hustling' and welfare, to low paid regular work. In the nineteenth-century there was an equivalent fear that the residuum abused the poor law and private charity. This encouraged the creation of The Society for Organising Charitable Relief and Repressing Mendicity in 1869. Although nationally based, the society was always strongest in London. It was premised on the unoriginal, if more scientifically pursued, belief that the poor could be

---

117. Priestley, Philip, 1985, at p.117.
118. Pike, Luke Owen, 1876, Vol. 2, at p.530.
119. Mayhew, Henry et al, 1862, Vol. 1, at p.115.
120. Davis, Jennifer, 1984, at p.319.
121. Hodder, George, 1845, at p.198.
122. Beames, Thomas, 1852, at p.54.
123. Engels, Friedrich, 1958, at p.104.
124. Swift, Roger, 1987, at p. 275.

divided into "deserving" and "undeserving".[125] The society believed that charity should be administered on the basis of 'character' as much as apparent need. The deserving could properly be aided by private philanthropy; the remainder were the province of the workhouse. It campaigned against the indiscriminate distribution of alms. The *British Quarterly Review* also divided paupers into those who were "wilful and vicious" and those who were "involuntary and helpless".[126] In the early 1870s, the Metropolitan Police Commissioner felt that "indiscriminate charity" remained a problem in the capital, as it created and sustained a class of people whose vocation it was not to labour.[127] There were regularly published cautionary tales as to the potential dangers of such blanket largesse.[128] Much of Mayhew's work also attempted to assist 'respectable' Victorian Londoners in making the difficult distinction between the two classes of pauper. This bifurcation of the destitute also led men like Philip Danvers to stress the need for a system of relief in which "vagabonds" were not incarcerated with those poor who had been "borne down by misfortune, sickness, or want of employment".[129]

The 'Typical' Crime

Given that the 'typical' criminal in Victorian London came from this underclass, it might be expected that most instrumental crimes would be *relatively* small in scale. On examination, this proves to be the case. In 1859, for example, the capital's 12,654 *reported* felonies (ignoring misdemeanours), of all types, affecting property, produced an average *claimed* loss (many were exaggerated) of £4-4s.[130] If embezzlement, a primarily 'middle class' rather than 'street' crime, is taken from this category, the average falls to £3-17s. This must be seen against an average worker's weekly wage of 20s to 25s.[131] The average for unrecorded crimes was probably very much less than these figures suggest.

As Mayhew appreciated, the rewards for burglary were usually relatively low because most of the houses raided were themselves quite

---

125. See *The Gentleman's Magazine*, September 1814 at p.228 for an earlier use of this distinction.

126. Anon, 1862, 'Phases of London Life', at p.341: Mayhew, Henry et al, 1862, at p.343.

127. PR.9.1869-77, Report for the Year 1872, at p.2.

128. Anon, 1872, 'How We Make Thieves', at p. 279.

129. Danvers, Philip, 1842, at p. 6.

130. PR.6, 1859.

131. Harrison, J.F.C., 1998, at p.68.

modest; as a result, thieves normally secured a: "...booty of such small value that they are necessitated frequently to commit depredations".[132] Given the large percentage of the proceeds of their crimes pocketed by fences and other middlemen, they might have to steal several times a day to survive.[133] Few habitual thieves in the 1850s 'earned' more than £2 a week.[134] As a result, the typical London criminal was a man pursuing a trade that limited him to threadbare clothes. The: "...ordinary thief seldom rises above very plain eating".[135]

That the proceeds of crime were normally relatively modest is not surprising. Even today, urban crime tends to be predominantly intra rather than inter-class.[136] In the Victorian period, with its more limited transportation 'out of area', this was even more the case. The victims of crime were predominantly other poor people. In the words of the Commissioner in 1895, Metropolitan crimes were: "...perpetrated for the most part at the expense of the poor, and not of the rich".[137] As a result, the incidence of crime was weighted heavily towards the slum areas of London. Opportunistic burglars often resided in areas like the Borough, Whitechapel, St. Giles and Shoreditch. They tended to target the houses of local working-class people.[138] Most of the juvenile thieves studied by Augustus Miles in the 1830s were arrested for crimes committed very close to their homes, most of which were in working-class areas. For example, Samuel Holmes lived, stole and fenced his goods in the Ratcliff Highway.[139] Despite the fears of the well to do about being 'garrotted', even this crime appears to have been heaviest in those areas where they rarely trod.[140] It only became a capital-wide preoccupation after a highly publicised attack on an M.P. in Pall Mall in July of 1862.[141]

---

132. Mayhew, Henry et al, 1862, Vol. 4, at p.338.
133. Charge to the Grand Jury of Birmingham, July 1839, reproduced in Davenport Hill, Mathew, 1857, at p.7.
134. Dixon, Hepworth, 1850, at p.22.
135. Archer, Thomas, 1865, at pp.26-27.
136. Lea, John and Young, Jock, 1984, at p.100.
137. *The Illustrated Police News*, November 30th, 1895.
138. Mayhew, Henry et al, 1862, Vol. 4, at p.338.
139. See on this Shore, Heather, 1997, at pp.202 & 203.
140. Sindall, Robert, 1990, at p.6. The name was first used in a letter to *The Times* by a barrister who was alleged to have been a victim in 1851. Prior to this date, such attacks had often been called 'thugee', after the suppressed Indian cult. Some complained that it was actually exhibitions on the cult of thugee, in London museums, that had given Metropolitan criminals the idea.
141. Mayhew, Henry et al, 1862, Vol. 4, at p.328.

Amateur Criminal Techniques

Most of the underclass's criminal ventures were characterised by poor preparation and planning. They were often committed impulsively and feebly executed, greatly increasing the risk of arrest. As a Pentonville prison chaplain observed, a combination of drunken habits and "gross ignorance" were likely to disqualify most London criminals from "success in thieving".[142] Specialism, or a skilled criminal technique, was rare. In 1877, Detective Inspector John Shore noted that contrary to the general notion of the public, his 16 years experience in London indicated that the criminal class varied their *modus operandi* as opportunity presented, the only exception being the capital's handful of top-level burglars.[143] Despite this, most burglaries were carried out by opportunists. Such men (and the occasional woman) were often lacking in the basic tools needed for their crimes. Instead of carrying proper jemmies, they improvised with screwdrivers and knives. They would work alone or in twos and threes to effect entry to premises in a variety of unsophisticated ways: standing on each other's shoulders to climb through an open first-floor window; breaking panes of glass and then forcing window catches etc. In 1874, there were only 13 recorded cases of larceny being effected in a London dwelling house by 'cat-burglars', intruders entering through attic windows from the adjacent roofs of unoccupied buildings, and 259 cases involving the use of false or skeleton keys (perhaps an indication of planning and preparation). These must be compared to 2,741 cases of entry through doors that had been left open and untended.[144]

At the end of the century, the poor 'quality' of most of London's ordinary criminals and their offences was still being stressed by men like Thomas Holmes, who felt that the common London burglar, lacking in "stature, strength, courage, or brains" would attempt crude break-ins that were devoid of skill and daring. He felt that they were a direct product of slum life.[145] Sir Robert Anderson, a former Assistant Commissioner (1888-1901), was equally dismissive of their abilities, believing that a good safe normally provided complete security against ordinary criminals. Unless they were unfortunate enough to be attacked by the capital's tiny number of professionals, most crime victims were paying the price of their own carelessness.[146]

---

142. Kingsmill, Joseph, 1854, at p.41.
143. pp.15.1878, at p.24.
144. PR.10.1874, Table No.19, at p.38.
145. Holmes, Thomas, 1908, at p.11 & p.33.
146. Anderson, Robert, 1910, at p.233.

Locations

The study of urban crime in the nineteenth century soon leads to the concept of the 'criminal area'.[147] Thus, Hepworth Dickson's mid-century account of the London prisons, and Thomas Bean's portrayal of the rookeries of London, painted a picture of geographically defined areas steeped in crime.[148] As one observer noted in 1862, many Metropolitan criminals appeared to select specific locations, bunching closely together so that it was: "...no uncommon thing for three or four contiguous streets to be wholly tenanted by them".[149]

Of course, such a phenomenon was by no means unique to London. All major British cities had their 'criminal' locations. Thus, Manchester had Deansgate and Liverpool had Waterloo Road.[150] In Manchester, as elsewhere, the "class of criminals" occupied some of the most squalid parts of the city.[151] However, London witnessed the apotheosis of this underclass and its haunts, if only because of the city's huge size.[152]

Some of these nefarious areas had long histories. For example, as early as 1785, Field Lane in Clerkenwell had been described as a "thieves' republic".[153] Little had changed 65 years later, when the journalist W.H. Dixon believed that it was still a: "...hot-bed of crime and demoralisation".[154] Although Dorset Street in the East End was to become notorious in the late 1880s, over half a century earlier, the Society for the Prevention of Juvenile Prostitution had focused on it as a problem area.[155] Other criminal blackspots were of much more recent origin.

Because they were resistant to both policing and social reform, these locations were seen as menacing Britain's major cities, especially London. Many thought that the work of the new police would be ineffectual until the legislature undertook the duty of breaking them up, or at least until it placed them: "...under sanitary regulations, and the more immediate and strict surveillance of the police".[156] This gradually occurred in many Metropolitan areas after 1850. Although London was socially very varied

---

147. Tobias, J.J., 1974, at p.221.
148. Radzinowicz, Leon with Hood, Roger, 1976, at p.75.
149. Pare, W., 1862, at p.11.
150. Dixon, W.H., 1850, at pp.224-228.
151. Neale, W.B., 1840, at p.8.
152. pp.10.c.1832, at p.34.
153. Hanway, Jonas, 1780, at p.xvi.
154. Dixon, W.H., 1850, at pp.224-228.
155. Ryan, Michael, 1839, at p.140.
156. Neale, W.B., 1840, at p.55.

at the close of the nineteenth century, its number of 'criminal' areas had fallen drastically. In the mid-century they had been widespread; towards its end, much more rare.[157] As a result, by the late 1880s, it could be claimed that not only was the criminal class no longer a large one, but that the: "...plague spots where they congregate are known and well defined".[158]

One reason for this phenomenon was that at the start of the nineteenth century many criminal elements could still be found in the historic 'rookeries' that were located in or adjacent to the City and parts of Westminster. These often dated back to an era when a local religious house had provided sanctuary. Even in the middle of the period, the Reverend Thomas Beames could note that many of the most aristocratic streets still had a background of wretchedness, so that few parishes were without a number of tenements that it would be difficult to describe as anything other than rookeries.[159] Although Westminster contained many opulent politicians and lawyers, it was also infested by more thieves than could be found in most other parts of the Metropolis.[160] They could be seen in the lanes and alleys that branched off from Orchard Street just as readily as in Whitechapel.[161] The 'Devil's Acre' was within a stone's throw of both Westminster Abbey and Parliament.[162] Similarly, the nefarious Berwick Street was located in affluent St. James's.[163] Alsatia, another historic rookery, was situated in Whitefriars, only yards from the Inns of Court, the home of London's senior lawyers, while Golden Lane was next to the Square Mile.

However, as the second half of the nineteenth century progressed, many of these were cleared and there was an increasing tendency for the criminal 'underclass' to be concentrated in clusters of streets within much larger, often outlying, poor areas.[164] In 1850, Thomas Beames had presciently noted that St. Giles, although one of the oldest and most extreme examples of a criminal area, no longer had any obvious reason for its condition. It was not on the banks of a river or connected with shipping, so affording a "harvest for crimps, thieves, and abandoned women".[165] It

---

157. Tobias, J.J., 1966 at p.41.
158. Barnett, Henrietta, 1888, at p.440.
159. Beames, Thomas, 1852, at p.106.
160. Mayhew, Henry, 1862, at p.353.
161. Wakefield, Edward Gibbon, 1832, at p.7.
162. Mackay, Alexander, 1850, at p.297.
163. Beames, Thomas, 1852, at p.106.
164. Tobias, J.J., 1974, at p.221.
165. Beames, Thomas, 1852, at p.19. It was located near modern Tottenham Court Road.

did not last another 20 years. From the mid-century, central rookeries were progressively demolished and their inhabitants displaced, many to the East End and the Borough, in a wider process in which both criminal streets and their surrounding slums were cleared. By the 1860s, Drury Lane and St. Giles had totally changed and order reigned. According to a local police Superintendent, only 15 years earlier they were a perpetual scene of riot and disorder, with public houses that were notorious for thieves, pickpockets, and burglars.[166] Slum parts of Drury Lane, Covent Garden and Bloomsbury that between them had produced 203 charges in 1875 saw just 19 a decade later, after extensive demolition and rebuilding.[167]

This process created new, and expanded existing, 'rookeries' in unreformed places such as Flower and Dean Street and Dorset Street in East London. It was to be these streets, more than anything else, that gave the East End its general (and slightly undeserved) reputation, so that by the late Victorian period the area was heavily associated with crime, squalor and social demoralisation, an: "...evil plexus of slums that hide human creeping things".[168]

In reality, such streets were not typical of the very poor areas within which they were located. Nevertheless, they tended to colour public perceptions of the wider area, explaining the divergence between reputation and empirical reality. On Charles Booth's figures, it is quite difficult to understand, at first sight, what was so special about the East End, even in the 1890s. It was significantly poorer than London as a whole, but not enormously so: 35.2% were in poverty or want there, compared to a London average of about 30%; 1.2% belonged to class A and 11.2% to class B (the lowest groups), compared to 0.9% and 7.5% respectively, although at 8.9% its 'middle class' was only half the London average. With figures like these, it is easy to see why men such as Walter Besant, with more experience and less sensitivity than (for example) Jack London, might stress the mundane aspects of the area, and its cultural rather than physical impoverishment.

The great majority of East Enders were well-intentioned if poor people: "...generally law-abiding; with narrow interest and limited outlooks, but with consciences which they keep alive, and a moral code which, if low, is nevertheless obeyed". Indeed, in an early anticipation of labelling theory, one observer was afraid that the exaggerated media response to the Whitechapel murders in 1888, with their portrayals of a crime-saturated, immoral and dangerous area, had a: "...tendency to make

---

166. Mayhew, Henry et al, 1862, Vol. 4, at p.237.
167. White, Jerry, 2008, at p.331.
168. Morrison, Arthur, 1901, at p.7.

the careless, the low-principled, and the weak-minded accept the role which public opinion has assigned to them".[169] The inherent 'normality' of these areas was to be evidenced by the numerous local 'vigilance' committees that were thrown up in the wake of the Ripper killings.[170]

The small clusters of 'criminal' streets found within these larger, very poor, but more 'respectable' working-class areas had distinctive qualities. For an example can be considered the notorious Flower and Dean Street rookery, which by the 1880s was considered by many to be the worst in London, unmatched for the number of the "dangerous class" found amongst its residents.[171] It was based around the main street, but included 27 courts and alleys. It may have been the location observed by Hugh Edward Hoare, a wealthy Old Etonian who, in the early 1880s, wished to become acquainted with the communities from which "violent unskilled" criminals came. This led him into one of East London's most notorious slums, a place that was "almost exclusively inhabited by the criminal classes".[172]

This pattern of slum areas inhabited by ordinary poor people, studded with localised congregations of criminals, was repeated in South London. Although most of the Borough's residents were labouring men and small shopkeepers, it had: "…low neighbourhoods in many of the by-streets, infested by the dangerous classes". Union Street was particularly bad, while Market Street was home to numerous prostitutes and thieves.[173] Similarly, P.C. Cavanagh could distinguish Ewer Street from the ordinary poverty of its surrounding area. Crime was endemic there, and violence could erupt without notice, especially after closing time.[174] This localised pattern of criminal areas continued to the end of the century. At a public meeting in 1897, a Mr. Barr from St. George's Parish Vestry opined that the courts abutting the Borough formed a: "…rabbit warren for the thieves and ruffians who infested the neighbourhood". Crime rates in these places were, apparently, uninfluenced by the general Metropolitan improvement that had occurred over the previous 40 years.[175]

---

169. Barnett, Henrietta, 1888, at pp.433-6.
170. Sugden, Philip, 1995, at p.19.
171. *Tower Hamlets Independent*, November 19th, 1881, quoted in White, Jerry, at p.7.
172. *Tower Hamlets Independent*, February 4th, 1882, quoted in White, Jerry, 1980, at p.7.
173. Mayhew, Henry et al, 1862, Vol. 4, at p.333.
174. Cavanagh, Timothy, 1893, at pp.24-25.
175. Anon, 1897, 'Inadequate Police Protection in South London', at p.681.

In modern America, it has been claimed that less than 3% of street addresses and the same proportion of the population in most cities produce over half their crime and arrests.[176] By 1900, a broadly similar, if much less marked, pattern would apply in London.

Low Lodging-houses

One characteristic of nearly all 'criminal areas' was the disproportionate congregation of 'low' lodging-houses within them. Indeed, in the case of the infamous Campbell Road in late-Victorian Holloway, their arrival in 1880 marked the transformation of the street into such an area.[177] They were cheap, frequently squalid, tenements with crowded multi-occupancy rooms, let on a casual (often nightly) basis, to the poorest and most rootless elements of London society. Although low lodging-houses could be found in all British cities, the acute accommodation shortage in London meant that they were a uniquely serious problem in the capital.[178] Such houses were also lucrative forms of investment for small Metropolitan landlords. They were widespread across the city, but especially prevalent in the bad parts of the East End and South London. Thus, John Binney could observe that St. George's in the East "abounds with them".[179] In 1888, *The Times* noted that "nearly every house" in Dorset Street was a common lodging-house, while many more could be found in adjacent alleys.[180] Similarly, nearly all the buildings in Hoare's (anonymous) East End slum street were registered lodging-houses, with 10 to 100 beds apiece. As the singer and 'slummer', Olive Malvery, observed, it was a business "best run in company" and rare to see isolated establishments.[181]

Their occupants tended to be disproportionately young, male, and single. In 1871, for example, Flower and Dean Street's 31 lodging-houses housed 902 people (out of a total population for the street of 1,078). One in three were men aged between 15 and 30. Only 308 were women, 200 of whom were aged between 15 and 40. Beds were available at 4d. a night, though a 'space' on the floor was even cheaper. There might be 8 to 12 people in each room, with sexes and ages often mixing indiscriminately,

---

176. Sherman, Lawrence W., 1992, at p.159.
177. White, Jerry, 1986, at p.12.
178. Anon, 1851, *Lost in London,* at p.377.
179. Mayhew, Henry et al, 1862, Vol. 4, at p.223. It was alleged that those in St. George's were owned by "disreputable Jews".
180. *The Times*, September 11th, 1888.
181. Malvery, Olive, 1906, at p.271.

especially prior to the 1850s.[182] It was not unusual for inmates to go to their beds after three or to leave before six in the morning.[183] The manager would normally take anyone who applied for a bed, if he had room and they had ready cash.

Such lodgings were frequently hotbeds of crime.[184] They were often described as being a "focus of contagion" where juvenile offenders were initiated into nefarious lives.[185] Several of the boy-criminals chronicled by William Augustus Miles in the 1830s had been drawn into offending by the lodging-house culture found in Whitechapel. Fifty years later, another informed observer feared that boys coming to lodging-houses were still being incited to turn to a life of crime.[186] A low lodging-house could also act as a "predatory centre" for its surrounding area. Cheap stolen goods would quickly find buyers there. Their keepers might even pawn them on behalf of resident thieves, breaking down bundles of stolen clothes into individual items and sending each piece with an inmate to a pawnshop for disposal.[187] For example, in the early 1850s, a 12-year-old noted that the female landlady of his low lodging-house in St. Giles would always "buy what the boys steal".[188]

Of course, there may have been a tendency for popular writers to suggest that the worst of such houses were typical of them all. A handful of them were even aimed at 'respectable' people. There was also a gradual improvement in their general condition, after Lord Shaftesbury managed to get the 1851 (14 & 15 Vict. c.28) and 1853 (16 & 17 Vict. c.1) Common Lodging-Houses Acts through Parliament. These statutes provided for compulsory registration and inspection. Even Hoare noted that the law regulating the number of beds for which a house was registered was "strictly obeyed" in his slum, for fear that an inspector might call. By 1872, Colonel Henderson was convinced that the "careful administration" of the two statutes had had a major impact on London crime levels.[189] Nevertheless, there was little room for complacency. Only three years later, the Commissioner opined that without strict and continuing supervision, the common lodging-houses would quickly become "active *foci* of moral as well as physical pestilence". Many continued to be

---

182. Miles, W.A., 1836, at p.7.
183. *The Times,* September 11th, 1888.
184. 'Amigo', 1847, at p.82.
185. Neale, William Beaver, 1840, at p.8. & p.54.
186. Anon, 1883, 'Homes of the Criminal Classes', at p.824.
187. Fredur, Thor, 1879, at pp.131-134.
188. Antrobus, Edmund, 1853, at p.96.
189. PR.9.1869-76, Report for the Year 1872, at p.8.

hotbeds of crime, especially in the East End, where inspection tended to be more cursory.[190] The impact of these statutes was also hindered by difficulties in the legal definition of such establishments, an issue that was only firmly settled by the Queen's Bench Divisional Court at the end of the century.[191]

However, even within London, the number of such houses was always *proportionately* fairly small when compared to other types of accommodation, and it also declined in most areas in the second half of the century. Thus, in 1854, according to one commentator, there were 10,824 Common lodging-houses, with an average of 82,000 occupants in the capital. This was probably their numerical peak. By 1888, according to the Farina Society, there were only 995 such houses, accommodating 32,000 inmates.[192] They declined further towards the end of the century, having only 30,000 places at most in 1893.[193] By its close, only 115 registered lodging-houses remained in London.[194] Even at their peak, they probably housed less than 4% of the capital's population; London's regularly employed work-force very rarely lived in them.

190. pp.15.1878, at p.82.
191. *The Times*, December 12th, 1899.
192. Wohl, A.S., 1997, at pp.74-76.
193. *The Standard*, October 4th, 1893, at p.6.
194. Malvery, Olive, 1906, at p.271.

CHAPTER THREE

THE COMING OF THE NEW POLICE

Introduction

London had a population of nearly one and a half million people when the Metropolitan Police force was established in 1829. Before this, policing had largely been the responsibility of an ill-assorted amalgam of the historic system of parish constables and night watchmen combined with the important but modest (in scale) professional policing innovations of the late 1700s and early 1800s.

The preamble to the 1829 Act for improving the Police in and near the Metropolis (10 Geo. IV, c.44), which founded the Metropolitan Police, summarized the problems that were thought to plague this system. It declared that the: "…local Establishments of Nightly Watch and Nightly Police have been found inadequate to the Prevention and Detection of Crime, by reason of the frequent unfitness of the individuals employed, the insufficiency of their Number, the limited sphere of their Authority, and their Want of Connection and Co-operation with each other". Thus, there were issues with the numbers, quality, and fragmentation of the various Metropolitan policing agencies. The historic parish-based system inherited from the early modern period and the limited professional forces added after the middle of the eighteenth century can be considered separately.

The 'Traditional' System

Prior to 1829, the poorer parishes of East London were particularly illustrative of the 'traditional' Metropolitan police system. Despite the huge increases in their population over the previous 50 years, they had changed little in a century, and provide ready ammunition for the 'Whig' portrayal of that system. Thus, in the early 1820s, Whitechapel's St. Botolph Without force was headed by a beadle (a salaried, full-time, parish officer), who was paid fifty pounds a year, and whose duties were, *inter alia*, to patrol the streets, spend evenings at the watch house, and supervise the watch. Supporting him were seven unpaid (by the parish) part-time constables and a paid street-keeper. The constables were appointed annually (often against their wishes) by the parish to execute warrants, attend court, and supervise the watch house once a week. If they had the resources, they could pay a deputy to do their duty for them. There were also up to 31 men employed in the nightly watch, operative between 10 p.m. and 4 a.m. in the summer, and 9 p.m. and 7 a.m. in the winter. There was no age qualification for these men, although they were *supposed* to be of good character and able-bodied. They were paid a nightly rate, usually earning between 10s. 6d. and 19s. a week.[1] Thus the two main components of the traditional system were the parish constables and the watch.

The Watch

The Watch was subject to harsh criticism right up to its abolition in 1829, as John Pearson's satirical portrayal of incompetent, corrupt, and feeble watchmen makes clear.[2] In his evidence to the Police Committee of 1816, the magistrate Sir Nathaniel Conant claimed that they were generally inferior, and often elderly, men who were usually found dozing in their watch-boxes when on duty.[3] Others suggested that anyone pursued by them would have to be a: "...cripple indeed, if ever the Watchmen overtook him on such an occasion".[4] The situation was not improved, as Robert Peel noted, by the widespread practice of appointing watchmen who would otherwise be constant burdens on the parish poor rate.[5] The Watch was also often used as a form of retirement home for parish servants who were "manifestly disabled by age or infirmity".[6] Watch pay was so poor that many of its members had 'day-jobs', doubling as porters and labourers, further diminishing their nocturnal efficiency. Fatigue combined with age, poor physical standards and a partiality to gin, consumed both on and off duty, may have contributed to their relative lack of mobility. There was a tendency for them to make only infrequent 'patrols' away from their boxes and benches.[7] Additionally, watchmen normally came on duty quite late, often well after dusk, despite this being a peak offending time, especially for juveniles.[8]

---

1. Radzinowicz, Leon, 1948-56, Vol. 1, at p.501, based on pp.9.1822, at p.192.
2. Pearson, John, 1827, at p.3.
3. Evidence of Sir Nathaniel Conant, pp.5.1816, at pp.30-31.
4. Egan, Pierce, 1821, at p.232.
5. *Hansard's Parliamentary Debates*, Vol. XXI, New Series, at p. 879.
6. pp.10a.1828, at p.22.
7. Chadwick, Edwin, 1829, at p.254.
8. Dudley, Thomas, 1828, at pp.iii-iv & p.12.

The Home Office papers on the notorious Ratcliffe Highway murders of 1811 contain descriptions by a watchman, Thomas Hickey, of the variety of tricks employed by his corrupt fellow officers to enhance their meagre pay, such as being bribed to look the other way by thieves.[9] In Shadwell, the existing watchmen were all discharged and replaced as a result of these revelations.[10] Although this incident also led to the establishment of the 1812 Police Committee, an observer could still argue, seven years after it reported, that: "To expect efficient protection from them [watchmen], would be to calculate on beholding strength resulting from imbecility".[11] Not surprisingly, many did not mourn the passing of a body that they considered "absolutely useless" and which, it was claimed, was often viewed with contempt and derision by thieves, even when its members were not openly corrupt.[12] Five years after abolition, the judge William Arabin was sure that the watchmen were "very inferior" in all respects to the new police, though he appears to have been inordinately impressed by the latter's ability to give clear forensic evidence.[13]

The Constables

The position of the traditional parish constables was often said to be as parlous as that of the watch. Like the watch, the office had an ancestry reaching back to the Statute of Winchester of 1285, something that critics in the 1820s would stress when emphasising that social change had rendered constables "worn out and utterly inadequate".[14] The duty was allotted to parish householders by rota, subject to an important element of discretion. In 1828, for example, Thomas Dudley thought that he had been made a Westminster constable purely because he had annoyed his local vestry. He believed that many men had had their businesses ruined because of the demands of their unwanted office.[15] In 1840, Joseph Butterfill, seeking compensation after being made redundant as a substitute Woolwich parish constable on the arrival of the expanding Metropolitan police, argued that his duty meant: "...losing his connection in trade for want of punctuality in attendance".[16]

---

9. James, P.D., and Critchley, T.A., 1971, at p.6 & p.19.
10. Radzinowicz, Leon, 1956, at p.39.
11. Leigh, Samuel, 1819, at p.97.
12. Wakefield, Edward Gibbon, 1831, at p.2.
13. pp.11.d.1834, at p.274.
14. Hardwicke, John, 1828, at p.495.
15. Dudley, Thomas, 1828, at p.15.
16. HO 61/25, 1840, Petition to the Marquis of Normanby, Home Secretary.

The system was, in some ways, made worse by the widely used expedient whereby those appointed to the office could pay a fine in lieu of service or, even worse (and far more commonly), appoint a paid deputy, such as Butterfill, to carry out the duty in their place. By the 1820s, a significant majority of Metropolitan constables were paid substitutes, though their numbers varied greatly between areas. As early as 1802, 150 of the 250 constables in the City of London were substitutes (and the figure there would be significantly higher a few years later). In the Liberty of Westminster, 31 of 80 men were substitutes, while in Southwark the figure was 46 out of 87. However, in poorer Finsbury, Tower Hamlets and Holborn their proportion dropped to less than 30% of the whole.[17] The consequence of widespread substitution was that: "...parochial police must be left almost exclusively to those who make it a business and profitable pursuit".[18] As they had to be paid by the person originally appointed to the office, they tended to be employed by the wealthiest and so, in contemporary eyes, most 'respectable' men, something that necessarily diminished the average quality of the constables even further.[19]

Although such men had to be approved by the relevant parish, substitution was more likely to produce constables who were personally corrupt and given to accepting bribes. This was, perhaps, not surprising, given that the annual pay for such 'stand-ins', even in the 1820s, was only between £8 and £10. Many substitutes were not inspired with the spirit of their office, or likely to: "...engage in the duties of thief-catching with gusto".[20]

Even where they were not substitutes, parish constables were normally reactive, responding to requests for assistance from crime victims and magistrates, rather than being permanently on duty, except when taking their turn to supervise the nocturnal watch house. Ultimately, it was a harsh fact that: "...unpaid constables are still only volunteer troops".[21]

Enhanced Parish Systems

However, criticism of traditional pre-1829 Metropolitan policing arrangements can be exaggerated, especially with regard to the early decades of the nineteenth century. After 1805, the Police Office magistrates (introduced in 1792) acquired the right to dismiss incompetent

---

17. Colquhoun, Patrick, 1803, at p.xiii.
18. Mainwaring, G.B., 1821, at p.549.
19. Anon, 1818, *The Constable's Assistant,* at p.13.
20. Grant, James, 1838, at p.386.
21. *The Times*, November 5th, 1821, p.6.

watchmen. Considerable progress had also been made in many individual parishes towards enhancing the organisation, supervision, financing and quality of the watch, especially in the central areas. These had usually been authorised by private Acts of Parliament, after petition from the parish concerned. As a result, the 1812 Police Committee, deciding against more radical change, recognised that improvements had been made in many parishes, and commended the "activity and vigilance" displayed by those willing to inspect and supervise their police arrangements. The committee felt that this merely needed to be extended to all Metropolitan parishes by legislation.[22]

By 1829, the most prosperous parishes had developed quite sophisticated systems of local policing, something that, in part, explains their resistance to reform that year. By then, many of their watchmen were physically fit and relatively youthful. For example, a list of those in the parish of St. Mary, Islington, in 1826, shows an age range of 19 to 40, with most men being in their twenties or early thirties. Even those who were taken from the charity rolls (a frequent complaint) were usually young and able-bodied.[23] Contrary to contemporary claims that they "very seldom" captured housebreakers, a perusal of the *Old Bailey Sessions Papers* quickly reveals numerous cases of burglars being detained by watchmen.[24]

Many of these improved parishes also experimented with uniforms and hierarchical supervision for their watch. Thus, the St. Marylebone parish force of the 1820s included one superintendent, six street-keepers, 17 sergeants, 180 watchmen and 42 part-time constables. Its ratio of one official per 369 inhabitants was considerably better than that achieved after the advent of the new police. Perhaps unsurprisingly, the St. Marylebone vestry argued that they should have been exempted from the provisions of the 1829 Act, as their parish was already well protected: "…both by day and by night, in fact its police was considered so efficient that its discipline and regulations formed the groundwork of the discipline and regulations of the New Police".[25] When introducing his Bill to the House of Commons in April 1829, even Peel readily conceded that some parishes had an "efficient parochial police" that was well able to protect the property and persons of their residents.

---

22. pp.4.1812, at p.96.
23. Paley, Ruth, 1989, at p.128.
24. Dudley, Thomas, 1828, at p.v.
25. See Reynolds, Elaine, 1989, at p.446 and p.459.

The Traditional System in 1829

As a result of a combination of historic problems and piecemeal reforms, the quality of parish-based policing in 1829 was very varied. A considerable number of watchmen and constables were still very poor (forming the basis for popular satire), many were at least competent and, in several improved parishes, albeit not usually in the worst areas of the Metropolis, they were very good, being well supervised and recruited from fit men of sound character.[26]

A major problem in leaving local authorities to enhance their own policing was that London's social stratification had increased rapidly during the eighteenth and early nineteenth centuries. Many vestries had neither the inclination nor the economic means to introduce the reforms pioneered by the better parishes. This allowed Peel to assert that isolated reforms might even make the situation in unreformed parishes worse, as they became sanctuaries for 'ne'er do wells' driven out of their improved neighbours. Consequently, it was necessary that localised "efficiency was made general".[27] He was not alone in this analysis. George Mainwaring argued that localised policing concentrations encouraged an orientation towards the needs of the richer citizens in London.[28] As will be seen, localism also precluded a force that could be effective at riot control.

Pre-1829 'Professional' Police

The 'traditional' policing arrangements of parish constables, watchmen and beadles, had been supplemented by piecemeal state-funded reforms in the late eighteenth century. These added limited full-time 'professional' forces to the Metropolis. They included: the Thames River Police, which had been established in 1800 (having started as a private venture by West India merchants in 1798) and which was intended to prevent crime in and around the Port of London; the constables attached to each of the seven new Police Offices (courts) set up by the Home Office in 1792, and the Bow Street Runners and patrols, who developed from the initial promise of support made to Henry Fielding by the Duke of Newcastle in 1753.[29]

These new forces continued to evolve and expand into the 1820s. Thus, after 1800, the Thames River Police grew to consist of a large force of

---

26. Emsley, Clive, 1987, at p.175.
27. *Hansard's Parliamentary Debates*, Vol. XXI, New series, 31 March-24 June 1829, at p. 872.
28. Mainwaring, G.B., 1821, at p.541.
29. Radinowicz, Leon, 1948-56, Vol.3, at pp.56-57.

Thames watermen, who manned boats in groups of four under the command of a surveyor (there were 86 of them by 1828), as well as a small number of land constables and three magistrates. At least two of the land-based constables would patrol near the police office in Wapping every night, all of which parish was in the Thames Police jurisdiction and covered by both boat and land patrols.[30] The number of officers employed at each police office in the Metropolis also increased to 12 (from an initial six).

After 1805, the Bow Street Office had also maintained professional Horse (including a 'dismounted' section) and Foot patrols, as well as the Runners. The Horse patrol (both mounted and dismounted) covered the capital's outskirts, the nocturnal Foot patrol, with a total of 100 men, operated in the inner London areas. The latter force patrolled in groups of five, with its area being subdivided into 16 sections, each of which had one patrol designated to it.[31] The Runners, the oldest government-funded police officers in the capital, emphasized quick reaction and detailed investigation.

In 1822, Robert Peel established yet another professional force, the 27 uniformed men of the Bow Street Day patrol. It consisted of 24 officers and three Inspectors, these being divided into three Divisions. They patrolled from 9 am until the night patrol's coming on duty, and were readily distinguishable by their blue coats and trousers, and red waistcoats. The small size of the Day patrol reflected, in part, the fact that it had been set up: "...more as an experiment as to the effect it would produce upon so small a scale, than as to its remaining permanent in the same state". The 'experiment' in diurnal policing was claimed as a great success, supposedly, so effective, that no swift increase was necessary, though a fourth Division was soon proposed.[32]

In 1829, and in the face of some parliamentary sceptics, Peel informed the House of Commons that if so small a body of men could effect such impressive results, it was fair to suppose that "great good" would flow from the establishment of a far larger patrol. Very importantly, it gave a foretaste of a more effective system of professional daytime policing, something that had largely been absent before 1822. Peel also felt that it was primarily the efficiency of the post-1805 Mounted patrol in deterring and apprehending criminals that lay behind the disappearance of highway robbers from the environs of the Metropolis.

These 'professional' officers worked in a variety of ways. The Bow Street Runners and, to a much lesser extent, the salaried constables

---

30. Radinowicz, Leon, 1948-56, Vol.2, at pp.529-31.
31. Gatrell, V.A.C. et al., (Eds) 1980, at p.181.
32. See Appendix to pp.10a.1828, at p.334.

attached to the 1792 Police Offices, emphasised detection, though the latter body conducted a small amount of preventative patrolling, along with the enforcement of warrants. The Runners carried out what would be considered to be mainstream detective work, though the word was very little used before the late 1820s. By contrast, the various 'patrols' (foot, horse and day) emphasised overt mobile urban surveillance and thus were primarily a preventative force.[33]

As with the better watches, these forces adopted policies that would be later adopted or replicated by the new police. Thus, the post-1829 requirement that recruits be physically sound, of a certain stature, and not elderly, was similar to that of the 100 man Bow Street Night patrol in 1828, where no man was appointed who was over 35 years of age, under 5ft 5" in height, and who had not satisfied a thorough medical examination at the hands of the force's surgeon. Like the new police, this force, made up of a hierarchy of one inspector, 17 'conductors' (effectively sergeants) and 82 constables, under the supervision of the Bow Street magistrates, promoted from within its ranks. The "most fit and intelligent" of the conductors were made Inspectors when a vacancy occurred, and the conductors were appointed, on the basis of good behaviour and length of service from amongst the constables.[34] Peel approvingly noted that the mounted patrol was also carefully recruited from healthy men of good character.

Small Numbers of Professional Police

Although many of these reforms were quite effective, they were also very limited in scale. In 1828, there were still only 427 professional, government-funded, officers, costing about £35,000 per annum, for the whole of London. All other Metropolitan protection was provided by the traditional system of beadles, parish constables, and watchmen.[35] As a result, the 12 officers appended to Union Hall Police Court served a population of 150,000 people and, allegedly, 300 resident thieves.[36] It was an impossible task. As John Wade noted in early 1829, the existing professional policing agencies in London were simply inadequate for the size of the city, and the extent of their responsibilities: "What can be more futile than the Bow-Street day-patrol of 24 men with 10,000 streets [to

---

33. See Reynolds, Elaine, 1989, at p.447.
34. Appendix to pp.5.1816, at p.333.
35. Sheppard, Francis, 1971, at p.33.
36. Allen, L.B., 1821, at p.38.

cover]"?[37] In almost identical terms, George Mainwaring felt that the frequency of serious Metropolitan crimes made it necessary to publicise the deficiencies of the capital's police system, lacking as it was in both "power and efficiency" because of its tiny number of full-time professional officers and its administrative fragmentation.[38]

Fragmentation of Policing

As this comment suggests, it was not just the number and quality of Metropolitan law enforcement officers, whether professional or traditional, that occasioned problems. Even if all of London's parishes had been able to establish effective watch systems, and the number of professional police officers had been considerably expanded, there would still have been no "unity of system" and no guarantee that they could act in "mutual concert and co-operation".[39] Indeed, in 1821, a Police Court magistrate was aware of "natural antipathy" between his constables and the traditional parish officers, despite their shared objectives.[40] Thomas Dudley cited the case of a zealous constable from St. Paul's parish in Covent Garden who resolved to clear 'low' coffee houses from the area during his term of office, as he felt that they were being used to fence stolen goods. He sought the assistance of the professional constables attached to the nearby police office. Initially, he received no support and was strongly discouraged. Sir Richard Birnie told him that his own men knew their duties and were not to be interfered with by parish officers. He was even 'assaulted' by these constables when he sought their help (though such aid was eventually forthcoming).[41]

The existing police arrangements were unacceptably disjointed.[42] For many reformers, allowing the parishes a continuing role would "reduce that unity of purpose" that was essential to deal with Metropolitan crime.[43] They felt that it was vital that the existing discordant elements of the London police system, watchmen, patrols, constables etc., be incorporated into "one vigorous and well-organised whole - a regular police force".[44] One of the primary aims of the 1829 Bill was to establish a central board,

---

37. Wade, John, 1829, at p.73.
38. Mainwaring, G.B., 1821, at p.9.
39. Mainwaring, G.B., 1821, at p.22.
40. Allen, L.B., 1821, at p.4.
41. Dudley, Thomas, 1828, at p.17.
42. Chadwick, Edwin, 1829, at p.254.
43. pp.11.d.1834, at p.12.
44. *Police Quarterly Review*, Vol. 37, 1828, at p.502 & p.504.

under the immediate direction of the Secretary of State, with a view to placing the: "...whole watching and patrolling of the Metropolitan District under its superintendence". All parochial distinctions would be done away with and compulsion introduced to police funding, at a flat Metropolitan rate of (initially) 8d. in the pound.[45]

Reform in 1829 was as much about centralising control, and bringing the inferior parishes up to a more uniform standard, as about a general improvement in quality. Many features of the 'new' police accorded with what might be termed existing 'best practice' amongst the professional patrols and reformed Watches in London. In some areas, at least, it is clear that the break between the 'old' and 'new' police was much less sharp than some accounts allow.[46]

The Debate on Policing Reform

According to the (largely twentieth-century) 'Whig' version of police history, 1829 brought 'order out of chaos'. As traditional notions of community responsibility in London broke down under the impact of urbanisation and industrialization, the capital's historic police system became ineffective at dealing with rising levels of crime, and increasingly dependant on poor quality officers, prompting constant attempts at reform from the middle of the eighteenth century onwards. These were baulked by political resistance, until the end of the 1820s, when the necessary changes were made.[47] This analysis, although not entirely well founded, had its basis in some contemporary opinion, albeit often exaggerated for political purposes. Thus, in Peel's view, the country had "entirely outgrown its Police institutions".[48] Similarly, when introducing the Police Bill to the House of Lords in 1829, the Duke of Wellington claimed that there was no branch of the English Criminal Justice system that was so defective as its police.[49]

However, although, to present day observers, the coming of the new police has the weight of "historical inevitability", this was not quite so

---

45. *Hansard's Parliamentary Debates,* Vol. XXI, New series, 31 March-24 June 1829, at pp.872-875. And 'Proceedings in Parliament' in *The Gentleman's Magazine,* Vol.99, Jan-June 1829, at p.360.
46. See on this Smith, Philip Fermond, 1985, at p.4, and, more generally Reynolds, Elaine, 1998.
47. Lyman, J.L., 1964, at pp.141-154.
48. Letter of February 1828, cited in Philips, David, 1980, at p.185.
49. *Hansard's Parliamentary Debates*, Vol. XXI, New series, 31 March-24 June 1829, at p. 881.

apparent in 1829.[50] Despite mounting concern about Metropolitan security, the new police were clearly not a simple response to public pressure. A process of gradual and incremental change, based on a mixture of preventative and detective policing philosophies, had dominated the debate until the middle of the 1820s. In 1829, this approach was suddenly superseded by radical transformation and a system that was (initially) overwhelmingly premised on preventative policing allied to a strong capacity for public order maintenance.

Political Resistance to Reform

For almost a century prior to 1829, any proposal for a new London police system had attracted fierce political criticism. This both delayed change and shaped the eventual form in which it was delivered. To some extent, objections depended on social provenance, though several concerns were almost universal.

Radicals feared the political consequences of centralisation. Conservatives were concerned about the impact of reform on local élites.[51] The government would gain power and a major source of patronage. The middle social 'orders', probably the least resistant in London to the concept of a regular police force, were anxious about the potential expense involved in implementing change, as well as the loss of local, parish vestry control (often their primary medium of political expression).[52] Concern about the erosion of 'traditional' English civil liberties, these being premised on a mixture of individualism and libertarianism, was widely shared across the classes. The greater provision for policing found in some continental systems was also considered to be inimical to the rights of 'freeborn' Englishmen. To modern eyes, there was still a remarkable tolerance for crime and disorder as the necessary price of liberty. The 1822 Parliamentary Committee, when deciding against radical change, expressly concluded that it was: "...difficult to reconcile an effective system of police, with that perfect freedom of action and exemption from interference, which are the great privileges and blessings of society in this country".

However, by the 1820s, the tide of opinion was slowly turning, as more observers decided that it was absurd to hear Englishmen boasting of their freedom when they were also at constant risk of having their property

---

50. Ignatieff, Michael, 1979, at pp.443-445.
51. Miller, W.W., 1987, at p.42.
52. Evidence of Sir Nathaniel Conant, pp.5.1816, at pp. 30-31.

seized and being "cruelly beaten into the bargain".[53] In a letter to the Duke of Wellington, in 1829, Peel expressly suggested that one aim of any new police force would be to teach people that liberty did not consist in having their houses robbed by organised gangs of thieves or in leaving the principal streets of London in the: "…nightly possession of drunken women and vagabonds".[54]

Reform in 1829

Change came suddenly. The 1822 Committee had concluded that the existing disjointed policing system was a hindrance in controlling crime and public order to a "much less degree than might have been apprehended". It was "certainly" not such a major problem as to justify radical reform.[55] However, unlike that of 1822, the composition of the 1828 Committee was heavily influenced by Robert Peel, the then Home Secretary and, predictably, favourable to his views. This largely explains the *volte-face* in only six years. It is also possible that the Bill's unthreatening title, the "Metropolis Police Improvement Bill", contributed to the minimal parliamentary opposition. Some M.P.s may not have appreciated quite how radical its provisions were. Lord Durham subsequently complained that the very late stage of the Parliamentary Session in which the Police Bill was introduced meant that it was: "…hurried through its several stages, so as to preclude the possibility of its details being properly discussed".[56]

More generally, policing reform was 'in the air' at the end of the decade. This was not confined to London. For example, in the year 1828 to 1829, improvement commissioners in Manchester, considering how to reorganize their own system, sent a delegation to survey police arrangements in Edinburgh, Glasgow, London and Birmingham, as these cities had a reputation for possessing the "best regulations on these subjects".[57] A body of recent literature, including John Wade's important *A Treatise on the Police and Crimes of the Metropolis* also helped set the scene for a centralised force.[58]

---

53. Anon, Thoughts on Prison Discipline, 1822, at p.40.
54. Quoted in Ascoli, David, 1979, at p.32.
55. pp.9.1822, at p.9.
56. HANSARD 1803-2005, HL Deb 15 November 1830 vol 1 cc493-500.
57. Barrie, David G., 2010, at p.265.
58. Smith, Keith, 2007, at pp.8-9.

Outline of the New Police

Long before the 1828 Select Committee reported, and the ensuing Bill on Metropolitan police reform appeared, Peel had well developed, if not publicised, ideas about the basic shape of any new force. He had outlined them in a letter to Sir John Hobhouse as early as December 1826.[59] Peel was adamant that the chief requisites of an: "...efficient police were unity of design and responsibility of its agents". Thus, it was to be a centralised, uniform, and uniformed, force covering the whole of the Metropolitan area in (initially) a 10-mile radius from St. Paul's Cathedral, with the notable exception of the City of London. It would treat these areas as "one great city" producing a London-wide force with a hierarchical command structure paid for out of a fixed parish rate.[60]

The exemption of the City from the rest of the Metropolis, although politically necessary (its opposition had killed much more limited reform in 1785), was a glaring and intellectually unjustifiable exception to this general philosophy. 'Fortuitously', the 1828 Committee gave Peel a pretext for excluding the Square Mile, allowing him to repeat its politic but exaggerated claim that the state of the nightly police there was "much superior" to that in Westminster and urban Middlesex. Nevertheless, the exception led the radical M.P. John Bright to refuse support for the Bill. Lord Durham also strongly criticised the City's exclusion in the House of Lords.[61] In 1839, Sir Robert Peel candidly admitted in parliament that the exemption of the City a decade earlier had been political, and had produced an anomaly whereby a small civic district, the permanent population of which did not much exceed 60,000 people, was governed by its own police, under a different system to that of the whole of its surrounding area, so that the: "...incongruity and absurdity of the position must be apparent, on a moment's reflection". He had originally hoped that the residents would appreciate this themselves, in the years after 1829, and agree to become part of the wider system.[62] However, this did not happen, despite recommendations from a variety of bodies for such a change.

Lord John Russell, the Home Secretary in 1839, also conceded that it would be much better to have one police force for the whole metropolis, as had been proposed in committee, but accepted that the outcry raised in the

---

59. Phillips, David, 1980, at p.185.
60. *Hansard's Parliamentary Debates,* Vol. XXI, New series, 31 March-24 June 1829, at p.872.
61. *Hansard's Parliamentary Debates,* Vol. XXI, New series, 31 March-24 June 1829, at p.1488 & p.1752.
62. HANSARD 1803-2005, HC Deb 28 May 1839 vol 47 cc1059-66.

Square Mile had prompted him to abandon what he thought would have been a great improvement to the capital's policing.[63] Instead, that year, after a number of minor changes, and an earlier reform in 1832, the City's supposedly 'superior' traditional system was replaced by a new style police force of its own, closely modelled on the Metropolitan force, but limited to the Square Mile. This ended the role of the City's wards in appointing constables and supervising watchmen in favour of a centralised force of officers. (Though many of these were recruited from former watchmen, and the force used the old watch-houses as their police stations).[64]

For the rest of the century, Metropolitan Police Commissioners periodically criticised the continuing anomaly of an exemption for the Square Mile, and Sir Richard Mayne unsuccessfully supported a parliamentary Bill in 1863 to effect the incorporation of its force into his own, arguing that it made no sense on grounds of efficiency and economy. (The City force cost rather more per man to fund and duplicated some Metropolitan police functions).[65] Nevertheless, this prompted vigorous opposition in the Square Mile and also, perhaps more surprisingly, from some London boroughs, which wanted to see less, not more, centralisation. At a huge meeting at the Mansion House, the Lord Mayor warned of the power that was given to the Home Secretary by a police force that was not locally accountable.[66] A public meeting held in Lambeth also resolved that amalgamation would be a direct-attack on local control at the behest of a government bent on centralising power.[67] The City fought off all the recommendations for amalgamation that were made by Parliamentary Select Committees and Royal Commissions during the remainder of the century.

Perhaps fortunately, demarcation between the two London forces was not always very strict in practice, whatever might have been the case in theory. As an M.P. (and former Lord Mayor) pointed out in 1863, they usually worked in harmony. He had regularly seen suspects produced at the Mansion House Police Court by Metropolitan Police constables who had followed, or arrested them, in the City jurisdiction.[68] Twenty five

---

63. HANSARD 1803-2005, HC Deb 03 June 1839 vol 47 cc1290-1.
64. Harris, Andrew T., 2004, pp.152-153.
65. *Hansard's Parliamentary Debates,* Vol. XXI, New series, 31 March-24 June 1829, at p.1488 & p.1752 and confidential memorandum by Richard Mayne to Sir George Grey, dated June 1st, 1863. The City of London Police survives to this day.
66. *Daily News,* April 22, 1863.
67. *The Times,* April 21, 1863, p.12.
68. 'The Proposed Amalgamation Of The City And Metropolitan Police', *Daily News,* April 22, 1863.

years later, when examining evidence in Goulston Street, just inside the Metropolitan Police area, shortly after one of the Ripper murders, Colonel Warren observed that: "There were several Police around the spot when I arrived, both Metropolitan and City".[69] More importantly, there was also statutory authority under the City Police Act allowing the two forces to call for large-scale assistance from each other in case of emergency, this being arranged between the Home Secretary and Lord Mayor.[70] This was particularly important when public order issues arose in the Square Mile, given the small size of its force. Thus, a visit to the City by Napoleon III of France led to a request from the Lord Mayor for assistance, so that the Metropolitan Police lined the route from Temple Bar to St. Paul's. Furthermore, as Sir George Grey noted in 1863, the head of the City force and the Chief Commissioner of the Metropolitan Police had always maintained a very good and co-operative relationship, reducing the potential inconvenience occasioned by the separation (though he was still a strong believer in amalgamation).[71]

Although these were the only substantial police forces in the Metropolitan area, there were a few other, smaller, policing bodies in the capital. For example, over a dozen railway police forces operated at various times in and around London train stations during the course of the century. They would liaise regularly with the Metropolitan and City forces. Thus, in 1851, when two robbers shot at Sergeant Edwin Earthy in East Acton, details of the attack and the weapons used in it were quickly passed on to the Great Western Railway police. Its officers swiftly made an arrest after they detained and searched a man at the Paddington terminus for uttering a fake sovereign, and found him to be in possession of an identical weapon.[72]

Public Order and Policing Reform

The rather fitful and organic, rather than calculated and systematic, development of the metropolitan police during the nineteenth century would suggest that claims of sustained political ambitions for their large-scale use, beyond immediate criminal justice objectives, can be

---

69. Warren's Report to the Home Office 11th June 1888.
70. Fletcher, Joseph, 1850, at p.242.
71. HANSARD 1803-2005, HC Deb 21 April 1863 vol 170 cc481-525.
72. OBSP, Trial of William Harris and Henry Round, 24th November 1851, t18511124-26. All subsequent references to the Old Bailey Sessions papers using this citation system are taken from the online 'The Proceedings of the Old Bailey' at www.oldbaileyonline.org.

exaggerated.[73] However, there was one exception to this general pattern. A desire to produce a potent anti-riot force was a vitally important factor behind the advent and form of the new police. The latter part of the eighteenth century had witnessed serious public disorder in the swiftly growing Metropolitan area. For example, in the Gordon Riots of 1780, 260 people were killed; most of them rioters shot by the military forces that eventually suppressed the disturbance.[74] A further 25 people were executed for their part in the affair. Perhaps most worryingly, it was the decisive action of the King, rather than the municipal authorities, that regained control of the situation.[75]

Less dramatic disturbances continued in the capital during the ensuing half-century. The army was called out in 1783 and 1793, when the pressing of men for the navy prompted riots, and there were further disturbances in 1794.[76] In 1798, five rioters, a constable, and a registered stevedore were killed in an exchange of fire at the Marine Police Office in Wapping. There were further riots in 1815, 1820 and 1821, these being associated with the return, subsequent death and funeral of the notorious Queen Caroline. Worryingly, some manifest clear political and anti-government undertones. There were yet more disturbances in central London in 1822 and 1825.[77] Indeed, the capital appears to have witnessed riots on some scale almost every year after 1815.[78]

Soldiers were regularly used to deal with these disturbances, the Life Guards becoming known as the 'Piccadilly Butchers' in the process. Even so, there was mounting concern about the use of the military for this purpose. In August 1821, a number of carbine and pistol shots were fired by troops dealing with disturbances in Hyde Park occasioned by the Queen's funeral, and *The Times* noted the potential for another 'Peterloo' type massacre to occur, with many civilian deaths.[79] The military included regular soldiers, the part-time foot 'volunteers' and the yeomanry cavalry. The latter, because of their prosperous backgrounds, were a bulwark of the existing social order, but also a 'blunt instrument'. They were often undisciplined, and lacking in crowd-control skills. Though the regular army was better trained, there were periodic anxieties about its loyalty, if only because of the social provenance of most of its recruits. Additionally,

---

73. Smith, Keith, 2007, at p.40.
74. Toynbee, Paget, 1925, at p.207.
75. Wilkinson, George, 1816, at pp.331-336.
76. Radzinowicz, Leon, 1948-56,Vol.2, at p.212.
77. Wade, John, 1829, at p.26.
78. Lyman, J.L., 1964, at p.151.
79. *The Times,* August 15th, 1821, at p.2.

military equipment was not ideal for such duties. Even the best trained soldier could: "...only act by using his arms. [and] The weapons he carries are deadly".[80]

Perhaps unsurprisingly in these circumstances, John Hardwicke suggested that continued use of the military was not reconcilable with the English constitution. He thought that it would be better to introduce a "really efficient civil force" that could replace troops, rather than continue with a "despicable" system that needed the backing of soldiers in disturbances of the slightest gravity.[81] An increasing intolerance of urban disorder, and concern about using soldiers to deal with it, was an important factor in the establishment and, even more so, the ultimate form, of the new police. Men such as Peel and Wellington believed that any reformed force should be able to control public disturbances. Peel expressly alluded to this when informing the House of Commons that his new police would mean it was possible to dispense with a: "...military force in London, for the preservation of the tranquility of the Metropolis".[82] A key distinction between the new police and the better sort of pre-1829 watchmen was that the latter had had no role in riot control.

This necessitated the introduction of a large, integrated, disciplined, hierarchical, centrally controlled and directed body of men who were accustomed ('drilled') to operate together in large numbers. It precluded parish or even borough-based reform. It also meant that a strongly 'preventive' system was likely to appear attractive, as the disciplined and regulated body it produced could be combined with a potent riot force, in a way that, for example, a largely detective body could not.

Even in 1829, there *were* alternative ways in which greater uniformity of policing standards across the capital might have been achieved without producing the centralised body that emerged that year. Old-fashioned watchmen *could* have been placed under many of the inspections and 'stimulants' that were to be applied to the new police.[83] Indeed, the 1812 Committee had noted that the standards imposed voluntarily in some parishes could be made universal in London if enforced by enough legislation.[84] However, such a body would not have had the capacity to

---

80. Report of the Departmental Committee on the Featherstone Riot (c 7234), 1893-4, at p.10. Cited, Manchester, A., 1984, at pp.241-242.

81. Hardwicke, John, 1828, at p.504.

82. *Hansard's Parliamentary Debates,* Vol. XXI, New series, 31 March-24 June 1829, at p. 883.

83. Robinson, David, 1831, at p.87.

84. pp.4.1812, at pp.1-4.

deal with crowds, and thus would not obviate the need for recourse to the army.

From the beginning, riot control was central to the new force. It was always intended that it would be placed under such discipline that, in an emergency, it could act: "…as an united corps- [to deal with] for instance, the late riots of Spitalfields".[85] The new police not only provided a 15% augmentation of total uniformed men under government control, at a time when the military was being cut back by parliament, but they were also more reliable and less 'provocative' than troops. One reason that the 1834 Committee felt the new police was one of the "most valuable" modern institutions was that there had been no use of the military to assist the civil power in London in the five years after 1829.[86] Although this record was not preserved intact to the end of the century, subsequent use of troops was quite exceptional, largely being confined to the riots of 1855 and 1888. In 1835, the speed with which election disturbances in the then very small town of Wolverhampton had led to the deployment of mounted dragoons, a fierce confrontation with the crowd, and three young men being shot and seriously wounded by soldiers, provided a salutary reminder, if any was needed, of the potential dangers of using the military to deal with riots and demonstrations.[87] As the 1868 Report noted, the use of the civil force was: "…in all cases where practicable, preferable to the use of soldiers". To this end it was even suggested, unavailingly, that a reserve of police pensioners, and paid special constables (akin to the militia), should be formed for use in emergencies.[88]

All of the police Divisions would provide a quota of men for special occasions, even when they were held well outside their own areas. This function required the training of police officers in quasi-military "Battalion drill", so that 500 or 1,000 men could be deployed at one spot effectively. Thus, more than 1,200 men assembled from all over London to preserve order during the King's opening of parliament in 1831.[89] In its first two decades the new force was frequently used to deal with political and other disturbances in both London and the provinces, especially those involving Chartists. This role continued to be of primary importance in the Metropolitan area for the rest of the century. Unlike military bodies, the police were also effective in dealing with 'routine' low-level public disorder, such as major gin-house disturbances.

---

85. *The Manchester Times and Gazette*, August 22, 1829.
86. pp.11.d.1834, at p.21.
87. Cox, David, 2011, at p.12.
88. pp.14.1868, at p.20 & p.27.
89. MEPO 7(2) Police Orders 1829-1833, 19th Oct.1831.

Dealing with a disturbance

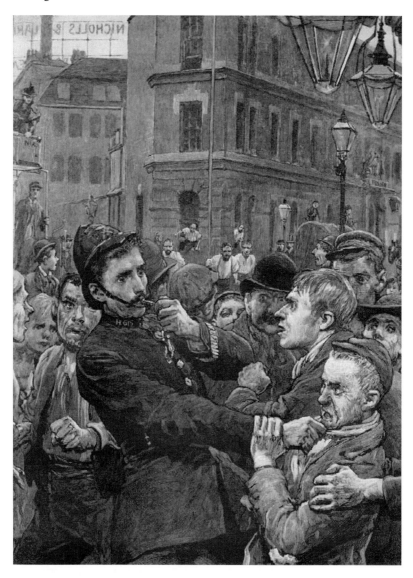

Dealing with a riot in 1866

Reform in 1829

In 1829, Sir Robert Peel informed the House of Commons that it was no longer possible to leave: "...all the responsibility in connection with the detection of offenders, or the prevention of crimes, in the hands of the parochial authorities". This understated the radical nature of the change that was planned. Almost all responsibility for policing would be transferred from the parishes to the new force.[90] It was to produce an unprecedented exercise in urban social control and massively accelerated a process of change in London policing that had been gathering pace since the 1770s. However, as has been noted, apart from its scale, comparatively little that it introduced was *totally* unprecedented, other than the unitary nature of the force. The achievement of 1829 was to universalise features of policing that had been the subject of limited and localised reforms and experiments in earlier years.

---

90. Ascoli, David, 1979, at p.1.

The New Force

Colonel Charles Rowan and the barrister Richard Mayne were appointed as joint Commissioners (the title was not used for a decade) on 7th July 1829, and moved into number four Whitehall Place, which swiftly became known as 'Scotland Yard' after the location from which its rear entrance was accessed. (In 1890 number four was replaced by a new Gothic-style building designed by Norman Shaw and located on Victoria Embankment). The pattern of having two Commissioners followed the already established practice of the Thames Marine Police, though it also meant they brought both legal and military expertise to the positions. Fortunately, the two men worked together in almost total harmony. Less successfully, Captain William Hay replaced Rowan when the latter retired in 1850. After Hay's death in 1855, Mayne became sole Commissioner, a pattern that was subsequently continued.

Sir Richard Mayne

At the end of August 1829, Rowan and Mayne were sworn in as Justices of the Peace, with the exclusive function of leading the Metropolitan police, rather than acting in any judicial capacity. In the twelve weeks before the first officers went on duty that September, they managed to design, organize, and equip their force, purchasing uniforms and police stations in the process. They took over many old watch houses (to the chagrin of several parishes) as well as acquiring some new premises. Mayne's legal training helped him to draw up the requisite regulations for the new force in a relatively short period. At about the same time, John Wray was appointed as Receiver for the Metropolitan Police District, tasked with dealing with the financial aspects of the new force. He served until 1860.

The Metropolitan police was established with an initial complement (when fully deployed over 18 months later) of slightly more than 3,000: "...young, strong men of good intelligence and with a written recommendation as to good character".[91] Obviously, they had to be men. The Women's Police Service would wait until the First World War. Nevertheless, most police stations employed women, on a part-time basis, to search females who had been taken into custody, though there were sometimes problems occasioned by the lack of female warders for women held overnight.[92] Thus, in 1842, when Emma Shell was brought to a police station on suspicion of theft, Inspector Henry Beresford "sent for a female to search her".[93] In 1889, the Home Secretary was confident that all police stations had female attendants who, although not resident on the station premises, lived close by and could be summoned to the station at night if their services were required.[94] Many were the wives of married officers. That year, a number of formally appointed Police Matrons were also employed to supervise and search female offenders. However, the male-only nature of the force occasioned some other problems. As a contemporary newspaper correspondent later noted, the (inevitable) lack of female detectives did not help policing, as women were often uniquely well placed to acquire information.[95]

Recruits to the new force had to be under 35 and over 20 years old, and more than 5ft 7" in height in their stockings (quite tall for an urban population of the era).[96] Thus, the constables who held the number '69' in

---

91. pp.11.d.1834, at p.29.
92. HANSARD 1803-2005, HC Deb 29 April 1889 vol 335 c674.
93. OBSP, Trial of Emma Shell, 24th October 1842, t18421024-2944.
94. HANSARD 1803-2005, HC Deb 18 March 1889 vol 334 c41.
95. *The Times*, October 11th 1888, p.5.
96. pp.11.d.1834, at p.29.

H Division for 15 years after 1858 ranged from a minimum of 5 feet 7 and ¾ inches to well over six feet.[97] It was sometimes suggested that the height requirement explained why so many officers were recruited from the country. Urban-bred men who reached the requisite stature were not normally from social backgrounds that provided fertile sources of recruits, though countrymen sometimes lacked the requisite degree of literacy.[98] By 1900, the (normal) age limit had been reduced to 27, the (usual) height requirement had been increased to 5 feet 8 inches in 1870 and, towards the end of the century, 5 feet 9 inches (with a power to waive this requirement where necessary), while recruits were also being subjected to an increasingly thorough and detailed medical examination, to ensure their potential for long service.[99] Men were rejected for *inter alia*, flat feet, narrow chests and even deformities of the face. Their written recommendation normally had to come from two "respectable" housekeepers and the candidate's last employer.[100] The majority of entrants were single men and, by the 1890s, they could not have more than two children at the time that they enlisted if they were married.

In 1838, in correspondence to 'patrons' who had put forward candidates for the force, explaining why their nominees had been rejected, three reasons predominated, as they were to for decades. The most frequent was that the candidate was declared "unfit by surgeon", two other important ones being "undersize" and "unable to read or write".[101] In 1869, for example, 4,550 men sought admission to the Metropolitan force. Of these, a majority were not even examined, as they were obviously not within the stipulated conditions governing age, stature, health, education, and provision of character testimonials. Of the 2,080 selected for examination, 940 were rejected and 1,140 accepted.[102] On a smaller scale, only 36 out of 140 men in Timothy Cavanagh's group of applicants in the 1850s were accepted.[103]

---

97. Register H Division, Nos 1-270, 1858 onwards, held at Met Collection Police Heritage Centre, Empress Building, London, SW6 1TR.
98. *The Times*, August 19, 1872, p.11.
99. Shpayer-Makov, Haia, 2004, at p.260.
100. *The Times*, June 17, 1831, at p.3.
101. Correspondence of the Commissioners MEPO 1 (30) No.51673, Letter dated November 23rd, 1838 *et seq*.
102. 'The Police of London', *Quarterly Review*, Vol.129, No. 257, 1870, pp.87-129, at p.97.
103. Cavanagh, Timothy, 1893, at p.2 and p.50.

Testing literacy and sight

Testing a potential recruit for height

At the beginning, many recruits had had previous experience serving with the newly replaced policing agencies. For example, in August 1829, the 70 men from the Bow Street foot patrol were handed over to the new police *en bloc*.[104] Many of the better parish watchmen were also recruited on an individual basis. In a letter of July 1829 to the vestries of the first batch of London parishes to come under Metropolitan Police control, the Commissioners asked for details of their existing watchmen and constables (presumably paid substitutes) that could be "well recommended", and who came within the age and height regulations.[105] A notice affixed to Church doors in the central parishes, and signed by Rowan and Mayne in their capacity as Justices of the Peace, warned remaining watchmen that their service would end after 29th September, when they would be replaced by a "new police".[106]

Recently discharged N.C.O.s and petty officers from the armed services provided another important source of recruits, especially for command positions, at least initially. According to Mayne, men from the army and marines made the best constables. Thus, P.C. John Brooke had spent more than 25 years in the Grenadier Guards from the age of eighteen, serving at Waterloo in the process, before enlisting in the Metropolitan police (he quickly left to take up a position in the Lincoln Militia).[107] Thirteen out of 17 initial superintendents were former sergeant-majors.[108]

However, as the force became more established, this preference for ex-soldiers declined slightly, partly because worries emerged about their ability to act independently, possible reservist liability, and partiality for alcohol. Sailors were sometimes considered more favourably, though a significant number of old-soldiers could always be found in police ranks. They made up nine per cent of the force in 1870, if militiamen are included. As the Duke of Bedford noted in 1901, a large number had been employed over the years with "most successful results".[109] In the 1880s, the City also took a significant number of its recruits from the ranks of the "strong and well-disciplined railway porters". These men were, by

---

104. Gash, Norman, 1985, at p.501.
105. Correspondence of the Commissioners MEPO 1 (1), Letter dated 29th July 1829.
106. 'The New Police And The Watchmen', Charles Rowan, in *The Morning Post*, September 29th, 1829.
107. OBSP, Trial of George Fursey, 4th July 1833, t183307045.
108. pp.11.d.1834, at p.29 & p.33.
109. HANSARD 1803-2005, HL Deb 25 June 1901 vol 95 cc1350-86.

definition, of very sound physique and used to working with the public under the control of superior officers.[110]

Although the traditional parish constables, watchmen and patrols were brought to an end in the central area between 1829 and 1830, some of the officers attached to Bow Street and the post-1792 police offices survived for up to a decade, even though, according to a police court magistrate, the continued separation resulted in considerable: "...inconvenience both to the public and the magistrates".[111] This was not assisted by thinly veiled hostility between the old and new forms of police, and a corresponding lack of co-operation. In the decade after 1829, some magistrates still preferred to work through their own principal officers, though three metropolitan policemen were 'promoted' to being Runners.[112]

The new Scotland Yard building of 1890

---

110. Shand, Alexander Innes, 1886, pp.594-608.
111. pp.12.1838, Vol. ii, at p.465. He felt that Court officers should be confined to being "doorkeepers and ushers".
112. Cox, D. J., 2010, at p.223.

In 1836, the Metropolitan force absorbed the Bow Street Horse Patrol. Two years later, the Report of the Committee on the Metropolis's Police Offices successfully recommended an amalgamation of the constables attached to the post-1792 police offices, the Bow Street Runners, and the Thames River Police, with the Metropolitan force, on the grounds of "greater efficiency".[113] The River Police became the new 'Thames' Division.

Discipline

From the beginning, Metropolitan officers were subject to an unprecedented level of personal discipline. This reflected concern about the potential for abuse in office, a belief that it would make for a more efficient force, and an attempt to engineer popular legitimacy. Indeed, Rowan had been selected as a Commissioner, in part, because of his military record as a disciplinarian with the 52nd Regiment (ironically, he was often to prove more flexible than his younger 'legal' colleague). Its strictness was evidenced by the high turnover of men. After an initial deployment of about 1,000 officers in 1829, over six Divisions in the central Metropolitan area, the full complement of more than 3,000 men (of all ranks) paraded in 1831, following a staggered introduction, on a parish-by parish basis, over the preceding months. Of these, however, 1,250 had resigned, many, (including 230 former soldiers) disliking the harsh regime, and a further 1,989 had been dismissed, within 18 months. There were only 562 of the original 2,800 constables left by 1834.[114] The force's clothing contractor allegedly complained about the cost of altering so many uniforms for re-issue to new recruits.

The most common ground for dismissal was drunkenness. Two men were fired for intoxication on the very first day of the force's operation and, in August 1829, a constable from D Division was dismissed for being drunk whilst giving evidence at the Westminster Sessions.[115] A significant number of dismissals continued to be for intoxication over ensuing decades. At Christmas, when temptation was most acute, officers would be expressly reminded that: "All must refrain from accepting drink offered to

---

113. Published on the 11th July 1838. Its 36 page report had been prepared by a committee of about a dozen eminent men including Sir Robert Peel and Viscount Howick.
114. pp.11.d.1834, at p.31.
115. Correspondence of the Commissioners MEPO 1 (30) No.52941, Letter dated 26th August 1829.

them on duty". Allegedly, if slightly apocryphally, one Boxing Day, Mayne dismissed 60 men who had ignored such a warning.[116]

However, 'intoxication' was usually a matter of degree, and did not always lead to dismissal, at least in its lesser forms or for a first offence. A rough distinction also appears to have been made between being 'under the influence of drink' and being 'drunk' when on duty. In 1882, for example, James Hartigan was reduced to a third class constable after 16 years of service, having been seen drunk on duty by two other officers.[117] Commissioner Warren (who was especially strict about alcohol abuse) tightened up regulations a few years later.[118] Nevertheless, they were subsequently relaxed again, so that in the Edwardian period lesser cases of drunkenness were often dealt with by fining the constables concerned three shillings a week for a year or, in the case of officers holding rank, with demotion.[119]

Insolence, absence from the beat without reasonable cause, and neglect of duty were also important grounds for dismissal.[120] Again, this was usually a matter of degree. Earlier in his career, for example, P.C. Hartigan had merely been moved to another station when found to be away from his beat for up to 45 minutes, on two separate occasions. In 1863, a newspaper correspondent could claim that in extreme cases a constable might be the subject of over 20 formal complaints without being dismissed.[121] Against this, some of the most egregious cases of neglect or violation of duty were also statutory criminal offences that could be prosecuted in the Police Courts, though there were only a handful of such actions every year. Thus, in 1872, P.C. Brown of T Division was prosecuted for refusing to go on duty without first giving notice.[122]

After the initial 18 months (that is by 1831), rates of dismissal from the new force began to fall, quickly being exceeded by normal resignations, as the Commissioners appreciated that an excessively high turnover was affecting the acquisition of institutional expertise. Even so, a large, albeit declining, number of officers continued to be dismissed or required to resign for misconduct throughout the rest of the century. They averaged 10% of the force a year in the first decade of its existence, but fell to less

---

116. MEPO 7/8, 21st December 1850. Cavanagh, Timothy, 1893, at p.78.
117. OBSP, Trial of James Hartigan, 11th December 1882, t18821212-157.
118. *The Times*, November 16, 1888.
119. *Penny illustrated Paper,* August 20th, 1910, p.245.
120. MEPO 7(2) Police Orders 1829-1833, 12th October 1832.
121. *Reynold's Newspaper*, July 19th, 1863.
122. *The Pall Mall Gazette*, November 18th, 1872.

than 5% in the 1850s and 1860s.[123] For example, in 1852, 231 men were dismissed.[124] By 1879, this had fallen further to only 153 officers, despite a considerable increase in police numbers.[125]

The force also made use of the lesser penalties of fines, reduction in rank (18 cases in 1852), loss of seniority, loss of a day off (later in the century), formal cautions and admonishments or reprimands to erring officers. For example, in 1861, Sergeant Lombard of C Division was reduced in rank for neglect of duty. He had failed to report a larceny and to take steps to trace the suspects.[126] Fines were commonly set at one shilling, a day's pay, five shillings, or (exceptionally) several days' pay. Erring officers might also be moved to a "distant" part of their Division, or even another Division altogether, as a punishment for misbehaviour or to remove them from unhealthy influences.[127]

Although the 1829 Act had contained disciplinary provisions for officers as well as penalties for those who hindered police efficiency, such as publicans who served them alcohol while on duty, these were greatly supplemented by the many rules contained in the Metropolitan Police Contract and Force Handbook from the same year, and the Metropolitan Police General Instruction Books of 1829 and 1836. There was also tight control of the private behaviour of individual constables, compared to both their immediate predecessors and even some of the later northern constabularies. For example, the 1829 Metropolitan Police Contract required that all officers' debts be paid "forthwith", and prohibited most part-time employments, a radical change from the old Watch, whose members had often worked during the day.[128] Thus, and typically, P.C. Payne 114 was dismissed in March 1868 for contracting debts that he failed to pay.[129]

Constables were drilled in uniform, placed on salaries, and often housed in dormitories in their station/section houses or 'police barracks', close to their Divisional HQs, if single, at least until quite senior in rank or experience. In exchange for a small weekly rent (usually just a shilling), they had their own beds and access to a kitchen and recreational areas, in buildings that were often supervised by a married sergeant or inspector and his wife. Some of these establishments even had limited accommodation for

---

123. Miller, Wilbur, 1997, at p.41.
124. pp.13.b.1853, at p.7.
125. Shpayer-Makov, Haia, 2002, at p.159.
126. Police Daily Orders, 4th July 1861.
127. See, for example, Police Orders, 16th May, 1861.
128. Booth, J.V., 1985, at pp.9-15.
129. MEPO 7(38) Police Orders, 13/3/1868.

married constables. Unfortunately, in 1862, an investigation revealed that many were extremely unhygienic.[130]

A constable is disciplined by the Commissioner

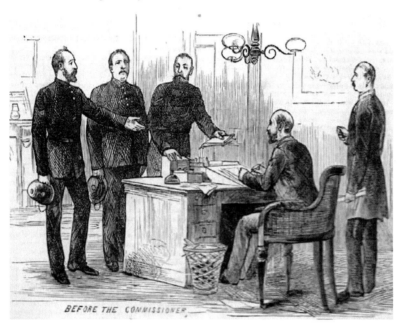

BEFORE THE COMMISSIONER

Police officers were forbidden or discouraged from frequenting insalubrious pubs or street entertainments and from using obscene language.[131] They were also banned from accepting fruit, oysters or coffee from the basket-women on their beats, even for payment, whilst on duty.[132] As the 1833 Committee appreciated, a 'new' police constable, unlike the old watchman, was a policeman for 24 hours a day.[133] This notion was gradually absorbed by rank and file officers. For example, in 1873, P.C. William Pye, drinking while off duty and in civilian clothes at the Crooked Billet public house in Shadwell, became suspicious when he saw several people attempt to pass an imperfect bank note. He followed them, and saw the same process repeated at another tavern, whereupon he arrested

---

130. Emsley, Clive, 2010, at pp.121-122.
131. Ignatieff, Michael, 1978, at p.192.
132. MEPO 7(2) Police Orders 1829-1833, 22/10/1831.
133. pp.11.1833, at pp.42 & 43.

them.[134] No pre-1829 watchman would have behaved in this manner.

The strictness of official control occasioned regular complaints over the course of the century. In 1852 it was claimed, although the Home Secretary vigorously denied it, that to their "great amazement" some constables from Stepney (K Division) were being given the choice of attending divine service at St. Thomas's Church, or a drill session in lieu.[135] In 1855, a group of constables at Paddington (D Division) became so incensed at the petty discipline imposed by their (largely Irish) sergeants, including regular deductions from their wages for infractions and being ordered to go to church like "schoolboys", that they wrote to Lord Palmerston, the Prime Minister.[136] In 1872, officers were still complaining about the: "…arbitrary conduct of the Divisional superintendents in dealing with trivial breaches of regulations".[137] Sir Charles Warren's Commissionership in the 1880s was one of the most rigid in this respect, and widely considered to be more stringent than useful by many experienced and senior officers.[138]

The author of a socialist (revolutionary) tract felt that senior commanders often imposed discipline in a more insidious way. If an officer offended or demonstrated too much independence, he would be transferred to another Division or sub-Division where, using the complex regulations that governed policemen, he could be closely observed until discharged after being "caught tripping in some trifling offence, or breach of police rules". Thus, he claimed that a P.C. Carter, who had objected to handing over to the wider force a public reward given to him for rescuing someone from a fire, was transferred to Brixton and, once there, watched until he was caught speaking to a tradesman, contrary to rules, and fined a day's pay. He was later dismissed for other reasons.[139]

In 1872, 1887 and 1890, concern about excessive discipline contributed to short-lived, localised, strikes, quasi-trade unionism, and even public meetings in Hyde Park, by policemen eager to discuss their grievances. In 1872, for example, 39 officers from T Division (Kensington) and 71 men from E Division (Bow Street) who had refused to go on duty were

---

134. OBSP, Trial of Mary Rivers and William Anderson, 24th November 1873, t18731124-4.
135. HANSARD 1803-2005, HC Deb 17 May 1852 vol 121 cc683-5.
136. Emsley, Clive, 1996, at p.96.
137. *The Morning Post*, November 19th, 1872, p.4.
138. Approved quotation from a 'Daily Paper' in published tract: Anon, 1888, *The Metropolitan Police and its Management,* at p.6 & p.8.
139. Anon, 1870, *The Revolution in the Police and the Coming Revolution of the Army and Navy,* at p.5.

dismissed with the approval of the Home Secretary (many were subsequently reinstated).[140] A force of constables from Poplar had to be drafted in as emergency cover, even though they did not know the areas they were policing. In 1890 and 1891, George Walden attempted to organise a formal Metropolitan Police Union, albeit with very limited success.[141]

Nevertheless, the heavy turnover of men also suggests that the new police *were* radically different to the forces that had gone before them. Clearly, behaviour that had been acceptable in some of the old institutions, especially the Watch, was not tolerated in the Metropolitan police. There was, inevitably, a downside to such tight control. One of its effects was to distance the police from the general public. This was exacerbated because, within a few years of its inception, the Metropolitan force showed a marked reluctance to recruit too many Londoners, favouring, in particular, those from rural areas and (in the early decades especially) Ireland. This was in marked contrast to the old, locally recruited, Watch. Londoners were seen as potentially febrile, cunning, untrustworthy, and unreliable, as well as being physically poorer specimens. This prejudice (if such it was) was to last into the Edwardian period: "A countryman is fresh clay to the potter's hands, the Londoner has much to unlearn before he can be taught".[142] As a result, even late in the nineteenth century, only 28 per cent of officers were London born (though half had resided in the Metropolitan area imediately before recruitment).[143]

Despite this preference, a majority of recruits were from towns and cities, albeit outside London, rather than hamlets and small villages. The rise of provincial police forces after statutes were passed in 1835 and 1839 requiring or permitting their establishment allowed the Metropolitan Police to make effective local enquiries, in their potential recruits' home areas, about the men they planned to take on.[144] Typically, of the 10 constables who successively held the Number '69' in H (Whitechapel) Division between 1855 and 1873, only one came from Middlesex. The other nine were from the Home Counties (the most common source), East Anglia, Dorset and Wales.[145] In 1870, the Metropolitan force also included 670 Irishmen (121 of them sergeants or above) and 152 "Scotchmen" (47

140. *Daily News*, November 21st, 1872.
141. *The Morning Post,* February 9th, 1891, p.3.
142. Dilnot, George, 1915, at p.79.
143. Shpayer-Makov, Haia, 2002, at p.51.
144. Gamon, Hugh, 1907, at p.15.
145. Register H Division, Nos 1-270, 1858 onwards, held at Met Collection Police Heritage Centre.

of them holding rank). The force had 11 "foreigners", some of them involved with the detective branch.[146]

Social Background

The social provenance of most officers made a contribution to softening the consequences of the distancing of police from public. From the beginning, Peel had stipulated that the new police should not include military officers on half pay, or gentlemen fallen on hard times. He felt that such men would be inherently unsuited to the duties of the office, and would make the other constables feel awkward. Several applications from such individuals in the year from 1829 to 1830 were rejected, although the Superintendent of R Division was a captain on half-pay. Their status improved very slightly in the decades after establishment. However, in 1890, James Monro still thought that he was being magnanimous when noting that, in view of their heavy responsibilities, constables were: "...entitled to be considered as skilled labourers". (He felt their pay was quite modest given their duties).[147]

Internal promotion was stressed from the beginning, apart from the appointment of Commissioners and, after 1855, the two new positions of Assistant Commissioner (a third was later added to head the C.I.D.), other officers being appointed purely from: "...those men who have distinguished themselves by good conduct in the lower ranks".[148] This could be done, by showing "zeal, activity, and judgment".[149] Indeed, for much of the period there were no examinations for promotion to most ranks, on the basis that it was performance, rather than theoretical tests, that was the measure of a man. Ordinary constables who made a mark, and avoided making enemies amongst their superiors, progressed to being sergeants, then inspectors, and finally superintendants (the head of a Division). As a result, in 1880, Inspector Squire White, from the Westminster Division, a man just over 40 years of age, stressed when giving evidence at the Bailey that, despite his rank and 20 years service, he had "entered as a constable".[150] The major ranks were themselves sub-divided for much of the period; for example, until late in the century there were three classes of constable.

---

146. 'The Police of London', *Quarterly Review*, Vol.129, No.257, 1870, at p.99.
147. Monro, James, 1890, at p.203.
148. *The Morning Chronicle,* August 12th, 1829.
149. General Instructions Book, 1st proof, hand-amended by the Commissioners, deposited at Met Collection Police Heritage Centre, at p.1.
150. OBSP, Trial of William Butcher et al, 3rd August 1880, t18800803-423.

Peel's insistence that men accrued some seniority in a rank before being promoted, to avoid purely formal appointments, was followed throughout the era, constables typically having to serve for several years before they could make sergeant. Even Detective Inspector Frederick Abberline, noted for his rapid rise through the ranks, was only promoted to sergeant after two years as a beat constable in N Division (Islington) during the 1860s. The time taken for most men to secure promotion varied greatly, though a large majority of officers remained as constables throughout their careers. P.C. George Clarke was on the beat for 13 years before making sergeant in S Division, in 1853. His brother Henry took 14 years to achieve the same rank. However, his youngest brother John made sergeant, in N Division, in just five years.[151] Internal promotion meant that the police force became a significant avenue of social mobility for a few working-class men.

Peel had felt that if the new officers were overpaid, they would inevitably attract the 'wrong sort'. He thought that a "three shilling a day man is better than a five shilling a day man" for the work they would have to do. John Wilson Croker's concern that this might be too low appears to have been partly supported by high subsequent wastage.[152] Salaries for junior ranks were never generous, even by international comparison. At the end of the period, a visiting American could note that the pay of Metropolitan policemen, up to the rank of Inspector, was "considerably below" that received by the New York Police.[153] In 1853, all of the constables in D Division signed a petition, presented to Richard Mayne, asking for an increase in pay: "...in consequence of the increased price of provisions".[154] In the early 1870s, a period of particularly acute tension within the force over wages, a new recruit would still earn only about £1 a week, this sum gradually rising to £1 7s 6d, while a Sergeant would start at £1 9s, and a Chief Inspector at three guineas. A modest increase of a shilling a week, granted in 1870, was only given in exchange for some men relinquishing one of two days' leave a fortnight.[155]

Police salary levels were periodically discussed in parliament during the course of the century, with some M.P.s feeling that they were woefully low, while others, along with most government ministers, thought that they were adequate for men from the relevant station in life, and pointed out

---

151. Payne, Christopher, 2011, at p.18.
152. Gash, Norman, 1985, at p.501.
153. Flynt, Josiah, 1903, at p.442.
154. *The Times*, July 29th, 1853, p.6.
155. *Daily News*, October 18th, 1872, and letter from a constable in H Division to *The Standard,* October 15th, 1872, at p.5.

that there was normally no shortage of recruits to the service. Thus, in 1880, Richard Assheton Cross, the Home Secretary, noting the recommendations of the Departmental Committee appointed in 1878 to inquire into the pay and organisation of the Metropolitan Police, saw: "...nothing in that Report to lead me to believe that any general rise of wages is at all necessary".[156] City constables were better paid, by about two shillings a week, than their Metropolitan counterparts, this being a reflection of the Square Mile's wealth.[157]

Although banned from most other employments (unlike the old watchmen), constables could be 'hired' for major functions, such as society balls, with the approval of their superintendent, supplementing their incomes in the process.[158] This was done: "...in their own time, and from 5s. to 10s. is generally given by the person interested".[159] Additionally, and not altogether properly, as they were not supposed to receive money without express permission from superiors, it seems that many policemen were offered and accepted tips for providing extra services, such as showing "special vigilance" when a house-owner was away.[160]

However, although no major increase in pay was given to the new police officers, when compared to the average earned by the better remunerated members of the old Watch, there were a few new perquisites, such as boots and a small coal and candle allowance: towards the end of the century, a pair of the former were issued twice a year. (In 1897 this was converted to a monetary allowance for footwear).[161] In 1833, 3,200 tons of coal was distributed at a total cost to the force of 4,531 pounds. Against this, in December 1830, officers were expressly forbidden to ask for a Christmas box from people who lived on their beats (as was common practice with the old watchmen).

Far more significantly, after 1839, officers who had completed at least 15 years of service and who were medically unfit to continue, or who had reached the age of 60, were usually provided with pensions on retirement.[162] This was given some statutory authority in 1847, and followed concern during the first decade of the force at the manner in

---

156. HANSARD 1803-2005, HC Deb 19 February 1880 vol 250 cc913-4.
157. HANSARD 1803-2005, HC Deb 27 June 1890 vol 346 c219.
158. General Instructions Book, 1st proof, hand-amended by the Commissioners, deposited at Met Collection Police Heritage Centre, at p.7.
159. Dickens, Charles (Junior), 1888, *Dickens's Dictionary of London*, p.xx.
160. *The Times*, November 19th, 1889, p.12.
161. *The Morning Post*, January 5th, 1897, p.6.
162. Shpayer-Makov, Haia, 2002, at p.159.

which some men who had been "disabled for life" in the line of duty were simply given a gratuity of 30 pounds and discharged.[163] As a result, in 1864, Detective Inspector Jonathan Whicher received the generous pension of just over 133 pounds a year when he retired due to "congestion of the brain" after 26 years' service, at the age of 49. (It may also have been a diplomatic response to unfair public criticism of his conduct of the Road murder investigation).[164] More commonly, a constable who retired in the 1850s, after 15 years' service, having been certified as disabled, might receive 27 pounds a year, though some received just 18 pounds.[165] In the 1870s, about 2% of the force was pensioned off each year in this manner.[166] In 1879, for example, 187 men who had served for at least 15 years were given pensions, while 183 who had served shorter terms were granted leaving-gratuities.[167] Typically, in 1847, a seven-year veteran with a good record received a gratuity of £28. However, before the Police Pensions Act of 1890 these were normally allowed on a discretionary basis, although nearly always given to deserving cases. The 1890 statute provided a legal right to a full pension (about half of final salary) after twenty-five years' service or, in some situations, on earlier medical discharge.

Throughout the century, new recruits were overwhelmingly working-class men, though there was a small, but not insignificant, minority from what might be termed the 'lower middle' class. Nevertheless, in the early years of the force, entrants with any level of education invariably justified joining by reference to their straitened circumstances. One, quite typically, noted that shortly after 1829: "I was, by reduced circumstances (the result of my own indiscretion) compelled to enter the ranks of the A Division of the Metropolitan Police Force".[168] Two decades later, in November 1848, when a group of third-class Metropolitan constables petitioned for an increase to their weekly pay of 16s 8d (after deductions), they observed that: "Most of the married men on joining are somewhat in debt".[169] In 1855, Timothy Cavanagh felt that, although his recruiters emphasised that the force was "not a refuge for the destitute", about 90 per cent of the men who had joined with him had done so through "stress of weather". He would have applied for admission to the Horse Guards as a private if he

---

163. *The Morning Post*, June 13th, 1835, p.5.
164. Summerscale, Kate, 2008, at p.225.
165. OBSP, Trial of Robert Woods, 30th January 1854, t18540130-317.
166. *The Morning Post*, August 24, 1877, p.6.
167. *The Morning Post*, August 19, 1879, p.2.
168. Anon, 1852, *Confessions of a Detective Policeman*, at p.3.
169. Emsley, Clive, 1996, at pp.95-96.

had failed to gain entry (the army often being the final resort for healthy young men).[170] Thomas Waters, who rose to become a Detective Inspector, was even more blunt when looking back on his career, noting that adverse circumstances: "...compelled me to enter the ranks of the metropolitan police, as the sole means left me of procuring food and raiment".[171]

Their low social provenance is not surprising. Even hostile observers accepted that police officers had onerous and unpleasant duties to perform, despite their modest pay.[172] At the end of the century, a working week of 60 to 70 hours was still normal.[173] By then, they averaged one day off a fortnight, or 26 days a year, and 11 days of paid annual leave (only introduced in 1890), making 37 days in total.[174]

As a result, although in 1872 the Metropolitan Police claimed to recruit from "almost every class in the Community", this really meant from every type of low-grade employment.[175] Their intake included butchers, clerks, grooms, tradesmen, agricultural labourers, former sailors, and discharged soldiers. For example, of the 10 constables who held the Number 69 in H Division between 1858 and 1873, five were former labourers, one was a boot-maker, one a carman, another a soldier, one a weaver, and the last was listed as having no occupation when recruited.[176] Even Jack Whicher had worked as a labourer before he joined the Metropolitan force at the age of 23. Interestingly, there was also some movement between English police forces, as opportunity and better terms presented themselves. In the 1840s, for example, P.C. George Trew served for several years in the City police. However, earlier in his life, he had spent seven years in the Metropolitan force, and nine months in a rural constabulary.[177]

Throughout the century, voluntary resignations increased in 'good times' (such as 1872), when officers left "owing to the high rate of wages earned by the working classes". In these years, constables, especially the better-educated and more able men, could find more congenial and lucrative work elsewhere.[178] Officers could leave the force on one month's

---

170. Anon, 1871, *Our Police System*, at p.694.
171. Waters, Thomas, 1853, at p.5.
172. Carpenter, E., 1896, at p.147.
173. Shpayer-Makov, Haia, 2002, at p.216.
174. HANSARD 1803-2005, HC Deb 18 June 1907 vol 176 cc295-9, 295.
175. PR.9.1869-76, Report for the Year 1872, at pp.4 & 5.
176. Register H Division, Nos 1-270, 1858 onwards, held at Met Collection Police Heritage Centre.
177. OBSP, Trial of Matthew Shrimpton and Henry Williams, 17th August 1846, t18460817-1457.
178. PR.9.1869-76, Report for the Year 1872, at pp.4 & 5.

notice with full pay. If they left without such notice, they would forfeit any outstanding money that was due to them.[179]

Perhaps not surprisingly, in these circumstances, Timothy Cavanagh could observe that during the 1850s: "...very few [recruits] spoke English properly".[180] The educational qualifications for new officers (essentially literacy) were much less strict than the increasingly demanding physical requirements. To remedy this, there were evening classes attached to some police stations for the many men with poor educations.[181] In 1882, a police court magistrate observed that although some officers were educated, most were "inferior" men who would be well advised to take advantage of these facilities.[182] Various other attempts were made to encourage learning. As early as 1842, the Reverend Edward Wakeham established the first Divisional Library in Hammersmith, to promote edifying reading amongst the area's officers.[183] However, detectives tended to be recruited from among the better educated uniformed officers, as did those filling administrative positions at Divisional H.Q.s, if only because of the large amount of reading and report writing that their work required. The very few men of 'good' education who joined the Metropolitan force would often serve in important clerical positions at Scotland Yard itself.[184]

Inevitably, there were some disadvantages to eschewing an officer-class. It made it difficult to secure men with a sufficient level of education to understand legal niceties, something that would occasion particular problems, later in the century, when it came to selecting detectives. Sir Frederick Adair Roe, the presiding magistrate at Bow Street, giving evidence to the 1838 Committee, warned that his experience of police superintendants and inspectors led him to conclude that it was: "...utterly impossible that they can have the opportunity of having the experience and direction of superiorly-educated men".[185] Almost half a century later, a newspaper correspondent, who had visited the scene of a Fenian bombing, was struck by the apparent ignorance and lack of perception in the investigating constables *and* their superior officers: "In fact, the latter appeared to have been promoted from the ranks and to have no tact or judgment about them". He urged the introduction of an army-type officer

179. General Instructions Book, 1st proof, hand-amended by the Commissioners, deposited at Met Collection Police Heritage Centre.
180. Cavanagh, Timothy, 1893, at p.2 and p.50.
181. Anon, 1871, *Our Police System*, at p.694.
182. Anon, 1882, *Metropolitan Police Court Jottings*, at p.39.
183. *The Standard*, September 7th, 1842.
184. Morris, R. M., 2006, at p.84.
185. pp.12.1838, Vol. ii, at p.480.

class.[186] This was not a new suggestion even then. Lord Dudley Stuart had made the same proposal in 1853.

Without the availability of entry at commissioned level, men of 'good' backgrounds were highly unlikely to join, even if they had been allowed to (often not the case). Although the middle classes might have eulogised their 'bobbies', they did not view it as a profession to be encouraged amongst their own relations. In the early 1880s, Fuller noted that most of his London relatives: "...forbade the very mention of my name in their home after I entered the police service". Nevertheless, towards the end of the century, explanations for enlistment based on economic necessity became less common, though this may have been partly due to a more precise targeting of potential recruits. Even Fuller felt that the situation had improved by the time he retired in 1908.[187] However, at the turn of the century, James Greenwood still believed that most policemen joined because they could "find nothing better to do". A new officer was still being paid at a similar rate to the better sort of labourer.[188] Of course, all things are relative. Compared to prison warders, for example, policemen were "generally respected".[189]

This combination of strict establishment discipline and modest social background also produced an inherent contradiction in their position. They were of the working class but separate from it, easily accused of being turncoats. This dichotomy was well caught by a socialist tract from 1870, which declared that the Metropolitan police were governed by a "brutal and despotic" power, and as a result individual officers were often automatons, without mind or reason. However, its author also noted, approvingly, that stirrings of dissatisfaction were emerging amongst the rank and file, apparently manifest, *inter alia*, in demands for better pay and concern about their pension arrangements.[190]

Training

Training for new Metropolitan police officers was minimal throughout the era, though this changed shortly afterwards. In the mid-century, it was usually only 10 days long, carried out in a class of about 30 men.[191] Most

---

186. *The Times*, February 5th, 1885, at p.13.
187. Fuller, Robert, 1912, at p.21.
188. Greenwood, James, 1902, at p.2.
189. Anon, *Five Years' Penal Servitude*, 1877, at p.124.
190. Anon, 1870, *The Revolution in the Police and the Coming Revolution of the Army and Navy*, at p.5.
191. Payne, Christopher, 2011, at p.17.

of it was spent on drill, usually conducted at Wellington Barracks, though some time was given to sabre practice, studying the Instruction Book and listening to occasional lectures from a superintendant. It was followed by a period (often just a week) spent in the company of an experienced constable, after which a man was sent out alone to walk his own beat. However, newly appointed constables would normally be based at the larger principal police stations, rather than outlying ones, "so as to instruct them better".[192] Towards the end of the era, basic training was extended to three weeks, followed by a period spent attending the police courts to learn forensic procedure.[193] To assist officers master their powers and responsibilities, various manuals, both official and private, were published, including popular (but very thorough) 'catechisms' on police duties and law, such as that produced by Horatio Childs.[194]

Morale

Establishing an entirely new force, with its own *esprit de corps*, took time. Because such an experiment was almost unprecedented, many officers and their commanders were exploring their responsibilities and making up their duties as they went along during the early years. It took decades for a body of mature, experienced, men to emerge who could pass on their knowledge to new recruits. This process was greatly slowed down by the rapid turnover of officers during the early decades. This was especially problematic, as most senior officers thought that it took several years service to make a good policeman.

In the final quarter of the century, however, there were signs that a core of experienced men aiming at full careers had been achieved. Turnover declined, so that in 1870, only 11.02% of the Metropolitan force left for all reasons (death, resignation, retirement, dismissal).[195] By the end of the century, it had fallen much further; increasingly careful selection meant that the wastage rate from those initially chosen to enter the force was only 28½ per cent over the entire first seven years of service.[196] Aided by an improvement in working conditions, more officers were making a 'career' of their service and staying on to a pensionable age. Many were taking advantage of the educational facilities available and joining the various athletic and sporting clubs for officers that proliferated in this period, and

---

192. MEPO 7/8, 19th July, 1850.
193. The Bristol Mercury and Daily Post, August 18th, 1898.
194. Childs, Horatio, 1903.
195. *Quarterly Review*, Vol.129, No.257, 1870.
196. HANSARD 1803-2005, HL Deb 25 June 1901 vol 95 cc1350-86, c1350.

which may be seen as indicative of a new level of institutional identification and morale. This had often been absent in the 1830s and 1840s. By the 1890s, for example, even the small A Division had its own swimming club, which organised an annual fête and competition in the open waters at Hendon.[197]

Prize-giving at the police orphanage

THE PRINCESS OF WALES GIVING PRIZES AT THE METROPOLITAN AND CITY POLICE ORPHANAGE, TWICKENHAM.—SEE PAGE 86.

Despite the low pay and long, unsocial hours, in some respects at least, the Metropolitan Police were pioneers when it came to improving employment conditions, especially during the second half of the century. For example, an orphanage for the children of officers who died in service was established in Twickenham in 1870 (it was shared with the City force). Queen Victoria was one of its first patrons and in 1874 it was accommodating 115 boys and girls.[198] By the end of the century, it could take 260 children. An annual ball to raise funds became a major London social occasion, attracting hundreds of people.[199] A convalescent home for

197. *The Morning Post*, August 12th, 1892, p.3.
198. *The Illustrated Police News*, April 4th, 1874.
199. *The Standard,* April 25th, 1896, p.5.

sick and injured officers was also opened in Hove, and short, paid holidays eventually introduced.[200]

A fall in the mean age of recruits from 26 years in 1833, to 24 in 1850, and then to 22 1/2 by the end of the century, is also indicative of the emergence of a career mentality amongst police officers.[201] The (normal) maximum recruitment age was reduced to 27 (informally this was already the case), so as to ensure a reasonable length of service. By the start of the twentieth century, the high morale and relative professionalism of the London policeman was obvious to an American observer, and clearly distinct from the levels achieved in most of the rest of Europe: "...one looks in vain on the continent for the splendid *esprit-de-corps* which permeates the entire Metropolitan Police Force of London".[202] The physique and intelligence of most Metropolitan officers meant that it was a: "...corps d'elite in the truest sense of the term".[203]

Accountability and Control

Both of the London forces differed from their provincial counterparts in the manner in which they were supervised and controlled. In the City of London Police, established in 1839, the Commissioner was appointed by the City Corporation, albeit with the approval of the Crown. However, in the Metropolitan force, the Commissioner was always appointed directly by the Crown upon the recommendation of the Home Secretary, and was answerable to that Minister. This was in marked contrast to the post-1829 provincial forces, which normally answered to Watch Committees in their boroughs and magistrates in the counties. (Though for three years after 1839, government-established police forces in Manchester, Bolton, and Birmingham, hurriedly founded to confront the Chartist threat, were also based on the Metropolitan model, before being handed over to municipal control).[204]

Even Sir Robert Peel accepted that removing the police from the power of local authorities meant that it was incumbent on Parliament to inspect and scrutinize the force, and that from time to time it should be subject to more general consideration by the legislature.[205] Illustrative of this, in 1887, the M.P. for Bethnal Green questioned the Home Secretary, Henry

---

200. Shpayer-Makov, Haia, 2002, at p.175.
201. Taylor, David, 1997, at p.49.
202. Fosdick, Raymond B., 1915, at p.197.
203. HANSARD 1803-2005, HL Deb 25 June 1901 vol 95 cc1350-86, c1350.
204. Weaver, Michael, 1994, at p.289.
205. HANSARD 1803-2005, HC Deb 18 November 1830 vol 1 cc575-82.

Mathews, over the routine arrest of a Pimlico woman who, he felt, had not been drunk but merely ill when detained near Victoria station. Mathews assured him that he had already inquired into the case and received a copy of a report from a magistrate that had been sent to the Commissioner, showing that the woman had already been turned out of the railway refreshment-room by the Station Inspector and then refused to leave, so obliging a nearby constable to arrest her.[206]

The rationale advanced for this difference in control between the Metropolitan and other forces lay in the great size and special characteristics of the capital, it being the centre of government, both imperial and national, as well as housing foreign legations, museums, art collections and major popular entertainments. Additionally, there was no correlation between the policed area and any units of local administration. Even after 1888, the 688 square miles of the Metropolitan Police District, extending into all adjacent counties (Kent, Essex, Hertfordshire, etc.) was very much greater than that of the new London County Council.[207]

The Commissioner of the Metropolitan Police had enormous powers when compared to the equivalent officers in most other British forces. Many of these were placed on a statutory basis, so that although he was: "…subject to the Home Secretary as his superior, and in that sense is not supreme, but within certain limits he is practically an independent autocratic ruler".[208] Additionally, considerable autonomy was allowed to the Commissioners for much of the early period, so that, in 1886, it could be argued that Sir Richard Mayne had been "virtually independent of the Home Office". However, it was also claimed that, after his death in 1868, Home Secretaries had become more assertive, gradually encroaching on the Commissioner's responsibilities, and that William Harcourt had even established a new department within the Home Office to supervise the Metropolitan force.[209] Even so, at the end of the period, an American student of the Metropolitan Police was still very impressed by the way in which: "…politics is not allowed to play any part in the management and direction of the organization".[210]

This unique form of control did not go unchallenged, many observers feeling that it was there for political, not practical, reasons. In the late 1870s, for example, the feminist and radical Josephine Butler commended the City of London force for preserving its independence from the

---

206. HANSARD 1803-2005, HC Deb 11 July 1887 vol 317 cc353-4.
207. Fosdick, Raymond B., 1915, at p.43.
208. Sims, George (ed.), 1902, Vol. 2, p.4.
209. HANSARD 1803-2005, HL Deb 18 February 1886 vol 302 cc555-77.
210. Flynt, Josiah, 1903, at p.448.

Metropolitan Police, and lamented the latter's lack of local control. A few years later, it was suggested that the granting of extra powers to the police, and their lack of accountability, meant that: "Year by year the English Police system has thus been approximated more nearly to the Continental system".[211] Butler proposed that what would now be termed the 'democratic deficit' in accountability be remedied by placing the force under municipal control and removing the role of central government.[212] However, such campaigns met strong opposition from many London policemen. Timothy Cavanagh, for example, was greatly concerned that the Metropolitan Police would fall under the control, and political manipulation, of the new post-1888 London County Council (a favourite suggestion of some radicals and socialists). He felt that Britain needed a designated Minister of Police with special responsibility for all of its constabularies.[213] After his appointment in 1890, Commissioner Edward Bradford was also forced to actively resist such proposals.

211. Anon, *Police Rule*, 1884, at p.2.
212. Butler, Josephine, 1880, at pp.38-39, p.47 & pp.52-55.
213. Cavanagh, Timothy, 1893, at p.132.

CHAPTER FOUR

ROUTINE POLICING
AND THE 'PREVENTATIVE' SYSTEM

Introduction

At street level, London was normally better 'patrolled' after 1829 than it had been under the old watch, a few rich parishes excepted, and this became increasingly thorough as the century progressed. Indeed, by the 1850s, there was concern that people were so used to leaving everything to the 'professionals' that they were becoming reluctant to intervene in street crimes, a classic illustration allegedly being the notorious 'Parliament Street murder', committed with bystanders looking on, not one of whom interfered, apart from an errand boy.[1]

The Commissioner of the Metropolitan Police headed the largest uniformed force in the world, albeit with the biggest area (eventually 688 square miles including its suburban and rural parts) to control. By most European and North American standards, London was a relatively highly policed city, though valuable comparisons are inherently difficult given the different range of tasks entrusted by varying countries to their respective urban police forces. Nevertheless, in 1911, Paris had 8,597 officers for a population of 4,154,042 people, producing a ratio of one officer to every 483 citizens, compared to a London ratio of one to 354 people. However, Berlin had a ratio of one to 324, and Vienna one to 342.[2] New York appears to have managed with significantly fewer men.

London was certainly much better policed than most English provincial towns and counties. In the year from 1874 to 1875 there was, on one assessment, one policeman for every 398 people in the Metropolitan Police district (their own figures might suggest 458), compared to one per 738 in the boroughs, and one per 1,244 in the counties.[3] However, the lack

---

1. Dickens, Charles, 1857, at p.1.
2. Fosdick, Raymond B., 1915, at p.100.
3. Stack, John, 1992, at p.130.

of a precise and constantly maintained ratio between police and public in the Metropolitan area, which experienced constant and rapid growth throughout the century, was the subject of some criticism, as force expansion sometimes lagged behind that of the built environment.[4] In 1880 alone, for example, 70 miles of streets were added to those that had to be watched or patrolled by the Metropolitan Police.[5]

Hierarchy

There was a considerable degree of consistency in uniformed policing from the 1830s to the end of the century. In 1909, *The Times* could note that an examination of Scotland Yard 10 years earlier would have revealed a force that was little changed from the 1850s.[6] From the outset, the Metropolis (the City apart) was subdivided into largely self-contained Divisions. The first six were created in 1829, and most of the remainder the following year. Further sub-division from this initial group of 17 occurred in 1865, when Clapham (W), Willesden (X) and Holloway (Y) were created, with the last Division, Bethnal Green (J), coming into existence in 1886.

Central control was kept by regular liaison with Scotland Yard. In the early decades, this was done via the Sergeant Clerk, a Divisional administrative officer who went to headquarters in person, each afternoon, to receive orders and information (there being no central printing press until 1858). In 1867, Divisional H.Q.s were linked to each other and to Scotland Yard by telegraph lines, though as late as 1886 these were not considered very efficient.[7] (The City police had used them a decade before the Metropolitan force). By 1913, 180 out of 194 Metropolitan police stations were also on the public telephone system. The exceptions were small stations of minor importance.[8]

---

4. See, for example, letter from Evelyn Ansell, *The Times*, 1902, December 26th, p.12.
5. *The Standard,* August 10th, 1881, p.2.
6. *The Times,* January 11th, 1909. It was: "…only within the last decade that precedent, tradition, and routine have been uprooted with a resolute hand where they interfered with efficiency". However, from a practical perspective, many of the early Edwardian changes were relatively small, and often largely administrative.
7. Cavanagh, Timothy, 1893, at p.16.
8. HANSARD 1803-2005, HC Deb 30 April 1913 vol 52 c1191.

The Scotland Yard Telegraphic Room

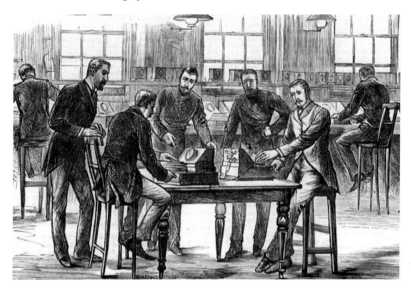

However, as the force (and city) grew ever larger, many began to feel that the Metropolitan Police was over-centralised. They thought that too many decisions were being referred back to the very highest ranks, often to the Commissioner himself, in Scotland Yard. It was claimed that a system that had worked well with a force of 1,000 men (as it had been in 1829) was "utterly unsuited" to one that was ten times that size. It was also alleged that there were too many "veteran lieutenants clinging to office and bygone traditions".[9]

To ameliorate this problem (it did not solve it) two Assistant Commissioners ('high-status' men appointed from outside the force) were added by the Police Act of 1856. In 1857, men at this rank received 800 pounds a year, somewhat less than half the salary of the Commissioner. In 1878, Lord Truro urged that their number be increased to four, in view of the huge amount of high-level administration that had to be done.[10] The head of the C.I.D. did, subsequently, become a third Assistant Commissioner.

In 1869, the apparent lack of senior officers to liaise between the Commissioner and the Divisions (partly a result of Mayne's earlier

9. *The Pall Mall Gazette*, January 19th, 1881.
10. HANSARD 1803-2005, HL Deb 30 July 1878 vol 242 cc629-37, c629.

reluctance to delegate) also led to the introduction of an extra tier of command via the geographical grouping of Divisions into four districts, each of which was placed under a 'District Superintendent'. However, these officers did not acquire significant duties, and so were more cosmetic than functional. Indeed, fifteen years after they were introduced, it was noted that their responsibilities were so minor that there were often vacancies in the positions for long periods of time without inconvenience.[11] Some argued for a genuine sub-division of the capital, in which the four areas would become distinct commands, under the leadership of the equivalent of a provincial Chief Constable.[12]

Each Division was assigned to a superintendent, under whom, originally, were four inspectors and sixteen sergeants. As a result, in 1838, the whole service contained 17 superintendents, 68 inspectors, and 323 sergeants, with about 3,000 constables.[13] The number of the lower command ranks gradually increased with the size of the force, so that by 1851 a personal inquiry into the "protective" police (i.e. those who were not detectives) by Charles Dickens suggested that there were 19 superintendents, 124 inspectors and 585 sergeants (along with 4,797 constables).[14] In the 1870s, a Division contained an average of 450 to 500 men, although the largest, Stepney, had 700. Whitechapel, the smallest, had only 300 officers, although the presence of detectives and command elements meant that it had by far the highest number of Inspectors. In exceptional times of severe disturbance, or after a major crime, the Divisions would assist each other.[15]

Police Stations

The 1841 census indicates that there were then 116 police stations of all types and sizes in the Metropolitan police area. By the end of the century there would be almost 200. Every Division had at least one station that operated as its central HQ, with subordinate stations and section houses for outlying officers to work from, or be accommodated in. Thus, in 1884, N (Islington) Division had its H.Q. in Stoke Newington High Street, with sub-Divisional stations in 11 other locations, including two in the Enfield Small Arms and the Waltham Gunpowder factories. Clapham (W) Division had 10 outstations as well as an H.Q. at Brixton, while the

---

11. pp.15.b.1886, at pp.ix-x, *The Times*, October 2nd, 1886.
12. *The Pall Mall Gazette*, January 19th, 1881.
13. Grant, James, 1838, at p.388.
14. Dickens, Charles, 1851, at pp.97-103.
15. Anon, 1871, 'Our Police System', at p.692.

geographically confined A Division (Whitehall) only had one sub-station.[16] In 1888, the very rough Dorset Street area of the East End was provided with no fewer than four police stations (most were section houses), so that it could be: "...well watched nightly, on account of the character of many of the inhabitants".[17]

Towards the end of the century, the 'classic' and distinctive purpose-built largely brick Metropolitan Police station, with its attendant blue light (used from early on), became increasingly common in the London area, as older buildings were replaced. This process was assisted by the powers of compulsory purchase granted under the Metropolitan Police Act of 1886, which were exercised 10 times to buy land for police stations in the four years to 1890.[18] A typical result of this expansion was that in 1891, X (Kilburn) Division took possession of a new station, next to Queen's Park. It was a commodious structure of brick and stone, with living accommodation for 40 men and a billiard room and library for their use.[19]

Prior to this time, police stations were often much less distinctive. For example, that at Hyde Park (until rebuilt in 1902) was an old one-storied brick building, with a verandah and grass lawn, surrounded by iron rails. It had originally been built as a military guardroom. In the 1870s, about 30 single officers resided there. Along with an Inspector's (or Enquiry) Office, Charge-room, cells, kitchen and dining room, it also contained a spacious library with a full-size billiard table and well-stocked bookshelves. There were adjacent stables for the horses of the Mounted Police.[20]

In the 1850s, Charles Dickens noted that Metropolitan police operations were largely based around 25 main stations, most of them acting as Divisional HQs. These were so "uniform" in their organisation that one could be taken as typical of all; he chose Bow Street for his study. During a nine-hour duty, some men were kept at the station to act as an emergency reserve, being sent out to deal with specific problems or calls for assistance, while the remainder would be 'on the beat'. Before starting their patrol they would be briefed on matters such as missing persons and the results of disciplinary proceedings against fellow officers. There would normally be two inspectors on duty at the same time, one of whom would visit beats in the Division and ensure that constables and sergeants were doing their duty properly, while the other would stay at the station to take the charges and to listen to any complaints made against officers by the

---

16. Kirchner, F.J., 1884, at p.vii.
17. *The Times*, September 11th, 1888.
18. HANSARD 1803-2005, HC Deb 11 April 1889 vol 335 cc213-4, c213.
19. *The Morning Post*, December 19th, 1891, p.2.
20. Owen, Edward, 1906, at pp.2-3.

public.[21]

Police station charge-room in 1872

The 'Beat' System

Each Division was: "...divided into subdivisions, each subdivision into sections, and each section into beats".[22] Constables were in charge of beats, sergeants of sections, inspectors of subdivisions, and as already noted, a superintendent headed the whole division. Thus, the beat was the smallest unit for area policing; there were usually eight of them to a section. They built on numerous eighteenth-century experiments with the old watchmen and, possibly, the military 'Shorncliffe' system of interlinked patrols and pickets that would have been familiar to Rowan. Significant Metropolitan streets were patrolled on an interlocking basis, each street or

---

21. Dickens, Charles, 1851, at pp.97-103.
22. pp.14.1868, at p.11.

series of streets being placed under the "especial guardianship of an individual officer".[23] Each police station had a *Beat Book* setting out all of the beats within its area.

At the bottom of the police pyramid there was, for most of the period, an average of one sergeant supervising every section of up to 10 constables. He would place them on their beats, monitor them while they were on duty, and see that they were relieved at the proper times.[24] However, occasionally, during the 1830s, officers had been divided into groups of as few as four men, each under the supervision of a sergeant.[25] More commonly, in the same decade, there had been nine constables, eight of whom would be allotted beats and one of whom would be kept (in rotation) as part of a small reserve in the police station, ready to deal with emergencies and replace injured or otherwise absent officers.[26]

The constables would parade in front of their sergeant, before and after going on their shifts, assembling at a particular spot, so that he could see that they were sober and properly dressed. Additionally, he might meet them at various designated points and would periodically patrol the section's area (often walking in the opposite direction to the men) to ensure that they did their duty properly, just as an inspector would often check up on him. At the end of the century, an ordinary (rather than a Chief or Divisional) Inspector might be in charge of about 26 constables and sergeants.[27]

The Commissioners had originally intended central beats to be covered in 10 to 15 minutes.[28] However, some daytime beats in semi-rural areas were up to seven and a half miles in extent. Nevertheless, in the centre of commercial London they would usually be very much smaller than this, and might cover a single small street, walked several times in the course of an hour, especially at night.[29] Thus, in 1866, P.C. James Collins from A Division noted that while on night-duty he patrolled Eversholt Street: "…about every quarter of an hour or twenty minutes".[30] The length of individual beats also diminished in proportion to the (perceived) level of

---

23. pp.14.1868, at p.692.
24. pp.14.1868, at p.12.
25. Grant, James, 1838, at p.391.
26. General Instructions Book, 1ˢᵗ proof, hand-amended by the Commissioners, deposited at Met Collection Police Heritage Centre.
27. Flynt, Josiah, 1903, at p.442.
28. General Instructions Book, 1ˢᵗ proof, hand-amended by the Commissioners, deposited at Met Collection Police Heritage Centre, at p.34.
29. Antrobus, Edmund, 1853, at p.43.
30. Eisner, Manuel, 2003, pp.130-132.

criminality of the local population, and the consequent "necessity of increased watching".[31] As a result, those in East and South London were usually relatively short, although, as a public meeting by concerned ratepayers in the Borough in 1897 shows, many people still felt they were far too long.

From the outset, it had been stressed that good London policemen would get to know every house, man, woman, and child on their beats, including their occupations, habits, and circumstances.[32] This knowledge was obtained by: "...constantly being employed in the same quarter and the same street".[33] For example, P.C. James Silver, giving evidence in a notorious murder trial in 1843, testified that he knew the victim well as a result of spending five years on the same Whitehall beat.[34] However, this could also make the work very tedious, and increase the risk of corruption due to excessive fraternization and familiarity with local people, leading to more movement of men towards the end of the century. In 1902, constables' beats were rotated every month.[35]

Perhaps because many of the initial recruits to the new force were taken from the former police establishments, some old habits seem to have died hard. The Commissioners complained in 1831 that some constables continued to "stand idling together while on duty". Men were warned not to enter into conversation with female servants, each other, or anyone else, except where their duties required it while on patrol.[36] The public, too, especially the well-to-do in 'good' areas, quickly appear to have expected higher standards of conduct in police officers than they had with their predecessors, so that the Commissioners were moved to warn that: "Complaints have been made that Constables are seen in conversation with females when on duty, especially in Hyde Park".[37] Nevertheless, this perennial issue, along with that of officers hobnobbing with maids in the kitchens of smart houses, survived for the rest of the century. In 1852, for example, a correspondent to *The Times* claimed that he had witnessed a constable spend an hour during the late evening talking to two female

---

31. pp.14.1868, at p.11.
32. General Instructions Book, 1st proof, hand-amended by the Commissioners, deposited at Met Collection Police Heritage Centre, at p.34.
33. Schlesinger, Max, 1853, at p.51.
34. OBSP, Trial of Daniel McNaughten, 27th February 1843, t18430227-874.
35. Flynt, Josiah, 1903, at p.443.
36. Extracts from Orders from the Commissioners, Whitehall Place, of 7th Jun, 6th, 11th, 17th October 1830 and June 15th 1831, Reproduced in PR.45.1844, at pp.103-106.
37. MEPOL 22/9/1857.

servants across the railings of their master's house, after which the constable: "...received from the window, by the hand of his loving and loquacious nymph, a handful of cake or other food". He felt that such practices were widespread and helped to explain why it could be so difficult to find a policeman in emergency.[38]

Inevitably, at least some of these allegations were unfounded or unfair. In 1831, officers were enjoined to wear a special badge to show when they were on duty, as there had been "constant complaints" from the public about constables talking together, though they were actually off duty albeit still in uniform; this swiftly became a striped armband and lasted until well into the twentieth century.[39]

Police patrol-work was primarily done at night, when the greatest risk of offending was perceived. For most of the era, almost two-thirds of the force was employed between about 10 P.M. and 6 A.M., though the length and hours of night-duty varied slightly over the course of the century. Typically, in 1891, only 40 % of men were employed to cover the 16 hours after 6 A.M.[40] The importance and physical hardship of foot-patrol to policing, and the distance normally covered over a duty, can be seen in a tract produced by a former constable, P.C. John Hunt. He had been required to resign in 1858, after 15 years of service, for failing to take proper care of his feet and not following the treatment for them prescribed by the Divisional Chief Surgeon (he vigorously disputed the allegation which had cost him his pension). He noted that London P.C.s had to: "...walk twenty-two and a half miles a night, no matter the weather, wet or dry".[41] This had been a feature of the force from the outset. Hunt's estimate as to distance covered was only slightly exaggerated. A Dr Farr calculated that on average a constable on night duty walked 16 miles over his beat.[42] Not surprisingly, perhaps, Timothy Cavanagh was to observe of his time in 1850's Lambeth that only someone who had done it could: "...possibly imagine the dreary work it is tramping about for eight long hours in such a filthy neighbourhood".[43]

In 1830, the Commissioners expressly forbade men to carry umbrellas while patrolling; instead, they were issued with oilskin capes and, for cold

---

38. Letter to *The Times*, July 16th, 1852.

39. Extracts from Orders from the Commissioners Whitehall Place, 7th June, 6th, 11th, 17th October, 1830, and June 15th, 1831, Reproduced in PR.5.1844, at pp.103-106.

40. *The Times*, August 11th, 1891, p.12.

41. Hunt, J., 1863, at p.4.

42. pp.14.1868, at p.13.

43. Cavanagh, Timothy, 1893, at p.25.

weather, a greatcoat. These were vital, especially in winter, if only because the Metropolitan climate was often damp, so that the: "…fog makes it home in the folds of the constable's great-coat; the rain runs from the oilskin cape which stands the policeman in the stead of an umbrella; the wind is cold and bleak".[44] To sustain themselves, some men on night duty took food with them, especially if patrolling outside wealthy areas. Thus, in 1882, P.C. George Hudson could note that, while on the beat in Deptford, he would: "…often see constables on duty eating meat and cheese at night-it is usual for them to carry meat out for their supper".[45] Others carried small bottles of cold tea.

This type of work also had physical conscquences for the men involved. In 1838, a Worship Street Police Court magistrate noted that: "The duty of the Metropolitan Police (the night duty), is very severe, and injures the constitution of many men".[46] Over 30 years later, little had changed. Samuel Smiles, the self-help guru, observed that policemen were especially prone to diseases of the lungs and air-passages, as a result of their exposure to inclement weather and urban pollution. Of the 63 police deaths in London in 1868, 27 were from consumption, and nearly half of the officers who reported sick in the winter months were suffering from bronchitis, sore throats, or rheumatism.[47]

Furthermore, and as the 1868 Report noted, although a constable working nights "remains on his legs" for eight hours (this was sometimes done in two four-hour shifts with a short break between them), his subsequent rest period might be interrupted, as he would frequently have to attend at a police court as a witness, and occasionally even be at a drill parade. Unsurprisingly, a significant number of prematurely superannuated officers were not injured but, like P.C.s Isaacson and Treadwell, pensioned on £27 a year in 1857, simply: "Worn out and unfit for further duty".[48] According to the M.P. William Burdett-Coutts, allowing pensions after 25 years' service was important specifically because a quarter of a century of police duty: "…generally unfits a man for any other employment".[49] Chief Inspector Wells also felt that normal police work: "…kills men in twenty-five years-they cannot do it any longer if they are compelled to do it in the streets". A few men taken off the beat after 15 or 20 years' service might

---

44. Schlesinger, Max, 1853, at p.57.
45. OBSP, Trial of James Hartigan, 11th December 1882, t18821212-157.
46. pp.12.1838, Vol. ii, at p.465. Some of these, he felt, could be usefully retired to act as court ushers.
47. Smiles, Samuel, 1870, at p.125.
48. MEPOL 8/10/1857.
49. HANSARD 1803-2005, HC Deb 19 June 1890 vol 345 cc1327-8, c1327.

be able to work on beyond this limit, if given an administrative role in a place where they could be "nice and quiet". However, it was rare to see a man reach even 24 years of continuous "hard plodding".[50] Of course, being pensioned for this reason was only allowed where an officer was not to blame for his decrepit condition. In 1861, for example, P.C. Fenn of F Division was dismissed summarily after the Surgeon-in-Chief found him to be unfit for further service "through intemperance".[51]

In 1834, sick rates averaged 3 per cent of the force during the six winter months, and 2 1/5 per cent in the summer ones.[52] This remained fairly constant during the rest of the century, sick rates still running at about 3 per cent in the 1870s.[53] As a result, in 1907, Metropolitan officers averaged 10 days of sick leave a year.[54] Many officers would receive a slightly reduced rate of pay while off duty, if only to discourage malingering. However, in 1899, the Home Secretary noted that although police regulations provided for a deduction of one shilling a day while on the sick-list, this was not usually enforced where an officer was suffering from injuries received in the execution of his duty.[55]

Except when in training, it was only in the very worst areas that constables would patrol in pairs. They would also be expected to deal with routine incidents without summoning assistance from colleagues, which would, of course, remove another man from his own beat. It was almost a "rule of the service" that this was only done in an emergency, and would usually have to be justified to the section sergeant, later on.

However, if called for, help would often arrive fairly quickly from adjacent beats or a local station, at least in highly policed areas, being summoned by 'springing' a rattle, blowing a whistle, or shouting. Thus, in 1840, P.C. Edward Blayney, on patrol in Whitechapel, swiftly responded when called by a "brother officer" on a neighbouring beat. He helped him detain two suspects.[56] More than 60 years later, P.C. Joseph Chambers, tackling a thief near Tower Hill who had grabbed hold of his testicles also quickly secured help: "I blew my whistle and [P.C.] Easterbrook came to my assistance".[57]

Constant surveillance of the urban environment was a crucial part of a

---

50. Monro, James, 1890, at p.202.
51. Police Daily Orders, 4th July 1861.
52. pp.11.d.1834, at p.28.
53. *The Morning Post,* August 24th, 1877, p.6.
54. HANSARD 1803-2005, HC Deb 18 June 1907 vol 176 cc295-9, c295.
55. HANSARD 1803-2005, HC Deb 04 August 1899 vol 75 c1474.
56. OBSP, Trial of William Johnson et al, 3rd February 1840, t18400203-631.
57. OBSP, Trial of Michael Meyer, 25th July 1904, t19040725-578.

policeman's job. It was popularly believed that a patrolling constable's glance could "take in everything" without overt staring.[58] Officers would usually walk at a regulation 2 1/2 miles per hour (it had initially been set at three), to some a "dreary dawdle", checking buildings and people for signs of forced entry or unfastened locks and windows, as they went along. Indeed, they would normally patrol on the kerb side of the pavement during the day but the inner side at night, specifically so that they could check doors and bolts more easily after dark. This role was sufficiently important to be calculated. Thus, during the year to the end of 1876, 16,769 doors in the Metropolitan police area and 8,530 windows were found open or not properly fastened and the householders duly warned.[59]

This approach to security was shared by the neighbouring City of London force, where the first action an officer took after going on night duty, as he patrolled a street of shops or warehouses, was to check all means of access and egress to the buildings: "...he flashes his lantern on each bolt and padlock. When he sees any fastening insecure, he puts a private mark upon it, and makes a note in his memory as well".[60] If constables failed to alert householders to any doors or windows that were in an unsafe condition, and their sergeant noticed, they might be fined.[61] In the City force, at least, many men also made secret marks on unoccupied buildings, so that they could establish if there had been any unauthorised entry.[62] Even so, police activity did not end the widespread use of private watchmen in commercial premises; many men, such as John Fair, who was employed by the Metropolitan Wood-paving company in Regent Street during the 1840s, continued to make a living from static security.[63]

From the beginning, patrol performance was closely monitored, effective officers being rewarded, sometimes with small sums of money, and poor ones admonished, disciplined, or dismissed. Thus, on 17th March 1831, P.C.s Farrant and Hobbs of C Division were given five shillings each for apprehending 19 pickpockets over the previous month. By contrast, the following day, P.C. Read was dismissed from the same Division for "gross neglect of duty". His offence was to allow a blatant burglary to occur on his beat in Regent Street, that same morning, although it was only 10 minutes walk in length.

---

58. *The Times*, December 25th, 1908.
59. *The Morning Post,* August 24th, 1877, p.6.
60. Shand, Alexander Innes, 1886, pp.594-608.
61. *Quarterly Review*, No.99, 1856, at p.166, reproduced Barrett, A., and Harrison, C., at p.241.
62. pp.15.1878, at p.183.
63. OBSP, Trial of Emma Shell, 24th October 1842, t18421024-2944.

Occasionally, the zeal of the patrolling constables' sergeants in effecting supervision was felt to be excessive. In the Police Orders for 13th August 1845, the Commissioners directed that the practice whereby Sergeants tried to "entrap" Constables on duty by watching them from "hiding places" was to cease.[64] Despite this warning, they sometimes continued to set such traps in ensuing years.

Rewards from police funds for meritorious action were usually quite modest, often, like Hobbs' payment, being the sum of five shillings, and sometimes as little as half a crown, although the Commissioner made 1,101 such payments in 1876 alone.[65] Occasionally, members of the central detective force might receive ten or twenty pounds after a particularly successful and lengthy operation. Slightly more important was the formal acceptance and passing on of rewards given by members of the public to individual officers, something that appears to have been almost institutionalised from its frequency, although each payment had to be specifically authorised by the Commissioners in Police Orders. Typically, these might range from one shilling to over a pound.[66] Occasionally, however, such largesse might extend to the award of something like the "very handsome gold watch" presented to Sergeant Hickeson by the 'gentry' of South Kensington, for his courageous conduct in arresting a notorious burglar.[67]

Nevertheless, some senior officers were nervous about accepting such rewards too lightly. In June 1830, for example, Superintendent William Murray turned down an offer of money gifts from the Surrey Justices for several of his men who had received injuries dealing with a small riot. Murray felt that giving a reward in such a situation would do more harm than good and might even encourage a return to the "old police system" in which officers would only intervene if they saw financial advantage. The men had not lost any police property in the disturbance and were, apparently, quite satisfied with their superintendant's thanks![68] Officers who spotted fires early on, before they had spread, were also usually rewarded with a payment of 10 shillings from insurance companies. This seems to have prompted at least one constable to start his own small blaze with a view to claiming the relevant sum.

Enhanced urban surveillance was greatly facilitated by nineteenth-century developments in street lighting. The advent of gaslight to London,

---

64. Best, C.F., 1985, at p.4 and p.6.
65. *The Morning Post*, August 24th, 1877, p.6.
66. MEPOL 7/15 Police Orders 1850-52, 24th May, 1850, 23rd September 1851.
67. MEPOL 7/38 Police Orders, 14th April, 1868.
68. Anon (A Vestryman of St. Ann's), *The Metropolitan Police,* 1834, at p.72.

first introduced in Pall Mall in 1807, made a significant contribution to
law enforcement.[69] Much later in the century, George Sims noted that the
greatest 'ally' of the police in the process of promoting public order in
London's streets had been the new electric street lamps, which were much
more efficient and numerous than their gas-powered predecessors.[70] This
was especially important as sidestreets and alleys were often merely
observed from junctions by beat constables, rather than being actively
covered. Lighting tended to be best in well-to-do areas, but was sometimes
very poor in the back streets of the East End and other marginal locations.

Although a constable's duties were often very tedious, he could
suddenly find himself in difficult circumstances that might require him to
act with intelligence, commonsense, and discretion.[71] This meant that as
well as having "robust constitutions", officers needed to have their wits
about them. They also had to be able to give clear evidence in court and
understand manuals on police law.[72]

Reaction to the New Police

Wherever the new police were introduced, they met widespread
hostility. This was most obviously marked in parts of the North of
England, but was strong elsewhere, especially in the London area.
However, the strength of this reaction does suggest that the changes in
policing style were immediate and real rather than cosmetic (as is
sometimes suggested). Constables were not merely re-labelled watchmen,
even of the better sort. Indeed, initial antipathy to their arrival prompted a
swift reconsideration of the merits of their predecessors. As a result, it
could be noted that: "An intense feeling of hostility to it [the police]
prevails in the Metropolis". The same author thought that this was present
in the "middle classes, as well as the multitude". Many 'respectable'
people actively applauded the initial animosity of the public towards the
"blue army".[73] Exactly the same points were made in a petition from the
parish of St. George, Middlesex, presented to parliament by their local
M.P. in 1834. He noted that, although certainly not universal, a: "…great
dislike for the force prevailed throughout a considerable portion of the
metropolis".[74]

---

69. Roberts, M.J.D., 1988, at pp.273-294 & at p.277.
70. Sims, George, 1910, at pp.24-25 & p.66.
71. Greenwood, James, 1902, at p.2.
72. Anderson, Robert, 1910, at p.148; and pp.11.d.1834, at p.28.
73. Robinson, David, 1831, at p.84.
74. HANSARD 1803-2005, HC Deb 13 March 1834 vol 22 cc125-30, c125.

Some asserted that this opposition was not genuinely representative of ordinary Londoners. *The Times,* for example, felt that it largely came from criminals, pickpockets and thieves, or those intimately connected with them, such as receivers of stolen property and brothel-keepers. The newspaper maintained that all 'respectable' people were glad to see the passing of the Watch.[75] Such an analysis received support from Edward Gibbon Wakefield, who claimed to recognise most members of a violent anti-police 'mob' at Temple Bar as hardcore thieves who resented the inconvenience created by the new force.[76]

Nevertheless, initial conflicts between the police and general public, evidenced by widespread disturbances, would suggest that hostility was certainly not confined to marginal urban elements. Amongst them were demonstrations against officers guarding the King's procession to parliament in 1830, when the police were attacked by labourers and small shop-keepers shouting "Down with the Peelers!" After riots involving political radicals at Cold Bath Fields, in 1833, P.C. Robert Culley was stabbed to death. Very significantly, a coroner's jury, made up of small tradesmen, which considered his demise, returned a verdict of "justifiable homicide", despite pressure to produce a finding of murder. Their decision met considerable popular celebration. A large public meeting held in Chatham, and addressed by a delegation from the Metropolis, cheered the coroner's jury and sympathized with all the "victims of police brutality in London".[77] Their verdict, which was overturned on appeal, was based not on Culley's apparently inoffensive personal conduct, but on the alleged "ferocious" and "brutal" behaviour of the police on the day, and doubts about whether the Riot Act had been read.[78]

In 1834, the basis for popular concerns about the police were summarised in the House of Commons by Colonel Evans. This former soldier conceded that the new police were an efficient force, but also noted that there was great anxiety that so large a body, combining a: "…system of espionage with their military character, should be under an irresponsible control, and at the disposal of the Minister for the time. The expense, too, was a great matter of objection".[79] As this comment suggests, there were objections to the cost, constitutionality, operation, and control of the new force.

---

75. Leading Articles, *The Times*, 5th, 6th and 10th November, 1830.
76. Wakefield, Edward Gibbon, 1831, at p.4.
77. 'Public Meeting At Chatham, In Support Of The Victims Of Police Brutality', *The Poor Man's Guardian*, June 15th, 1833.
78. 'Inquest on Culley, the Policeman', *Jackson's Oxford Journal*, May 25th, 1833.
79. HANSARD 1803-2005, HC Deb 13 March 1834 vol 22 cc125-30, 128.

Cost

The financial cost of the police was to be one of the most important and under-estimated (in the modern era) popular grievances. The M.P. John Wilks was probably right in thinking that the: "...additional expense was in a great degree the cause of the unpopularity of the new police".[80] It was swiftly claimed, with a little truth, that they were "infinitely more expensive" than their predecessors.[81] An anonymous but hostile observer, considering 15 parishes selected "casually" from the Metropolitan police area, compared the total of their contributions to the watch in 1828 with those they made to the new police in 1831. He concluded that the former stood at £48,874, while the latter was £99,847.[82] A near doubling of the previous cost to London as a whole, to over £200,000 per year in the early 1830s, and £240,000 by 1838, seems likely, though comparisons are quite difficult to make. This was particularly annoying because Peel, when introducing the 1829 Bill, had suggested that the tax imposed under the new Act would be less than the old watch rate. The force also seemed to be significantly more expensive than an equivalent number of regular soldiers.

However, after 1833, central funds provided a quarter of expenditure, initially up to a maximum of £60,000.[83] This allowed parochial assessments to be reduced to 6d. in the pound, as had originally been intended. By 1854, the government was contributing £100,928.[84] This took some of the 'heat' out of the debate, although many provincial M.P.s, such as Ralph Thicknesse, representing Wigan, bitterly resented being asked to pay for a police force from which their constituents did not benefit, and disliked being told that they should view it as analogous to funding the country's army or navy. Against this, as Peel pointed out to the Commons, the Irish police were also subsidized out of the consolidated fund.

In some Metropolitan areas, the increase in cost was particularly extreme. To a considerable extent, the semi-rural parishes on the fringes of London subsidised the rest of the city after 1829, paying much more into the fund than they got back in policing services. In 1830, for example, the Ealing vestry complained that the cost of their old watch to the parish had not exceeded £100 a year, whereas, under the new system, they were

---

80. HANSARD 1803-2005, HC Deb 18 November 1830 vol 1 cc575-82.
81. Robinson, David, 1831, at p.82.
82. Anon ('A Metropolitan Rate-Payer'), 1834, at p.4 and p.18.
83. Grant, James, 1838, at p.388.
84. *The Times*, March 2nd, 1854, at p.10.

paying £880 in police rate annually.[85] Several of these parishes unavailingly asked to be allowed to 'opt out' of the system. More than a decade after its introduction, the vestry of Woolwich petitioned unsuccessfully against the arrival of the new force in 1840, as a result of an expansion of the Metropolitan Police area. They claimed that their highly effective 'traditional' form of policing made it unnecessary, and were very reluctant to face the heavy financial costs involved in funding the new force.[86] As late as 1844, a large petition, signed by those living in St. Marylebone, complained of the "heavy burthen" to which their parish had been subjected to maintain the force, and demanded an inquiry into funding.[87] Indeed, the issue never entirely went away. In 1899, for example, the M.P. James Bigwood noted in a parliamentary debate that all of the outer Middlesex hamlets had to pay 5d. in the pound to support the Metropolitan force, even though, in many of them, a "policeman was seldom seen".[88]

Constitutionality

In 1843, Sir Robert Peel was persuaded that, 14 years into its operation, the Metropolitan force manifested the utmost respect for the law, and that there was no evidence that anyone had: "...been by their means impeded in the exercise of any right which the constitution gave them".[89] However, not everyone was so sanguine. Along with concerns about cost, there were numerous constitutional objections to the new force, especially in its early years. These were summarised in a major article in *Blackwood's Edinburgh Magazine* in January 1831, which claimed that the new policing system was one of the greatest inroads ever made into the fundamental principles of the British constitution.[90]

There were several reasons for this political antipathy. It was partly the result of a: "...natural tendency in the minds of the people to look with suspicion on a body with very enlarged powers".[91] There was a fear that the new police gave excessive power to the Crown, and that the constable was really a soldier in disguise, albeit armed with a truncheon rather than a

---

85. Paley, Ruth, 1989, at p.114.

86. HO 61/25, 1840, Petition against the New Police to Marquis of Normanby, Home Secretary.

87. HANSARD 1803-2005, HC Deb 05 March 1844 vol 73 cc590-7, c590.

88. HANSARD 1803-2005, HC Deb 16 May 1899 vol 71 cc754-835.

89. HANSARD 1803-2005, HC Deb 15 August 1843 vol 71 cc744-60, c744.

90. Robinson, David, 1831, at p.84.

91. Grant, James, 1838, at p.391.

musket. Indeed, to some observers he was more dangerous than the soldier. His constant presence on the streets meant that he also appeared to be a "general spy".[92] This was made worse because he was answerable directly to the Home Office, rather than local Justices (see below).

As a result, and as the 1833 Committee noted, a combination of cost and constitutional objections meant that, at first, the very existence of the new force became a "matter of serious consideration".[93]

Gradual Acceptance

Despite such initial unpopularity, the process of acceptance appears to have started fairly early among the upper and middle classes, being, in part, a reflection of Peel's success in producing a politically non-threatening body of men who knew their places vis à vis their 'betters'. In part, it was also a result of their *apparent* success in defeating crime. Certainly, the new police were a more efficient force than *most* of those that they replaced and, as a result, there was some immediate support for the institution. In 1830, for example, a long-term resident of Lambeth, who was delighted with their conduct, was most struck by the improvement in diurnal security (greatly neglected under the 'traditional' system): "We have now no mobs or rioting in the day time".[94] (Though to other Londoners, having officers on duty during the day appeared to be a terrible waste of money).[95] In May of the same year, a letter from a Hampstead householder commended the watchfulness and courage of two local constables who had foiled a burglary at his home, confronting a three-man gang in the small hours, even though "handled very roughly" in the process.[96]

There was enough positive news for the 1834 Select Committee to produce a generally favourable verdict on the force, five years after establishment, although this is, perhaps, unsurprising, given that its members included many of the 1828 Select Committee which had initially recommended its formation (including Sir Robert Peel himself). It concluded that the principal objectives of a "methodized system of Police" had been attained, making the force one of the "most valuable of modern institutions".[97]

---

92. Ibid, at p.83.
93. pp.11.c.1833, at pp.4-5.
94. Anon (A vestryman of St. Ann's), 1834, *The Metropolitan Police,* at pp.69-70.
95. HANSARD 1803-2005, HL Deb 15 November 1830 vol 1 cc493-500.
96. Anon (A vestryman of St. Ann's), *The Metropolitan Police*, 1834, at p.74.
97. Smith, Keith, 2007, at p.16.

Both Commissioners observed that middle-class grievances gradually shifted during the 1830s, moving from concern at the oppressive use by the police of their new powers to regular complaints about their lack of efficiency and unwillingness to take even more drastic steps to combat crime. An early sign was that although, initially, the Metropolitan police were regularly drafted into the provinces to deal with local disorder, by the late 1830s this was often done to the marked chagrin of London parishes. St. Leonard's Shoreditch even drafted a resolution condemning the practice in 1839, because of the attendant loss of protection in the Metropolis.[98]

By the 1850s, middle and upper class Londoners usually considered the police a laudable and essential national institution, something that was evidenced in popular literature such as *Punch*. This was still not quite a universal sentiment, even amongst these social groups. For example, Lord Dudley Stuart, the MP for Marylebone, was a persistent critic, and particularly concerned about the high level of the police rate. He sought the appointment of a select committee to consider the general management of the Metropolitan force.[99] Nevertheless, by then, the process of acceptance amongst the well-to-do had often advanced so far as to produce an almost uncritical attitude towards the institution. Thus, William Ballantine recorded a street altercation in which a policeman was clearly in the wrong, but where a member of the public of 'military bearing', who had not even witnessed the incident, stepped forward and presented his card to the officer offering to give evidence on his behalf.

For some other, quite specific, groups, acceptance of the Metropolitan Police also came fairly swiftly. For example, requests for assistance from publicans, eager for the police to attend their beer gardens, also grew very rapidly, and ultimately had to be paid for at three shillings per night in 1838.[100] As a result, by the late 1830s, the pseudonymous 'Fidget' was both concerned and amazed at the way people in London were regularly being told that it was an "admirable force".[101]

Working Class Hostility to the New Police

For the London working class acceptance of the police came far more slowly. They would need the rest of the century and beyond to be reconciled to the 'plague of the blue locusts', and the process would be far

---

98. Emsley, Clive, 1996, at p.54.
99. *The Morning Post*, June 16th, 1853, p. 4.
100. Correspondence of the Commissioners MEPO 1 (30) No.51913, Letter dated 6th Sept. 1838.
101. 'Fidget', c.1838, at pp.7-8.

from complete even then. At the close of the era, much 'hooligan' activity in rough areas, especially assaults on officers, appears to have been a manifestation of continuing antipathy to policing.[102] The relative decline in such hostility in the latter part of the century was *not* the result of a softening of police methods, but rather their tacit acceptance as legitimate by those who were policed. Officers were increasingly seen as permanent, if often disliked, aspects of the urban landscape, rather than 'novel' liberty-takers.

There were many reasons for working-class antipathy. The police were perceived by many poorer Londoners to be "property protectors", acting for the middle and upper classes.[103] Most importantly, they created a bureaucracy of official morality that impinged heavily on the traditional street-centred patterns of urban working-class life.[104] Like any external imposition of new normative values, this was a painful process. Officers were often thought to be loitering about the streets, waiting to 'trump up' charges for what were perceived to be technicalities.[105] In 1837, even Charles Dickens could claim that people were being confined in police stations, in grim conditions, over the most trivial matters.[106]

One reason for this was that the simplest task the new police faced was that of establishing enhanced public order and decorum in the streets. This was much easier than dealing with the capital's more sophisticated forms of crime. Vagrants and drunks could be cleared from pavements, beggars arrested, public games, gambling and fighting limited or even stopped, 'furious' driving could be prevented, and prostitution (very loosely) controlled. For example, 707 beggars were charged in the St. James's Division in the three months between March and May 1832. The same year, 9,000 vagrants were arrested in the Metropolitan Police District as a whole, considerably more than in the 12 months before 1829.[107]

Such policing necessarily impinged directly on the urban working class. Many of their entertainments and occupations were necessarily conducted in public, whether street or tavern, to a much greater extent than those of prosperous Londoners, if only because the former's homes were cramped and squalid.[108] These were also places where the police were most active. For example, the control of drinking in public houses

---

102. Pearson, Geoffrey, 1983, at p.86.
103. *Poor Man's Guardian*, September 24th, 1831.
104. Storch, Robert, 1975, at pp.61-90.
105. Robinson, David, 1831, at pp.84-86.
106. Dickens, Charles, 1837, at p.92.
107. pp.11.d.1834, at pp.56-57.
108. HO 61/25, 1840, Resolution of the vestry.

appeared to be specifically aimed at workingmen because, by the 1850s, they were almost exclusively the preserves of the lower classes. The increasing insistence of the Middlesex Justices on public-house closure at 11.00 p.m. ignored the fact that they were often the beer cellars of the poor, some of whom worked very late hours.[109] However, publicans were forced to observe these closing hours -eventually set down in the 1839 Police Act- for fear that a "cat's-eyed inspector" would catch them out.[110] By contrast, gentlemen could always drink claret at their clubs or in their homes, whatever the hour.

Similarly, the banning of off-course, non-credit, betting in 1853 impinged primarily on the lower classes who most resorted to it; the upper orders could wager in person at the racetrack or by credit.[111] In parts of an increasingly proletarian South Islington, towards the end of the century, there were numerous affrays between the police and public in the small streets running off the Caledonian Road over games of 'Pitch and Toss', where money was gambled.[112]

The threatening impact that the new police were to have on 'traditional' street-centred life in the capital was particularly linked to their desire to "move on" individuals and disperse assemblies, even if they were ostensibly harmless.[113] Noisy street-entertainers, such as organ-grinders and ballad-singers, were ubiquitous in early nineteenth-century London. The police often dealt with them either by "moving on" those who attracted crowds or by arresting them for common law nuisance or statutory violations.[114] Street-vendors received similar treatment. In October 1838, George Davies and other itinerant dealers in fruit and vegetables petitioned, unavailingly, to be allowed to sell their goods "as usual" in front of the houses in Queen's Buildings.[115] Similarly, the primary concern of Mayhew's costermongers of the late 1850s, and a major reason for their hatred of the police, was that they: "...drive us about, we must move on, we can't stand here, and we can't pitch there".[116]

It was a sufficiently common command to form a cameo for Dickens, in 1853. A London 'ragged boy' named Jo is arrested by the police because

---

109. Adolphus, John, 1824, at p.58.
110. Hodder, George, 1845, at p.138.
111. Meason, M. Laing, 1882, at pp.195-196.
112. See on this Cohen, Philip, 1981, at pp.116-122.
113. See for example Storch, Robert, 1975, at p.83.
114. Vorspan, Rachel, 2000, at p.910.
115. Correspondence of the Commissioners MEPO 1 (30). Letter dated Oct.6th 1838.
116. Mayhew, Henry et al, 1862, Vol. 1, at p.20.

he refuses to move on, although he has been "repeatedly cautioned" to do so. His defence is that he has nowhere to 'move on' to, having been "moving on, ever since I was born".[117] Some decrepit individuals could take up to six such 'moves' to reach a neighbouring beat. By the end of the century, the police were also often moving on anyone found sleeping outside at night.[118] Under the Metropolitan Police Act 1839 (2 & 3 Vic. C 47), a refusal to 'move on', when ordered to do so, could be deemed to be resisting a constable in the execution of his duty, something that might attract a fine of £5 or a month's imprisonment.[119]

Sport provided another arena of conflict from the outset of the new force. For example, in May 1830, the police authorities at Camberwell tried to prevent cricket from being played on the area's celebrated Green, until Peel personally wrote to Rowan, drawing attention to their officiousness.[120] Such disputes lasted throughout the era. At the end of the Victorian period, an increase in street games of the newly popular Association Football caused further disturbances with police officers. In 1908, Thomas Holmes could note that during the previous year, more than fifty boys were summoned and fined at one London court alone for playing football in the streets.[121]

There were often few alternative venues for these types of recreation, as open spaces were scarce in working-class areas. As Holmes appreciated, the streets were the "playgrounds of the poor". He was also realistic about the invidious choice that many slum youths faced: either to stay in their: "...insufferable homes or to kick up their heels in the streets". Given the police response, this often meant a choice between becoming physical 'degenerates' or 'hooligans'.[122]

As a result of this rather officious activity, the police have been termed, with *some* justification, the agents of a "middle-class assault" on popular mores, enforcing a mass of petty enactments bearing almost entirely on working-class life. This meant that it was sometimes simply a matter of chance as to whether ordinary men got on their 'wrong' side, as the: "...duties of the police have been made to tally with upper-class, as opposed to working-class, notions of right and wrong".[123] The police also introduced an unprecedented degree of continuous surveillance into

117. Dickens, Charles, 1996 (1853), *Bleak House*, at p.308 & p.311.
118. London, Jack, 1903, at p.52.
119. Thompson, R., 1840, at pp. 26-27.
120. Gash, Norman, 1985, at p.504.
121. Holmes, Thomas, 1908, at p.174.
122. Holmes, Thomas, 1908, at p.169.
123. Reynolds, S., Woolley, B., & Woolley, T., 1911, at p.86.

working-class communities.[124] Some contemporary observers thought that their presence aggravated or even created disturbances that would not otherwise have occurred.[125]

Nevertheless, it would be wrong to say that such police activity impinged solely on the working classes. In 1840, for example, the vestry of St. Leonard's parish, Shoreditch, passed a resolution expressing concern about the "oppressive effect of the New Police Act" and, in particular, the reluctance of constables to allow shopkeepers to display goods on the pavement, as they had previously done.[126] In passing, it should also be noted that there was nothing unique to England, let alone London, in such a *modus operandi* in urban areas. Patrols carried out by the Parisian police and gendarmes in the 1820s, for example, looked for cabarets that were open after hours, and arrested vagrants, drunks, prostitutes, and anyone else who appeared to be suspicious and who could not give a good account of themselves.[127]

Such police campaigns inevitably encouraged an increased level of criminal prosecutions. This danger had been apparent long before 1829.[128] Thus, the 1822 Committee appreciated that any expansion of the police would mean that large numbers of petty offenders who had previously been ignored would be charged.[129] In 1829, even Sir Robert Peel warned that great care was to be taken to ensure that: "…constables of the police do not form false notions of their duties and powers". Despite this, almost a decade later, the lawyer John Adams thought that new police powers meant that "foolish and idle charges" were being brought, instead of being quietly forgotten.[130]

Not surprisingly, the police were often lampooned for concentrating on 'soft' targets, and conducting ludicrous operations, such as the removal of an apple-stall and the attendant "capture of the fruit-woman".[131] Similarly, in 1850, a concerned member of the public complained (unavailingly) to a police magistrate about the "brutal ill-treatment" meted out by a policeman to a 13-year-old boy with an apple-barrow. The lad was held overnight and

---

124. Hay, Douglas, 1980, at p.58.
125. Robinson, David, 1831, at p.86.
126. Emsley, Clive, 1996, at p.60.
127. Emsley, Clive, 1987, p.272. They also checked that doors and gates were secure.
128. Anon, 1804, *A Letter to A Member of the Society,* at pp.15-17.
129. The 1822 Police Committee had asserted that previous years had witnessed an "alarming increase of street robberies within the Metropolis", pp.9.1822, at p.9.
130. Adams, John, 1838, at pp.19-20.
131. *Punch,* June, 1843, at p.132.

produced before the police court the following morning for causing an obstruction, while his barrow was left abandoned in the street. It was also claimed that, since they had acquired authority over cab-ranks, the police had exercised a "savage tyranny" over cabmen.[132] Twenty years further on, another observer could note that, although most police officers were reasonably well tempered, no one acquainted with the streets of London could be ignorant that the instances of: "...bullying and overbearing conduct towards unfortunate costermongers, applewomen, and others are far more frequent than could be wished".[133]

Even some strong supporters of the Metropolitan force complained that far too much of its work was devoted to dealing with 'status' and petty street offenders, rather than 'real' criminals, such as the roughs who lived by robbery and burglary. Too much time was taken up with: "...men who may make a bet in the street, or against publicans who keep their houses open a few minutes after hours".[134] The same author cited the amazement of visiting French policemen at seeing an otherwise orderly group of men, who had been casually gaming in public, being arrested and marched off to Bow Street Magistrates Court. He approved of the apparent reversal of priorities in Paris, where trivial 'crimes' were (allegedly) widely ignored, and resources concentrated on the graver ones. In Paris, the larger the robbery, the more likely it was to be solved, whereas the contrary situation prevailed in London.[135]

Class Bias in Policing

Unsurprisingly, in these circumstances, it did not take long for an anonymous tract to claim that it was an inherent tendency of the new police system to neglect the detection of crime "except among a particular class".[136] Even a judge could be convinced that some laws, albeit introduced from worthy motives, were simply used as "engines of oppression against the poor".[137]

At times, the differential enforcement of the criminal law between social classes could become overt. John Glyde, writing in 1856, was well aware that children of the poor were treated differently when compared to their middle and upper-class counterparts. In one situation, the deviant was

132. 'Police Outrage', *Reynolds's Weekly News,* October 6th, 1850.
133. Acton, William, 1870, at p.216.
134. Meason, M. Laing, 1882, at pp.195-196.
135. Meason, M. Laing, 1881, at pp.299-300.
136. 'Fidget', c.1838, at p.8.
137. Parry, Edward Abbot, 1914, at p.199.

brought before his parents or teacher, was admonished or punished informally, and the offence passed over without public disgrace; in the other, the: "… 'delinquent' is taken before a magistrate, punished by the law, and disgraced and hardened as a man would be".[138] His views were shared by Micaiah Hill, who talked openly of England's "class legislation" which was made to bear with: "…severity upon our juvenile population, if made up of children of the poor". For them, succumbing to the quite natural temptation created by publicly exposed penny tarts in open windows, or toys in exposed baskets, would often result in prosecution.[139] Similarly, Mary Carpenter, despite her preoccupation with the 'dangerous classes' and their cultural transmission of social indiscipline, appreciated that among the: "…lowest class, the moment a child is detected a thief he is prosecuted".[140] Over half a century later, rich hooligans "running amok" were still much more likely than the poor to be dealt with by way of a fine, rather than immediate imprisonment.[141] Boat Race night was one thing, but when the Hackney boys clashed with those from Bethnal Green "that's another tale".[142]

Police Coercion

In many working-class areas, police coercion was only thinly disguised. As one observer noted in 1871, it was astonishing to see what an immense amount of: "…vigilance, legislation, and force are actually in constant employment, to keep down the vice and crime which belong to the poorer class".[143] James Greenwood, visiting Leman Street Police station, saw cutlasses hanging over the chimneypiece in the office, and a group of new 'arrivals', both officers and suspects, all of whom were bleeding, so that the police station looked like a "butcher's shambles".

In 1833, a usually supportive newspaper accepted that there might be some truth to allegations that the police exercised their authority "too rudely and vexatiously towards the humble classes".[144] Even admirers of

---

138. Glyde, J., 1856, at p.133.

139. Hill, M., and Cornwallis, C.F., 1853, at p.17.

140. Evidence to Select Committee on Juveniles, Answer to Question 816, by Mary Carpenter; reproduced in Tobias, J.J., 1972, *Nineteenth Century Crime,* at p.46.

141. Parry, Edward Abbot, 1914, at p.205.

142. Holmes, Thomas, 1908, at p.167.

143. Anon, 1871, Our Police System, at p. 693.

144. 'Popay And The Police', *Cobbett's Weekly Political Register*, August 31st, 1833.

the force noticed that a normally polite and friendly constable could be rather different if encountered at night in a poor area. Most unflatteringly, in 1851, the apparent brutality of members of the Metropolitan force was even compared unfavourably to that of the armed French police, where, it was alleged (if not not entirely plausibly) an officer regarded himself as a "servant of the community".[145]

Gradual 'Acceptance' by the Working Class

Despite these conflicts, in many areas of London the police made steady, and sometimes deliberate, progress in gaining popular acceptance during the course of the century. Within a few decades of 1829, many workingmen of the 'respectable' sort (often skilled or semi-skilled workers) were willing to complain about the lack of policing in their areas, compared to the wealthier parts of London. This process was not confined to the Metropolis. Police in other British cities, such as Middlesbrough, also won a grudging measure of working-class support.[146]

It was not *purely* self-delusion that led Sir Henry Smith to believe that, in foreign countries, the police were regarded as representing the government, whereas in London they "belong to the people", so that they could generally count on the citizens' support. Interestingly, he thought that the reason that such support was often lacking in America was that "ultra democratic theories" had destroyed the notion of the police being public servants.[147] Similarly, in 1890, after his retirement, the former Metropolitan Commissioner, James Monro, was to opine that the Metropolitan Police could operate on its relatively small staff only because of the widespread public recognition that policemen were their "friends and protectors". They were seen as a disciplined body of men engaged in protecting the "masses" as much as the "classes" against those who were not so law-abiding.[148]

This popular support, although only gradually, and always incompletely, won, was important. It was widely believed that the (often) paramilitary R.I.C. was handicapped by its frequent absence. The need for legitimacy was also accepted by the Royal Commission on a Constabulary Force of 1839, which asserted that no police force could function properly: "Without the assent or aid of the Community". This was especially

---

145. 'The Police Again', *The Era*, August 31st, 1851.
146. Taylor, David, 2004, at p.766.
147. Smith, Henry, 1910, at pp.264-266.
148. Monro, James, 1890, at p.617.

important when it came to the provision of criminal intelligence.[149] The elderly Edwin Chadwick, looking back over thirty years on his involvement in that Report, was also convinced that any police force: "...must owe its real efficiency to the sympathies and concurrent action of the great body of the people".[150]   In 1873, this was given equal importance to the good qualities of the police officers themselves when it came to explaining the success of the Metropolitan force. Its members had: "...upon the whole secured for themselves the confidence of the people of this capital, who, therefore, have always been ready to aid them".[151]

Encouraging 'Legitimacy'

Undoubtedly, the post-1850 economic improvement (see chapter 10 below), and the increased levels of cultural and social security that flowed from it, helped preserve the 'English model' of policing to the end of the century. However, there were other factors behind its survival. Once the disturbances of the early Victorian years had passed, men came to the fore at the Home Office and in many British police forces who believed that the political surveillance and overt repression of the European *haute police*, or the blatant political involvement of their American counterparts, was both undesirable and unnecessary.[152]

To encourage acceptance they promoted a service ethos in the police, successfully resisted any process of militarisation, pursued a policy of minimum force, and, towards the end of the century, edged back from excessive political partisanship.

Service Orientation

To promote popular legitimacy, Edwin Chadwick had argued that a police force should actively "cultivate its beneficient services". Police involvement in assisting with accidents, disasters, and fires would also relieve the "monotony of mere sentinel work". (Especially as crime declined and the innate tedium of patrol work increased).[153] Such a 'service' approach was certainly followed by the Metropolitan police, which became involved in many basic forms of social work.[154] As James

---

149. pp.12.b.1839, at p.185.
150. Chadwick, Edwin, 1868, at pp.16-17.
151. *Daily News*, December 12th, 1873.
152. Emsley, Clive, 1996, at pp.261-262.
153. Chadwick, Edwin, 1868, at pp.16-17.
154. Jones, David, 1982, at p.22.

Monro noted, they touched ordinary people by helping infirm people across busy roads and providing many other services.[155] A selection of statistics is indicative. In 1868, for example, 2,805 lost people (many of them children) were returned to friends and families. In 15 months at the end of the 1860s, the police seized 20,871 assorted stray dogs, which were either destroyed or returned to their owners. In 1869, they took 2,079 people, the bulk of them accident victims, to hospital.[156] They frequently used their own 'hand-ambulances' to do this. In 1894, the very busy Lost Property Branch, based at Scotland Yard, received 29,716 items, including 2,393 purses, of which 15,987 were successfully returned.[157]

The Metropolitan Police Lost Property Office, Scotland Yard

---

155. Monro, James, 1890, at p.617.
156. Smiles, Samuel, 1870, at p.105.
157. *The Illustrated Police News*, November 30, 1895.

Lost children being looked after by the Metropolitan Police

More generally, dozens of unnamed bodies were photographed each year before burial to allow them to be identified later if relatives made enquiries, while the police often woke workmen up in the early morning with "thunderous knockings" (though they were also usually paid 4d a week for this service).[158] On a more sophisticated basis, the Metropolitan Police Returns for 1859 could note the number of suicides attempted but prevented by patrolling officers, and the number of fires reported and extinguished by the police "before the arrival of the engines".[159] At a very personal level, most ordinary Londoners could only be stirred by the courage of men like P.C. John Welch, who suffocated in a sewer while trying to rescue three workmen in 1849.

Political Non-Partisanship

The Metropolitan force was relatively careful to keep out of party politics. Any police officer caught canvassing in a political cause while on duty was dismissed (unlike some American forces).[160] However, political non-partisanship went much further than this, especially as the century advanced. The police were increasingly keen to avoid unnecessary conflict with working men generally over political issues, especially after the bad publicity occasioned by the Trafalgar Square disturbances of 1888. As a result, there were deliberate attempts to steer the force back towards having at least the appearance of being a more neutral body. This was made easier because most officers were themselves originally working-class men. James Monro, in particular, stressed that the police were: "…not the representatives of an arbitrary and despotic power, directed against the rights or obtrusively interfering with the pleasures of law-abiding citizens".[161]

The Metropolitan force appears to have been careful to avoid any hint of bias during the dock strike of 1889. Monro was resistant to pressure from the dock employers to police the dispute more 'vigorously', refusing to prosecute over placards designed to deter (or intimidate) 'black legs' that read: "As men we beg you to clear out at once, or we must inform you that the consequences will be extremely serious". The police were also careful to distinguish the small number of 'roughs' from ordinary strikers. Despite having been imprisoned in 1888 for assaulting officers in Trafalgar Square, John Burns, the strikers' leader, appears to have co-operated with

158. Morrison, Arthur, 1901, at p.12.
159. Metropolitan Police Returns, Table No. 20, for 1859.
160. Flynt, Josiah, 1903, at p.448.
161. Fosdick, Raymond B., 1915, at p.167.

them. Significantly, when informed that 500 extra policemen were being sent to the scene he commented that it would mean (through sympathy) "500 extra tanners for the strike fund".[162]

Use of Minimum Force and a Civilian Culture

The primarily civilian and unarmed nature of the Metropolitan force had been one of its characteristic features from the outset. Initially, this was vital to acceptance. Indeed, its opponents still felt that the force established in 1829 was far too 'military' in appearance. In 1833, for example, William Cobbett complained of the novelty of seeing peace-officers in uniform: "...embodied in companies and battalions, marching in rank and file, commanded by Serjeants and colonels—under the mock name of superintendents".[163] Anticipating this, those responsible for police uniform had initially considered red and gold (the Bow Street foot patrol wore red waistcoats), but rejected this as too 'military' in favour of a dark blue, stiff-collared, brass-buttoned, tailed-coat with clear numerical and Divisional identification, and a heavy, strengthened leather, but still conventionally shaped, black top hat; tunics and lighter 'Roman' helmets were still more than 30 years away. (Until 1861, officers could wear lightweight white trousers during the summer months as an alternative to the normal heavy blue winter issue).

In its first decade, it was frequently stressed that the force should not follow the example of the Irish Constabulary (it became 'Royal' in 1867), despite Peel's own involvement in the latter's establishment. Thus, Viscount Clements, the M.P. for Leitrim, warned parliament in 1839 that he had: "...seen the evils of an armed police in Ireland, and he had no wish to see the same system adopted in this country".[164] Many senior officers agreed. In 1882, the Home Secretary noted that he had consulted the Commissioners (full and assistant) and Superintendents in the Metropolitan force about arming the police, after a constable was shot and wounded, and they had been "unanimously against the proposal".[165]

As a result, guns were very rarely carried on a routine basis, though the 'unarmed' nature of the Victorian police has been slightly exaggerated, especially in the Metropolitan area. Firearms were issued at a variety of times during the century. Thus, in the early years, Inspectors were permitted to carry pocket pistols while on duty. Periodically, a specific

---

162. Ballhatchet, Joan, 1991, at pp.54-59. A tanner was six old pence, or 2 1/2 p.
163. HANSARD 1803-2005, HC Deb 14 June 1833 vol 18 cc797-811.
164. Hansard, vol. XLIX (1839) 1197.
165. HANSARD 1803-2005, HC Deb 02 November 1882 vol 274, cc622-4.

scare, such as the Fenian problems of 1867, led to the arming of considerable numbers of ordinary policemen in the London area. Several hundred officers received basic revolver training during 1868.[166] In 1883, the problems posed by the more serious types of conventional crime, apparently evidenced by the murder of P.C. George Cole by an armed burglar in December the previous year, prompted the issuing of firearms to some officers engaged on routine duties, especially in outlying and isolated parts of London, such as Camberwell. An official questionnaire issued to officers in the outer Divisions that year even produced a majority in favour of being routinely armed.[167]

Generally, however, the men who were issued with revolvers appear to have been carefully chosen from the more sensible, experienced, and collected members of the force. As a result, weapons were only very rarely used or even drawn. Abuse of firearms was dealt with extremely severely, and officers were only permitted to use their weapons in self-defence.[168]

This civilian orientation had not been achieved without challenge, especially in the force's early years, while later in the century some provincial forces and their Chief Constables (often former soldiers) and several other commentators petitioned, with some political support, to be reformed into light auxiliary military units. For example, in about 1860, Valentine Baker, of the 10th Royal Hussars, suggested that both the Metropolitan and county forces receive military training so that they could act as a militia in the event of invasion. The Home Office vigorously resisted these proposals, one such suggestion, from the same year, being endorsed by a Whitehall official: "It has been frequently suggested to organise the Metropolitan Police *militairement*, and always repudiated. It seems to me highly unconstitutional".[169]

Even so, by the 1870s, and under the influence of Colonel Edmund Henderson, the London force had become markedly more martial in its organisation than previously, with: "…more effective drill, and a greater military smartness throughout".[170] Of course, and as was noted in parliament, if it was to function properly, a large police force that operated in a population of three million people, could not be "wholly devoid of a military character". Nevertheless, after basic training, it was claimed that most officers still spent only 20 to 25 hours at drill in the course of a

166. MEPOL 7/38. Orders for 7/1/1868.
167. Emsley, Clive, 2010, at pp.158-159.
168. Emsley, Clive, 1985, at pp.137-140.
169. Emsley, Clive, 1996, at p.59.
170. Anon, 1871, 'Our Police System', at p.692.

year.[171] However, the trend towards a more military force accelerated under Colonel Charles Warren, in the late 1880s. Warren even redrafted their drill manual, loosely basing it on that for infantrymen.

Some observers, like Josephine Butler, deprecated such moves along with sartorial changes such as the post-1863 'Roman' helmet: "We see the tunic and the helmet superseding the civil hat and coat introduced by Sir Robert Peel, and attempts made from time to time to arm the police with swords or revolvers". She felt that the mounted police were becoming increasingly like the household cavalry, overtly parading in large groups in Hyde Park, and that the distinctions between the constable and the soldier were being obliterated.[172] According to a radical journal, under Colonel Warren the force had become increasingly like the R.I.C., and was being used for purposes for which it was never intended.[173] The *Pall Mall Gazette* supported claims that Warren's Commissionership had witnessed over-centralisation and the adoption of military-type discipline for officers, despite the fact that: "Battalion drill avails nothing when the work to be done is the taking down of a midnight assassin".[174] However, Warren's departure in 1888 eased some of these tensions.

Continuing Hostility

All of these measures helped promote popular acceptance of the police. Nevertheless, much working-class hostility continued to the end of the period and beyond. Even the former C.I.D. man, Walter Dew, could recall that as a child in London in the 1870s and 1880s he had had an "instinctive dread of the London policeman".[175] Similarly, an Edwardian observer could note, when distinguishing between East and West End views of the police, that: "The Police down East are no longer the servants of the community, they are masters; at the best kindly champions, at the worst tyrants". In such areas their word was often law, encouraging swollen heads amongst young constables.[176] As John Cairns, a late Victorian stipendiary magistrate, was to note: "An officer with a "swelled head" was a public danger".[177] Acceptance of the police in the worst 'criminal' slums was largely absent: "In other parts of London if a street assault is

---

171. HANSARD 1803-2005, HC Deb 09 May 1873 vol 215 cc1733-50.
172. Butler, Josephine, 1880, at pp.38-39 & 47.
173. *The Link*, 24th March, 1888.
174. Porter, Bernard, 1988, at pp.86-88.
175. Dew, Walter, 1938, at p.1.
176. Gamon, Hugh, 1907, at pp.23 & 24.
177. Cairns, J. A. R., 1922, at p.263.

committed the first idea is to call the police, but here that would be the last thing that would be thought of".[178]

Even where there was little personal risk, many people were reluctant to actively assist the police. Despite P.C. John Sweeney calling out 'Stop Thief' in a crowded part of Hammersmith, when pursuing a suspect in the late 1870s, local: "...people made an avenue for him".[179] In rough areas, the police could not even expect assistance from the public when they were themselves physically attacked. Typically, when two officers, ejecting a pair of drunks from a pub in Brixton, were viciously set upon, the incident was witnessed by a crowd of more than a hundred, but: "...although called upon, not one came forward to help the police".[180] In the very worst locations, if officers were seen to be disadvantaged, some elements of the public might even join their attackers. In 1890, when a constable remonstrated with an East End drunk for pushing people off the footpath, the officer was knocked down and kicked, at which: "A number of roughs got round and also assaulted him".[181]

Nevertheless, although there was still considerable distrust of the police amongst many members of the working class in 1900, a *degree* of tacit acceptance had been won from all but its very lowest elements.[182] It should, perhaps, be noted that this fall in popular hostility towards the new police was a widespread urban phenomenon, and not confined to London, even if very marked in the capital. For example, there was a steady decline in antipathy towards officers in the 'rough' town of Middlesbrough after the 1860s.[183]

---

178. Hoare, H.E., 1883, at p.231 and pp.234-235. Nevertheless, "violence was nearly always confined to native weapons", i.e. feet and fists.
179. Sweeney, John, 1905, at p.8.
180. 'Attack on the Police', *Illustrated Police News,* March 1st, 1895, at p.2.
181. *Illustrated Police News*, June 21st, 1890, at p.4.
182. Jones, David, 1982, at p.22.
183. Taylor, David, 2004, at p.764.

CHAPTER FIVE

POLICE COURTS AND THE GROWTH IN POLICE POWERS

Introduction

The 1820s witnessed a shift in political opinion in favour of enhancing public security and order at the expense of 'traditional' notions of liberty and personal freedom.[1] By 1842, the barrister John Adolphus, aware that changing social mores in the political nation were influencing the law's prescription of what was acceptable amongst the working class, was forced to hope that the country had not yet reached the point of imprisoning them: "…for slight irregularities, attended with no violence, injury, or public scandal".[2] Despite his concern, there was a growing willingness to criminalise hitherto accepted behaviour and to countenance an increase in police powers and interventionism, as civil libertarian and constitutional objections were marginalised. By the end of the period, an observer could note that it was fortunate that the Metropolitan Police worked for the capital's good, as: "An organisation so powerful in the hands of despotic authority would make life a daily burden, and the word "liberty" would be an empty sound".[3]

New Offences

Many offenders in Victorian England were in conflict with the law because of the criminalisation of acts that a century earlier would not have been illegal or, if proscribed, only rarely enforced. As a prison report noted, much of the apparent increase in inmate numbers in the middle of the century had occurred because: "Offences which were formerly passed

---

1. Gatrell, V.A.C., 1990, at p.244.
2. Adolphus, John, 1824, at p.10.
3. Sims, George (Ed.), 1902, p.8.

over, are now made the occasion of frequent commitment to gaol".[4] Some 27 years later, Luke Owen Pike appreciated that the number of late Victorian criminals could only be made to appear 'formidable' by including those who were guilty of offences that: "...our hard-drinking great grandfathers would have regarded as merits rather than faults".[5] After the 1850s, in particular, and at the instigation of an increasingly interventionist Home Office and a variety of other pressure groups, new powers to combat various forms of 'victimless' crime, and to deal with matters that had previously been questions of individual morality, were swiftly added to the penal repertoire. This was manifest in Acts affecting or criminalising, *inter alia*, the sale and consumption of alcohol, begging, prostitution, gambling, the sale of pornography, the post-release supervision of felons, cruelty to children and animals, as well as several blood sports.[6]

By way of illustration, in the 1850s and 1860s there were attacks on the sale of obscene material although, until then, the police had not usually had the power to arrest those traders who earned a livelihood by selling "immoral" books and prints. Before the law was tightened up in 1857, Holywell Street off the Strand had been a major centre for the sale of pornography.[7] Change meant that one of its most notorious figures, William Dugdale, died in 1868 while serving a sentence of hard labour in the Clerkenwell House of Correction.[8] The compulsory supervision and inspection of the city's lodging-houses, with attendant prosecutions, was another area of heavy state intervention.[9] Some of these statutes may even have been counterproductive. The Lotteries and Betting Act of 1853 was aimed at suppressing all forms of ready-money betting outside enclosures. However, once cash betting was made illegal, it became street-oriented, and thus public, encouraging participation and making it harder to oversee.[10]

Similarly, there was a major attack on alcohol-related misconduct. Thus, public inebriety *simpliciter* became a crime, irrespective of whether the drunkard was being disorderly. In 1869, the police in London made 9,538 arrests for simple intoxication.[11] They were also encouraged to be more rigorous about enforcing existing legal powers, so that there was a

---

4. Beggs, Thomas, 1849, at p.19.
5. Pike, L.O., 1876, Vol. 2, at p.484.
6. Jones, David, 1982, at p.25.
7. Mayhew, Henry et al, 1862, Vol. 4, at p.210.
8. White, Jerry, 2008, at p.318.
9. PR.9.1816-76, Report for the Year 1872, at p.2.
10. McKibbin, R., 1979, at p.148.
11. Miller, Walter, 1997, at p.91.

tripling of convictions for drunkenness between 1855 and 1875. A District Superintendent attributed the apparent increase in cases of public intoxication (of all types) over three years, up from 23,007 in 1869 to 33,867 in 1872, purely to changes in the law, especially those contained in the 1872 Licensing Act, which brought more instances to notice, and which meant that publicans who would previously allow drunken people to remain on their premises: "...until they became partially sober, or were taken to their homes now turn them into the streets, or call on the Police to take them off".[12] There was other important legislation in this area, such as the Habitual Drunkards Act of 1879. In one of the most drastic developments, the Inebriates Act of 1898 allowed convicts who were deemed to be 'habitual' drunkards to be sentenced to detention in an inebriate reformatory for up to three years, in addition to any other punishment they received.[13]

The police also abandoned previously accepted and tolerant practices towards drunks, such as carrying them home in wheelbarrows; at one time these had been kept in readiness at the local police station for this very purpose. By the latter decades of the century: "...in the estimation of a policeman, a very little inebriety constitutes drunkenness".[14] As a result, in 1877, it could be noted that nearly all of the apparent increase in drunkenness was a result of the: "...increased activity of the police under recent legislation".[15] At the same time, there was a campaign against previously high levels of illicit distilling in the metropolitan area.

In sexual matters, State intervention also advanced apace, especially in the final years of the century. In 1885, for example, William Thomas Stead, the editor of the *Pall Mall Gazette*, 'discovered' an extensive trade in child prostitutes, centred on London, many allegedly seduced into their profession between the ages of 13 and 16. He then published his evidence in a notorious article.[16] This resulted in the Criminal Law Amendment Act of 1885, largely intended to combat the exploiters involved in prostitution. The statute made it an offence for a landlord to permit prostitution on his premises. Additionally, and partly influenced by Stead, Parliament raised the age of consent from thirteen to sixteen in the 1885 Act (it had been twelve as late as 1875). It also attempted to control prostitution in other ways, such as the passing of statutes in the 1860s that provided for the

12. PR.9.1869-6, at p.92.
13. Garland, G., 1985, at p.20.
14. Anon, 1882, *Metropolitan Police Court Jottings*, at p.49.
15. *The Morning Post*, August 24th, 1877, p.6.
16. Stead, W.T., 'The Maiden Tribute to Modern Babylon', *Pall Mall Gazette*, July 6th 1885, at p.4.

compulsory inspection (and treatment) of women in garrison towns, in an attempt to reduce the incidence of venereal disease amongst servicemen.[17] There were serious, but ultimately unsuccessful, proposals to extend these provisions to prostitution in big cities, including London.

Judicial decisions swiftly caught the 'spirit of the times'. In *R v Coney* (1882), for example, eleven senior judges sitting to determine an appeal, concluded that prize-fighting (as opposed to gloved boxing) was illegal and that all persons aiding and abetting such a fight were guilty of assault, the consent of the fighters to their bout being irrelevant.[18]

One indication of the significance of this combination of new crimes and the stricter enforcement of old ones, was that fully a third of the people taken before a court in London in the mid-1880s were charged with being drunk and disorderly or for not sending their children to the newly compulsory schools (the 1870 Education Act being strictly enforced).[19] Similarly, it has been argued that over half of all imprisoned juveniles in the mid-nineteenth century were in custody due to an unprecedented willingness to extend the practical age of criminal responsibility to younger children, and the criminalisation of previously legal forms of behaviour.[20]

Police Powers

The Metropolitan police inherited or acquired enormous powers to deal with street crime and disorder. For example, the 'catch-all' provisions in the Vagrancy Act of 1824, such as the offence of being a 'suspicious person', were particularly significant, not least because the new police sometimes "stood on the limits of [its] authority".[21] By the early 1830s, an average of 2,500 people were being convicted annually in London as reputed thieves or suspicious characters.[22] Even so, the Commissioners campaigned for yet greater legal powers. For example, in 1838, Rowan complained that it was "absurd" that officers were not allowed to arrest without warrant those accused of misdemeanours, such as common assault, that they had not personally witnessed.[23]

---

17. Fisher, Trevor, 1996, at p.32.
18. 8 QBD 534 (the 'Prize Fighting Case').
19. Jones, David, 1982, at p.6.
20. Wiener, Martin J., 1990, at p.52.
21. pp.12.b.1839, at p.173.
22. King, Peter, 1998, at pp.116-166 and at p.134.
23. pp.12.1838 at pp.84-85.

At their formation, in 1829, all police powers had been contained in seven Acts of Parliament. By 1861, these had increased to 75, and in 1878 there were well over a hundred.[24] They ranged from the 1834 Beer Act, which allowed officers to enter any Public House at will, to the very important Metropolitan Police Act 1839 (2 & 3 Vic. C 47), which contained many provisions creating, or codifying existing, offences that were only punishable summarily. Among them were such diverse matters as discharging firearms in public, wantonly ringing bells and using indecent language in the streets.[25]

A year after the 1839 statute was enacted, one (quite measured) commentator felt that it was so draconian that everyone in London should be made aware of its provisions, if only because it would: "...expose all classes to the most rigorous penalties and imprisonments for minor offences".[26] Concern over the 1839 Act was to continue for the rest of the century. As a stipendiary magistrate observed in the 1880s, it conferred upon the police powers that were "unknown to the general law of the land". One of its most important provisions was found in section 24 of the statute (though its roots lay far back in the previous century), whereby anyone brought before a magistrate charged with having anything in his possession that might: "...reasonably be suspected of being stolen or unlawfully obtained, and who shall not give an account to the satisfaction of such magistrate how he came by the same shall be deemed guilty of misdemeanour". The penalty for this offence, which reversed the burden of proof, was a £5 fine or a maximum of two months' imprisonment. It was used extensively where evidence was inadequate to found a more serious (and indictable) offence, such as receiving or theft.[27]

Its operation can be seen in a case from March 1837, in which the Home Office received a petition from a businessman who described himself as a collector of broken glass and old metal, asking for the return of a cart that had been "forfeited" by his employee, one Henry Samuels. This had been seized after Samuels was summarily convicted of unlawful possession of 34 lb. of brass. He had been arrested by a Metropolitan Police officer while carrying the metal, and produced at the Queen Square Police Office, where the sitting magistrate, David Gregoire, initially adjourned the case to give him an opportunity to produce evidence that the metal was honestly purchased. Two days later, Samuels appeared before him again, with a witness whose evidence was rejected by the magistrate.

---

24. Petrow, Stefan, 1994, at p.32.
25. Stephen, J.F., 1883, at p.265.
26. Thompson, R., 1840, at pp. 26 & 7.
27. pp.15,1878, at p.183.

Samuels was ordered to pay a 40-shilling fine and the cart was seized.[28] In London, 1,754 people were convicted of unlawful possession of goods in 1859 alone.[29]

This 'crime' created an enormous potential for injustice, as it was feared that many people were unable to give a "satisfactory" account, even when it was true. This was especially likely as workmen might be annoyed by the initial request, and reply facetiously to police officers. In the early 1880s, it prompted a magistrate to stress that, when it came to such charges: "...too great caution cannot be exercised".[30] Unfortunately, not all Justices were as careful.

Taken together, the Penal Servitude Act of 1864, the Habitual Criminals Act of 1869, and the Prevention of Crimes Act of 1871, also greatly tightened police supervision over 'ticket-of-leave' men and released prisoners with two or more previous convictions for felony. They provided for the registration of everyone found guilty of significant offences and improved on existing techniques to identify those previously convicted. Released convicts under such supervision had to report on a monthly basis to the police and prove that they were living an honest life. The police were empowered to arrest without warrant a licensee who was thought to be living in a generally dishonest manner.[31] Supporting these statutes, a *Habitual Criminal Register,* an alphabetical list of those liable to the statutory penalties contained in the 1869 and 1871 Acts was drawn up. At first, everyone convicted and given a prison sentence was included on it. However, this soon resulted in the Register being "swamped". As a result, after 1877, it was changed to include people whose reputation as habitual criminals could be taken as established, i.e. those convicted on indictment of a crime where a previous conviction was proved against them and those who were released from a formal sentence of penal servitude, even if it was their first sentence. The volume for 1892 contained 3,851 names.[32] Nevertheless, it appears to have been an unsatisfactory system, and many London police stations kept their own private registers of suspicious local characters.[33]

As this suggests, a constant problem for both the police and courts when it came to enforcing these extended judicial and police powers over 'hardened' criminals was that the means of identifying them had been

---

28. Smith, Bruce P., 2005, at p.151.
29. PR.6.1859, Table No.8, at pp.20-21.
30. Anon, 1882, *Metropolitan Police Court Jottings*, at p.71 & p.73.
31. Petrow, Stefan, 1994, at p.50.
32. MEPO 6/4, Habitual Criminal Register for 1892.
33. Stevenson, J., 1986, at p.47.

outstripped by the new ability of the bureaucracy to record their offences and of the legislature to pass laws governing them. This led to several attempts at developing improved means of personal identification, something that was only to be properly solved, at the turn of the century, by the advent of fingerprinting. As a result, along with the registers of habitual criminals, companion volumes recording "distinctive marks" were issued from the 1880s, to assist in their recognition. These could be cross-referenced from the main habitual criminal register. They identified a range of marks, scars, tattoos, deformities and peculiarities in nine parts of the body. Thus, Arthur Abiss had a: "Birthmark back right shoulder, cast right eye". If the physical characteristics of criminals believed to be using an alias appeared to tally with a man recorded earlier under another name, application would be made to the governor of the prison from which he had been freed for a photograph or the assistance of someone who was personally acquainted with him, such as a warder. Additionally, inmates in prisons such as Holloway, especially if on remand, would be regularly inspected by experienced local detectives, so that one recorded that: "One of the most disagreeable experiences is being passed under review by the plain-clothes men, with a view to recognition, which takes place twice a week".[34]

Such measures were obviously laborious and inherently unreliable, leading, after initial resistance, to the adoption of anthropometry in 1893, a process that had originally been developed in France by Alphonse Bertillon, during the 1880s. Under this system, the respective proportions of a convict's body measurements were measured with callipers, so as to facilitate his identification if he re-offended and was captured. The Metropolitan force added thumbprints to the Bertillon system in 1893.[35] A Registry was established of these measurements, although only 18,000 British criminals had been measured by 1900, and it was clearly an inadequate system. The use of photography also increased.

By the end of the century, Sir Robert Anderson, a former Assistant Commissioner and head of the C.I.D., was blunt about the effect of the awesome array of police powers available to the Metropolitan force. He ridiculed those who suggested that introducing such a system to Ireland would be morally wrong, when they were seemingly oblivious to its existence at the very seat of English government. He felt that the fact that there was no great city in the world in which life and property were so safe as London (very possibly true) was largely due to it being governed: "...not

---

34. 'In Holloway "On Remand"' *Pall Mall Gazette*, October 27th 1892.
35. *Daily News*, November 20, 1895.

by ordinary law but by police law. For London, like Ireland, could not be governed without a Coercion Act". By a 'Coercion Act', he meant one limited to a specific geographical area and which armed the police with 'extraordinary' powers: "...unknown to the ordinary law, and sometimes foreign to the spirit of that law". He felt that the most obvious illustration of this was that under the 1839 Act a constable might call anybody to account whom he found loitering after sunset. If he considered that his explanation was unsatisfactory, he could arrest him and bring him before a police magistrate, who might send him to hard labour for a month, without any right of appeal.[36] The same Act made being drunk in a public place, in the capital, subject to a fine of 40s. (with imprisonment in lieu), compared to the normal five-shilling national fine.[37]

Police powers and duties became so extensive that the 1908 Royal Commission on the Metropolitan Police could freely acknowledge that they limited: "...in almost every direction the freedom of action of Londoners". However, it was not just the existence of these powers, but a new determination to enforce them, that was unprecedented. As the battle against street crime and disturbance was slowly 'won', the police were able to focus resources elsewhere, on previously neglected targets. For example, a new level of general order on the streets allowed some increase in police action against prostitutes.[38] In the closing decade of the nineteenth century, the numbers in the Metropolitan Force and, more pertinently, their ratio to the public (even allowing for the concurrent increase in population), also began to increase slightly, allowing a higher degree of activism.[39] Such an increase *may* have encouraged an extension of policing into previously untouched areas.

Josephine Butler was exaggerating, but not outrageously so, when she observed that there was a standing threat to liberty from "police rule", which was in danger of becoming a rival to formal government.[40] It was a far cry from any notion of police officers as 'citizens in uniform' paid to give full-time attention to duties that were incumbent on everyone.

---

36. Anderson, Robert, 1910, at pp.94-95.
37. Thompson, F.M.L., 1988, at p.329.
38. Emsley, Clive, 1991, at p.72.
39. Discussed in Petrow, Stefan, 1994, at p.37. It should be remembered that the Metropolitan force had a number of 'national' security responsibilities.
40. Butler, Josephine, 1880, at p.46.

The Police Courts

The police had no (legal) power to punish on their own account, although cuffs, rolled capes and fists appear to have been regularly used for illicit chastisement. Nevertheless, police effectiveness was heavily dependant on swift and efficient judicial support. However thorough an area's policing, uncertainty and attrition in its criminal litigation process can substantially reduce the value of deterrence, and so undermine the work of local officers.[41]

Jury trial, the historic English method of fact adjudication, was procedurally slow, relatively expensive, and uncertain in outcome. The progressive abandonment of limitations on barristers' rights to represent clients, culminating in the passing of the 1836 Prisoner's Counsel Act, also meant that trials on indictment gradually became longer and more technically complicated. This was problematic, as to be effectively enforced, minor offences needed a direct power to which: "…much discretion must unavoidably be allowed, immediately to punish them".[42] In nineteenth-century London, this was provided by the system of stipendiary magistrates that had been established in the capital by the Middlesex Justices Act of 1792.

Summary Jurisdiction

The 1792 'Police Offices' or Courts (as they became popularly known during the early nineteenth century) along with the older (but similar) Bow Street Office were initially staffed by three paid magistrates, and had both executive and judicial functions, being involved in investigating crime and supervising policing, as well as judging summary, and deciding interlocutory, matters. These functions parted company after the Report from the Select Committee on Metropolis Police Offices of 1838 came out firmly in favour of making the: "Magistrate's duties as purely judicial as possible".[43] By 1839, the Police Courts had taken their final shape, altering little into the twentieth century.[44] Indeed, after this date, calling them 'Police Courts' was rather misleading (if highly telling), as they had, in theory, "nothing to do with police". Some observers, such as Henry Brougham feared that the phrase lowered them in the public estimation.[45]

---

41. Goldkamp, John S., 2011, pp.115-122.

42. Hardwicke, John, 1828, at p.496.

43. pp.12.1838, at p.14.

44. Davis, Jennifer, 1984, at p.309.

45. HANSARD 1803-2005, HL Deb 23 March 1855 vol 137 cc952-77, c952.

In the 1840s, they sat from eleven in the morning until five in the afternoon at up to a dozen locations, of which the most important were: Bow Street; Covent Garden; Queen Square; Great Marlborough Street; Hatton Garden; Union Street in the Borough; Worship Street; and Lambeth Street in Whitechapel.[46] These courts were staffed by 23 stipendiary magistrates in the 1850s.[47] (The maximum allowance under the 1839 Police Act was 27).[48] They were usually former barristers.

Their jurisdiction expanded steadily after 1829. Thus, the 1839 Police Act gave them important powers to deal with most misdemeanours, unlawful possession of goods, 'suspicious' or drunk and disorderly behaviour, common assault, gambling and vagrancy, albeit that some of these had been matched in earlier provisions. In 1859 alone, for example, the stipendiary courts convicted 2,614 prostitutes and 5,577 people who were drunk and disorderly.[49] In the 1850s, they gained jurisdiction over nearly all offences committed by juveniles, except murder.[50] The Criminal Justice and Juvenile Offenders Acts of 1855 also gave them power to try some small thefts. There was further expansion under the 1879 and 1899 Summary Jurisdiction Acts.

Some of this increase in jurisdiction was permissive, rather than compulsory. By 1900, 80% of indictable matters in England were being dealt with summarily, with the defendants' necessary agreement (often given because of the statutory limitations on sentencing in police courts).[51] Additionally, defendants might be reluctant to be held in custody during the longer delays pending trial on indictment.[52]

As a result, summary cases included quite serious assaults and not insignificant thefts as well as numerous very minor matters.[53] The modern situation in which 98% of criminal disposals (given its broadest interpretation) are determined summarily had largely arrived. Thus, in 1855, the metropolitan magistrates dealt with 97,090 cases, of which only 19,278 were sent for trial jury trial, 77,712 being disposed of summarily.[54] In 1872, in the Whitechapel (H Division) area alone, 5,260 people were charged before the magistrates' courts, but only 265 were committed for

---

46. Mogg, Edward, 1844, at p.112.
47. Davis, Jennifer, 1984, at p.311.
48. *The Morning Post*, March 13th, 1893, p.8.
49. PR.6.1859, Table No.8, at pp.20-21.
50. Wiener, M.J., 1990, at p.259.
51. Bentley, David, 1998, at p.20.
52. Crompton, Henry, 1905, at p.7.
53. Guest, A., 1891, at p.86.
54. Davis, Jennifer, 1984, at p.312.

trial on indictment.[55] Police Courts also became increasingly willing to intervene in what had previously often been accepted and ignored facets of working-class life, such as wife-beating, being aided in this by statutes such as the Act for the Prevention and Punishment of Aggravated Assaults on Women of 1853 and the Wife Beaters' Act of 1882.[56] Women could also come to the Police Courts to have their husbands bound over to keep the peace.

These developments helped make the courts central to everyday life. This aim had been explicitly identified by the Select Committee on Metropolitan Police Offices of 1838, which hoped that they would: "...encourage in the common people a habit of looking to the law for protection". Although the wider society continued to employ informal sanctions long after the advent of the new police, the unprecedented availability of relatively easy, swift, and inexpensive summary prosecutions appears to have lowered the level at which formal sanctions would be invoked.[57] It seems that at least one fifth of all larceny charges under the Criminal Justice Act, and two thirds of cases generally, were brought by working-class prosecutors, though most of these came from above the level of the 'casual' poor. Of course, the convenience of summary procedures also attracted many actions from employers, such as the London docks, which were increasingly willing to prosecute pilfering workers using these forums.[58]

Not surprisingly, perhaps, there were doubts about the quality of justice that the newly expanded police courts administered. In the 1830s, they led Charles Dickens to observe that within the walls of the police courts: "...enough fantastic tricks are daily played to make the angels blind with weeping".[59] Although exaggerated, some of his concerns were well founded. The growth of summary jurisdiction meant that fairly serious cases, carrying up to a year's imprisonment, were being mixed up with those of the "most trivial description", such as the prosecution of disorderly women. However, they did not necessarily receive markedly different consideration.[60] The speed of summary proceedings was particularly striking.

As the century advanced, some of the worst of these abuses were corrected. Nevertheless, constitutionalists continued to worry that

---

55. PR.9.1869-76, Report for the Year 1872, Divisional Report, at p.98.
56. Tomes, Nancy, 1978, at pp.338-342.
57. Davis, Jennifer, 1989b, 'Prosecutions and their Context', at p.416.
58. Davis, Jennifer, 1984, at p.319.
59. Dickens, Charles, 1837, *Oliver Twist,* at p.92.
60. Adams, John, 1838, at p.12.

administering justice at "high pressure" in these forums was not conducive to fairness. Sometimes, in minor matters such as drunkenness, a charge would simply be read out, followed by a single sentence from the arresting officer, after which the magistrate moved straight to sentence (usually a modest fine). Notes of the evidence were not normally kept, making appeals difficult.[61] To the end of the period, Police Court magistrates often ignored the complicated English rules of evidential admissibility.[62] They were also more likely than juries to make an assessment of the 'man' before them, rather than the facts with which he was charged. Even this might be based on unreliable sources. John Porton petitioned the Home Secretary after a policeman falsely swore he had seen him with men of notoriously bad character.[63] Sometimes, their approach to other procedural niceties was 'robust', something that was aided by the frequent absence of defence legal representation. An American visitor noted that police courts had much less time for the: "…disgusting postponements and legal subterfuges by which so many guilty [illegal] gamblers escape imprisonment in the United States".[64]

These concerns were aggravated by the low quality of some stipendiary magistrates, especially in the first half of the century. Charles Dickens' appalling 'Mr. Fang' was not typical of those who presided over Metropolitan police offices, even in the 1830s, though loosely based on a real magistrate who was eventually dismissed by the Home Office. Nevertheless, there is some support for his harsh portrayal.[65] In the late 1830s, the relatively modest annual salary of £800 was widely blamed for their (sometimes) poor quality.[66]

However, by the 1850s, experienced and reasonably able barristers, earning £1,400 a year, were more commonly found in the office.[67] Some magistrates, especially in the second half of the century, presided over their courts with a consciously benign spirit. Thus, A.C. Plowden often dispensed practical advice on extra-legal matters, feeling that the time taken up on this was a reasonable price for promoting faith in the administration of justice.[68] Unfortunately, another bar to recruiting high-

61. Guest, A., 1891, at p.86.
62. Gamon, Hugh, 1907, at p.151.
63. HO 61/25 letter dated 21/2/1840.
64. Flynt, Josiah, 1903, at p.448.
65. Ballantine, William, 1890, at p.53.
66. *Hansard's Parliamentary Debates*, Vol. L, 3rd.Series, 7 Aug.-27 Aug 1839 at p.446.
67. Davis, Jennifer, 1984, at p.311.
68. Plowden, A.C., 1903, at p.26.

quality men, the lack of a proper career structure, was not remediable.[69]

The situation was not improved by the low-level of remuneration provided for police court clerks. Unlike the salaries for magistrates, their pay did not increase significantly between 1839 and 1883, although their employment frequently required them to work late into the evening or to take papers home.[70] Additionally, the courts themselves were often physically cramped and dilapidated. In 1873, for example, there were complaints in Parliament about conditions that were allegedly a "disgrace to this great metropolis". Some were not even kept properly clean or painted.[71] In 1880, one former Chief Clerk described Wandsworth Police Court as an "unwholesome dungeon" that had been condemned 30 years earlier but still remained in service, exposing court personnel to the foul emanations coming from a huddled mass of "crime, drunkenness, filth and poverty".[72]

The 'new' Bow Street Police Court

NEW COURTHOUSE AND POLICE STATION, BOW-STREET.—SEE NEXT PAGE.

69. pp.12.1838, at p.16.
70. *Daily News*, March 20, 1883.
71. HANSARD 1803-2005, HC Deb 21 April 1873 vol 215 cc777-93, c777.
72. *The Standard*, October 20th, 1880, p.6.

Magisterial Support for Police

Very significantly, the police could usually be confident of the
magistrates' support for their efforts to promote order and decorum on
London's streets. Thus, as a young army officer, the future Q.C. and,
ironically, Metropolitan stipendiary magistrate, Montagu Williams, had
experience of this in the 1850s. While on leave in London, a fellow officer
(who later became a parson) sought to intervene when he saw a constable
"brutally ill-treating" a prostitute, shortly after midnight. When he sought
to remonstrate with the policeman, he was himself seized (very roughly),
as was Williams. To their astonishment, both were charged with assaulting
the police. Next morning they appeared before the magistrate at
Marlborough Street who, after hearing the evidence of the constables and
defence witnesses: "…decided, Heaven knows why, in favour of the
police, fining us five pounds and binding us over to keep the peace."[73]
Unsurprisingly, Josephine Butler spoke darkly of the: "…complicity of
magistrates with the police in extra-legal or illegal arrests and
imprisonments".[74]

However, this was not *invariably* the case, especially in the early
decades of the new force. There were always limits as to how far even the
summary courts would countenance 'intrusive' police behaviour. Thus, in
1870, the publican of the Black Horse, Haymarket, successfully applied
for a summons at Marlborough Street Police Court against Inspector Parry,
of C Division. Parry would, apparently, personally visit the public house
four to five times a night, sending a sergeant at other times. He would
enter the bar, sneering at the patrons "as if they were convicts", deterring
custom. The publican only withdrew his application after the Divisional
Superintendent appeared in Court, apologised for what had occurred, and
accepted that such conduct was wrong (one police visit a night to licensed
premises normally being deemed sufficient). This analysis was fully
supported by the Stipendiary magistrate.[75]

A lack of co-operation from London's magistrates also appears
to have been at least partly behind the modest use of the 'habitual
criminal' legislation of 1869 and 1871 in the capital, when compared to
northern cities. In December 1869, Superintendent Howard of H Division
noted that Metropolitan magistrates were almost unanimous in feeling that
it was unacceptable to punish a man merely for being in the streets, even if

---

73. Williams, Montagu, 1890, pp.45-46.
74. Butler, Josephine, 1888, at p.41.
75. *Illustrated Police News*, February 12th, 1870.

he had previous convictions and kept bad company.[76] The almost London-wide campaign against costermongers, launched by the police in the 1860s, also failed largely through their lack of support. In a more localised example, in 1874, two Worship Street magistrates dismissed police summonses against costermongers for obstruction, on the ground that they had no right to issue them unless they had first tried to remove offending barrows and been obstructed by their owners (the physical risk of doing this was often too high for the police). Some magistrates also resisted the periodic police clampdowns on prostitution that occurred during the 1870s and 1880s, by using a highly legalistic interpretation of the law to dismiss the cases against many of those arrested.[77] Although the rate of conviction in contested summary trials rose steadily, if not dramatically, from 53% in 1857 to 64% in 1870, a substantial minority of cases did result in acquittal, while the increase in conviction rates may reflect improved forensic presentation of cases and pre-trial screening.[78]

Nevertheless, with these reservations, the Police Courts greatly facilitated a process in which, with the establishment of the 'new' police, and the increasing ease of criminal prosecution, the working class and their activities were subject to official interference and discipline to a hitherto unprecedented extent.[79] It was freely accepted, even in 1838, that the police magistrates largely discharged their duties by administering "criminal law amongst the poorer classes of the population".[80] Little had changed over 60 years later. The Edwardian judge Edward Parry had no doubt that police courts, at least when dealing with summary only matters, were often a "machine for teaching better manners to the poor".[81] They did this in a cheap, non-technical and swift manner, with fewer procedural safeguards and often, in practice, a reduced standard of proof.

From the mid-century onwards, these courts also became increasingly unwilling to entertain complaints of police brutality or abuse of power by working class people, or to resist other police demands.[82] By 1891, it was claimed that the magistrates' acceptance of police evidence had reached the point at which some members of the public felt that it was almost: "…useless to defend themselves against a police charge". Some alleged

---

76. Stevenson, J., 1986, at p.48.
77. Davis, Jennifer, 1984, at p.329.
78. Miller, Wilbur, 1997, at p.91.
79. Davis, Jennifer, 1984, at p.317.
80. pp.12.1838, at p.16.
81. Parry, Edward Abbot, 1914, at p.214.
82. Ibid., at p.329.

that they had become "mere slaves of the police".[83] This was exaggerated. However, even a former stipendiary could note that if someone was wronged by an officious officer, took his number and, in exchange, was charged with an "elastic" offence such as "insulting words and behaviour" there was always a risk that, in a busy police court, the presiding magistrate might: "...be as indifferent to your egotism as was the constable".[84]

Summary trial of illegal gamblers

83. Guest, A., 1891, at pp.86 & 90.
84. Cairns, J. A. R., 1922, at p.267.

CHAPTER SIX

EFFECTIVENESS OF LONDON POLICING

Introduction

How far did nineteenth-century policing and judicial initiatives contribute to the post-1850 reduction in Metropolitan crime? In many cases, both 'Whigs' and 'radicals' (amongst modern historians) are agreed that the police *did* make a major contribution to urban security, albeit largely disagreeing about how this was received by the policed. There was also ample contemporary support for such a connection.

Within a few years of its foundation, Francis Place thought that any improvement in Metropolitan crime rates was due to a: "…better regulated police, [combined with] a better description of Police Magistrate".[1] According to William Arabin, Metropolitan street robberies were comparatively rare by 1834, something that he attributed: "...entirely to the vigilant conduct of the police".[2] Such an analysis was to be reiterated throughout the era. From the vantage point of the 1870s, another observer felt that the enormous improvement of the capital's "blue coated protectors" on its old watchmen and constables was obvious, and explained why most people could walk abroad in tolerable security.[3]

However, this analysis is (and was) certainly not universal. Some nineteenth-century writers and many modern academics (have) emphasised alternative explanations, whether social, economic or cultural, for the capital's improving security (see chapter ten below). Additionally, even if the police *did* have a major impact on Metropolitan crime rates, there is a considerable debate as to how exactly this occurred.

---

1. Place, Francis, 1972, at pp.14-15.
2. pp.11.d.1834, at p.299.
3. Anon, 1874, *London Guardians of the Night*, at p.574.

Control of Public Space

Throughout the Victorian period, the Metropolitan Force was overwhelmingly oriented towards controlling public space and the opportunistic criminals who operated in it. At the same time they targeted certain street crimes, such as larceny from the person, and the 'casual' offences committed by the numerous vagrants and prostitutes found in public areas. Many historians have suggested that they were highly successful in this aim, promoting decorum and public order by dealing with disturbances, status and street offences. Some contemporary observers supported this analysis. Thus, shortly after 1829, a correspondent to *The Times* stressed police effectiveness in dealing with minor disorder and incivility. They had, he claimed, reduced widespread public drunkenness and aggressive begging, and were cracking down on gaming, spirit shops and the "tossing of half-pence in obscure allies".[4] Sixty years after their establishment, William Ballantine was also persuaded that the state of the streets had been greatly improved by the advent of the new police, with undesirable elements and activities such as illegal gambling being removed.[5] Similarly, George Sims, looking back from the Edwardian period, felt that the police were entitled to much of the credit for the reduction in aggressive soliciting and kerb-crawling that had occurred in areas like Piccadilly Circus and Pimlico. These were places where, only a few decades earlier, it had been impossible for 'decent' people to walk after dark.[6] At about the same time, the former London prison chaplain John Horsley also attributed an improvement in general morality, or at least its "outward manifestation", over the last decades of the nineteenth century to the permanent vigilance of the police.[7]

Ubiquity of Police

Generally speaking, the Metropolitan Police were able to enter the very worst and roughest areas of Victorian London at will, though there were always a few alleys and streets that they avoided unless present in force.[8]

---

4. *The Times*, 13th November 1830, Letter by 'A Friend to Liberty but not to Licentiousness'.
5. Ballantine, William, 1890, at p.36. He acknowledged that little attempt was made to shut down gambling establishments that were properly housed and frequented by the "better class" in places such as Leicester Square.
6. Sims, George, 1910, at pp.24-25 & p.66.
7. Horsley, John, 1913, at pp.271-275.
8. Hoare, H.E., 1883, at p.227.

For example, in the 1870s and early 1880s, the long-standing Flower and Dean Street rookery in East London was considered to be so dangerous that it was sometimes not: "...safe for the police to venture here alone".[9] The worst of the small streets and passages in East London had lurid sobriquets, such as 'Blood Alley'. Policemen always patrolled this particular location in pairs, because: "The alleyites gave very short shift to the policeman who ventured to interfere with their innocent pleasures".[10]

In any event, the police were often unable to pursue suspects effectively in such areas, even if they could enter them. In East End criminal slums many of the houses were interconnected, so that if a man had a short headstart it was extremely difficult to catch him.[11] Similarly, if the police pursued a fugitive into a cheap lodging-house, it was often impossible to identify and arrest him if he swiftly got into a vacant bed or ran though the building and out of a rear exit.[12] The Flower and Dean Street rookery was considered to be especially difficult for this reason, so that it was often: "...useless for the police to follow beyond a certain point".[13] In one rookery, it was claimed that thieves were so confident that they could escape if chased that they would spend several minutes publicly dividing up the proceeds of major robberies in the street.[14]

In some particularly rough places, senior officers deliberately adopted a policy of containment, rather than pursuing direct confrontation with local residents. For example, the notorious Jennings' Buildings in Kensington, largely inhabited by poor Irishmen, was often completely avoided by constables, who might limit themselves to patrolling its immediate environs. While 'slumming' in a dangerous East End rookery, Hugh Edward Hoare also noted that the police did not even "profess to patrol the street". Instead, they aimed at keeping criminals and disorderly people from spilling over into the more respectable areas nearby, by stationing men at its outlets.[15]

Individual policemen, patrolling their beats, could also show a great deal of personal discretion in avoiding dangerous areas and incidents. Timothy Cavanagh, who served in the Metropolitan force after 1855, freely admitted to having allowed a fight to continue in a slum alley

9. *Tower Hamlets Independent*, 4th February 1882, quoted in White, Jerry, 1980, at p.7.
10. White, Jerry, 1980, at p.90.
11. Hoare, H.E., 1883, at p.826.
12. Fredur, Thor, 1879, at pp.131-134.
13. *Tower Hamlets Independent,* 4th February 1882, in White, Jerry, 1980, at p.7.
14. Hoare, H.E., 1883, at p.826.
15. Hoare, H.E., 1883, at p.231 and pp.234-235.

inhabited by Irishmen, after being told by one of his colleagues that a policeman had been murdered there on an earlier occasion.[16] As this suggests, constables were particularly hesitant about intervening in back street fights.[17] One officer in the 1880s, explaining his reluctance to break up such a disturbance, in a notoriously 'rough' area, candidly noted that: "...one man's no good down there, and I don't want another bashing. I've had one since I've been in the force, and that's quite enough".[18]

Slum policing often required the police to establish a *modus vivendi* with area criminals and 'roughs', to some degree, given the limitations on their manpower. Low levels of disorder and crime were tolerated in a way that would not have been acceptable in other parts of the capital. They adopted a more limited set of goals in these locations, concentrating on the maintenance of public order and dealing with serious crimes, such as murder, focussing less of their energy on enforcing the law against 'routine' and status offences.

Nevertheless, the number of urban locations in which the police could only operate circumspectly diminished steadily as the 1800s advanced. As *The Times* noted in 1888: "In great towns it is not long since they often had to walk warily and be very discreet in their operations".[19] By then, however, most areas of London were under police 'control', albeit sometimes intermittently. Indeed, by 1865, even the notorious Ratcliffe Highway was controlled in a way that, although not ideal, was still very effective. The police were neither conspicuously absent nor too overtly apparent. In emergency, the sound of officers' rattles would bring "speedy aid" from their colleagues.[20] Henry Mayhew and his collaborators produced a similar assessment of the same area, at much the same time, feeling that everything: "...reflected great credit upon the police, who seem to have the most unlimited jurisdiction, and complete control over the low people and places in the rough East-End of London".[21]

Later in the century, the thoroughness of the beat system of policing (and its limitations) in the worst parts of the East End was to be clearly evidenced at the inquest examinations of officers who had been patrolling near the scene of the 'Jack the Ripper' murders. When a veteran constable, P.C. Neil, who had discovered one of the bodies, was "severely questioned" as to his 'working' of his beat, he was adamant that he had been on the very

16. Emsley, Clive, 1991, at p.70.
17. Gamon, Hugh, 1907, at p.14.
18. Vigar-Harris, Henry, 1885, p.30.
19. *The Times,* December 3rd, 1888; Wiener, M. J., 1990, at p.260.
20. Archer, Thomas, 1865, at p.123.
21. Mayhew, Henry et al, 1862, Vol. 4, at p.231.

spot where he found the corpse not more than half an hour earlier. His beat was a short one, and could be crossed in less than 12 minutes (a fairly normal length for a 'rough' urban area).[22] He was able to alert colleagues immediately by flashing his lantern and being: "...answered by the lights from two other constables at either end of the street".[23]

Effect of Police Presence

As a result of this regular police presence it is certainly *possible* that many Londoners who had been accustomed to commit petty crimes with relative safety decided to change their lifestyles.[24] Charles Booth, for example, believed that the "pressure of police supervision" was of primary significance in controlling and regulating the incidence of crime amongst the capital's semi-criminal group.[25]

In the early Victorian period, even a modest level of policing was a relatively new phenomenon in some places. It is also, perhaps, a mistake to assume that Victorian attitudes to the threat posed by the police were the same as those of the modern era. Because the police were *perceived* to be successful in improving public order and in targeting certain types of street offences, such as larceny from the person, and the sort of crimes committed by vagrants and prostitutes, potential criminals *may* have been less tempted to embark on such activity when times were harsh. Thus, the police could have exercised a 'restraining' influence on the many men and women whose involvement in crime was occasional and opportunistic and who were periodically faced with economic stress.[26] The police presence also forced criminals to adopt smaller and swifter ventures.

That casual street crime might be susceptible to enhanced policing had been mooted long before 1829. In 1821, for example, George Mainwaring concluded that although many people thought it inevitable that offences would occur because of innate human criminal propensities, this was not necessarily true, rare "atrocious offences" occasioned by deep-rooted depravity apart. The great mass of offences found in a wealthy Metropolis did not fall into this category. About 90% of those committed

---

22. Interestingly, there were also three night watchmen on duty close to the spot.
23. 'The Whitechapel Murder', *The Times*, September 3rd, 1888.
24. Jones, David, 1982, at p.143.
25. Booth, Charles, 1889, Vol. 1, at pp.33-36.
26. Jones, David, 1983, at pp.151-68.

in the London area were the opportunistic work of an urban underclass, and it was to this group that an "efficacious police will alone apply".[27]

Henry Mayhew's work suggests that, by the 1850s, many policemen also accepted this analysis. They did not direct their energies towards dealing with expert thieves, who often found obtaining legitimate work impossible because of their criminal records. Instead, it was the lazy: "...low petty thief, the area-sneak, and that genus that more especially excites the spleen and rouses the ire of your modern policeman".[28] Mayhew's views were partly supported by a police court magistrate who observed that the 'rougher' elements in London occasioned more annoyance to the general public and were: "...more obnoxious to the police, than the worst and most criminal members of the community".[29] In the same vein, an interested cleric, keenly aware of the police force's failure to combat London's small quota of professional criminals, believed that they had, at the least: "...contributed by increased efficiency to bringing lesser offenders before the bar of justice".[30]

The advent of a regular police force may have been particularly significant, at least initially, because many Metropolitan street criminals were extremely amateurish and unsophisticated in their ventures. As a result, some were relatively easily detected or deterred. It has even been suggested that, in the relationship between those who enforced the law and those who broke it, the nineteenth century saw the balance of technological advantage (in a broad sense) come to lie with law-enforcers: "...'criminals' had not as yet erected defences against the assault delivered upon them".[31] There were some dramatic illustrations of this. In March 1831, for example, P.C.s Farrant and Hobbs, acting alone, apprehended 19 pickpockets in the West End.[32] Unfortunately, the police were to be less successful in combating professional crime, and even in addressing 'amateur' crime of a non-street type or that evinced any sophistication.[33]

Contemporary Faith in Prevention

If their speeches to Parliament are taken at face value, both Peel and Wellington possessed great confidence in the ease with which an effective

---

27. Mainwaring, George B., 1821, at pp.138-140.
28. Mayhew, Henry et al, 1862, Vol. 4, at pp.226-227.
29. Anon, 1882, *Metropolitan Police Court Jottings*, at p.75.
30. See generally, Gregory, Robert, 1886.
31. Gatrell, V.A.C., 1980, at p.336.
32. Best, C.F., 1985, at p.4.
33. Jones, David, 1983, at pp.151-68, quoted in Kayman, M., 1992, at p.93.

preventative model could be introduced to the capital. According to the latter, it was: "...perfectly practicable to prevent, in a very great degree, the commission of crimes, by a new regulation of the police".[34] Robert Peel expressed similar views in the Commons. The Commissioners also repeatedly stressed the importance of prevention in the General Instructions of 1829. An absence of crimes in the new police Divisions, rather than successful detections and prosecutions, was to be the measure of policing success.

Many contemporary observers felt that the new police experienced swift success. Within a decade it was being observed that: "Person and property are now incomparably safer than they were under the old system. [so that] The new police are now the objects of universal approbation". It was also claimed that there had been a "vast diminution" in the amount of crime in London (and a great increase in the number of cases in which offenders were detected and prosecuted to conviction). So 'apparent' were these trends, that some felt they removed the: "...prejudices so strongly and generally entertained against the new force".[35]

The presence of the police in London does appear to have led to a major initial increase in the prosecution of indictable offences, suggesting considerable police activism and, possibly, that some forms of crime were readily addressable by an improved system. In 1828, the last complete year under the 'old form' of London policing, the number of committals for trial was 5,896, whereas in 1831, the first complete year under the new system, before the police had "checked the luxuriant crop of vice fostered under the old system", they amounted to 12,846.[36] Whatever the cause, in the 40 years prior to 1850, on one assessment at least, robbery declined from 3.5% of crimes tried at the Old Bailey to less than 0.5%, showing a marked contrast to burglary. This might suggest that the improvement in security in the streets, the amphitheatre for robbery, was much greater than elsewhere.[37]

As a result, within a few decades it was almost received opinion, in Edmund Antrobus's words, that the Metropolitan police had become an: "...important element in the control and prevention of crime".[38] According to another observer, the impact of a new and efficient police was second only to (significantly) education in reducing the criminal class and by

---

34. Hansard's Parliamentary Debates Vol. XXI, New series, 31 March-24 June 1829, at p.1750.

35. Grant, James, 1938, at p.391.

36. Adams, John, 1838, at p.9.

37. Rudé, G., 1985, at p.26.

38. Antrobus, Edmund, 1853, at p.42.

making its activities and life unviable. Many pickpockets admitted that: "'Lots of us turns honest now 'cause it's no go'".[39] Such a view may have been slightly optimistic, and certainly premature, as much of the impact of the force still lay in the future in the early 1850s. However, over the next 40 years, as the police continued to improve in efficiency and crime declined, it probably became more widespread.

By the 1860s, even those who felt that thieves were of a greater general competence than previously, considered that, despite their high numbers, there was a great mass of: "...risks to which, notwithstanding his gifts, the London thief is perpetually exposed".[40] Although their chances of being arrested for any given offence were fairly small (Wakefield thought the risk was between 2% and 10% a time), those who did become involved in regular and serious criminal activity in the mid-century would often have fairly short careers.[41] By 1849, Thomas Beggs believed that 'reliable' estimates suggested that the average career of "habitual depradators" in London was about five or six years from start to finish, whether they were ended by transportation or long-term imprisonment.[42] According to *The Times,* the rise in the apparent importance of habitual criminals in the 1890s was a reflection of the impact the police had had on the capital's occasional, opportunistic and amateur criminals: "The police are too strong and too active, the risks too great, for the amateur burglar to succeed".[43]

Limitations on Policing

However, such optimism, though increasingly widespread, was not universal. The ability to conduct highly visible patrols and to physically 'control' public space or to put down occasional large-scale disturbances was, and is, not necessarily synonymous with an ability to prevent much 'routine' crime. In 1878, Lord Truro thought that even the 'protective' police were excessively stolid for effective crime control. Although they might be seen marching on pavements in an impressive manner, there was an absence of that: "...vigilance, sharpness, briskness, and attention to duty which was desirable in a great Metropolis like London".[44]

---

39. Anon, 1853, *The Dens of London,* at p.180.
40. Anon, 1862, *Review of Those that Will not Work,* at p.353.
41. Wakefield, Edward Gibbon, 1831, at p.35.
42. Beggs, Thomas, 1849, at p.24.
43. May 30th, 1896, Quoted in Wiener, Martin J., 1990, at p.343.
44. HANSARD 1803–2005, HL Deb 30 July 1878 vol 242 cc629-37, 629.

Of course, the regular presence of patrolling officers must have been of *some* value, in an increasingly socially stratified city, where, in its less salubrious areas, requests for help from crime victims might not receive a ready response from the public. Nevertheless, modern research has rarely found a direct relationship between patrol levels and crime rates except where they are kept at saturation levels or in areas that were previously 'black-spots' for criminal activity.[45] There is little evidence that increasing the incidence of foot patrol *directly* decreases crime.[46] This is not entirely surprising; in the 1980s, it was calculated that the average London constable on foot patrol might expect to pass within 100 yards of a burglary in progress only once in every eight years.[47]

There *were* instances of this happening in Victorian London. In the early hours of November 1878, for example, P.C. Edward Robinson captured the notorious Charles Peace, a professional burglar and murderer. Robinson noticed a light come on suddenly at the back of a house and became suspicious. The heroic constable then overpowered his man despite being shot in the arm by Peace. Other potential escape routes from the building had been blocked earlier by another constable and a sergeant, summoned by Robinson from adjacent beats.[48]

Similarly, in some highly localised pockets of nineteenth-century crime, the simple presence of an officer did produce significant results. Thus, the Adelphi Arches, a series of subterranean chambers and vaults near the Strand, which in the early decades of the nineteenth century had been frequented by large numbers of thieves and prostitutes, had become an "innocent and harmless" location by the 1860s. This was achieved by placing a policeman there, on permanent night duty, to prevent undesirables from entering the area.[49] The presence of officers patrolling a larger, but still geographically confined, high crime rookery could also be significant, as had been anticipated prior to 1829.[50] This also accords with modern experience with the intense policing of crime 'hot-spots'.[51] The prevalence of such locations in the 1820s *may* have contributed to the (apparent) initial success of the new police after 1829. Unlike the 'thieves' sanctuaries' of the eighteenth century, Victorian rookeries were kept under

45. Hough, Mike, 1987, at pp.70-72.
46. See on this Reiner, R., 1993, at p.1096.
47. Clarke, R. & Hough, M., 1984, at p.xx.
48. OBSP, Trial of John Ward (Charles Peace), 18th November 1878, t18781118-51.
49. Mayhew, Henry et al, 1862, Vol. 4, at p.239.
50. Dudley, Thomas, 1828, at p.iii.
51. Durlauf, S. N. & Nagin, D. S., 2011, at pp.34-35.

fairly constant surveillance. The dramatic reform of the longstanding St. Giles' rookery, in the 1850s, was *partly* attributed to a "vigilant and energetic police force".[52] Certainly, many 'roughs' found their areas of "exclusivism" significantly curtailed by the police.[53]

Even in larger criminal areas, a constant level of police surveillance did, at least, mean that bulky stolen commercial goods, such as carts, could readily be identified, especially if taken into residential parts. Lock-ups, where stolen goods might be secured, could also be located and searched. Poor juveniles and adults who suddenly appeared to be living above their means could be stopped and investigated. Such measures probably meant that life was made harder for criminal elements, necessitating greater caution and inhibiting their activities, so that: "The whole system of the Metropolitan Police is one which must greatly enhance the difficulty of a successful course of crime or plunder".[54]

Nevertheless, it is apparent that preventative patrolling was not, and is not, *directly* a crime panacea. This was fully appreciated at the time.

Contemporary Doubts about Prevention

There were swift doubts about Peel's 'preventative' model. This was, perhaps, not surprising. It ran counter to many policing initiatives, reaching back to the Fielding brothers' work at Bow Street in the 1750s, which were aimed at collating information so that London's criminals might face the "Certainty of Speedy Detection". Detective work had received bad publicity in ensuing years, as a result of incidents such as the 'blood money' conspiracies of 1816, in which Bow Street 'Runners' such as George Vaughan had enticed men into committing crimes with a view to swiftly effecting arrests. Vaughan was eventually convicted of being an accessory to burglary.[55] Even so, before 1829, there were many who challenged the effectiveness of a preventative system, and who questioned whether the new policemen would be any improvement on their watchmen predecessors. Even as the new force was being planned, the need for a detective body to deal with any crimes that did occur was widely accepted. Many proposals for reform envisaged a combination of detection and preventative patrolling as the best approach to urban policing.[56] Even the

---

52. Mayhew, Henry, 1862, Vol. 4, at p.329 and p.226.
53. Watts, W.H., 1864, at p.179.
54. pp.11.d.1834, at p.7.
55. OBSP, Trial of John Donnelly and George Vaughan, 18th September 1816, t1816191-6.
56. See for example *Quarterly Review*, Vol. 36, 1828, at pp.494-496.

1812 Committee, which came down heavily in favour of the latter, noted that it was wrong to believe that the two systems were not compatible. They complimented each other.[57]

By 1829, there were also other policing models available that put more emphasis on detection. The French 'Brigade de la Sureté', founded by the detective François Eugène Vidocq, was one. Vidocq was placed in command of a force of plainclothes' officers (initially staffed by ex-convicts), in 1817. This body met considerable success in its first year of operation, infiltrating much of the Parisian underworld despite its small size. It was swiftly increased to 28 men.[58] (Some French professional policemen bitterly resented the use of an ex-convict and other former criminals as detectives).[59]

After 1829, fresh sceptics, who wished to see detection placed much higher up the priority list, swiftly emerged. Thus, in 1831, Edward Gibbon Wakefield declared that detection, prosecution, and punishment must always be: "...more effectual in repressing crime than any measure of mere prevention". The latter could never be more than an important auxiliary in the war against crime. He felt that the lack of encouragement and provision for detection in the new police was a "crying defect" and (presciently) advocated the establishment of a specialist force of detectives.[60] Men like Wakefield would maintain a constant challenge to the 'Peelite' school of policing throughout the rest of the century, winning a series of gradual but limited victories in the coming decades, as the inherent limitations of the preventative approach became increasingly apparent. Cumulatively, these would effect a partial transformation of the system by the end of the era.

Significantly, several (though by no means all) provincial forces placed a higher priority on detection immediately after their foundation than did the Metropolitan police. For example, the Birmingham police gave serious attention to developing their detective skills from their establishment in 1839. Their commander, Commissioner Francis Burgess, encouraged officers to be familiar with known criminals, to carry out careful crime scene investigation, and ordered the immediate reinstatement of suspended constables if they subsequently caught the perpetrators of offences committed on their beats.[61] (Although this also occasionally happened in

---

57. Cited in pp.10a.1828, at p.23.
58. Griffiths, Arthur, 1898, at pp.348-358.
59. Emsley, Clive, 'Policing The Streets Of Early Nineteenth-Century Paris', 1987, at p.278.
60. Wakefield, Edward Gibbon, 1831, at p.1 & p.35.
61. Weaver, Michael, 1994, 'Science of Policing', p.303.

the capital).[62]

Even Rowan realistically accepted that the preventative system was not suitable for the countryside, so that a: "...rural police was rather to prevent crime by detecting offenders than to prevent it by their actual presence in every village".[63] This was due to the scarcity of population, the large geographic areas involved, and the paucity of police officers to cover them. Some even argued against issuing uniforms to rural police, so as to aid their concealment when on duty. This was not purely an academic point for the Metropolitan force. The major growth in their area in 1840, followed by smaller scale expansion, meant that some outlying areas of almost open countryside came under their control, along with several decidedly bucolic crimes. In 1874, for example, Colonel Henderson, the Commissioner, reinforced the small force at Waltham Abbey with twenty uniformed constables and several detectives to deal with a series of arson attacks, in which haystacks and ricks were set alight.[64]

However, rural areas merely reproduced, on an extreme scale, problems that were attendant on preventative policing throughout the Metropolis. For example, it had always been a matter of complaint that the pre-1829 Watchmen's patrols were familiar to nocturnal criminals because they conducted them at "known and fixed intervals" while wearing a type of uniform.[65] In 1816, the magistrate Sir Nathaniel Conant claimed that thieves would often observe a watchman until he was out of the way. This was easy because the lantern he carried showed his location at a great distance.[66] In 1821, George Mainwaring noted that it was unlikely that any lurking criminal would attempt to: "...execute his purpose, when he knows that the watch is in the way, and will soon be out of the way".[67] The following year, in his evidence to the Committee of 1822, the Chief Clerk at the Bow Street Office, John Stafford, suggested that if the foot patrol were too obviously uniformed, it: "...would operate against their being successful in discovering or apprehending offenders".[68] This was an argument for an enhanced detective and covert function for any new police force, rather than for an even more distinctively uniformed and regimented

---

62. OBSP, Trial of George Davis, 13th June 1842, t18420613-1727. P.C. Thomas Malley, of H Division, worked in plainclothes to find the perpetrator of a robbery that had occurred on his beat, and as a result of which he had been suspended.
63. Rawlings, Phillip, 1999, at p.80.
64· Elliott, Bryn, 2001, p.11.
65. Chadwick, Edwin, 1829, at p.254.
66. Evidence of Sir Nathaniel Conant in pp.5.1816, at pp.30-31.
67. Mainwaring, G.B., 1821, at p.541.
68. pp.9.1822, at p.24.

body. Nevertheless, the rigid post-1829 beats of the new police provided an increase, rather than a reduction, in predictability. Many claimed that the new police were even less flexible than their predecessors.[69]

Rigidity of Patrol

Although they did not shout the hours, unlike their predecessors, this having been expressly forbidden in the General Instructions, the new police and their bull's eye lanterns (introduced in 1840 to replace earlier eighteenth-century models), with a wick fuelled by an oil-filled container, were prey to exactly the same limitations as the old watchmen. Officers could be seen, and even heard, from a distance. The heavy uniform footwear of the police meant that, for nocturnal criminals, the: "...tramp of the Bobbeian boots may readily be recognised full half a mile away and *Bill Sykes* has ample time to put his crowbar in his pocket, and vanish round the corner".[70]

Each constable was given a card on which the streets he was to patrol were marked; aside from emergencies, he was not supposed to depart from his set route. The regularity of their patrols can be gauged by the words of an attempted suicide, late in the century, who planned to jump off a bridge into the Thames from a position that lay on the path of a beat constable: "I hid from you until you had passed and I knew it would be a quarter of an hour before you came this way again".[71] The results of an enquiry held in 1844, after a robbery victim from the Commercial Road complained to the Commissioners about the lack of police protection in the night streets, is also suggestive. The constable on whose beat the crime had occurred could only explain his absence by suggesting that he had been at the wrong end of it at the relevant time. As he had always been a "strictly attentive, good man" this was accepted.[72] That prostitutes watched officers 'off' their beats, before plying their trade, was also a popular explanation as to why the Ripper's victims were alone and unobserved when accosted in 1888.

The predictability of the system was especially vulnerable to the operations of professional criminals. For example, after the 1850s, organised but illegal gambling made use of 'doggers-out' to keep patrolling officers under observation.[73] More seriously, many burglars would have someone posted to keep a lookout for the local policeman. They could

---

69. Ballantine, William, 1890, at p.51.
70. Punch, April 12th, 1873.
71. Greenwood, James, 1888, at p.16.
72. Mepol 4/6, Complaints Against Police, Jan 23rd, 1844.
73. McKibbin, R., 1979, at p.148.

calculate where in the cycle of his (typically) 15 to 20 minute patrol he might be. If necessary, they would "decoy him away by conversation".[74] In the 1850s, some burglars employed women, known as 'canaries', to assist them in this fashion. They could keep a lookout and carry a carpetbag of tools to the targeted premises, exciting less suspicion than a man. Where necessary, they could also distract a patrolling officer.[75] In an emergency, such women might feign public drunkenness, while posing as prostitutes, to prompt investigation and arrest. In the 1880s, Michael Davitt claimed that, in *extremis*, they would even pull a beat officer's whiskers, ensuring that they were taken into custody, and so removing the constable from the area.[76]

Once skilled burglars had entered a building they would fasten their means of access, so that patrolling officers had no suspicion of what was passing within.[77] There were numerous recorded instances of thieves spending the best part of a night in commercial premises, methodically taking what was of value, before waiting for an opportunity to slip out.

Not surprisingly, in these circumstances, the value of beat officers was questioned almost immediately. To many, one of the most irritating aspects of the 'novel' preventative system was the apparently pointless and mechanical nature of much of its patrol work. One observer, discussing Peel's "idlers" in the late 1830s, complained that, although 50% more expensive than a normal labourer, they spent their time walking the streets in a "slow monotonous step".[78]

More considered doubts about their value quickly emerged. The 1834 Police Committee accepted that both assaults committed in the heat of the moment and opportunistic street larcenies, were not easily prevented by patrolling. In such cases the police could only operate indirectly, via an increase in detection and thus deterrence.[79] By 1838, even the Commissioners were willing to concede that most forms of instrumental crime, such as embezzlement, forgery, stealing from carts, and theft by servants and employees, were beyond the immediate reach of the police.[80]

Of course, there were foolish, grossly incompetent, or simply unlucky criminals, who were caught in *flagrenti delicto* by routine policing. Thus, John Mason and Richard Kidd were arrested in Blackfriars in 1836, having

---

74. Mayhew, Henry et al, 1862, Vol. 4, at p.336.
75. Thomas, Donald, 1998, at p.73.
76. Davitt, Michael, 1886, at p.38.
77. Mayhew, Henry et al, 1862, Vol. 4, at p.336.
78. 'Fidget', 1838, at p.7.
79. pp.11.d.1834, at pp.7-8.
80. pp.12.1838, at pp.464-465.

tried to pick a pocket in full view of an officer. Others carried out crimes against the person within easy summoning distance of a policeman. Nevertheless, their numbers were probably quite small, especially as criminals became familiar with the *modus operandi* of the new force.

No doubt, some other potential criminals were deterred by an exaggerated fear of police patrols (the 'scarecrow' function) occasioned by their very obvious presence. Decisions about offending are not made on an entirely rational basis. In Thomas Wontner's words, criminals did not (and do not) calculate "with a merchant's eye of profit and loss".[81] Indeed, even in the modern era, it has been noted that intense and highly visible police activity appears to produce an increased fear of apprehension, and so a reduction in crime, that goes beyond any realistic assessment of the prospects of being caught.[82] However, as Wakefield noted in the 1830s, although the police might oblige thieves to take new precautions, their efforts did not usually prevent them from offending.[83]

Some observers had always appreciated that it was impossible for the police to watch every street, all of the time, and that most felons were intelligent enough not to commit their crimes in full view of patrolling constables.[84] As a result, they argued that urban surveillance was the "least important of measures of [crime] prevention", especially as it often required impractically large numbers of officers to be at all effective.[85] This was cruelly exposed by the Ripper murders of 1888, especially the (fourth) killing, of Annie Chapman, which occurred when the local area was being subjected to saturation policing. Huge numbers of police, both from the uniformed and plain-clothes branches, were on patrol from dusk to dawn that day. Yet the Ripper must have passed through the police ring twice. As Walter Dew noted, although the superstitious thought this required supernatural powers, the reality was that: "...however thorough a police patrol may be, it is quite impossible to keep every door in every house in every street under continual surveillance". Anyone, with a little luck, could have done the same.[86] This was borne out again after the fifth murder. As officers poured into the area where the body had been discovered, several hundred pounds was stolen from under their noses in a raid on Aldgate Post Office.[87]

---

81. Wontner, Thomas, 1833, at p.214.
82. Durlauf, S. N. & Nagin, D. S., 2011, at p.31.
83. Wakefield, Edward Gibbon, 1831, at p.6.
84. Sindall, Robert, 1990, at p.107.
85. Wakefield, Edward Gibbon, 1831, at p.6.
86. Dew, Walter, 1938, at p.114.
87. *East End News,* 5th October, 1888.

As a result of these defects, by the close of the century, some experienced criminals felt that patrolling officers were of "no account".[88] There were also periodic claims that a higher proportion of Metropolitan criminals were beginning to show enhanced levels of skill and sophistication, something that did not bode well for the wider system.[89] Compounding such problems, the very nature of London streets, especially their frequent lack of 'observable space', did not facilitate effective patrolling. In 1863, even Sir Richard Mayne noted that houses in the suburban and rural areas of the Metropolitan Police District were vulnerable, because burglars could enter them via gardens and yards, well out of sight of patrolling officers. This allowed them to carry out their crimes unimpeded, and then to leave at their leisure.[90] Unfortunately, this was not just a rural problem; others, considering the houses in London's many miles of fully urban streets, were struck by how: "...easy of access nearly all these buildings are".[91] In 1834, the magistrate Henry Moreton Dyer observed that routine street policing was also much less effective against criminals who gathered in public houses or other off street premises, rather than in public, to plan and organize their burglaries and thefts.[92]

Taking these points into consideration, it seems likely that much Victorian uniformed policing was not particularly effective in *directly* combating conventional crime, anymore than it is today. Can it then take any credit for the latter's general decline, and the steady drop in rates of (*inter alia*) larceny and robbery? It would be possible to reject any significant police role in this process, and to rely on alternative paradigms, of which there are several. Thus, it has been argued that improved policing was merely a minor facet of a general change after 1870 that made crime a less attractive proposition for the lower classes. Other factors included matters as diverse as the move in fashion towards tighter fitting clothes, making theft from the person and the concealment of stolen items more difficult, and the 1870 Education Act, which withdrew potential juvenile thieves from circulation (see chapter 10 below).[93]

Nevertheless, there are more subtle paradigms that might allow the Metropolitan Police to claim a significant amount of credit for the

---

88. Rook, Clarence, 1899, at p.256.
89. Petrow, Stefan, 1993, at p.107.
90. Confidential memorandum by Sir Richard Mayne to Sir George Grey, dated June 1st, 1863, at p.3, in Met.Pol.Lib.
91. Meason, M. Laing, 1883, at p.757.
92. Emsley, Clive, 1996, at p.28.
93. Sindall, Robert, 1983, at p.25.

improvement in urban crime levels. In particular, they may have made a major contribution *indirectly*. One way in which this might occur would be by breaking up the street cultures in which many offences originated, and which acted as a constant incitement to crime. Linked to this possibility is the modern 'broken windows' theory of policing and urban crime control, pioneered in the 1980s by James Q. Wilson and George Kelling. This has been at the root of a re-emphasising of the importance of foot patrol and the control of incivilities, manifest in various 'zero tolerance' initiatives by police forces in America and, to a much smaller extent, Britain.[94]

Urban Street Culture

It is apparent that the 'boisterous' sub-criminal street culture of early nineteenth-century London could foster more serious, but still opportunistic, conventional crimes. For example, the 1816 Committee on Juvenile Delinquency concluded that public gambling was especially influential in precipitating youths into crime.[95] Street people were able to conduct constant surveillance of their urban environment, and so were also alert to criminal possibilities suddenly presenting themselves. Furthermore, many thieves did not operate alone, or even in pairs. By their very nature street crimes were often corporate ventures. For example, the London pickpockets who abounded in or near theatres, operas and public gardens frequently worked together. Commonly, one might create a diversion, another pick the victim's pocket, and yet another receive the stolen item immediately afterwards.[96]

In the years immediately preceding 1829, large but amorphous street groupings also appear to have been common. Thus, the 1816 Police Committee questioned the magistrate William Fielding about "enormous associations" of young Metropolitan criminals known as the 'Cutter Lads'. Similarly, in 1817, a Bloomsbury constable complained of local gangs of boys up to 60 strong.[97] L.B. Allen recorded bands of 15 pickpockets working together, following the various Queen Caroline processions in 1820.[98] As late as November 1828, Thomas Brooks, of Coleman Street was crossing Hoxton to the City at 11 a.m. when he was suddenly knocked

---

94. Wilson, James Q., and Kelling, George L., 1982, at p.29.

95. Anon, *Report of the Committee for investigating the Causes of the Alarming Increase of Juvenile Delinquency in the Metropolis*, at pp.18-19.

96. Barrington, George, 1809, at p.18 & p.19.

97. Shore, Heather, 1999, at p.43.

98. Allen, L.B., 1821, at p.7.

down by between "thirty and forty persons", and robbed of a valuable gold watch and five sovereigns.[99]

Arguably, these publicly operating offenders and, even more so, large criminal bands, were highly susceptible to a more efficient and overt police force that could call on extensive support. It is reasonable to suppose that one of the earliest effects of tighter control of the streets and other public space would be to reduce the viability of such large 'loitering' groups, which, by their nature, were inherently difficult to conceal or direct. Indeed, this had been anticipated. In 1828, Randle Jackson claimed that there was an overt breakdown of order in London's streets, with the: "… almost unchecked parading of the streets by the notoriously dissolute". He concluded that this encouraged crime and required a more aggressive and interventionist approach by the police, so that public spaces were cleared of the "disorderly and criminal".[100]

Within a decade of its foundation, James Grant, examining the *apparent* success of the new force, felt that the "extensive confederations" which had previously existed amongst criminals had been broken up after 1829. As a result, there were no longer cases of: "…thieves being leagued together, and carrying on an organized system of war against property, in bands of twenties or thirties". Housebreaking and burglary in the late 1830s was usually carried out by individuals acting alone, or in small partnerships of two or three men.[101] Grant was clearly optimistic, and probably exaggerated the situation both prior to and after 1829, but some of his analysis was sound.

Although at first sight it might seem strange that the new police could have had quite the influence that was claimed for them in deterring London's gangs of street roughs, they had one great advantage over their immediate predecessors. They could call on extensive support in *extremis*, so that street encounters were (nearly) always 'won'. Ultimately, as most informed commentators appreciated, urban policing rested on coercion, and gaining a psychological ascendancy over the 'vicious' elements in society was vital. After 1829, the knowledge that to fall foul of an individual officer was to "invite the enmity of a whole Division" was a potent threat.[102] Confronting an officer meant taking on an institution, not just a man. To Captain Melville Lee, writing at the turn of the century, the analogy with maintaining order in a colony was clear. The policeman, managing a hostile crowd, or keeping order in a slum peopled by thieves,

---

99. *The Police Gazette; or, Hue and Cry*, October 14th 1828.
100. Jackson, Randle, 1828, at pp.11-12, & p.19.
101. Grant, James, 1838, at p.387.
102. Gamon, Hugh, 1907, at p.30.

was rather like a European in a crowd of "Asiatics". If the police force lost prestige, its officers would also lose respect; criminals did not fear the: "...prowess of the individual policeman, they fear the organization behind him-take that away, and the constable becomes merely a big man armed with nothing more formidable than a wooden truncheon". However, because, from their earliest days, the Metropolitan police had always 'won' their conflicts with the public, at whatever level they occurred, it came to be accepted, even in 'rough' districts, that it would be futile to resist them.[103]

Because of their constant street presence, the new police were also particularly well equipped to regulate, if not prevent, prostitution. This was especially important in London as it was often at the base of general criminal lifestyles and wider underworld networks. As a member of the London Society observed in the 1830s, prostitutes themselves were often "ferocious thieves". Additionally, such women frequently worked for men who were criminals in much wider terms, whether robbers or pickpockets. Sometimes, these pimps and 'bullies' would rob the men lured back to their girls' quarters, especially in insalubrious areas. In a few houses of ill repute, it was even rumoured that murders were carried out.[104] According to an East End correspondent, many of the women in the rough Minories area in 1859 were prostitutes or street thieves controlled by local bullies who "lived by robbery and violence".[105]

Prostitution was not the only form of street 'entertainment' to provide the background to more serious forms of crime. Prize, cock-and-dogfights, ratting competitions and gambling could all do so. Even in the 1860s, an observer taking a trip with the 'Fancy' to attend a Prize Fight noticed that there were numerous openly criminal elements in the crowd.[106] Many of these activities had been conducted quite overtly prior to the advent of the new police.[107]

In like manner, and as modern concerns about 'aggressive begging' indicate, street mendicancy can easily involve an element of threat, sometimes making the dividing line between robbing and begging very fine. For example, in 1887, one newspaper correspondent complained that his wife, while at home in Kensington, had been abused and threatened by a 'rough', who remained in their hall for 10 minutes, until the police

---

103. Melville Lee, W. L., 1901, at pp.382-383.
104. Ryan, Michael, 1839, at pp.175-176.
105. Letter, 'The Social Evil', *East London Observer,* October 29th, 1859.
106. Ormsby, John, 1864, at p.633.
107. pp.11.d.1834, at p.4.

appeared in response to her summons.[108] Again, patrolling officers were well placed to deal with such activity.

An officer finds a child sleeping rough

The police were also especially well equipped to deal with the capital's numerous destitute and vagrant juveniles, who were often the raw material for crime. In the early to mid-Victorian period such youths could still be found huddled together at night in unfinished buildings or sleeping rough under arches, surviving as best they could, usually by begging, scavenging, or crime.[109] However, the police increasingly brought them before the magistrates. Arresting youths like the inebriated 12-year-old Robert Darkin, so drunk in Covent Garden that he could not stand up, posed few

---

108. Emsley, Clive, 1996b, at p.101.
109. Anon, 1882, *Metropolitan Police Court Jottings*, at p.61.

difficulties.[110] By the 1860s, these children could also be 'catered for', in the longer term, by applying the provisions of the Industrial Schools Act (29 and 30 Vict. c.118), under which any child under 14 found begging could be brought before a court and sent to a reform school.[111] As a result, by 1887, Dr. Barnardo could observe that Covent Garden was much better policed than it had been in the 1860s, when a colony of children had lived rough there quite openly. They had disappeared 20 years later.[112]

Of course, a reduction in visible deviance does not *necessarily* mean that a real diminution in offending has taken place. The Commissioner of the City Police, Sir Henry Smith, looking back on changes over the second half of the nineteenth century in formerly vice ridden areas such as the Haymarket, thought that although they were outwardly much better than they had been 50 years earlier, the evil was often still there. It was merely less "flagrant" and not so obvious to the casual observer.[113] Nevertheless, with this (exaggerated) reservation, it appears that eliminating the more overt signs of vice and petty crime was something that uniformed patrol was inherently good at.

An Exercise in 'Zero Tolerance'?

The new police may have operated in a more indirect manner to control serious crime. According to the modern 'broken windows' analysis, although conventional policing does not have a major *direct* influence on offending rates for most serious types of crime, by promoting public order and decorum, by 'cracking down' firmly on minor infractions and public nuisances, which it can do very efficiently, policing can have a major *indirect* influence on levels of serious crime. This is because the "moral street-sweeping" at the core of such police-work promotes enhanced levels of community solidarity and intolerance for deviance, and in turn prevents an area's 'respectable' elements from moving to pleasanter localities, or withdrawing from the use of public space and community involvement.[114] Thus, police action strengthens informal social controls which *do* have an important influence on more serious crime rates, as well as encouraging co-operation between police and public and general resistance to law breaking.

---

110. Hodder, George, 1845, at p.133.
111. Anon, 1882, *Metropolitan Police Court Jottings*, at p.61.
112. Barnardo, Thomas John, 1887, at p.2.
113. Smith, Henry, 1910, at p.181.
114. Reiner, Robert, 1992 b, at p.763.

Conversely, low-level disorder and crime are: "…usually inextricably linked, in a kind of developmental sequence". If a neighbourhood is unable to prevent aggressive beggars and drunks from annoying pedestrians, thieves might reason that it is also unlikely to summon police to identify a potential 'mugger' or to interfere when the mugging actually occurs. Allowing behaviour that signals "no one cares" erodes community solidarity.[115]

The 'Broken Windows' analysis reversed much of the policing orthodoxy of the 1960s and 1970s, when it had frequently been argued that the 'over-reach' of the criminal law was a major justice problem. Significantly, this was usually identified as a 'relic' from the previous century, whereby too many status offences had been created, minor nuisances criminalised, and far too much discretion left to individual officers. That such laws were often used to "clean the streets of undesirables" was considered a vice rather than a virtue, as it was especially open to abuse.[116] The surviving sections of the 1824 Vagrancy Act were often cited as classic examples of enabling statutory provisions that encouraged such policing.

Kelling and Wilson were primarily concerned with 'ordered' communities becoming 'disordered', which was the twentieth century American trend until its final decade, and thus vulnerable to "criminal invasion". However, and of course, the paradigm applies in reverse, so that as disordered communities become ordered, crime declines. Indeed, it was a belief that the process could be reversed that inspired the police campaign in New York during the 1990s. Using this analysis, the overt presence of officers on the streets after 1829 *may* have made a significant, if indirect, impact on conventional crime. In Victorian London, order came out of disorder.

As per the Wilson/Kelling paradigm, the Victorian police, with their unprecedented powers and enormous public exposure through foot patrol, were well placed and equipped to deal with "disreputable or obstreperous" people who undermined the civility of urban life. They were on the same streets for such long periods that they usually knew who the 'regulars' on their beats were, whether respectable or not. As in the paradigm, they required the latter to observe certain rules of decorum. The existence of vague 'catchall' powers (especially those set out under the Metropolitan Police Act of 1839), allowing the arrest of suspicious people, drunks or vagrants, although offending against principles of equity, gave them the power to deal with public nuisances. They were also often not excessively concerned with legal niceties, having recourse to cuffs and capes if they

---

115. Wilson, James Q., and Kelling, George L., 1982, at p.29 & pp.31-34.
116. See, for example, Morris, Norval, and Hawkins, Gordon, 1970, at p.3, p.6 & p.12.

thought it absolutely necessary. Some of their actions would not have withstood a legal challenge. This was possible because of the inability of the policed to have recourse to legal remedies; 'rights' in the poorer parts of Victorian London were often for "decent folk" or the occasional professional criminal who could afford a lawyer.[117]

Arguably, as with the Wilson/Kelling analysis, the primary concern of Metropolitan police officers was 'order-maintenance'. This was something that often took precedence over dealing directly with conventional crime, which was a very much harder task to accomplish. Foot-patrol can be highly effective in elevating the general level of public order, even if it means that an officer: "...prohibits all sliding, puts down vaulting over posts, leapfrog, grottos, chuckfarthing".[118] This, in turn, can have an indirect 'knock-on' effect on conventional crime.

Additionally, some evidence from modern 'zero tolerance' initiatives suggests that although most status and minor offenders do not commit serious crimes, a large proportion of 'hard core' criminals share in the petty deviant 'life-style'. Thus, although the police might not arrest or convict criminals for burglary or robbery, they are able to 'harass' them for street gambling, public drunkenness and disorderly behaviour. Doubtless, in some cases, arrests for such minor offences are (and were during the nineteenth century) specifically targeted at those suspected of more serious deviance, making their lives harder, and impressing upon them the extent of police power. Such operations were a feature of the new Metropolitan force from its inception, as Wakefield noted in 1831, the: "...New Police harass the thieves".[119] Significantly, even the Commissioners sometimes felt it necessary to warn officers that they should not "point out persons as suspected" unless they were very certain that they were criminals.[120]

In England as a whole, statistics indicate that 'traditional' preventative policing, if measured by non-indictable prosecutions, peaked in the final year of the century, when a record 761,322 summary only prosecutions were brought. Perhaps significantly, the lowest ever number of indictable crimes in England and Wales (76,025) was also recorded in the same year. Arguably, the years after 1900 witnessed a fall in such policing, at the expense of pursuing indictable crimes and, much later, motorists. It is at least possible, that any modest rise in indictable crime that occurred in

---

117. Wilson, James Q., and Kelling, George L., 1982, at pp.30-31 & pp.33-34.
118. 'The Model Policeman', *Punch,* June 17th, 1848.
119. Wakefield, Edward Gibbon, 1831, at p.30.
120. MEPO 7/8 13th June, 1850.

following decades was linked to this disengagement from preventive policing.[121]

Reservations about Broken Windows

Some caution is necessary before accepting the Wilson/Kelling paradigm in its entirety, whether in a modern or a historical context. Although serious crime and low level anti-social behaviour tend to occur together, this is not *always* the case. It is also possible that excessively rigorous public order policing risks alienating people, especially when carried out amidst conflicting sets of cultural values. This might cut off police-public co-operation, and the supplies of information and witnesses on which effective policing is often reliant.[122] At least some of these considerations applied in Victorian London. Indeed, some contemporary observers, such as M.L. Meason, specifically alluded to them, feeling that too much "old-womanly" legislation was being enforced in the city, and that it made the police "exceedingly unpopular with a class of men who might otherwise be of the most use to them". Perhaps rather mistakenly (given Peel's views), he felt that the Metropolitan Police had "never been intended" for such an interventionist role.[123]

Additionally, there was the risk of deviancy amplification, as those imprisoned for newly prosecuted or created minor offences lost their 'characters' (vitally important for service and some other positions in Victorian London) and thus their prospects of future employment. Exposure to imprisonment might also "lessen its horror" and thus its deterrent value. Because of this, as early as the 1830s, some were complaining of the "injudicious legislation" that was boosting the criminal returns by up to a quarter.[124] As will be seen in the next chapter, there are also some major question marks over 'routine' police effectiveness generally in Victorian London.

---

121. Taylor, Howard, 1999, at p.117.
122. Mathews, Roger, 1992, at p.35 & p.47.
123. Meason, M. Laing, 1882, at pp.195-196.
124. Wontner, Thomas, 1833, at p.256.

CHAPTER SEVEN

REVISIONIST INTERPRETATIONS

Introduction

The analysis in chapter six suggests that the police had a significant impact on Metropolitan crime rates, even if indirectly, by dealing with street incivilities and controlling public space. While such an analysis is highly plausible, it should be noted that neither claim goes entirely unchallenged. Not all of the statistical evidence supports modern notions of Victorian police effectiveness, while the degree to which the police could and did engage with street incivilities is at least open to question. Both issues warrant further examination.

Crime Statistics and the Police

Although some statistics suggested initial police success in the early to mid-1830s, immediately after their introduction, the two phenomena, a decline in recorded crime and the advent of the new police, do not correlate precisely, suggesting that they may not *necessarily* have been linked. Although many crimes of serious violence *were*, apparently, declining in the years immediately after 1829, it would appear that the advent of the new police in London occurred at a time when such crimes were already falling, and had been for decades (see chapter one). When it comes to other offences, the situation is much more complicated. Despite some contemporary claims that the new police met swift success wherever they were introduced, committals for many offences from Metropolitan Police Courts continued to grow for at least five years after 1829. Thus, common assaults increased from 3,426 in 1831, to 5,121 in 1833. More significantly, common larceny grew from 6,953 cases in 1831, to 7,852 in 1833. Such figures prompted Lord Durham to complain that the new body was less efficient than its predecessor.

Against this, some serious offences, such as burglary, did fall fairly quickly, from 133 cases in 1831 to 104 two years later. More spectacularly, larceny in a dwelling house declined from 866 to 195 cases. Several observers argued that preventative 'harassment' was more effective for these rarer, graver, and more premeditated crimes, as greater preparation and perpetration time was required, while the parties attempting them were: "...more likely to be of that class known to the police, who would therefore observe and progressively impede their operations".[1]

There *was* a general fall in recorded crime, against previous trends, in the years between 1835 and 1838, but this merely preceded another increase. The general pattern of recorded property crime in London appears to have continued either upwards, or at least unabated, for the first twenty years of the Metropolitan force's existence, before starting its steady fall during the 1850s. Indeed, at the apparent zenith for instrumental crime in the late 1840s, after the force had been in existence for almost 20 years, the by then elderly Lord Brougham employed an almost apoplectic description of the contemporary state of law and order and the inadequacies of the criminal justice system, feeling that the: "...inefficacy of the means that the laws afford for restraining evil doers becomes every day more deplorably manifest".[2]

Forced onto the defensive, proponents of the new police argued (probably correctly) that it was merely that unprecedented numbers of cases were being detected and prosecuted. However, this invited Sir Peter Laurie's retort, to the 1838 Select Committee, that detection had not been the underlying ethos of the 1829 reforms. The New Police was established to: "...prevent crime, but when a great increase of crime was found to have taken place, the answer was 'but it is all detected now'".[3] Similarly, in 1831, Wakefield felt that although the police were apprehending more criminals, as a preventative force they appeared "hardly more efficient than the old".[4] Two years later, the anonymous 'Newgate Schoolmaster' agreed with this analysis, suggesting that they were "not an efficient preventative" force.[5]

Control of Street Incivilities

Irrespective of statistics, using the 'broken windows' analysis in a historical context is at least premised on the Metropolitan police being highly effective in dealing with street incivilities, even if they were not able to directly confront more serious or skilful forms of crime. However,

---

1. pp.11.d.1834, at pp.7-8.
2. Brougham, Henry, 1847, at p.2.
3. Robinson, Cyril, 1979, at p.9, and Miller, William, 1987, at pp.43-45.
4. Wakefield, Edward Gibbon, 1831, at p.5.
5. Anon., *Old Bailey Experience*, 1833, at p.192.

even this analysis has not gone entirely unchallenged. Throughout the period, police effectiveness was limited by a lack of numbers and, partly linked to this, a frequent reluctance to 'engage' with street disorder. These limitations require elucidation and, at the least, encourage a measure of caution before attributing too much of the post-1850 reduction in crime to the policing of incivilities by the new force.

Limitations on Manpower

London was easily the most heavily policed city in Britain. In 1871, there were 10,350 officers in the Metropolis (including the separate and relatively small City force) compared to a total of just 15,860 provincial policemen; in 1901, the figures were 16,900 and 27,360 respectively.[6] Nevertheless, even in Victorian London, there were severe limitations on the manpower available for patrol, so that many thought the Metropolitan force was "none too strong" for its extensive responsibilities.[7] In 1882, a stipendiary magistrate noted that, despite their numbers, the Metropolitan police were: "…not more than barely sufficient to detect crime and insure public order in public places".[8] In 1840, after the 1839 Metropolitan Police Act had extended the Metropolitan Police area to a radius of 15 miles from Charing Cross, 2,084,312 people in an area of 439,823 acres containing 294,125 houses, were being policed by just 4,338 men. In 1880, the figures were (acreage increasing only slightly) 4,433,535 people in 607,014 houses, being policed by 10,943 men. Thus, in 1840, there were 489 people to each constable (already up from 448 a decade earlier). In 1880, there were 457 people per man. The population per constable was much the same in 1880 as it had been at the start of the period, having briefly gone over the 500 mark between the early 1850s and the early 1860s.[9] Ratios did improve somewhat in the last two decades of the century so that, near the end of the period, there was one officer to each 396 people.[10]

However, after 1861, the force had responsibility for the security of naval bases and dockyards outside London, such as Chatham and Devonport, and also of Woolwich Arsenal and the Enfield small-arms factory, reducing the 'headline' figure of available men. The numbers involved in these duties were not negligible. At the end of 1876, of the

---

6. Briggs, J., et al., 1996, at p.151.
7. *The Standard*, October 4th, 1893, at p.6.
8. Anon, 1882, *Metropolitan Police Court Jottings*, at p.37.
9. PR.7.1825-79, at pp.10-11.
10. Briggs, J., et al., 1996, at p.154.

complement of 10,268 metropolitan police officers, 1,263 were involved in government work, 668 of them in the dockyards.[11] The following year, only 8,122 of its then complement of 10,446 men were actually assigned to Divisional duties, the rest being used for police headquarters ('Scotland Yard') and admiralty or military work.[12] In 1888, Woolwich alone had 174 officers, Portsmouth 155, Chatham 188, and Pembroke Dockyard 34 (out of a total force of 14,106 men).[13] Some observers even feared that the number of men available for 'proper' police purposes, as opposed to those guarding government establishments or public buildings from dynamite outrages, had fallen significantly, in proportion to the public, in the years between 1849 and 1887.[14]

Even ignoring these men, numerous ordinary officers were not available for routine patrol. Although the Victorian police were not faced with anything like the level of bureaucratic responsibility, and its attendant paperwork, of their modern counterparts, and were starved of leave, there were still heavy administrative demands on their time.[15] Officers had to be kept back to man their police stations, to liaise with other stations, and to guard prisoners, while each Division would try to keep from 8 to 16 or more men (depending on decade) available at its headquarters to form an emergency reserve. Some officers would be off work, sick or injured. Others would be attending court to give evidence or present charges.[16]

Regulative Duties

Compounding these manpower difficulties, police duties, and the regulatory burden imposed on them, grew inexorably as the century advanced, further draining resources for 'conventional' police work. Most of these new duties had "little in common" with normal policing.[17] For example, by the 1880s, there were 300 men permanently assigned solely to traffic duties around the capital, directing the flow of (horse-drawn) vehicles through its often narrow and congested streets. This was a vital task. Despite the absence of the internal combustion engine, 1,135 people were killed in London streets in the decade to 1877, and 21,827 severely

---

11. *The Morning Post*, August 24, 1877, p.6.
12. Butler, Josephine, 1880, at p.18.
13. Dickens, Charles (junior), 1888, at p.197.
14. *Launceston Examiner* (Tasmania), 22nd November 1887, p. 3.
15. 'Hard Times for Policemen', *Daily News*, October 31st, 1872.
16. Melville, W.L., 1901, at p.239.
17. PR.9.1869-76, at p.11.

injured. Most had been hit by wagons, carts, omnibuses or vans.[18] In 1889 alone, 150 people were killed in Metropolitan traffic accidents. That same year, the busy crossing at Regent's Circus required the dedicated service of 26 constables over a 24-hour period, at an annual cost of £2,600.[19] Josephine Butler questioned whether it was necessary that the men involved in superintending the traffic should form part of the police at all, and feared that it might lead to the fire brigade being incorporated into the Metropolitan force (as some had already proposed).[20]

Other officers were employed as 'Smoke Jacks', the name given to the policemen whose special duty it was to note breaches of the Smoke Nuisance Abatement Acts, or were involved in the inspection of lodging-houses (under the 1850s' Acts), dangerous structures etc.[21] This left even fewer men available for normal patrol duties. As a result, in the late 1880s, James Monro proposed a rise in the police-rate to fund the recruitment of an extra 1,000 men, arguing that their work could not be accomplished "efficiently" unless such an increase was allowed.[22]

Nocturnal and Diurnal Policing

In 1868, after taking into account illness, administration and leave, there were, at the most generous estimate, about 7,500 men 'on the ground', policing a city of 3,507,828 people and 472,240 buildings.[23] Even this figure is highly misleading because, of course, men could not be permanently on duty. The force had to provide 24-hour policing in the capital, although most officers did eight to ten hour shifts. Their distribution throughout the day was not uniform. The majority of policemen worked at night. Thus, in 1840, of the 4,300 officers available, there would only be 900 men on daytime duty at any one time, these being divided between morning and afternoon shifts.[24] Similarly, although the force numbered 8,883 men in 1864, two thirds of them were on night duty, which was then between 9 p.m. and 6 a.m. This was a typical distribution between diurnal and nocturnal manning levels. As a result, in 1868, there was, at the very

18. *The Morning Post*, August 24th, 1877, p.6.

19. Monro, James, 1889, at p.4.

20. Butler, Josephine, 1880, at pp.52-55.

21. Clarkson, Charles Tempest and Richardson, J. Hall, 1889, at p.247 & p.255.

22. Octavia Hill in the *Nineteenth Century* for September 1889, reproduced in Monro, James, 1889, at pp.1-9.

23. PR.9.1869-76, at p.12.

24. Inwood, Stephen, 1990, at p.129. He incorporates figures drawn up by Jennifer Davis.

most, one man on duty for every 2,245 people in the capital during the day, with twice that number at night.[25] Similarly, in 1887, and ignoring the 457 men on 'fixed point' duty, daytime beat patrols in the Metropolitan Police area, at any one time, were being carried out by just 1,478 officers.[26]

Even allowing for more intense levels of population density than are found in the modern era, the expanding city had "interminable" miles of streets to be patrolled.[27] In 1834, Colonel Rowan had claimed that every street, road, lane, court and alley was "visited constantly day and night by some of the police". However, he later qualified this by acknowledging that not every spot was physically reached, though most were "viewed".[28] In reality, even in the late 1880s, there were only 7,916 miles of patrolled beat in London, with major streets usually being patrolled down both sides by different officers.[29] Thousands of miles of pavement were not patrolled at all. Quite a few of the smaller London streets were left entirely uncovered, except by a cursory glance from a main-street junction.

Poor Communications

The effective deployment of available officers was further constrained by the era's limited means of communication. For most of the period, individual beat officers could only communicate with neighbouring colleagues, when at a distance, via rattles (inherited from the old watch), of which even the improved patterns could only be heard distinctly to a maximum of 400 yards, and very faintly to 700, as tests carried out in 1883 established. (They worked via the operation of a wooden tongue pressed by a spring against a ratchet-wheel which, when swung round by a handle, gave out a penetrating noise). Even after these were replaced in 1885, the audible range of the new police whistles, designed and made by Joseph Hudson, was relatively clear to just 900 yards (and faint at 1000). Covert communication could only be effected at night, by the discreet flashing of officers' bull lamps.[30]

Complaints about Policing Levels

Given these limitations, it is, perhaps, not surprising that there were

25. PR.9.1869-76, at p.12.
26. *The Times*, September 16th, 1887, p.8.
27. Meason, M. Laing, 1883, at pp.756-7.
28. pp.11.d.1834, at pp.27 & p.34.
29. Stuart, James, 1889, at p.635.
30. Bunker, J., 1998, at p.6.

regular complaints, throughout the century, that officers could be hard to find when most needed, and sarcastic comments about a policeman's clothes being of such a: "…deep, "Invisible Blue" that persons have lived for years in London without seeing one".[31] For example, in 1848, a newspaper correspondent complained that he and a group of friends had been pestered by a drunken prostitute, near Haymarket, for considerably more than a mile, in the middle of the day, before they could find an officer to take charge of her.[32] Similarly, on a winter evening in 1852, another correspondent went in search of a policeman after members of the public caught and held a thief. He walked down several major thoroughfares near Bond Street for 15 minutes looking "intently" for an officer, without finding a single man.[33] Many members of the public: "…constantly, and with justice, complained of the inadequacy of Police protection".[34] At the end of the century, there were still areas, such as the Borough, in which witnesses could be intimidated and where it was claimed that the police were effectively powerless, although: "…all these places would become quiet if only the numbers of the police were raised".[35]

Of course, and inevitably, some public expectations of the new force were unrealistic. For example, shortly after their foundation, a newspaper correspondent was shocked that two weeks after he had "wasted" much time reporting the theft of a large table clock that had been stolen from his Bethnal Green home, the police had still not recovered it![36] Complaints would reach a crescendo whenever there was a 'scare' about levels of street robbery, with allegations that officers spent too much time in the servants' quarters of grand houses while patrolling and avoided the rougher parts of their beats.[37] They were particularly acute during the garrotting panics of 1856 and 1862.[38]

In an attempt to ameliorate such concerns, dozens of 'fixed points', permanently manned by a stationary officer, some with sentry-type boxes to keep out the elements, were introduced by Colonel Henderson in 1871. These supplemented the beat system, so that the public knew where

---

31. 'The Model Policeman', *Punch,* June 17th, 1848.
32. *The Times*, December 20th, 1848, p.2.
33. *The Times*, Jan 1st, 1852, p.3.
34. Octavia Hill in the *Nineteenth Century* for September 1889, reproduced in Monro, James, 1889, at pp.1-90.
35. *The Morning Post,* July 21st, 1898, p.4.
36. Letter, *The Times,* 13th November, 1830.
37. MEPOL 4/6 Complaints Against Police, July 16, 1845.
38. Sindall, Robert, 1987, pp. 351-359.

officers might be found at set hours. Most were manned from 9 am to 1 am, although a few were established on a more restricted basis. For example, there was always a man near St. Peter's Church in Grosvenor Road, Westminster, during these hours.[39] If an officer carrying out this duty responded to a call he was supposed to be replaced immediately by the next patrol to pass. Not everyone approved of them, not least because they were manpower intensive. One superintendent also felt that the posts were excessively static and so unhealthy for the men involved, and a rather inefficient use of resources. He thought it would be better if officers were confined to moving about an area within a radius of 50 or so yards of a fixed point.[40]

Despite such measures, concern about police absence or inactivity lasted until the end of the century. Thus, in October 1897, a conference of delegates from South London vestries was held to call public attention to the lack of police protection in their areas. This prompted leading local ratepayers to complain to the authorities. One asserted that the area's police force was "largely understaffed". Another claimed that the police were not providing sufficient protection for the rates they paid. A delegate from Lambeth even proposed that local ratepayers should form their own "special police force", the embarrassing presence of which would "sharpen up the official police".[41] Very occasionally, Londoners did make their own arrangements. For example, one Sunday in 1870, 20 residents of Upper Street, Islington, finding that the powers of the police were insufficient to check local rowdies, sallied forth by pre-arrangement, armed with canes, and "belaboured" their area roughs. It was claimed that this subsequently prompted Colonel Henderson to order his subordinates to adopt more energetic measures to preserve the local peace.[42]

Significantly, in any exceptional crisis that required very large amounts of manpower, the police were still dependant on calling out the military or on recourse to special constables (regulated by the Special Constables Acts of 1820 and 1831), though these were almost entirely untrained, normally operative only during short-term emergencies (the City apart), and required notice to raise. At most, they wore a white band on their arms and carried a paper warrant card to signify their status to the official police and public.[43] They were also volunteers, although the 1843 Enrolled Pensioners Act allowed the compulsory enrolment of the out-pensioners of Chelsea

39. Dickens, Charles (Junior), 1879, at p.xx.
40. *The Times*, October 29, 1870, p.12.
41. Anon, 1897, *Inadequate Police Protection in South London*, at p.681.
42. *The Penny Illustrated Paper,* November 12th, 1870.
43. 'Meeting of Special Constables', *The Morning Post*, March 20th, 1848, p.2

Hospital as special constables in emergency. Their employment reached its apogee in 1848 when, although the Chartist demonstration on Kennington Common attracted only 20,000 people, there were 150,000 special constables "spontaneously enrolled" against the movement.[44] Their number included many middle-class men, such as Alfred Andrews, a journal compositor and reporter, who was on duty at a disturbance in Bird Cage Walk that year.[45]

Special Constables go on duty in 1848

The distribution of policing resources in the capital had been 'evened out' to a very considerable extent after 1829. Nevertheless, officers were still not uniformly spaced out over the city. The most crime-ridden areas, if isolated from 'good' locations, were often the worst policed.[46] There was still a tendency for resources to be disproportionately concentrated in the better (and politically more influential) areas. In 1868, one East London paper declared that outside the favoured parts of the West End, where rich people could be found, the: "…popular joke about the invisibility of a

44. 'The Chartist Demonstration', *The Times,* April 11th, 1848.
45. OBSP, Trial of Samuel Strapps, 12th June 1848, t18480612-1552.
46. pp.11.d.1834, at p.35.

Special Constables are signed up

policeman is a dull and sober reality".[47] Twenty years later, many felt that the East End was still under-policed in comparison with other parts of the city, prompting a local paper to declare that the city's 13,000 officers were "inadequate and disproportionately distributed".[48] Police statistics indicate that although in densely crowded Whitechapel there were more police per *square mile* in the mid-century than almost any other part of London, it had, along with Lambeth, one of the lowest ratios when compared to *population* (the highest being found in Westminster).[49] Generally speaking, it seems that Victorian policing tended to be heaviest in areas where the working class lived in close proximity to significant elements of the middle and upper classes.

The number of men available could make a huge difference to police effectiveness. In 1877, Colonel Fraser, Commissioner of the relatively small City Force, candidly admitted that the main reason for the lower level of burglary in the City, compared to the Metropolitan Police area,

---

47. *East London Observer*, December 5th, 1868.
48. *East End Advertiser*, September 29th, quoted in Fishman, William, 1988, at p.178.
49. Jones, David, 1982, at p.139. This is largely explained by its extremely high population density. On the use of the Whitehall Division as a reserve, see Melville, W.L., 1901, at p.239.

was that his force had a very much smaller space (671 acres) and population to police, for its size. As a result, uniformed officers in the City were: "...much closer together than they are in the Metropolitan police district".[50] This was later reiterated by Sir Henry Smith, who freely conceded that the police were always "very thick on the ground" in the Square Mile.[51] In 1877, the City force was made up of 710 uniformed officers and 77 in plain clothes.[52] By 1888, it consisted of a Commissioner, a Chief Superintendent, a Superintendent, 14 Inspectors, 92 Sergeants, and 781 Constables.[53] Thus, it had almost a tenth of the men of the Metropolitan Police, but far less than 1% of the latter's area, and only 1% of its night-time population, to control (its daytime population of commuting workers was very much higher). This very high officer to street ratio was a luxury the Metropolitan force simply did not, and could not, enjoy over the rest of the capital.

It is at least arguable that it is unlikely that a force as (relatively) small and stretched as the Metropolitan Police could, unaided, have single-handedly waged a successful 'war' against costermongers, prostitutes, hawkers, drunkards, rowdies, urchins, beggars, street theatres, and misbehaving publicans. It certainly explains why they were sometimes hesitant about doing so.

Reluctance to Engage

Even if present, the police were usually fairly selective about enforcing sanctions for minor street and status offences. This prompted some observers to feel, mistakenly, that they hated doing so.[54] They appear to have divided up London into 'respectable' and 'non-respectable' areas for this purpose, with some locations being ranked in between. The former could expect a relatively high degree of protection and 'officiousness'. The latter would witness laxer control and a higher threshold for intervention.

Just as marginal elements who were harassed in 'good' areas because of their appearance, recreations or occupations, might resent police heavy handedness, those attempting to pursue the 'respectable' life amid social disadvantage often resented the laissez-faire attitude of their local force. In 1888, Octavia Hill observed that where the police were willing to concentrate resources they could do much to "purify the worst streets".

---

50. pp.15.1878, at p.183.
51. Smith, Henry, K.C.B., 1910, at p.113.
52. pp.15.1878, at p.182.
53. Dickens, Charles (junior), 1888, at p.198.
54. Meason, M. Laing, 1882, at pp.195-196.

However, she also noted that they largely confined their efforts in poor areas to the main arterial routes, so that in the back alleys and minor streets of the East End it was possible to see large groups of "hulking lads" freely gambling, swearing, and terrorising respectable pedestrians. The authorities did not have enough men to: "...patrol such streets regularly, and keep the same order as in the wider streets". Hill felt that an increase of at least 3,000 officers would be needed to do this.[55] Similarly, in 1880s' Rotherhithe, in South East London, there was still, apparently, a permanent risk of serious interpersonal violence, and hundreds of thieves and loafers could be found lounging about street corners, in a manner that: "...would not be allowed anywhere but in a place such as this".[56]

At least some of the evidence for the 1830s and beyond suggests that the police (of all ranks) not only lacked the numbers, but often did not have the desire, to act as agents for the 'respectable' life, even in some of the better parts of the city. After 1829, a flood of orders emanating from the Commissioners in Whitehall Place sought to stamp notions of discretion on the new force. Officers were cautioned not to react to "silly expressions of ridicule" that they received from the public. Bad language was to be ignored. Where necessary, Inspectors were told to explain the: "...necessity of discretion and forbearance in an officer of the law".[57] Such forbearance seems to have been shown on a regular basis, and minor verbal abuse was widely overlooked.[58] For example, in 1834, P.C. John Grove initially ignored a group of four drunken men and women in Pimlico, even though they swore when he told them to go home. It was only when they refused to 'move on', and continued to shout obscenities, that his visiting section sergeant insisted on an arrest being made.[59]

In orders issued on 31st March 1831, the Commissioners directed that Inspectors should not take into custody anyone brought in by an officer on a: "...vague charge of 'obstructing the Constable in the execution of his duties'". On June 3rd of that year they were forced to reiterate this command. The Commissioners stressed that an officer was not authorised to arrest anyone without being able to prove some specific act by which the law had been broken. Desk officers were forbidden to discharge people

---

55. Hill, Octavia, in the *Nineteenth Century* for September 1889, reproduced in Monro, James, 1889, at pp.1-9.
56. Fuller, Robert, 1912, at pp.23-24.
57. Extracts from Orders from the Commissioners, Whitehall Place, 7th June, 6th, 11th, 17th October, 1830, June 15th, 1831, Reproduced in PR.5.1844, at pp.103-106.
58. OBSP, Trial of John Cronie, 30th June 1831, t18310630-14.
59. OBSP, Trial of Robert Cummins, 4th September 1834, t18340904-144.

arrested for disorderly conduct who gave undertakings as to their future behaviour, so that even weak cases had to come before the scrutiny of a magistrate, further deterring constables from excessive officiousness. Warnings were even issued about the abuse of the (swiftly notorious) command to 'move on', after such orders were given to groups of people who were merely conversing in the street.[60]

The Commissioners also fielded many complaints from members of the public who were keen for a more interventionist stance. In January 1830, when Henry Manskill complained that the police allowed basket-women to sell items in public carriageways, their measured response was that officers were normally encouraged not to interfere where: "...no annoyance is caused to passengers or housekeepers".[61] Similarly, from early on, they received complaints from parish vestries about inadequate police action against beggars. Replying to such a claim from the clerk to St. George's, Hanover Square, in a letter of 5th June 1832, Richard Mayne stressed the legal difficulties in taking action. It was also manpower intensive. Arrested beggars were often accompanied by children, who the police then had to take home to the distant parishes where they usually resided, rendering officers "useless for a great part of the day".[62] In 1838, when Sir Anthony Carlisle and other notables wrote to the Commissioners to complain about the beggars, prostitutes, and disorderly persons that (allegedly) infested Regent Street, and demanded that the police be more proactive in removing them, the Commissioners responded by saying that their officers already had directions to intervene: "...whenever the law will authorise them".[63] Clearly, such a position had not been reached in Regent Street.

In the same year, Rowan vigorously opposed a proposal that the police regulate the capital's brothels.[64] He was also prepared to turn a blind-eye to behaviour in public-houses in 'rough' areas, that was not properly licensed, such as dancing, provided it was not "grossly immoral". Reluctant to be "over squeamish", even the presence of known prostitutes in such establishments did not alarm him, provided it was reasonably discreet. This moved one critic to claim that his lack of competence as a police commissioner "must be apparent to all".[65]

---

60. Miller, Wilbur, 1997, at p.63, and at pp.104-106.
61. Correspondence of the Commissioners MEPO 1 (1) Letter dated 2 Jan. 1830.
62. pp.11.d.1834, at p.55.
63. Correspondence of the Commissioners MEPO 1 (30) No.52941, Letter dated November 3rd 1838.
64. pp.12.1838 at p.252.
65. Ryan, Michael, 1839, at p.208.

Rowan's pragmatic approach appears to have survived throughout the century, even if the threshold for police intervention fell significantly as London became more orderly. In 1872, for example, Superintendent Edward Worels was still able to record 290 brothels in the Stepney (K) Division area alone, often open until 3 a.m., with lights and reflectors in their entrance passages to indicate their presence. Indeed, many prostitutes from these houses actively solicited in the adjoining thoroughfares, causing "annoyance" to local residents, without being challenged by the police.[66] Sir Charles Warren, influenced by both the availability of police resources and their relationship with the general public in poorer areas, even tried to initiate a limited policy of laissez-faire in the summer of 1887, despite a strong personal dislike for prostitution. Although two hundred brothels in East London were 'closed' in that year (it was usually a very temporary phenomenon), it was largely as a result of pressure from the government and purity groups, rather than the police hierarchy.

It frequently took the efforts of bodies like William Coote's National Vigilance Association to encourage any police action at all. In areas where they were slow to move, this organisation was often there to shame the authorities into acting.[67] The development of similar private initiatives to prosecute other forms of conduct no longer deemed acceptable by polite society is also indicative of a general police reluctance to intervene in such areas. Thus, it was the NSPCC (founded in London in 1883), not the police, which issued a summons, paid for a solicitor, and prosecuted Mary Scoley of Millwall for savagely beating her illegitimate daughter.[68] Similarly, in the 1870s and 1880s, summonses under the 1857 Obscene Publications Act were often taken out by the Society for the Suppression of Vice (active from 1802). In late 1877 they initiated prosecutions against the re-issuers of a penny dreadful, *The Wild Boys of London*.[69] After 1890, the National Anti-Gambling league was behind many of the court cases initiated against illegal betting establishments.[70]

Police caution was probably based, in part, on realism. In areas like the East End casual street-centred prostitution, for example, continued to abound for social and economic reasons. The demand for sexual services, and the economic incentives to provide them, meant that any 'crack-downs' merely re-arranged the personnel involved, rather then eliminating the activity. Typically, an attempt in the 1850s to reduce prostitution in

---

66. PR.9.1869-76, Report for the Year 1872, at p.100.
67. Haggard, Robert F., 1993, at p.6.
68. *East End News*, 11th August, 1893.
69. Springall, John, 1994, at pp. 326-349.
70. Petrow, Stefan, 1992, at p.67.

Shadwell by prosecuting the manager of 30 local brothels, though successful in securing his conviction, did not result in the nuisance being abated. The principal prosecution witness and police informer took over their management himself after the trial.[71]

Well-publicised police campaigns against other forms of nuisance were often of short duration, such as those launched against 'penny-gaffs' in the East End in 1838 and 1859. Sir Richard Mayne openly admitted that quashing them for not having licenses would produce only short-term benefits, as many would swiftly re-open. Equally, despite constant complaints from costermongers about the legal action taken against them, only three were actually convicted for hawking without a license in 1859, suggesting that the police usually just "moved them along".[72] Illicit gambling and drinking dens ('spielers') flourished throughout the era, especially in the East End and parts of South London. By the close of the century they were providing one of the earliest avenues for the expansion of organised crime in London. Official licensing hours, though generous in London (Sunday apart), were still frequently ignored in poorer areas, even after 1872.

Even when the police did attempt to intervene, their success was often limited. As one magistrate noted, unruly behaviour by 'roughs' was something that: "...no police vigilance can baffle, and which no severity of punishment can suppress".[73] According to an East End observer, the "quiet, orderly, respectable" inhabitants of his locality were continually disturbed at night by rough elements, despite the "complicated police machinery" in the area.[74]

Sometimes, attempts by the Commissioners to limit the responsibilities of their new force drew harsh criticism. There were always many amongst the 'well-to-do' willing to condemn their failure to deal with urchins who obstructed central thoroughfares with games of marbles or by playing at hoops.[75] Similarly, the reluctance of police officers to arrest beggars, even if they were pestering 'gentlemen', could excite anger, some officers being threatened and abused by their social 'superiors' for confining themselves to telling mendicants to 'move on'. The behaviour of the Metropolitan force was, apparently, different in this respect to some provincial constabularies. Many London beggars thought that provided they avoided

---

71. Mayhew, Henry et al, 1862, Vol. 4, at p.230.
72. PR.6.1859, Metropolitan Police Returns for 1859, Table No.8, at pp.20- 21.
73. Anon, 1882, *Metropolitan Police Court Jottings*, at p.75.
74. Letter, 'The Social Evil', *East London Observer,* October 29th, 1859.
75. Letter 'Paternal Predilections Of The Police', *The Times*, October 18th, 1842, p.5.

committing a "glaring annoyance" the police would usually leave them alone.[76]

So apparent is this official restraint that even radical critiques of Victorian policing have had to accept that working-class recreations were not under "direct assault" all the time. This would have placed "absurd demands" on their time. Instead, it is suggested that they employed the pressure of constant surveillance and loose regulation rather than overt suppression.[77]

Police Discretion

As these examples indicate, in many areas, where the local culture remained resistant to reforms, enhanced police powers were not only ineffective, they were frequently not even exercised. Indeed, after an early (circa 1830), and apparently unsanctioned, outburst of enthusiasm, the Metropolitan police seem to have appreciated that they could only be used with circumspection. Thus, in 1831, 72,824 people were taken into custody by the police, an astonishing degree of activism in a city of about one and a half million people. However, this figure was to remain fairly constant throughout the next 40 years, not falling below 60,000 or rising above 80,000, so that in 1872 it was still only 78,203 people, despite the huge general growth of the city, its population and police force, along with a major expansion of the police area in 1840.[78] Even allowing for a major reduction in crime, the average policeman appears to have become steadily less, rather than more, interventionist, as his official powers increased.

Although the police did have the authority to arrest for peccadilloes, it was usually exercised sparingly, being highly dependant on a complex interaction of personal, social and geographic factors. An example can be seen in the police reaction to the 'Skeleton Army' disturbances of the early 1880s. This body, largely recruited from the lower working class, and funded by the Brewers, demonstrated against the Salvation Army in the early 1880s, pelting them with paint, mud and stones. Although Salvationist marches normally had adequate protection, officers, often forced to give up their Sunday leave to police them, appear to have lacked enthusiasm for their duties, and some Salvationists even found themselves under police arrest, as a threat to public order.[79]

---

76. Anon, 1848, *Sinks of London Laid Open,* at p.22.
77. Storch, Robert, 1976, at p.487.
78. PR.11.1875, Table No.17, at p.35.
79. Richter, Donald C., 1981, at p.82.

Similarly, despite (or because of) long-standing antipathy between costermongers and police during the late 1880s, the responsibility for moving their barrows from street markets was largely left to local vestries, as the: "... commissioner has resisted any attempt to thrust the duty upon the police". (Where necessary, they did make a show of force to support vestry officials trying to clear barrows).[80] Even in very central areas like Piccadilly and the Strand, the police were much less likely to interfere with soliciting prostitutes after midnight.[81] In the autumn of 1847, there was a flurry of complaints to *The Times* from 'respectable' ratepayers about the willful failure of the police to deal with the "disgusting" behaviour of soliciting prostitutes.[82]

The need for officers to use their powers with discretion was emphasised throughout the century. Thus, in the General Orders of 1829, it was stressed that they should not stand on the 'limits' of their authority. Towards the end of the century, in 1893, a judge, Sir Henry Hawkins, writing in a police-training manual, expressly reminded constables that they were not always bound to arrest for an offence: "You ought to exercise your discretion, having regard to the nature of the crime, the surrounding circumstances, and the condition and character of the accuser and the accused".[83] The following year, another manual advised police officers that although they were possessed of great powers to interfere with the public, they should normally adopt a "conciliatory and forbearing" approach, and warned them that being officious on every little occasion would excite popular ill-feeling. The use of persuasion was often more effective.[84] Despite the availability of 'catch-all' statutory powers that could be 'shaped' to fit most 'suspicious' street people, like that found under section 4 of the 1824 Vagrancy Act (see chapter six above), such charges were used quite sparingly.[85] Of 67,703 people taken into custody in 1874, only 836 were held for being "suspicious characters", compared to 26,155 for being drunk and disorderly or for public drunkenness.[86]

In the modern era, patrolling constables are aware that in sensitive high-risk urban environments there are 'slow-go' areas, where considerable

---

80. Clarkson, Charles Tempest and Richardson, J.Hall, 1889, at p.254.
81. London, Jack, 1903, at p.77.
82. See, for example, letter in *The Times*, November 13th, 1847.
83. Quoted in, Reiner, Robert, 1994, at p.724.
84. Bicknell, P., 1894, 11th edn., at pp.10-11, reproduced in Taylor, David, 1997, at pp.157-158.
85. Brogden, M. and Brogden, A., 1994, at p.37.
86. PR.10.1874, Table No.22, at pp.40-41.

discretion must be exercised.[87] The same applied to the 'rough' areas of Victorian London. For example, in the East End, a constable breaking up a fight between drunkards, amid the jeers of a watching crowd, would normally merely ask the two men to go their separate ways. To arrest every inebriated person who fought in the streets would require them to "pack the cells to suffocation". Many observers felt that "tactful" officers maintained the best public order, diplomatically ignoring drunken threats, even to their own person.[88] In 1859, this 'toleration' led a local newspaper in the Minories area near the Tower to demand greater police activism in dealing with the: "…filthy language and disgusting conduct of that class who set all moral decency in open defiance".[89]

In the notorious criminal slum of Jennings' Buildings in Kensington, despite a heavy local concentration of policing, a lack of resources meant that a degree of accommodation was reached between police and residents, if only because officers could not sustain a permanent level of confrontation. As a consequence, they allowed behaviour that was clearly criminal, such as Irish faction-fights, and which they would not have tolerated outside the Buildings' immediate confines, to occur without ready intervention.[90]

Far from gratuitously rushing to intervene when opportunity arose, jurisdictional disputes between City and Metropolitan officers, who were reluctant to take responsibility for each other's problems, continued to be an issue to the end of the century. In the 1890s, for example, Sergeant Leeson (as he then was) witnessed an unconscious drunken woman being secretly carried backwards and forwards across the City and Whitechapel boundary by their separate police forces, to avoid the trouble of arresting her.[91]

A discretionary application of the law was also necessary because many of the cases reported to the police had a domestic provenance, something that often made intervention impractical. These might include former co-habitees 'stealing' each other's property and pawning it. Then, as now, the police were nervous about getting involved in such situations, if only because the people involved often: "…made it all up afterwards, and gave the police a great deal of trouble for nothing".[92] In areas such as domestic violence, many officers would be especially circumspect, unless the situation was exceptionally grave, or the offender persisted in his

---

87. Morgan, R., & Newburn, T., 1997, at p.169.
88. Sims, George, 1910, at p.79.
89. 'The Social Evil', *East London Observer*, October 29th, 1859.
90. Davis, Jennifer, 1989, at pp.15-21.
91. Davis, Jennifer, 1989, at p.27.
92. Archer, Thomas, 1865, at p.106.

behaviour. Informal resolutions were usually preferred. Thus, when P.C. Cummins came across William Bradford, who had been noisily and savagely beating his wife, he berated but did not arrest him, though he warned Bradford that if he beat her again that night he would lock him up.[93] In some areas the difficulty of taking even conventional crime to court was readily acknowledged, and further limited police activity. The presence of numerous drunken sailors in the H Division area, who would lose their property but not subsequently press charges, even if the police had arrested a suspect, was a major riverside problem.[94]

Until late in the Victorian period, enthusiasm for policing minor disturbances and misdemeanours was also restricted by the absence of a 'Time-Card' system. This meant that an officer who effected an arrest at night, and who would then have to present the detained man before a magistrate the following morning, would not be given compensation for time spent at court. If he was lucky, his case might be heard by 11.00 am, but if he was unfortunate, it might not come on until 1.00 pm, impinging heavily on his rest and leisure. As a result, many constables on night duty were "leniently disposed" to minor offenders. This situation was eventually rectified by recording time spent at court, and counting it towards the working week. Significantly, the introduction of the timecard was said to have doubled the amount of business dealt with by some London police stations.[95]

Physical Attacks on Police

From the beginning, the considerable physical dangers involved in non-discretionary policing in slum areas also encouraged restraint amongst patrolling officers. Imposing new norms of public behaviour meant that in: "...endeavouring to check the brutality of the roughs of the locality, who too often delight in a personal conflict with their constitutional enemies, the police frequently receive injuries of no minor description".[96] The new police were immediate targets for violence. Constables were so regularly assaulted in the early years of the force that, for a time, they patrolled some parts at night armed with cutlasses (these were later replaced by swords). In 1830, an officer with a beat on Mill Wall, near the Isle of Dogs, was accosted by four men (possibly sailors) who, without speaking, seized him and threw him off the wall into the Thames. Had the: "...tide

---

93. Tomes, Nancy, 1978, at p.336.
94. Evidence of Detective Sergeant, in pp.15.1878, at p.85.
95. Greenwood, James, 1902, at p.12.
96. Anon, 1882, *Metropolitan Police Court Jottings*, at p.45.

been up at the time, the policeman must have been drowned".[97] That same
year, the force's first non-accidental operational death occurred (one of
three in its first decade), P.C. Grantham being kicked to death by Irish
brawlers in Somers Town on 29th June. His killers escaped conviction.
Indeed, the Coroner's jury were concerned about his intervention in a
'domestic' quarrel.[98] Shortly afterwards, PC John Long was killed in Grays
Inn Road by a group of three men (possibly burglars), one of whom was
subsequently convicted of murder.[99] About ten officers were killed (other
than in accidents) during the first twenty years after 1829. Although quite
a modest total, there were many more cases of serious violence with less
drastic consequences. In 1831, for example, a shoemaker from Theobald's
Road, who had a longstanding grudge against the "Blue devils" generally,
and a local constable in particular, stabbed the officer with an awl.[100]

   As some of these cases indicate, relations between the 'Cockney Irish'
and the police were particularly difficult, encouraging special caution.
According to W. H. Watts, in the first years of the force a score of
constables had been "destroyed" (killed or maimed) in struggles with the
capital's criminals, especially in Irish districts. He claimed to have
regularly seen a: "...well conducted constable with every feature beaten
out of human proportions".[101] Amongst the mid-century 'street' people,
particularly the costermongers, there was also great antipathy towards the
police, something that often expressed itself in violence. According to
Mayhew, to: "...serve out a policeman is the bravest act by which the
costermonger can distinguish himself". Some had been imprisoned a
dozen times for this offence. Grievances against the police would be
nursed over a long period of time and eventually settled by violence.[102]
Hugh Edward Hoare, in his anonymous East End criminal slum, could cite
cases of men harbouring grudges against individual officers, stalking and
then attacking them from behind. In one, an assailant hit and hospitalised a
constable who had earlier warned him about a misdemeanour, giving him
a: "...tremendous blow on the head with a heavy kitchen poker".[103] Those
who had injured officers would be regarded as heroes, and collections got
up for them if they were sent to prison.[104] In 1868, at least 1,130 Metropolitan

97. *The Standard*, December 13th, 1830.
98. Wilkes, John, 1977, at p.22.
99. OBSP, Trial of John Smith, 16th September 1830, t18300916-15.
100. OBSP, Trial of John Cronie, 30th June 1831, t18310630-14.
101. Watts, W.H., 1864, at p.179 & p.221.
102. Mayhew, Henry et al, 1862, Vol. 1, at p.16.
103. Hoare, H.E., 1883, at pp.234-5.
104. Anon, 1853, *The Dens of London*, at p.175.

Police officers suffered from fractures, dislocations, and wounds. Of these, the greater number (though not all) received their injuries whilst attempting to apprehend criminals (rather than in accidents). Eighty officers were permanently disabled to some degree.

The worst parts of the East End and South London were an exceptionally harsh environment for the police, if only because they contained a higher proportion of their "natural enemies".[105] In Brick Lane and Bermondsey it was, apparently, unusual for officers to go a month without acquiring some type of injury, even at the turn of the century.[106] An extreme illustration of this came in 1851, when P.C. Henry Chaplin died after being attacked with stones and clinker by a disorderly crowd of coal-porters and labourers at Vauxhall Walk.[107] In 1872, Superintendent Charles Digby recorded that 203 sergeants and constables had been assaulted during the previous year in the Whitechapel Division alone, some of them so severely that they were rendered unfit for duty for several weeks.[108] Unsurprisingly, when Benjamin Leeson was sent there in 1890, he noted that it was: "The dread of most young constables".[109] Similarly, Timothy Cavanagh observed that his Inspector had come from Whitechapel: "...where, of course, he had gone through some very rough work".[110] In 1882, a quite disproportionate number of the 3,581 people arrested that year for assaulting Metropolitan police officers came from the Stepney area alone.[111] Even in the early 1900s, policemen were still viewed as the "natural enemy of mankind" in East End slums, and it was normal to wish to beat up a "rosser".[112] Arthur Harding recalled a policeman who tried to break up an illegal street game of 'crown and anchor' being viciously attacked. A similar experience befell another of his police acquaintances, who was beaten up by some men from Hackney. Harding found him lying unconscious in the street.[113]

Such attacks were usually considered part of an officer's job, and many minor assaults were not even reported. In East London, there were some particularly extreme illustrations of this phenomenon. According to Arthur Harding, on one occasion an Edwardian 'beat' officer even ignored a revolver shot that had been fired at him. Even if prosecuted, serious

---

105. *The Morning Post,* August 24th, 1877, at p.6.
106. Greenwood, James, 1902, at p.6.
107. 'Brutal Murder Of A Policeman', *The Standard*, May 6th, 1851.
108. PR.9.1869-76, Report for the Year 1872, at p.99.
109. Leeson, B., 1933, at p.17.
110. Cavanagh, Timothy, 1893, at p.18.
111. Jones, David, 1982, at p.123.
112. Malvery, Olive, 1906, at p.287.
113. Samuel, Raphael, 1981, at p.197.

attacks were often not punished very severely. For example, in 1858, a drunken Irish labourer, a "wild cadaverous fellow", who had recently been released from prison on a ticket-of-leave, viciously assaulted three constables in the King's Arms in Limehouse, kicking one of them in the head. He received three months imprisonment.[114] Samuel Smiles, writing in 1870, felt that despite the risks that they ran on behalf of the public, popular sympathy was only rarely extended to injured policemen.[115] Most officers were stoical about this. P.C. Robert Woods received "many blows" while arresting burglars during his career. On one occasion, he had his skull fractured and was in hospital for over six weeks. However, as his sergeant advised him, this was simply the "tradition of the force".[116]

Of course, serious (rather than minor) anti-police violence should not be exaggerated. Lethal force, especially using firearms, was rarely shown towards constables. Howard Vincent, the director of the C.I.D., and a man who was strongly opposed to any routine arming of the police, made a survey of all the occasions between October 1878 and September 1883 in which guns had been used against Metropolitan officers by burglars. He found just ten instances, as a result of which two officers had been killed, six wounded, and two had had their clothes torn by bullets. (Some others died as a result of being stabbed or bludgeoned).[117]

Additionally, the situation improved gradually during the course of the century, assaults (of all types) on the police declining nationally from 66 per thousand in the mid 1860s to 40 per thousand at the end of the century.[118] The national trend was more than reflected in the London area, though the capital's level of attacks on police witnessed a significantly slower decline than did its other (civilian on civilian) types of assault. By the close of the century, Charles Booth noted that the relationship between most Hoxton criminals and the police was regulated by informal 'rules of the game', and that anti-police violence was a "breach of these rules".[119]

Nevertheless, with this caveat, it would appear that the threat of violence was serious enough to produce a measure of circumspection amongst Metropolitan officers, in many situations, encouraging them to exercise discretion and a degree of caution in their operations, especially in rough areas.

---

114. 'Savage Assaults On Police-Constables By A Ticket-Of-Leave Convict', *The Morning Chronicle*, September 6th, 1858.
115. Smiles, Samuel, 1870, at p.126.
116. OBSP, Trial of Robert Woods, 30th January 1854, t18540130-317.
117. Emsley, Clive, 1985, at p.137.
118. Emsley, Clive, 1996b, at p.294.
119. Quoted in Evans, Alan, 1988, at p.15.

Conclusion

All of the above factors must be considered when assessing the validity of claims about the effectiveness of uniformed patrolling and the impact of the policing of street 'incivilities' on conventional crime. The police may have had the theoretical legal power to intervene in most areas of life, but in reality, their willingness to do so was highly contingent on multiple factors and, in particular: numbers, location, personal fears, pressure from above, concern about alienating local people etc.

Such revisionist interpretations notwithstanding, the impact of street policing on Metropolitan crime was still very significant. However, it was not quite as overt or swift as is sometimes suggested by modern 'ideal-typical' portrayals, conducive though these might be to academic theory. It was a gradual process of increasing interventionism, rather than a sudden assault on street disorder. A major indication of the inherent limitations of uniformed patrol was to be the gradual return of detective policing after 1829, something that increasingly supplemented the 'Peelite' model.

CHAPTER EIGHT

THE RETURN OF THE DETECTIVES

Introduction

Prior to 1829, policing arrangements in London had involved both situational prevention by patrols and watchmen, and post-crime detection by the Bow Street Runners, a few police office constables, and the tiny number of private thief-takers still working in the capital. For example, the trial of John Warren for forgery, in 1803, involved evidence from a Bow Street officer named Croker who had carried out covert surveillance of Warren's lodgings in Holborn, during the evening, and then followed him to a shop where he watched him spend a forged pound bill.[1] Despite this, in the immediate post-1829 era, the 'preventative' ethos triumphed over detection. The wording of section 42 of the 1829 Act made it clear that the new force was to be confined to replacing the watch, not the Runners. Resources for detection were sustained at no more than pre-1829 levels, and eventually reduced in favour of uniformed work.

However, a growing recognition of the inherent limitations of the 'preventative system' and the ineffectiveness of thinly manned routine patrol (see chapter seven above) meant that the merits of a system based on detection were swiftly reconsidered. Throughout the century, many men, like Colonel Fraser, Commissioner of the small City Force, were convinced that: "...you get a greater percentage of convictions out of a detective system than out of a uniform system".[2] By contrast, they felt that the high visibility of uniformed officers meant that: "...rogues were put on their guard, and forewarned to move to spots safer for their depredations".[3]

Detectives had always had their supporters in the Metropolis. Much of the evidence received by the numerous pre-1829 police committees cast serious doubts on the value of uniformed patrol, when compared to covert surveillance, and the former's triumph was largely due to political

---

1. Medland, W., (Ed.), 1803, at p.110.
2. pp.15.1878, at p.183.
3. 'Popay and the Police', *Cobbett's Weekly Political Register*, August 31st, 1833.

considerations and its compatibility with an effective riot force (see chapter three above). Experience after 1829 was to show that the Metropolitan police had great difficulty dealing with criminals showing any level of ability. As Charles Dickens was to observe, if an urchin picked a pocket, it was easy enough for a constable to shout 'Stop thief'. Crime that was more sophisticated required detective skills.[4] From the 1840s, there was also a mounting fear that the gap between police techniques and those employed by criminals was increasing.[5] In so far as there was any truth to this, it may have reflected increased public (and criminal) familiarity with the working of the new police.

Early Plainclothesmen

Although Peel had stressed in the parliamentary debates of 1829 that he would not countenance a system based on spying, and the commissioners had been determined to avoid "objections to our police on the score of espionage", the value of covert detection was never entirely rejected, even in the new force.[6] From its foundation, officers had been detailed to act in civilian clothes. The author of one set of detective memoirs even claimed that he had been an amateur private detective prior to 1829, and had been offered the position of Inspector in the new police by Colonel Rowan specifically for this reason. Although there was no official detective brigade: "...we all acted in that capacity when occasion required us to do so".[7] Thus, as early as December 1829, P.C. John Cole arrested two thieves one night, while walking through Buckeridge Street, St. Giles, in "plain clothes".[8] In May 1831, Inspector John Thompson detained a fleeing and pursued thief, who ran up to him, unaware of his status because of his lack of uniform.[9] On a larger scale, there were 112 officers doing duty in plain clothes at the State opening of Parliament in 1831.[10] Some plainclothesmen were particularly active. Sergeant Charles Otway from A Division seems to have been acting as a *de facto* Scotland

---

4. Dickens, Charles, 'The Modern Science of Thief-taking', Reproduced in Waters, Thomas, 1853, at p.189.

5. pp.15.1878, at p.26 & p.42.

6. Handwritten note added to General Instructions Book, 1st proof, hand-amended by the Commissioners, deposited at Met Collection Police Heritage Centre, at p.19.

7. 'Inspector F', 1862, at p.2.

8. OBSP, Trial of Michael Kelly and John Collins, 14th January 1830, t18300114-108.

9. OBSP, Trial of John Dennis, 12th May 1831, t18310512-85.

10. MEPO 7(2) Police Orders 1829-1833, 19th Oct.1831.

Yard detective on a fairly regular basis in the years immediately prior to 1842. For example, in 1837, he was sent by the Commissioners to assist in the investigation of the murder of 15-year-old John Brill near Uxbridge (then outside the Metropolitan police area).

As this suggests, even the Commissioners swiftly acknowledged the need for such men. In 1833, for example, when Rowan and Mayne were called to give evidence on the Popay scandal, involving an alleged police *agent provocateur*, they noted that the most difficult crimes they faced were burglaries carried out on Sunday evenings (presumably when servants were at evensong) by men armed with skeleton keys. To deal with such crimes, patrols were more effective if carried out by officers in plain clothes. It was, they claimed, already a matter of "public notoriety" that many men did their duty in civilian garb, and that when it came to catching felons: "...three to one are taken in plain clothes".[11] Superintendent Andrew McClean supported this analysis, and believed that: "A man in uniform will hardly ever take a thief". As a result, he frequently sent plainclothes men to watch suspected criminals after they were seen in his Division. There would usually be 13 of them on duty at night, and two during the day.[12] This policy was controversial. The M.P. Colonel George Evans considered McLean unfit to hold office specifically because he was in the habit of employing so many plainclothes men: "Such conduct could not be too strongly deprecated, and he must say, that it tended greatly to increase the prejudices against the police-system".[13]

Despite the hostility of men like Evans, wider doubts quickly developed about the efficacy of uniformed patrol work. During the 1830s, several Police Office magistrates, such as Roe and Dyer, suggested that the Metropolitan force was useful for: "...watching, prevention, preservation of the peace". However, another body, which they still had in the form of the 'Runners', was needed for detecting more serious and sophisticated crimes.[14] In 1833, a magistrate from the Lambeth police office concluded that operating as an efficient preventive force *necessarily* meant that the new police were poor detectives. By 1837, even the Under Secretary of State at the Home Office, Samuel March Phillips, was willing to admit that the Runners were far more experienced and expert in detecting crime, and searching out forensic proof than were the new police.[15]

---

11. pp.11.1833, at pp.79 & 80.
12. pp.11.1833, at pp.48-49.
13. HANSARD 1803-2005, HC Deb 22 August 1833 vol 20 cc 834-9.
14. Emsley, Clive, 1996, at p.28.
15. Cox, D. J., 2010, at p.219.

Similar doubts about the worth of uniformed policing were to be expressed throughout the remainder of the nineteenth century. In 1878, for example, a Divisional detective in East London was convinced that: "...one plain clothes man is worth a dozen uniform men". He reiterated the already long established view that the predictability of the latter meant that, although they had a valuable role in protecting the city against disorder, and were very good night-watchmen when it came to looking after property, they were of: "...no use whatever in detecting crime".[16]

There was also widespread concern that conventional policing was excessively oriented towards 'controlling' criminal locations and their resident underclass at the expense of more sophisticated investigative techniques. Thus, although the unusual circumstances of the 1888 'Ripper' murders swiftly convinced many informed observers that the crimes had not been committed by 'normal' East End criminals, the usual practise of keeping a "sharp look-out" in the area's criminal haunts was maintained, even though it was very expensive of manpower.[17]

Hostility to Detectives

Despite doubts about the effectiveness of uniformed policing, the return of detection to centre stage was delayed by acute fears about its constitutional propriety. These were found across the political spectrum. Thus, the radical Henry Hersee, a member of the National Political Union infiltrated by Sergeant William Popay, viewed every policeman who worked: "...in a dress other than that of a policeman, as a spy". He complained that he had seen several officers attired as tradesmen and carpenters, though he seems not to have appreciated that they were often at liberty to wear civilian clothes when off duty (many chose not to do so).[18] His views mirrored those of much of the political nation. The Committee that investigated the complaints against Popay, which included Sir Robert Peel amongst its members, concluded that the employment of policemen in plain clothes was only acceptable on an occasional basis, when strictly confined to detect offences or prevent breaches of the peace: "...should these ends appear otherwise unattainable". Its members also insisted that police undercover work should always be passive.[19] Popay, a former school teacher from Norfolk, had played an 'active role in encouraging the

---

16. pp.15.1878, at p.85.
17. *The Times*, September 11th, 1888.
18. pp.11.1833, at pp.42-43.
19. pp.11.1833, at p.3.

more extreme and violent elements of the National Political Union in Camberwell (most of whom were "faithful" in their allegiance to the Crown), urging them to learn marksmanship and use of the broad sword.[20]

Just as the advent of a uniformed service to the streets of London had required a major compromise over accepted notions of public rights and civil liberties, so effective detective work required another major shift in popular attitudes towards covert policing, even if, to some senior officers, such concerns were merely a manifestation of the 'paranoia' inducing pressures of modern life.[21] It also necessitated an acceptance of the inherent risk of corruption that was present in most detective work and the less savoury stratagems that were often a vital part of this form of policing, such as payments to informers, police-criminal fraternisation, and the use of infiltration.

Throughout the period, there was acute concern about where these tactics might lead. For example, any form of active entrapment was always considered to be unacceptable, and sometimes this was construed very broadly. Thus, in 1851, Jack Whicher and a colleague were accused of 'spying' and 'entrapment' after staking out the London and Westminster Bank in The Mall. Whicher had seen a former convict casing the bank, and then kept observation on the man and another 'old lag' for several weeks. Subsequently, the two detectives lay in wait until they caught the pair red-handed, fleeing from the bank with their loot. Instead of commending their initiative, several newspaper correspondents complained about the manner in which the policemen let the crime proceed, rather than nipping it in the bud.[22] In the same year, a barrister reiterated the 1834 Committee's conclusions, and warned that it was reprehensible for detectives to tempt susceptible men into crime, so that they could be arrested. Detection was only acceptable where the commission of an offence could not be prevented.[23]

The belief that detective work was 'underhand' was still producing acute concern thirty years further on again. Although Commissioner Edmund Henderson acknowledged its importance, he was also mindful that the very concept was "entirely foreign" to Englishmen.[24] The general public felt "repugnance" for the use of many detective ruses, and to the police exercising the same degree of ingenuity that criminals employed

---

20. Emsley, Clive, 2010, at p.57. HANSARD 1803-2005, HC Deb 27 June 1833 vol 18 cc1254-63.
21. Anderson, Robert, 1910, at p.221.
22. Summerscale, Kate, 2008, at p.53.
23. *The Times*, July 5th, 1851, p.7.
24. Petrow, Stefan, 1993, at p.93.

against society.[25] Indicative of this can be considered the case of Major Henri Le Carron, who had infiltrated Fenian groups in America on his own initiative, with great success, and at enormous personal risk. Nevertheless, he was roundly criticised by elements of the national press for taking the (vitally necessary) Fenian oath when doing so. Even Anderson, a former head of the C.I.D. and City Police Commissioner, thought that this was the: "...one act in le Caron's service which I regret".[26]

In 1880, further concern was occasioned by the case of Thomas Titley, a chemist who was convicted of supplying an abortifacient at the behest of *agent provocateurs* acting for the Metropolitan police (one of them was a female searcher in the force), after officers had become suspicious about his activities.[27] He was sentenced to just 18 months' imprisonment having been: "Strongly recommended to mercy by the Jury, on the ground of the provocation by the police inducing him to the crime".[28] There was also a popular petition for mitigation of his sentence.

Such attitudes influenced the willingness of good policemen to volunteer for detective duties. Even after their pay was enhanced in the late 1870s, Chief Superintendent Williamson noted that many very sound uniformed officers were reluctant to become involved in detective work, not merely because of the "uncertainty and irregularity" of the hours and poor promotional prospects, but also because of the "odium" that was attached to it. The work was repugnant to some men, who disliked the manner in which it would regularly bring them into contact with the: "...lowest classes, encourage unnecessary drinking and compel them, at times, to resort to trickery practices which they dislike".[29]

Perhaps, in part, because of such attitudes, it was widely believed that post-crime detection was the weak link in London policing, and an area where things really were ordered better abroad, particularly in France. It was frequently asserted that many of the sophisticated crimes that occurred in the capital, such as the famous Hatton Garden Robbery of 1882, would have been solved in most other European cities. Even late in the century, Arthur Griffiths could observe that it was popularly believed that the: "...least efficient department of English Police is that which is concerned with the detection of crime, and our detective service is often compared with corresponding agencies abroad in order to point the moral that we should do well to imitate the methods of our neighbours". However, as he

25. Clarkson, Charles Tempest and Richardson, J. Hall, 1889, at p.264.
26. Anderson, Robert, 1910, at p.155.
27. 'Law and Police', *The Pall Mall Gazette*, December 16, 1880.
28. OBSP, Trial of Thomas Titley, 13th December 1880, t18801213-133.
29. Petrow, Stefan, 1993, at p.98.

also pointed out, the same Englishmen who complained most about incompetent detectives would be the first to object if their powers were enhanced. French detectives were assisted by effective but arbitrary powers, such as the right to detain and interrogate a suspected person at will, which the Metropolitan police did not possess.[30]

A particular limitation on London (and English) detective work, until late in the century, was the reluctance of the courts to accept admissions made as a result of active police questioning. This was to become a major part of twentieth-century C.I.D. work and was a commonplace aspect of nineteenth-century detective work on the continent. However, in 1837, the Commissioners had stressed that even Inspectors should: "...not on any account suffer any statement in the nature of a confession, to be extracted from the person charged". (This did not preclude unprompted, spontaneous, voluntary admissions).[31] In 1840, a confession that had been misleadingly extracted by Sergeant Charles Otway from a suspected murderer, Richard Gould, attracted strong judicial and Scotland Yard criticism, as well as being excluded from evidence. In 1871, a Police Court Magistrate, Mr. Arnold, refused to entertain confession evidence by a woman accused of concealing the birth of her illegitimate child, which had been made to an Inspector at a police station *after* being cautioned. An influential legal journal, reporting (and applauding) the case, roundly condemned any development of an "inquisitorial" police, allowed to ask questions of detained suspects and seriously proposed that they should not be allowed to adduce in court *any* communication made to them by a detained person.[32] As late as 1893, Mr. Justice Cave declared that it would be "monstrous" if the law permitted a police officer to examine a prisoner, without anyone else being present, and then to produce the results of that examination against him.[33]

As a result of such views, at the end of the nineteenth century, London detectives were still far more circumscribed as to their powers of arrest, search, questioning and detention than their German and French counterparts, leading one American observer to note: "British practice has no parallel on the Continent".[34]

Other explanations for a degree of institutional inertia in the Metropolitan Police over detective work are not hard to find. One of the most obvious is that Richard Mayne, the young barrister appointed by

---

30. Griffiths, Arthur, 1898, at p.358.
31. Miller, Wilbur, 1997, at p.91.
32. *The Law Journal*, Vol. 6, 1871, at p.177.
33. *R v Male* (1893) 17 Cox CC 689, at 690.
34. Fosdick, Raymond B., 1915, at p.306.

Peel, and sole Commissioner after 1855, was still in office when he died in December 1868, at the age of 72. In 1842, Mayne had been instrumental in persuading the Home Secretary to support the establishment of a small force of detectives to observe known or suspected criminals (see below).[35] However, by the 1850s, he was somewhat autocratic and reluctant to delegate even minor responsibility to his two Assistant Commissioners, let alone superintendents, to receive advice, or readily countenance significant change. His attitude towards policing was still largely shaped by the debates of the 1820s and early 1830s.

As a result of the deficiencies found in the English detective system, some observers felt that once thieves or other criminals had evaded the area security provided by patrolling officers, which was not particularly difficult, and got well away from a crime scene, they were usually safe. Similarly, if a previously unknown murderer managed to keep out of the way for a few hours after he had killed his victim, the: "…detection of crime seems to be a problem which our so-called detectives have not the capacity in most cases to solve".[36]

Nevertheless, despite widespread hostility, provision for detective policing expanded steadily, if very slowly, throughout the century, as the limitations on uniformed operations became increasingly apparent and the Peelite 'model' of preventative policing was progressively adulterated.

Formal Provision for Detectives

The dependence of Peel's model of policing on surveillance meant that there continued to be a niche for the Principal Officers attached to Bow Street (popularly known as the Runners) and, to a very much smaller extent, those linked to the other post-1792 public or police offices. They operated as detectives, under the supervision of the Metropolis's stipendiary magistrates, for a decade after the advent of the new Metropolitan force. The Runners were enormously experienced and often able men. They even increased their work-rate in the London area during their final decade, albeit usually focussing on high-value thefts and fraud, rather than crimes such as murder. (The latter felony, and its inchoate fellow, made up only two per cent of their work, or six cases, in the Metropolitan area between 1792 and 1839).[37]

---

35. Petrow, Stefan, 1993, at p.92.
36. Meason, M. Laing, 1883, at p.757.
37. Cox, D. J., 2010, at p.126.

Nevertheless, for the three years after their abolition in 1839, there was no formal body in the Metropolis entrusted with detection. In this respect, London made less provision for detection than some much smaller English provincial cities, let alone other European capitals. However, in 1840, the bungled investigation into the murder of a peer by his Swiss valet, during which several police searches initially overlooked vital evidence, followed by the shambolic pursuit of the murderer Daniel Good in 1842, along with abortive investigations into several other killings, occasioned widespread popular alarm.[38] There was a growing feeling that the inherent nature of the Metropolitan police, especially the requirement that it patrol the London area on a continual basis, rendered it: "...almost incapable of engaging in such enquiries as can alone lead to the discovery of offenders".[39] A newspaper correspondent went further, speaking of its "total and unequivocal failure as a detective force".[40] In 1842, this finally led Sir James Graham, the then Home Secretary, to authorise the foundation of a small formal central detective branch, based at Scotland Yard.

The Central Detective Branch

Initially, the central detective force had a complement of only two inspectors and six sergeants, directly answerable to the Commissioner(s). Just one of them, Nicholas Pearce, was a former Bow Street Runner who had earlier transferred to the police. The force added an inspector and sergeant in 1864, and a chief inspector and several more sergeants in 1867. By April 1869, it numbered: one superintendent, three chief inspectors, three inspectors, six first class, and thirteen second class, sergeants.[41] They required the express authority of a Commissioner or an Assistant Commissioner to start an investigation. However, in its early days, anyone in England could call on its services, if they could afford the cost of a detective, just as they had with the Runners, though this practice was abandoned after a few years.[42] Additionally, and far more significantly, the force could be asked to assist provincial police forces in investigating serious but "very obscure" crimes outside London by, *inter alia*, the Home

---

38. Morris, R. M., 2006, at p.80. 'The Murder At Roehampton', *The Times*, April 28, 1842, at p. 6.
39. *The Times*, May 8th, 1840, at p.6.
40. *The Times*, May 30th, 1840, at p.6.
41. *Quarterly Review*, Vol. 129, No. 257, 1870, p.99.
42. Lansdowne, Andrew, 1893, at p.7.

Secretary.[43] Thus, in 1860, Detective Inspector Jonathan ('Jack') Whicher became famous for his investigation into a notorious child murder at Rode in Wiltshire. Whicher, a native Londoner, had been one of the founder members of the Central Detective Force in 1842, having joined the Metropolitan Police five years earlier.

This involvement in provincial cases, along with its small size, inevitably limited the central force to major criminal investigations in the capital for much of the period prior to 1868. Most of its officers were quite versatile. Thus, a few months either side of the Rode murder investigation, Jack Whicher solved the theft of a Dutch 'old master' that had turned up in London, and investigated the theft of six boxes of opium from the London Docks.[44] However, within the central force (and later those C.I.D. officers allocated to Scotland Yard) a degree of specialism was sometimes desirable and, as it expanded, possible, especially in the latter decades of the century. As a result, some individual officers developed expertise in distinct areas of crime. For example, John Taylor ('Jack the Sleuthhound'), who retired in 1896, specialised in high-profile burglaries, though not to the exclusion of other types of case. Other men focussed on fraud, forgery or coining offences.[45] Members of the central force usually described themselves as being from the "detective police" when speaking to the public. This was in contrast to the "preventative" uniformed police.

Continuing Use of Plainclothesmen

The modest, formal, central provision for detectives is slightly misleading. Almost from the start, as previously noted, a significant number of Metropolitan officers had worked in plain clothes on an informal basis. However, this practice continued and expanded, even after 1842. As the 1878 Report observed, throughout the force's early decades there were men: "...who were called plain-clothes officers, who did detective duties in Divisions". Additionally, Inspectors could be ordered to perform their duty in plain clothes. If they did so, they were required to carry a special brass tipstaff and their warrant card, so that they could be readily identified.[46] As a result, in 1846, P.C. Francis Manser, investigating coining offences in the Westminster Road, admitted that although, at the time, not in uniform, he was not one of the new detective force: "I am

---

43. *Quarterly Review*, Vol. 129, No. 257, 1870, at p.99.
44. 'Extensive Opium Robbery in the London Docks', *The Morning Post*, August 4th, 1859, p.7; *The Standard*, January 15, 1861, p.7.
45. Shpayer-Makov, Haia, 2011, at p.49.
46. MEPOL 7/38 Orders 14/4/1868.

sometimes about the town in plain clothes, but not often".[47] Similarly, in 1854, when P.C. William Brown of R Division, who had kept a baker's premises under observation while out of uniform, was asked whether he was a detective during cross-examination, he denied it, but admitted that he sometimes went "out in plain clothes by order".[48] (Even so, the Commissioners made clear that plain clothes were not to be worn gratuitously on duty by ordinary policemen).[49]

This process gradually became formalised, so that every Division was allowed to employ a: "...certain number of constables in plain clothes to make inquiries and hunt up offenders".[50] In 1856, there were normally six plainclothes men in each Division, making a total of about 108 detective "auxiliaries" for the capital. They could take upon themselves the role of detectives, as and when required and, after 1842, also assist the investigations of the new central force.[51]

Nevertheless, their appointment remained on a largely *ad hoc* basis, uniformed men putting on plain clothes at the direction of their superior officers.[52] Some were appointed for only a few weeks, perhaps when burglary was rife in a certain location. For example, in 1866, an officer noted that, because there had been many burglaries in the St. Pancras area, an: "...extra number of policemen were stationed in plain clothes".[53] Such men were primarily concerned with 'routine' crimes rather than very grave offences such as murder, rape and serious fraud.

By his final years, even the elderly Mayne had come to see that the provision for detectives was too small-scale and lax for the crime problems posed by a rapidly growing city. As a result, he became more sympathetic towards their work.[54] In the 1860s, he recommended an increase in the number of central detectives, and the formal establishment of 'Divisional' detectives in place of the former plainclothesmen, separate from the small central force, though he lacked the support to establish this body before his death. Change occurred in 1869, under Mayne's replacement, Colonel Edmund Henderson. This followed public and parliamentary concern at the failure of the police to prevent a Fenian attack

47. OBSP, Trial of George Sanders, 5th January 1846, t18460105-468.
48. OBSP, Trial of Thomas Truelove, 23rd October 1854, t18541023-1170.
49. MEPO 7/8 8th June, 1850.
50. pp.14.1868, at p.15.
51. *Quarterly Review*, No.99, 1856, pp.174-5, reproduced in Barrett, A. & Harrison, C. (Eds.), 1999, at p.254.
52. OBSP, Trial of George Sanders, 5th January 1846, t18460105-468.
53. OBSP, Trial of Matthew Hayes, 19th November 1866, t18661119-38.
54. Anderson, Robert, 1910, at p.129.

on Clerkenwell prison in December 1867, despite accurate intelligence from the Irish police, and the ensuing recommendation of the Departmental Committee on the Police of 1868, which proposed that local (i.e. non-central-force) plainclothesmen be formed into a separate Division of their own, under the control of a specially appointed superintendent. It also accepted that detective numbers were: "...wholly inadequate to the present requirements of the metropolis, and their constitution scarcely adapts them to cope with conspiracies and secret combinations". Compounding such problems, their pay was felt to be insufficient to attract high quality men. To address this, it was suggested that detective constables be divided into several grades, with increased pay available for the higher divisions.[55]

The Divisional Detectives

Under the post-1868 scheme, plainclothes police would still not normally be under the control of the central force, and would still be appointed in the Divisions, as had occurred for decades, but this would be on a more permanent, less improvised, basis. Additionally, service with them would constitute the: "...probationary service for enrolment in the [central] detective police". Indeed, where necessary, some of these officers could be placed under the temporary command of the central force by their own superintendents.[56] Of course, initially, most recruits to this force were, like Sergeant Thomas George Foster, former Divisional plainclothesmen.[57]

Although the central force remained very small until the end of the 1870s, the new Divisional detectives were considerably more numerous.[58] In 1870, they constituted 20 sergeants and 160 first-class constables, with a handful of higher officers (all officers in the central detective force at this time were at least sergeants).[59] There would usually be at least half a dozen such men per Division, and their numbers subsequently increased further. It was these officers, rather than those from Scotland Yard, who were most likely to make a detective input in low-level Metropolitan crimes.[60]

---

55. pp.14.1868, at pp.21-22.
56. pp.14.1868, at pp.21-22.
57. pp.15.1878, at p.82.
58. pp.15.1878, at p.1.
59. *Quarterly Review*, Vol. 129, No. 257, 1870, at p.99.
60. Smith, Philip Fermond, 1985, at p.66.

Ongoing Concern about Detective Resources

Despite this development, detective numbers were still thought to be inadequate, while the investigative abilities of individual officers were often considered to be poor, and their operations unsophisticated. There were also problems with their selection, supervision, career structure, training, conditions of service, and pay.

A lack of incentives meant that the quality of Divisional detectives, in particular, did not improve significantly after 1869, the consequences of which were also to affect the composition of the early post-1878 C.I.D. In the 1870s, for example, they received only 6d a week more than very experienced uniformed officers (then on a little under £2), although the "hours and duties of the detectives are more severe". Promotion, except for the fortunate few who managed to get sent to the central detective branch, was very rare, and opportunities above sergeant almost non-existent. Not surprisingly, the duty was no more, and sometimes considerably less, attractive to constables than ordinary uniformed work. Most good men went back into uniform after a period as a Divisional detective.

It was also alleged that their initial recruitment was often the result of being a particular Inspector's favourite, so that they were usually "good stupid men" who never got into trouble, rather than specially suited to their task. Frequently, they were not even used for proper detective work at all, but for every "trifling occurrence" that came up, sometimes even being employed to carry messages from station to station.[61]

Furthermore, the institutional bifurcation between Divisional and Central detectives occasioned jealousy and rivalry between the two groups. The Divisional men had to be handled with enormous tact, as they resented having their brains 'picked' for information by the Scotland Yard detectives, who would often claim all the credit for any ensuing arrests.[62] This was particularly unfortunate, because the central detective branch officers did not normally spend much of their time dealing with 'ordinary' criminals in peripheral areas, being primarily involved with high-profile cases such as murder and large-scale fraud or cases that were nearer to the centre of the Metropolis. As a result, few of them were acquainted with the "faces, residences, or habits" of run-of-the-mill criminals. When assigned to a specific case, they were largely dependant for this information on local detectives. Indeed, part of the latter's duty included regularly visiting prisons to familiarise themselves with area criminals.[63] This relationship

---

61. Smith, Philip Fermond, 1985, at pp.39-40.
62. Smith, Philip Fermond, 1985, at p.38.
63. pp.15.1878, at p.37.

between centre and Division was already longstanding in 1869. For example, in 1856, Jonathan Whicher, a central force detective, and sergeant Henry Jackson from H Division, were both in plainclothes in the Kingsland Road, when they followed and arrested two local suspects. Jackson subsequently carried out a search based on information obtained from these men. Clearly, he was providing local knowledge to assist Whicher.[64] Nevertheless, as a result of this division, many informed observers felt that co-operation between the two types of detective was rare, and that Scotland Yard officers sent down to the Divisions to assist in investigating a serious crime were considered to be "interlopers" by the local men, who might even keep back important information from them.

Divisional detectives were also less suited, by training and (often) aptitude, to infiltration. Indeed, becoming well known on their 'patch' to local criminals, it was often not remotely practicable. Further reform was necessary, and this followed the Ibbetson inquiry of 1877, set up as a result of the notorious 'Trial of the Detectives' the same year. This involved high-level corruption (tipping off fraudsters about police activity), and was a major shock to the system, as the men involved were at the apex of the central force, all of them of many years' seniority, and so well known to the public.[65] The whole function, organisation, and regulation of Metropolitan detectives was examined in often unflattering detail. There was little dispute, amongst those giving evidence, that existing arrangements were unsatisfactory and that results from detective work were often poor. The ensuing report, published in 1878, noted that the 69 enquiries launched by the Central Detective Force over the previous two years had led to just 19 people being arrested, of whom three were later discharged.[66] It ultimately led to the formation of the Criminal Investigation Department (C.I.D.) in April 1878.

The C.I.D.

The C.I.D. absorbed both the Divisional and the Central detective forces under its umbrella, producing a single body presided over by the newly created Director of Criminal Investigation (later to be a third Assistant Commissioner's position). Initially, this post was held by Howard

---

64. OBSP, Trial of Joseph Hopkins and John Stewart, 7th April 1856, t18560407-471.
65. *The Morning Post*, December 15th, 1877, p.4.
66. pp.15.1878, at p.1 and p.38.

The 1877 'Trial of the Detectives'

Vincent, a 29-year-old former soldier and qualified barrister.[67] However, some (the clear majority) of C.I.D. men continued to be assigned to Divisions, and others, many of them men of high rank, including a chief superintendent and three chief inspectors, to the central force, so that there was still a *de facto* separation.[68] (For much of the period, detectives in the central force were nominally part of A Division).[69] Along with the four senior officers, there were 12 detective inspectors, 15 detective sergeants and 32 detective constables at Scotland Yard in 1885.[70]

Howard Vincent

---

67. 'The Chief of the Criminal Investigation Department'', *The Penny Illustrated Paper and Illustrated Times*, July 8th, 1882, p. 20.
68. 'Reorganisation Of The London Detective Police Force', *The Leeds Mercury*, April 8th, 1878.
69. 'London Detectives', *Daily News*, April 3rd, 1886.
70. 'The Criminal Investigation Department', *The Morning Post*, September 2nd, 1885, p.5.

Even so, there was fairly regular movement between the two groups. Thus, Inspector Frederick Abberline, famous for his involvement in the 'Ripper' investigation, spent 14 years working as a detective in the East End with H Division C.I.D. and its Divisional predecessor, before being posted to the Central Force in 1887. His knowledge of the area meant that he was sent back to H Division the following year to investigate the serial killings. Interestingly, during his career, he only dealt with one other murder that came to a contested trial, most of his almost 30 appearances as a witness at the Old Bailey being in cases of theft or fraud.

The new detective force gradually expanded in size after 1878. During Howard Vincent's tenure as Director, numbers went up from 216 to 294 men.[71] By 1889, its 300 officers included 30 Inspectors, and further expansion was planned.[72] The following year, Andrew Lansdowne could note that some individual police Divisions in London had complements of detectives that were larger than the whole central force had been in Dickens' time.[73] Five years later, the C.I.D. consisted of 472 officers. Additionally, the City of London detective force, which had been established in 1848, had about 80 men. Unsurprisingly, its speciality was commercial fraud.[74] In 1854, for example, a pair of its best detectives tracked down two Antwerp merchants who had absconded with £5,500 to Whitechapel, and recovered the stolen money.[75]

Despite this expansion, detective numbers were still fairly limited, even at the end of the period, given the amount of suitable work available for them in the capital. In the late 1880s, Monro had been dismayed that the Metropolitan police, although facing the most sophisticated criminal threat in England, had the lowest proportion of officers devoted to detection of any major urban force; just 2.42% compared to Manchester's 2.7%, Liverpool's 3.55% and Birmingham's 4.5%. He wanted every London police station to have a C.I.D. man to deal with difficult crimes and to acquire intelligence about suspicious characters.[76] In 1909, there were still fewer than 600 detectives, in a force of 17,000 men, i.e. about 3.5%. By contrast, in the modern period, in England and Wales generally, dedicated detectives amount to about 15% of all police manpower.[77]

---

71. Petrow, Stefan, 1993, at p.95.
72. Clarkson, Charles Tempest and Richardson, J. Hall, 1889, at pp.260-261.
73. Lansdowne, Andrew, 1893, at p.7.
74. Griffiths, Arthur, 1898, at p.370.
75. *Daily News*, May 8th, 1854.
76. Petrow, Stefan, 1993, at p.95.
77. Morgan, R., & Newburn, T., 1997, at p.88.

Because the need for undercover work in the Metropolis was enormous, even after the advent of the C.I.D. some ordinary uniformed constables continued to be put into plainclothes on a temporary basis, for occasional duties, such as clearing the streets of betting and prostitution. Sometimes, such work was a proving ground for future applicants to the C.I.D.[78] As with the early plainclothes men, problems were occasioned by normally uniformed officers already being known to the public via their patrols. This risk could be reduced somewhat by having recourse to men who were not commonly seen on the streets. Thus, the future detective John Sweeney, when initially assigned to T Division (mainly Hammersmith) in the late 1870s, was normally responsible for clerical work rather than patrol duties, because of his relatively high level of education. However, his intelligence and the unfamiliarity of his face meant that he was also often chosen for "special work". For example, Sweeney was employed to go undercover to prove the suspected illegal Sunday trading of a publican. He was assisted in this by another officer, known as the "sketcher", who was also usually employed at the police station, drawing designs of suspected premises for police raids. Additionally, Sweeney helped a junior C.I.D. detective in watching gangs of 'roughs' who were terrorising parts of Hammersmith on Sunday evenings. On their first 'outing', they arrested 12 men. Nevertheless, despite such modest and intermittent exposure, after seven years' service Sweeney felt that all the area's criminals had "come to know me pretty well". He went to Scotland Yard as a probationary detective in 1884.[79]

In a particularly grave emergency, quite large numbers of 'beat' constables could be attached to the C.I.D. and operate out of uniform, as happened in August 1888, when many officers were temporarily employed in this manner in the East End, in an attempt to catch the 'Ripper'. So desperate was Sir Henry Smith, the Commissioner of the City Police, to find the murderer (though only one killing occurred within his jurisdiction) that nearly a third of his small force was assigned to this duty. They were given instructions to do everything that under ordinary circumstances a constable should not do, even though Smith feared that this would be "subversive of discipline". Thus, officers were encouraged to smoke on duty, go into public houses, and gossip with anyone they met.[80] In November 1888, a plainclothes man was even pursued by an agitated crowd in the mistaken belief that he was the serial killer.[81]

---

78. Fosdick, Raymond B., 1915, at p.298.
79. Sweeney, John, 1905, at pp.4, 8, 14 & 15.
80. Smith, Henry, 1910, at p.147.
81. *The Times*, 15th November, 1888.

Professional Competence

Because they made good copy, detectives tended to attract considerable, and sometimes unwarranted, media interest. After the mid-century, many prominent detectives, especially those from the central force, actively cultivated, and were cultivated by, journalists. They enjoyed a symbiotic relationship; the detectives' exploits were reported to the public, promoting their careers, while journalists got a 'story'. (Occasionally, police enquiries were also assisted by publicity).[82] Perhaps, in part, for this reason, some informed observers felt that both the importance and ability of Metropolitan detectives was greatly exaggerated in newspapers and journals.

Despite Charles Dickens's enthusiasm for the "extraordinary dexterity, patience, and ingenuity" of the small central force of Scotland Yard detectives in the 1850s, the reality was always rather different, with regular accusations of blundering and incompetence being levied against them and their successors, both at the central and Divisional level.[83] Many observers were openly sceptical about their real levels of expertise, feeling that there was normally no such thing as sending to London for: "…skilled detectives who, by some magical art, can hunt out crime undiscoverable by a decent set of competent policemen working in the ordinary way".[84] Indeed, one commentator thought that even the very top detectives usually looked like "common constables in plain clothes".[85]

Others believed that detectives performed adequately in those cases in which a degree of acquired knowledge about the 'criminal class' was all that was required, but were often woefully out of their depth: "…when the exercise of their calling demands patient inductive thought".[86] Most had a certain type of shrewdness, and an extensive knowledge of the haunts, habits, and associates of the "vulgar order of criminal". However, this did not equip them to deal with sophisticated felons or those who might not have offended on earlier occasions.[87] This concern gradually permeated popular consciousness. In late Victorian fiction, the private detective often outmatched the C.I.D. man, as with Sherlock Holmes and Inspector

---

82. Shpayer-Makov, Haia, 1999, pp.963-987.
83. Dickens, Charles, 1850, 'A Detective Police Party', at p.409; Collins, Phillip, 1994, at p.206.
84. 'What Detectives Really Do!' *Glasgow Herald*, December 28th, 1863.
85. *The Graphic*, July 3rd, 1880.
86. 'Detectives v. Criminals', *Daily News*, October 13th, 1860.
87. 'Public Prosecutors and the Detection of Crime', *The Pall Mall Gazette*, August 20th, 1873.

Lestrade, even though, in reality, private investigators almost never became involved with murder enquiries or worked with the official police.[88]

In a sample of 144 Metropolitan burglaries and robberies, conducted between 1856 and 1876, no arrests ensued from scene of crime examination and standard detective work, and only three from police enquiries. In most cases, where arrests occurred, it was because the victim knew the perpetrator, could describe him in detail, or (somewhat less commonly) because the criminal had been stopped (usually by chance) by uniformed officers.[89]

However, the new post-1878 C.I.D. appears to have met some early success. By 1882, Howard Vincent felt that its initial unpopularity had swiftly given way to general respect, both within the wider force and on the part of the general public. In the previous year, its 260 detectives had conducted 2,940 investigations and arrested 6,497 people.[90] In 1889, there were claims that its men were consistently apprehending 6,000 people a year.[91] Some assessments were even more impressive, one being that between 1879 and 1884 detective arrests in London increased from 13,128 to 18,344.[92] According to Robert Anderson, much of the credit for the reduction in crime in London during the final decades of the century could be attributed to the C.I.D., the figures showing what "marked success" attended their work during the first twenty years.[93] He was not alone in this belief. Several others claimed that the continual fall in crime during the 1890s was largely a result of: "The ever-increasing efficiency of the Criminal Investigation Department keeping the thieves in awe".[94]

Much depends on definitions, and the necessary degree of detective involvement before an arrest can be 'claimed' by the force. Additionally, arrests did not necessarily translate into prosecutions, let alone convictions. Perhaps significantly, officers from the C.I.D. are only specifically mentioned at the Old Bailey as witnesses in about 80 cases between their advent in 1878 and the end of the century. Nevertheless, it is clear that, by the turn of the century, there had been a significant improvement in the

---

88. Shpayer-Makov, Haia, 2011, 'Revisiting The Detective Figure In Late Victorian And Edwardian Fiction', at p.166.
89. Gatrell, V.A.C., 1990, at p.288.
90. 'The Criminal Investigation Department', *The Morning Post*, November 5th, 1883, p.6.
91. Clarkson, Charles Tempest and Richardson, J. Hall, 1889, at pp.260-261.
92. Petrow, Stefan, 1993, at p.95.
93. Anderson, Robert, 1910, at p.141.
94. *Daily News*, November 20th, 1895.

quality of detective recruits, compared to those of the 1870s. In 1900, the typical new C.I.D. entrant was 27 to 28 years of age, had spent at least a year in uniform on the beat, and had passed a competitive exam as well as being recommended to the position by his immediate superiors.[95] Additionally, detectives would spend time on probation at the start of their careers, being assessed for suitability. Warren's views on the need for 'stolid' characters had largely been rejected. Those officers who failed to show that they had enough intelligence to produce successful captures were returned to uniform at the end of their probationary period.[96]

By then, the C.I.D. was also noted for its relatively cosmopolitan composition. Although the Irish contribution had diminished slightly after the onset of the Fenian problems, there were men from a number of European countries in their ranks, including several Polish Jews. Some appear to have been recruited specifically, or in part, because of their linguistic abilities. Thus, C.I.D. Inspector Charles Von Turnow, involved in dealing with a gang of Poles who had forged Russian roubles, noted that he had translated some important letters in the case from German because it was his native tongue.[97] However, like uniformed officers, only a minority, albeit significantly more than in the wider force, were native Londoners, and most were still: "…recruited from the working classes throughout the country".[98]

Operations

Unlike many continental countries, the 'English' system of detectives, based on the Metropolitan model, was heavily decentralised, largely utilising the district boundaries of the uniformed branch. Most Metropolitan detective work after 1878 was done by the squads permanently attached to the 22 London Divisions, each largely confining itself to cases emanating from within its designated area, so that much of it was similar to that of the pre-1878 Divisional detectives and pre-1869 plainclothes men.

However, all detectives were necessarily less locally bound than were uniformed officers, frequently going out of their areas to conduct enquiries, carrying warrant cards to identify themselves (tipstaffs having been withdrawn in the 1870s), very much more freely than their 'protective' colleagues. They would normally be under the control of a

---

95. Fosdick, Raymond B., 1915, at p.306.
96. *The Times*, January 1st, 1909.
97. OBSP, Trial of Vincent Yankowski and others, 15th December 1879, t18791215-114.
98. 'London Detectives', *The Bristol Mercury and Daily Post*, August 18th, 1898.

detective inspector who was immediately answerable to the uniformed superintendent in charge of the Division, although the latter officer would rarely actively intervene in their operations, usually confining himself to disciplinary matters.[99]

By 1914, the 22 Divisions each had between 12 and 30 detectives permanently assigned to them, the remaining personnel (somewhat less than half the total) operating from Scotland Yard. Divisional men dealt with local crime, and made it their business to know their area's thieves. They would reinforce other Divisions, or be reinforced, as necessary.[100] Such local detectives would also regularly attend the main London holding/dispersal prison at Holloway (then a male establishment), using their knowledge to identify criminals who had previously been convicted and so were subject to more draconian punishments.[101]

The 'Central Office Squad' might be called in to assist with very serious local cases, supposedly being the force's 'teeth' for solving particularly grave and difficult crimes. Scotland Yard also held the late Victorian specialist units that supported detective work. These were manned by a new breed of police bureaucrat, and demonstrated a novel determination to process statistical information and to identify habitual criminals and recidivists.[102] In 1886, they included the clerical or 'Correspondence' department and the 'Convict Supervision' section (dealing with ticket of leave men). The fingerprint department was added at the start of the Edwardian period.[103]

Detective Techniques

Most modern work on Victorian detectives has tended to concentrate on the small central detective branch and, after 1878, the central pool of C.I.D. detectives, especially the post-1883 Special Branch (initially established as the Special Irish Branch), the first specialist sub-division of the C.I.D. and tasked with dealing with Fenians, anarchists and criminal émigrés. The low level, mundane, but much more 'typical' detective work carried out by the bulk of Divisionally based detective officers, and even many central force men, has often been neglected. Despite Dickens' attribution of almost superhuman intuition and perceptiveness to detectives in the central force, the working methods, and techniques of all detectives

---

99. Fosdick, Raymond B., 1915, at pp.275-277.
100. Dilnot, George, 1915, at p.26.
101. Spearman, Edmund R., 1894, at pp.358-9.
102. Petrow, Stefan, 1994, at p.83.
103. Sweeney, John, 1905, at p.16.

(central and local) were usually fairly simple.[104]

Informants

Many detectives actively cultivated intelligence from criminal contacts. By the latter part of the century most were heavily dependant on "narks" or "noses", i.e. informers and informants. Although these phrases were used rather loosely, even interchangeably, the former were sometimes defined as arrested criminals who had struck 'deals' with their captors. The latter was often considered to be a regular "auxiliary of the detective", an individual who lived on the margins of the criminal world and periodically provided information for remuneration. It was for this reason that it was accepted that any successful detective officer "must be prepared to expend money".[105] Indeed, in the early 1860s, Henry Mayhew and his collaborators suggested that it would be prudent for parliament to establish a "Detective and Inquiry Fund" specifically to reward detectives, because they were: "...almost always out of pocket through their researches".[106]

Although informants were regularly employed in political cases in the 1850s, their use for 'conventional' crime appears to have become widespread during the 1860s. By the early 1870s, most detectives of the rank of sergeant and above, whether Divisional or central, made regular use of them, normally paying between one and five shillings for information, depending on its value. Publican informants, an especially regular source of information, would also expect 'favours' at licensing meetings, such as the 'overlooking' of after-hours drinking. Colonel Henderson, when Commissioner, felt that this was simple "bribery", and only to be used in exceptional cases, but did not forbid or condemn the practise outright. (He also believed that the information it furnished was usually only useful in minor cases).[107] In 1877, Divisional Detective Sergeant Thomas Foster, from the rough 'H' Division, gave details as to how his detectives gained knowledge about local members of the "criminal classes". Normally, it was simply by visiting the places where they gathered. They then obtained information from local contacts with whom they were personally acquainted. The Division kept a "general thieves register of names" to facilitate this.[108] By 1893, so much use was

104. Collins, Philip, 1994, at pp.196-205.
105. 'Thieves and Detectives', *Reynolds's Newspaper*, November 30th, 1862.
106. Mayhew, Henry et al, 1862, Vol. 4, at p.242.
107. Petrow, Stefan, 1993, at pp.99-100.
108. pp.15.1878, at p.82.

being made of informants that they were referred to as the "base of detective duty".[109]

Howard Vincent, in his *Police Code and Manual of Criminal Law* of 1881, accepted that detective officers "must necessarily have informants". However, like Henderson, he discouraged their meeting in public houses or providing alcoholic refreshments rather than money. He also stressed that they should have their identity protected in court, officers declining to answer questions in cross-examination on this point unless the trial judge directed to the contrary.

Nevertheless, and despite their increased use, much informant evidence and information was unreliable or concocted. Sometimes, they might even work for criminals, effectively acting as 'double agents' and feeding deliberately misleading information to the police. There was also a risk that they would act as *agent provocateurs* to prove their worth. As a result, suggesting that a witness was a 'copper's nark' was often a valuable line of defence in cross-examination, as it was likely to discredit their testimony. George Elliott, who appears to have received periodic "instructions" from a local sergeant, felt it necessary to stress that he was not a 'nose' and provided information and assistance out of a sense of civic duty and friendship with the officer concerned, rather than for mercenary reasons: "I do not know what a *nark* is—I know that there are people who supply the police with information—I do not know whether they get paid for it, I never did".[110]

Covert Surveillance

Much Victorian detective work in the London area involved covert surveillance of known suspects and dubious, or even fairly 'ordinary', locations, often by the local plainclothesmen prior to 1868, the Divisional detectives before 1877, and those C.I.D. men permanently attached to the Divisions afterwards. As with much modern policing, simply keeping a weather eye on the 'usual suspects' was a prudent and often highly effective technique. Not surprisingly in these circumstances, Detective Inspector Lansdowne felt that: "A memory for faces is indispensable to the detective".[111]

Typically, in 1862, a detective arrested two known pickpockets he had been watching for some time, after they attempted to steal a timepiece

---

109. Petrow, Stefan, 1993, at p.100.
110. OBSP, Trial of Charles Gwynn and James Bowen, September 13th, 1880, t18800913-506.
111. Lansdowne, Andrew, 1893, at p.47.

while under observation.[112] In 1887, when Christopher Willcox, a Detective Officer working in the London and St. Catherine Docks, saw Cornelius McCarthy and William Simmonds "loitering" nearby, he decided to keep them under observation because of their previous criminal associations. When 72 bottles of oil were subsequently missed, uniformed officers were swiftly sent to McCarthy's home to arrest him.[113] Similarly, when Divisional Detective Sergeant James Ham was on duty in plain clothes in Cook's Road, Kennington Park, late one evening in 1873, he saw three men loitering. He "knew them all" as bad characters, and secretly followed the trio, until he saw them attempting to climb a wall. He confronted them and attempted to hold on to one man, being stabbed and, significantly, abused by name in the process. He was as well known to them as they were to him.[114] This sort of work was also common in the Square Mile. George Trew, a City constable, frequently worked in plain clothes there, when it was his duty to: "...watch persons about London, and find out, as far as I can, suspicious characters".[115]

Such tactics could occasion concern amongst the public. In 1879, just after the advent of the C.I.D., David Daniel, a released convict who had been employed by a Church-based Ragged School as a caretaker, complained that that he was regularly being followed by, what his clerical employer termed, "this new Investigation Department". On one occasion, he had even been prosecuted for possessing 'skeleton keys', though these turned out to belong to the school where he worked, and were legitimately in his possession. (Colonel Henderson later dropped the action as altogether misconceived).[116] At the same time, Josephine Butler noted that other Londoners had begun to complain about the unpleasantness of being: "...placed on the list of suspects, and being dogged by strangers six feet high, and of military aspect, while pursuing one's lawful calling".[117]

Very commonly, and despite their modest numbers, detectives merely reinforced uniformed street patrols and thus 'conventional' policing by

---

112. Mayhew, Henry *et al*, 1862, Vol. 4, at p.192. They were subsequently sentenced to three months imprisonment by a stipendiary magistrate at Westminster Police Court.

113. Anon, 1887-1888, *Central Criminal Court Sessions Papers*, at pp.200-202 & p.218.

114. OBSP, Trial of James Sales, 27th October 1873, t18731027-693. Ham was rewarded with three pounds by the Old Bailey court.

115. OBSP, Trial of Matthew Shrimpton and Henry Williams, 17th August 1846, t18460817-1457.

116. OBSP, Trial of David Daniel, 15th September 1879, t18790915-760.

117. Butler, Josephine, 1880, at p.47.

providing covert *area* surveillance, rather than actively investigating or following known individuals. This was especially frequent in crowded places. For example, in one case, a detective officer, under cover, seeing a loitering gang of suspicious youths in the Ratcliffe Highway, took immediate action with a cane, running across the road and: "...dealing smart cuts to two or three of their number".[118] Whenever there were large gatherings of people, detectives would be distributed amongst the crowd. In such cases, it was the general rule to station plain-clothes men as near as possible to uniformed policemen from their own Division, so that they might be assisted when making arrests.[119] Although at first sight a wasteful use of men, this type of operation was felt to be both necessary and valuable, as the high visibility of uniformed officers meant that criminals could easily evade them.[120]

Indeed, Divisional detectives, when not engaged in post-crime investigation, were often given a specific district to patrol, in plain clothes, so that they might "supplement the action of the uniform constables on the beats". If they saw a known criminal, they would follow him, although, unless possessed of something firmer than mere suspicion, this would not normally be beyond the territorial boundaries of their Division.[121] Significantly, even prior to the advent of the Divisional detectives, the policemen in each Division who put on plain clothes were often called the "'plain-clothes patrol'". (It may have been these normally uniformed officers who produced the popular belief that you could always tell a London detective by his regulation footwear).[122] Sometimes, even some of the force's supposedly élite central detectives would be sent out as "special patrols" in areas where crime was particularly rife. On such occasions, their mission was to watch out for an area's known criminals and to: "...patrol generally for the purpose of the prevention as well as the detection of crime".[123] Detectives doing such work were given to stopping men who were carrying large bundles, which they were then made to account for under s.24 of the Police Act 1839 (see chapter five above).[124]

Even then, there were many observers who felt that this was not 'true' detective work. Some complained that, rather than being a "secret body"

---

118. Archer, Thomas, 1865, at p.123.
119. *Quarterly Review,* No. 99, 1856, pp.174-5, Reproduced in Barnett, A. & Harrison, C. (Eds.), 1989, at p.254.
120. pp.15.1878, at p.87.
121. pp.15.1878, at p.36.
122. Lansdowne, Andrew, 1893, at p.7.
123. pp.15.1878, at p.38.
124. pp.15.1878, at p.183.

engaged in solving serious crimes, such detectives differed little from ordinary policemen, except by working in civilian clothes, almost always becoming very well known to the public and local criminals in the process. Some observers feared that a lack of 'proper' detective work allowed many criminals to escape arrest. It was even claimed (albeit rather improbably) that London was no better provided for detectives in the 1880s than it had been 50 years earlier, unlike Rome, Berlin and other major Continental cities.[125]

Certainly, there were several embarrassing high profile cases in this decade. For example, during his years in London, the notorious thief and murderer Charles Peace lived quite openly, even visiting Scotland Yard, while perpetrating hundreds of lucrative burglaries, before being caught by chance rather than detection. As one contemporary observer noted, Peace had: "...boasted of his contempt for the police, and his confidence seems to have been abundantly justified".[126] Some urged the adoption of the Irish system of regularly rotating detective officers from area to area, feeling that that way they would not become so well known to criminals (and also less inclined to become corrupt).[127] Many compared them unfavourably to the (allegedly) sophisticated and pro-active Parisian detectives, something that is partly (but not entirely) supported by the memoirs of various French policemen of the period.[128]

Crime Scene Investigation

Detectives often attended the scene of significant local crimes with ordinary uniformed officers. Many solvable cases could be concluded using little more than 'commonsense'. (Even in the modern period, techniques such as fingerprinting, DNA tests and the psychological profiling of offenders are used in as few as 5% of detections).[129] Thus, in 1887, when Sophia Tolliday came home to discover that her front window had been broken from outside, the catch opened, her bedroom rifled, and two sovereigns were missing from their hiding place, detectives did not require much thought to investigate two recent lodgers who had stayed with Tolliday shortly before the crime was committed.[130]

---

125. Meason, M. Laing, 1883, at pp.756-7.
126. Peace, Charles, c.1880, at pp.2-3.
127. 'The Detective Police', 29th January, 1880, *Pall Mall Gazette.*
128. Canler, M., 1862, at p.193.
129. Morgan, R., & Newburn, T., 1997, at p.118.
130. OBSP, Trial of Elizabeth Jarvis and Annie Young, 12th December 1887, t18871212-150.

By the turn of the century, detectives would often investigate serious crimes using a: "...gigantic snowball enquiry, working backwards from the persons immediately available". They would follow up any leads thrown up as they went.[131] Contrary to popular belief, they seldom found it expedient to adopt disguises. Although Robert Fuller was originally from the Central Detective Force that operated before the formation of the C.I.D., he had only done so on six occasions during his lengthy career. A disguise room was kept at Scotland Yard, but was rarely used.[132] Nevertheless, in 1890, two South London C.I.D. men disguised themselves as an architect and his assistant, with measuring tapes and other paraphernalia, to monitor and detain a notorious thief who had a record of escaping arrest.[133] More commonly, detectives might simply change their hats to provide some measure of concealment.[134] However, where necessary, well-disguised detectives could readily penetrate the worst criminal slums without exposure.[135]

Victorian detectives lacked many of the most basic modern forensic aids, such as finger printing. Although the uniqueness of human prints had been known since the 1820s, it was only in 1896 that Edward Henry devised a reliable means of classifying them, resulting in the opening of the Finger Print Branch in 1902, after he became an Assistant Commissioner at Scotland Yard. Within a very short time, promising material, such as fragments of broken glass, was being sent to this unit for examination, and the officers there were preparing blown up photographs of the prints for forensic comparison.[136] The new system was highly efficient. Recovered fingerprints could often be matched with those on file within a matter of minutes.[137] In June 1902, the first conviction based almost entirely on fingerprint evidence was secured. Harry Jackson, a burglar, received seven years' imprisonment after Detective Sergeant Charles Collins, who had specialised in fingerprints for six years, matched a print taken from a window sash with one on file.[138]

Despite these limitations, Victorian detective work could, occasionally, be highly sophisticated. For example, Jack Whicher's (much maligned) examination of the crime scene in the Rode murder case was a model of its

---

131. Dilnot, George, 1915, at p.49.
132. Fuller, Robert, 1912, at p.214.
133. *The Star*, February 12th, 1891, p.1.
134. Dilnot, George, 1915, at pp.24-28.
135. Anon, 1853, *The Dens of London*, at p.173.
136. OBSP, Trial of Michael Meyer, 25th July 1904, t19040725-578.
137. Flynt, Josiah, 1903, at p.445.
138. OBSP, Trial of Harry Jackson, 9th September 1902, t19020909-686.

kind for thoroughness and intelligent deduction.[139] He also set the pattern for detective inspectors being supported by a sergeant when in the field. Sometimes, detective work was even proactive. For example, in the early 1860s, Detective Sergeant Hardwick, while returning to Vine Street Police Station, overheard one of three men in a public house say "we must put off the job". This roused his professional attention. He concealed himself, and then followed them from the pub, watching them reconnoitre a leather-seller's shop nearby. The following day he identified the men involved. He then went to his Superintendent and got permission to follow up on what he suspected was a planned burglary, also being given the support of a uniformed sergeant and some constables. They obtained the use of a parlour, which overlooked the premises concerned, and kept watch round the clock. A few days later, they seized two burglars red-handed, as they exited the building.[140]

Occasionally, even the pre-1877 Divisional detectives could be fairly ambitious in their operations. In one case, an officer spent several nights living as a vagrant in a cheap, and rough, lodging-house, looking for and eventually identifying a murderer by his tattoo.[141] On rare occasions, detective operations might extend to elaborate entrapment/enticement schemes. Thus, George Dilnot noted a case in which a detective dressed up as a "Jew receiver" to get information. He smoked a cigar, wore gold jewellery, and said he was one 'Cohen' from the East End, while touring Southwark. This led to a gang of thieves who had burgled nearby St. George's Cathedral.[142] However, as already noted, the ethics of such operations were often questioned by contemporary observers, greatly limiting their use.

Some detectives do appear to have acquired a large measure of 'instinct' as a result of their work. In January 1885, for example, Detective Inspector Abberline arrested James Gilbert Cunningham, the perpetrator of a Fenian explosion at the Tower of London, after carrying out a swift mass interview of the hundreds of people at the crime scene. His suspicion was aroused by the suspect's: "...hesitation in his replies and his general manner".[143]

139. Summerscale, Kate, 2008, at pp.64-67.
140. Watts, W.H., 1864, at p.229.
141. Clarkson, Charles Tempest and Richardson, J. Hall, 1889, at p.238.
142. Dilnot, George, 1915, at pp.48-49.
143. Hand written note by Abberline in his scrapbook, doc 313.88 held at Met Collection Police Heritage Centre, London, SW6 1TR, at p.58.

Recruitment

The enquiry presided over by Sir Henry Selwin Ibbetson looked into the entire working of the detective branch, in part with a view to securing the appointment of a "superior class of persons" to the force in future.[144] The apparent lack of native intelligence amongst London detectives also considered by the enquiry which, unsurprisingly, concluded that because all detectives came from the uniformed force they necessarily attracted men from broadly similar social and educational backgrounds as ordinary constables. Modern analysis confirms this, although the detective force contained a somewhat higher percentage of men drawn from the lower middle class, those possessed of a more than very basic education, and officers who had grown up in the Metropolitan area.[145] It was normal for such recruits to have had at least two or three years' experience as uniformed officers before selection. In an extreme case, George Clarke spent 22 years in uniform before becoming a central force detective in 1862.

Although some senior officers, such as Superintendent Frederick Williamson, then head of the detective branch, maintained that there was no argument for recruiting detectives from a different class of men to the uniformed police, others disagreed.[146] They felt that the traditional type of police recruit -strong, reliable men, often taken from the countryside- were not necessarily well suited to London detective work.

However, there were other hindrances to attracting high quality men. In 1883, Howard Vincent, the newly (and briefly) appointed head of the C.I.D. observed that given the dangerous nature of the work involved, and the risk of personal legal liability, as well as the forensic difficulty of proving detected cases in court, it was not surprising that there were problems in selecting men possessed of the requisite and demanding qualities: "Considerable knowledge of the world, good education, good address, tact, and temper are also essential to a detective officer".

The physical dangers he alluded to were real. Andrew Lansdowne took retirement after apprehending a fraudster who tried to shoot him. He wrestled with the man for 15 minutes in front of a crowd of onlookers, apparently too alarmed to intervene, before a coalman came to his assistance.[147] More typically, in September 1888 two constables, operating in Bethnal Green in plain clothes, spotted a wanted burglar enter *The*

---

144. *The Morning Post*, August 7th, 1877, p. 5.
145. Shpayer-Makov, Haia, 2011, at p.87 and p.299.
146. pp.15.1878, at p.4.
147. Lansdowne, Andrew, 1893, at p.201.

Feathers public house. When they followed him into the building he shouted to his companions, and the pair were assaulted by up to a dozen men. One suffered a very severe head injury and the burglar escaped.[148] When John Taylor retired from the detective force in 1896, it was noted that, earlier in his distinguished career, he had been badly injured when single-handedly arresting the Holloway coining gang, and had also been stabbed by a thief on another occasion.[149]

Limited attempts to take men directly from civilian life, without previous service as uniformed constables, with a view to securing a better educated, higher quality of recruit, or those with foreign languages, were largely unsuccessful. The Departmental Committee on the Police of 1868 had recommended such recruitment, reflecting the already widespread belief that the qualities that made for effective uniformed officers were not necessarily conducive to good plainclothesmen. It was also subsequently attempted under Sir Howard Vincent, but abandoned fairly swiftly as a "complete failure".[150] As Colonel Warren observed in his article in *Murray's Magazine*: "...few if any [direct entrants] have been found to be qualified to remain in the detective service". Experiments involving the selection of former military officers and their social equivalents were particularly unsuccessful. A group of six such recruits were thought to have been been "eminently unsatisfactory". Men of this class would not usually be of the best stamp, normally having failed in 'proper' gentlemen's professions first. As a result, they were: "...less trustworthy, less reliable, and more difficult to control".[151] Of the six, one lapsed into alcoholism and committed suicide; another had to be pensioned off for bad health, while others drank excessively or wrote up false reports. Half left during their first year of service.[152]

Additionally, of course, such men had no knowledge of ordinary police operations, although they necessarily had to work closely with uniformed officers, something that put them at an enormous disadvantage. George Greenham was a direct entrant to the Central Detective Force in 1869, probably because of his facility with languages (necessary for those dealing with emigrés). Although a rare success, he freely admitted that his early years were difficult, due to this lack of basic knowledge.[153]

---

148. *The Illustrated Police News,* September 22nd, 1888.
149. *Lloyd's Weekly London Newspaper*, January 5th, 1896, at p.11.
150. 'London Detectives', *The Bristol Mercury and Daily Post*, August 18th, 1898.
151. Clarkson, Charles Tempest, and Richardson, J. Hall, 1889, at p.263 & p.264.
152. Shpayer-Makov, Haia, 2011, at pp.70-71.
153. Greenham, George H., 1904, at p.7.

Not everyone accepted the widely voiced criticisms of detective quality. In his 1888 article Warren specifically addressed allegations that London detectives lacked sophistication. His response was remarkably complacent, even seeking to make a virtue of it, and claiming that temperamentally the genius of the English race did not lend itself to "elaborate detective operations" like those practised on the Continent. Instead, Englishmen possessed other qualities that were essential to such work, amongst them being: "...dogged pertinacity in watching, thoroughness of purpose, an absence of imagination, and downright sterling honesty".[154] As a result, he believed there was little need for radical change, except, perhaps, to deal with the increasingly large number of suspicious foreigners resident in the capital. In 1889, Inspector Charles Tempest Clerkson was willing to extend the list of 'unusual' crimes, which required more intellectual dexterity than was commonly available, and where a "matter of fact mind" might be a hindrance to success. Nevertheless, even he believed that for the detection of common types of crime: "...paid informers, and every other kind of 'nose' the police employ do their work very well".[155]

However, it is at least arguable that a more valuable background for many Metropolitan detectives would have been similar to that of Detective Sergeant Andrews, who told the 1877 enquiry that: "I spent a great part of my youth in London, and I knew a great deal of London life, and I found that very useful to me after I became a detective officer".[156] Others felt that more intelligent, and better educated, men would also make superior detectives. Certainly, the detective branch could appear quite amateurish when confronted by sophisticated crime. There appears to have been some truth to *Punch's* celebrated Du Maurier cartoon of a London detective who was known to the world by his standard issue footwear. As 'Alf' the youthful Lambeth criminal observed: "...what is the use of a split in uniform trousers and the regulation seven-league boots?"[157] (Ironically, prisoners at Dartmoor made police-boots during the 1870s).[158] According to Dew, all of the detectives in his part of late Victorian East London were known to local criminals, who even gave them sobriquets; he was 'Blue Serge' after his favourite attire.[159] In the 1890s, there were tensions within the C.I.D. over the alleged preferment of provincial police officers who

---

154. Warren, Charles, 1889, at p.587.
155. Clarkson, Charles Tempest and Richardson, J. Hall, 1889, at p.275.
156. pp.15.1878, at p.52.
157. Rook, Clarence, 1899, at p.255.
158. Anon., *Five Years' Penal Servitude*, 1877, at p.124.
159. Dew, Walter, 1938, at p.90.

had been specifically brought in to deal with anarchists and Fenians because they were not already known to the wider public.[160]

Many observers believed that the system found it difficult to cope if ordinary criminals showed any sophistication in their operations. According to the *Saturday Review*, in 1868, the typical police detective was: "...seldom a match for a criminal with more than the average intelligence of his class".[161] They felt that an excessive emphasis on public order policing and on routine preventative patrolling was damaging to the wider force, and wholly inadequate against a hard-core of intelligent London criminals who were steadily refining their techniques.[162]

It was also frequently asserted that, until the advent of James Monro as (a very short-lived) Commissioner, in late 1888, those at the head of the Metropolitan force were invariably out of touch with detective work.[163] Certainly, Colonel Edmund Henderson was restrained in his use of them, as even Josephine Butler accepted; she feared that a more assertive Metropolitan Police Commissioner would employ them more intrusively.[164] Although a popular commander, Henderson apparently never took to the details of police work and "least of all to thief catching".[165] After his replacement by Colonel Warren, in January 1886, it was claimed that the situation got steadily worse. William Stead's *Pall Mall Gazette* ran a series of articles between 1886 and 1888 that were bitterly critical of the Metropolitan police. Although they ranged from attacks on the handling of public order policing to the decor at Scotland Yard, the low priority of detection was foremost amongst them. Senior officers, in particular, were criticised as 'Dodos' in their attitudes, the only exception being the then C.I.D. Chief, James Monro, allegedly "the one competent man" in the force because of his detective background. Charles Warren was derided for his preoccupation with public order and drill, neglect of ordinary crime, and attitude towards the C.I.D., particularly the manner in which he regulated it with 'red tape' and a host of limiting rules. Amongst them, the journal claimed, was that he would not permit any officer under 5' 9" in height to join, that the rules on paying rewards to informers were too restrictive, that a detective needed formal permission from the centre to pursue a suspect outside the London area, and that the periods that officers

---

160. 'Criminal Investigation Department', *Reynolds's Newspaper*, September 15th, 1895.
161. Petrow, Stefan, 1994, at p.68.
162. Anderson, Robert, 1910, at p.129.
163. Anderson, Robert, 1910, at p.129.
164. Butler, Josephine, 1880, at p.47.
165. Greenham, G.H., 1904, at p.124.

had to spend in uniform before becoming detectives were so substantial that they became well known to criminals and assumed the overt manner of uniformed policemen, complete with a regulation gait. The magazine joined those who complained that the detective branch had no room for "clever little ferrets of men".[166] (It should, perhaps, be noted, that there were also allegations that detectives were being recruited from reliable and stolid rather than 'clever' men in Paris at this time).[167]

In fairness, Warren expressly denied some of these allegations, especially those pertaining to physical size and degree of previous experience on appointment.[168] Nevertheless, he does appear to have had little interest in, and sometimes even a positive dislike for, something as unregimented as detective work. (This was shared by many ordinary constables who thought they were "not uniform and "unperfessional"").[169] Even some of Warren's officers believed that: "The Chief continually snubs the detective branch". A competent detective inspector took years to train, but under the Warren regime it was often alleged that the force was getting men of the utmost respectability, but with very little personal acumen, even though they had to cope with the keenest-witted foreign criminals, while even native offenders were increasingly sophisticated. Dealing with such felons required correspondingly: "...brighter qualities, and these are not to be found amongst the men who are now being taken into the ranks".[170]

It is also apparent that, throughout his short period as Commissioner, Warren had extremely bad relations with James Monro and his C.I.D. Warren distrusted their operational independence and natural secrecy and bridled at their apparent resistance to military-style discipline. As tensions developed between the two men, Warren complained to the Home Office about Monro's 'insubordination'. This appears to have prompted the latter's resignation, in August of 1888, which was handed in with an attached list of complaints about Warren's lack of interest in the C.I.D. and the restrictions that he imposed on it. Despite initial resistance, the Home Secretary, Sir Henry Mathews, eventually accepted the resignation, probably believing it to be the easiest course available. Robert Anderson replaced Monro (who returned as Commissioner just three months later).[171]

---

166. Porter, Bernard, 1988, at pp.86-88.
167. *The Illustrated Police News*, January 10th, 1874.
168. *The Times,* October 10th, 1888, p.5.
169. 'The Model Policeman', *Punch,* June 17th, 1848.
170. Approved quotation from a 'Daily Paper' in Anon, 1888, *The Metropolitan Police and its Management,* at p.6.
171. Pellew, Jill, 1982, at p.48.

However, shortly afterwards, the failure to solve the Jack the Ripper murders brought further criticism of the Metropolitan force generally, and its detectives in particular, despite a major police effort to find the killer. For example, after one of the later murders, a large number of plainclothes men were quickly on the streets, making inquiries in the neighbourhood.[172] According to a report by Chief Inspector Swanson, sent to the Home Office on the 19th October 1888, 80,000 handbills were distributed in the East End, extensive house-to-house searches conducted, and 2,000 lodgers questioned. Even Anderson freely conceded that C.I.D. morale was low at this point.[173]

Matters were made worse because, as Anderson was also frank in acknowledging, the detective department had always been an object of jealousy in the wider Force, something that was especially apparent during 1887 and 1888. He felt that a clear indication of this, at the highest level, was that the Commissioner's report for 1887 had mentioned the quality of police boots and the replacement of truncheon pockets with special cases, but did not contain a single word about crime detection in the Metropolis.[174]

Criticism of the detective abilities of the police came from within as well as from outside the force. A recurrent theme of internal critics, in the early years of the new C.I.D., when the majority of its officers were still former Divisional detectives, was their generally poor quality. According to Fuller, many of the old detectives in 1881, particularly those taken from 'rough' districts: "...seemed destitute of everything but a certain amount of low cunning, [and] a smattering of thieves' slang".[175] His views were supported by the lawyer William Ballantine, who also thought that the detective Branch was lax about publicising information on serious crimes, a situation that he contrasted unfavourably with the old Bow Street Runners. They were too willing to reveal details, such as whether a deceased victim had made a dying declaration implicating his attacker, which might be of assistance to criminals.[176]

By the turn of the century, it was also widely believed that Scotland Yard was being outstripped in the employment of new technology and crime indexes by many continental forces, especially those in Germany and France.[177] The situation was not improved by deficiencies in the professional competence and forensic knowledge of the uniformed officers

---

172. 'The Whitechapel Murder', *The Times*, September 3rd, 1888.
173. Anderson, Robert, 1910, at p.136.
174. Anderson, Robert, 1910, at p.139.
175. Fuller, Robert, 1912, at p.27.
176. Ballantine, William, 1890, at p.233.
177. Fosdick, Raymond B., 1915, at p.313.

who provided the immediate support for detectives. For example, they might make mistakes when attending a crime scene, as they frequently lacked the: "...detective instinct, and very often valuable time has been lost in the tracking of the fugitive criminal". It took the first six of the Ripper's murders for them to appreciate that there was a need to photograph a victim's corpse *in situ*, before moving it to the mortuary.[178]

Of course, there were exceptions to this general picture. Even in 1881, the otherwise troubled Rotherhithe police had two very experienced local detectives, Frank Brias and Jimmy Tooley. They had served there for 20 years, gaining a unique knowledge of the area, and seeing many local thieves grow up from boyhood. They were 'tough but fair' men who were willing to nurse informants at their own expense by the: "...occasional judicious expenditure of a coin or two".[179] Additionally, after 1878, greater care was being taken to secure the better men available from the uniformed branch. According to (former) Detective Inspector Andrew Lansdowne it was as a result of his quick success in uniform, in which he was made first sergeant and then acting Inspector that he was sent to Scotland Yard.[180] John Sweeney in Hammersmith, was also 'noticed' because he was a diligent and effective uniformed officer, typically pursuing a thief who he saw steal a pair of boots to his lodgings and arresting him.[181]

Detective Misconduct

Misconduct, whether motivated by zeal or personal gain, appears to have been an occupational hazard of detective work throughout the era. As early as 1833, there had been a scandal over the activities of the plainclothes man William Popay (see above). In 1855, P.C. Charles King, a regular C Division plainclothes man, was convicted and transported for using his position to organize a group of youthful thieves and pickpockets, even pointing out potential targets to them.[182] In 1863, three experienced, if not very senior, "detectives" (presumably, local plainclothesmen) were convicted at Southwark Police Court for attempting to extort money from a tavern keeper by threatening his licence. They were sentenced to a month's imprisonment and dismissed from the force.[183]   Most seriously of

178. Clarkson, Charles Tempest and Richardson, J. Hall, 1889, at p.272.
179. Fuller, Robert, 1912, at p.28.
180. Lansdowne, Andrew, 1893, at p.6.
181. Sweeney, John, 1905, at p.4.
182. OBSP, Trial of Charles King, 9th April 1855, t18550409-484.
183. *The Dundee Courier & Argus*, May 20th, 1863.

all, and in a major shock to the system, several very senior and well known members of the central detective force at Scotland Yard, including Chief Inspectors Druscovitch, Palmer, and Clarke, stood trial in 1877 on a variety of charges, including taking bribes, suppressing evidence and giving advance notice of impending police raids to criminals. Nearly all were convicted.[184] Even at the start of the following century, an otherwise laudatory Edwardian newspaper article could concede that: "...there are men in the C.I.D. who do not always do it credit".[185]

To an extent, many of these risks were unavoidable, leading *The Times* to declare that the use of detectives could never be more than an "unpleasant and dangerous necessity". The independent nature of their work meant they were the most difficult of police departments to supervise effectively. They also necessarily had to move in the criminal underworld. As Detective George Greenham was to note during the Trial of the Detectives: "When I want to get information I often have to mix with very bad company".[186] Detectives might even have to pretend to be involved in crimes, practising "habitual duplicity" in the process. Some officers found the lifestyle corrupting, and too much for their moral fortitude to resist.[187] The bribes could be very substantial, especially those offered by professional criminals. For example, £100 was offered (unavailingly) by Solomon Silver to a group of detectives about to search his premises for stolen goods.[188] As a result, while all gifts to policemen required written permission before they could be accepted, the Commissioners ordered that special care be taken that those to detectives had not been actively solicited.[189]

Some detectives also fabricated evidence and, it was claimed, even instigated crimes that they then 'solved', simply to curry favour with their superiors.[190] In 1910, a former detective sergeant named William Harris published details of an entrapment scheme, used by colleagues earlier in his career, in which ex-convicts were given forged crown pieces by a police informant and then immediately arrested and prosecuted as coiners. The prosecution statements in these cases were a "tissue of lies".[191] Allegations of detective perjury were especially frequent. The constant

---

184. Lansdowne, Andrew, 1893, at p.7.
185. *The Times*, January 1st, 1909.
186. Dilnot, George, 1928, at p.182.
187. *The Morning Post*, December 15th, 1877, p.4.
188. *The Times*, December 6th, 1911, p.4.
189. MEPO 7/15 May 27 1850.
190. Leading Article, *The Times*, August 15th, 1877.
191. *Penny Illustrated Paper,* October 1st, 1910.

temptation to take 'short cuts' in securing the convictions of men that they genuinely believed to be guilty, or even simply nefarious, was ever present. David Nicoll, a London anarchist of the 1890s, claimed that he had been the victim of deliberate perjury by two detectives as to the contents of a speech he had made in Hyde Park. He thought they had treated him unfairly, simply because of his politics.[192] Even Detective Inspector Fuller candidly admitted that during his career he had: "...formed erroneous opinions, more than once or twice".[193]

It was, in part, for this reason that detectives were often very unpopular with poorer Londoners. Alf, the Lambeth 'hooligan' of 1899, loathed 'splits' and distinguished them from ordinary policemen. He approvingly recalled an incident in which, when in custody, he had witnessed a detective telling a witness that the apprehended suspect on an identity parade was "fourth from end". When he pointed this out to the (uniformed) station inspector, the latter officer swiftly "re-shuffled the pack".[194] However, as *The Times* observed, there were ways of reducing corruption, even if it could not be eliminated. Obvious safeguards were for detectives to be closely monitored and to keep in regular contact with their superiors, informing them of their every step. Their use could also be confined to an essential minimum.[195] Both approaches were followed in London, though this inevitably limited their effectiveness.

Detectives were certainly not totally unsupervised, even in the era of the informal plainclothes men. In 1855, for example, Charles King's immediate (uniformed) supervisor, Sergeant William Godfrey, noted that men would be told to investigate certain incidents, such as a specific robbery, and then be left to their own devices for four or five hours a day. They would report back in the evening, or the following morning, as to what they had done during this time, which information would be entered into a record book. Nevertheless, in the 1850s, this was not usually very specific; a plainclothesman was not normally required to detail precisely whom he had spoken to, or exactly where he had been, during his enquiries.[196] By the 1880s, the situation was rather more formal. Detectives would be issued with a diary at the start of each month and forced to keep a day-by-day account of their movements and the investigations in which they had been engaged, along with any expenses that had been incurred. The local Inspector of Detectives was required to

192. Nicholl, David, 1892, at p.5.
193. Fuller, Robert, 1912, at p.196.
194. Rook, Clarence, 1899, at p.261.
195. Leading Article, *The Times*, August 15th, 1877.
196. OBSP, Trial of Charles King, 9th April 1855, t18550409-484.

keep a record of his own, detailing the work of his men. Each month, all of these diaries would be submitted to Scotland Yard for scrutiny and cross-referencing.[197]

The detective branch, as a whole, managed to avoid a repetition of the events of 1877, corruption becoming largely a localised phenomenon. This allowed Arthur Harding to contrast the C.I.D. men from Commercial Street station, who were "proper policemen", if rather rough, with the "villains" from Leman Street Station, who had been corrupted by the receipt of stolen property and the ready availability of money.[198] Many officers resisted temptation, though most of those that didn't have left few traces. Unfortunately, abuses in office were certainly not confined to detectives, as the next chapter will show.

---

197. 'London Detectives', *Daily News*, April 3, 1886.
198. Harding, C., & Wilson, L., 1988, at p.200 & pp.204-205.

CHAPTER NINE

ABUSE OF POLICE POWERS

Modern police studies have identified significant levels of corruption, pettiness, perjury and even outright violence during a previously perceived 'Golden Age' of English policing between 1930 and 1960.[1] Given their Victorian antecedents, this is not at all surprising. All of these phenomena were manifest during the nineteenth century. A few Metropolitan police officers even had personal recourse to theft while on duty. For example, there was a cluster of such cases shortly after establishment. Thus, in October 1829, P.C. John Jones became the subject of public ridicule after stealing a scrag of mutton from a Somers Town butcher. In 1830, P.C.s Richard Barrett and John Lyddiard were convicted of using their positions to steal money from a man they encountered in Rosemary Lane, in the small hours of the morning. They were sentenced to transportation.[2] However, police-perpetrated thefts were comparatively rare, given the size of the force and the opportunities presented by nocturnal patrol. Much more serious was abuse of position by individual officers.

To have an impact on delinquent street culture required that the police possess great discretionary power. In the modern era, Wilson and Kelling freely conceded that the style of assertive, discretion-based, urban policing that they favoured was a potential recipe for corruption and abuse, and not: "…easily reconciled with any conception of due process or fair treatment".[3] Unsurprisingly, the problems thrown up by such policing also plagued the Victorian police. Most London magistrates of the period recognised that the Metropolitan force recruited some men who were "unworthy of its traditions and ideals".[4] Unfortunately, the difficulty was often structural rather than confined to a few 'bad apples'.

---

1. See generally, Weinberger, Barbara, 1996.
2. OBSP, Trial of Richard Barrett and John Lyddiard, 16th September 1830, t18300916-218.
3. Wilson, James Q., and Kelling. George L., 1982, at p.35.
4. Cairns, J. A. R., 1922, at p.264.

Many had foreseen such problems prior to 1829. As a journal correspondent pointed out in 1818, although the prevention of crime might be better than its cure, it would mean taking steps that were "odious and repulsive" to civil liberties.[5] For many members of the Metropolitan lower working class, these were a luxury during the nineteenth century. Although well-dressed members of the public would usually be met with politeness, the ragged and outcast might experience gratuitous force from officers who were, for them, the "despot[s] of the streets". Some might even experience open "oppression and brutality".[6]

Kelling and Wilson hoped that by their selection, training, and supervision, the police would be inculcated with a clear sense of the proper limits to their power.[7] Arguably, and unfortunately, the Victorian Metropolitan police were deficient in both of the first two categories, i.e. careful and selective recruitment and, even more so, training, which was always extremely rudimentary during the 1800s (this changed in the Edwardian period). Where they *were* strong, was in their level of supervision, something that was backed up by an almost iron discipline. Though unpopular with many officers, this may well have been vital. Without it, London policemen could easily have degenerated into petty tyrants. It still could not prevent a woeful litany of abuse.

Much also depended on the direction that the force was given by its commanders. Fortunately, throughout the era, the abuse of position by junior officers was very actively and vigorously discouraged by senior ranks. It is hard to read the instructions given to the newly founded force without concluding that, whatever the reality on the ground, Mayne and Rowan genuinely wished to limit unnecessary confrontation with the public as much as possible. Officers were enjoined to provide their service numbers to anyone asking for them and were forbidden to wear their capes in such a way that those numbers were hidden, men who did so being presumed to have something "shameful" to hide and subject to dismissal. Constables were advised to be polite at all times (instances of "rudeness" in response to civil questions having been reported). Sergeants were warned to be quiet when deploying their men in the streets. Officers were also cautioned not to enter into 'altercations' whilst on duty; instead, they were to demonstrate total command of temper. They were forbidden to use their truncheons except in *extremis*, and were told to be helpful to those who called at their watch (later section) houses. When on patrol they were to make way for members of the respectable public on the pavement. With

---

5. *Gentleman's Magazine*, Vol. 88, July 1818, at p.219 and p.410.
6. *Spectator*, 30th April, 1864, Vol. XXVIII at p.496.
7. Wilson, James Q., and Kelling. George L., 1982, at p.35.

this caveat, they were also warned that they should treat members of the public equally, whether rich or poor, and not use language that would "provoke or offend" anyone arrested.[8]

Such advice was regularly reiterated throughout the century. Thus, in February 1853, officers removing basket-sellers were warned to keep their cool by the Commissioners. In June of the same year, they were further advised not to employ "unkind" language. Despite her reservations about the police, even Butler felt that the Commissioner in 1880, Colonel Henderson, was a man of "high principle", so that abuses of police power were less common than they would have been under a "less prudent or conscientious chief".[9]

Perhaps because of such directives, many establishment figures appear to have convinced themselves, fairly swiftly, that all was well with the force. William Arabin could: "...scarcely recollect a case where they have been too hasty and zealous in the discharge of those duties". He claimed that this view was shared by most of his fellow Old Bailey judges. Similarly, Colonel James Clitheroe, a Middlesex magistrate, could not "speak too highly of the police". He denied they were over-zealous and even claimed not to have heard complaints that this was the case.[10] Such opinions led the 1834 Select Committee to conclude that there had been fewer police "abuses of authority" than might have been predicted.[11]

However, despite establishment confidence, and even with strict guidance from higher command, the Victorian police were regularly criticised by neutral observers for victimising poorer working men for arbitrary reasons and for capriciousness in their exercise of power. The increase in police activism after 1829, combined with the limited educational background of most officers and the demands of internal promotion encouraged this, and hindered the establishment of cordial relations with the working classes. In the words of an experienced stipendiary magistrate in 1882, many police officers were presented with abundant opportunities to exercise: "...despotic and arbitrary power, with a knowledge, too, that great activity and zeal are most likely to attract the attention of their superiors, and so probably lead to promotion".[12] Slightly melodramatically, Josephine Butler claimed that the discretion given to

---

8. Extracts from Orders from the Commissioners Whitehall Place, 7th June, 6th, 11th, 17th October, 1830 and June 15th, 1831, Reproduced in PR.5.1844, at pp.103-106.
9. Butler, Josephine, 1880, at pp.38-39 & 47.
10. pp.11.d.1834, at pp.274-276, and p.357.
11. pp.11.d.1834, at p.10.
12. Anon, 1882, *Metropolitan Police Court Jottings*, at p.47.

officers to deal with prostitutes meant they often became an organized body of women-hunters, with the most arbitrary and: "…irresponsible powers, to pursue, to accuse, to condemn, and to hurry off to the most horrible and unnatural form of inquisition, any woman who may, or may not be, an immoral person".[13] Although Butler's fears were exaggerated, she was not alone. Some 16 years later, another commentator was to lament that the growth of the police in both numbers and power was becoming a serious threat for any people that wished to remain free and independent, producing a system with deep rooted "briberies, tyrannies, [and] iniquities".[14]

The Victorian Metropolitan Police inevitably developed their own equivalent of the much vaunted (by modern sociologists) 'canteen culture'. Indeed, the lawyer William Ballantine analysed it a century before it became a commonplace of police studies. He observed that whenever men were: "…associated in a common object, an esprit de corps naturally arises, and this not infrequently colours the testimony of individual members".[15] It also affected their understanding of what was 'acceptable' in any given situation. In 1838, for example, the judge John Adams observed that although those in official communication with the police 'establishment' would bear testimony to the "excellent conduct" of its superintendents and other senior officers, they were much less sanguine about ordinary constables and any plans to extend their legal powers. Even ignoring potential "partiality, ill-will, or prejudice", something which, Adams felt, their social provenance made impossible, there were other problems with the large and (at that time) very transitory number of ordinary police officers. In particular, how could society guard against their ignorance, over-zealousness, or inexperience? Like Ballantine, he appreciated that the abuse of police powers for oppressive purposes would bear particularly heavily on the lower classes, to whom the expense and difficulty of procuring bail was especially great.[16] Abuse of police power could manifest itself in brutality, corruption, perjury and the fabrication of evidence.

---

13. Butler, Josephine, 1880, at p.48.
14. Carpenter, E., 1896, at p.147.
15. Ballantine, William, 1890, at p.227 & p.236.
16. Adams, John, 1838, at pp.19-20.

Perjury

It was frequently alleged that police officers lied on oath. According to John Sheen, found guilty at the Old Bailey in 1872 of a counterfeiting offence, all they cared about was securing a conviction: "Colonel Henderson has the police to back him, and supplies them with funds to commit perjury. A man cannot come here and get justice".[17] Of course, this is the eternal cry of those who receive guilty verdicts. Nevertheless, many independent observers also felt that police perjury was a regular phenomenon in the capital, and it even entered popular consciousness, *Punch* noting that a constable normally had a: "...vivid recollection of what another Policeman remembers, and if the testimony of an Inspector is impugned, he shows a great love for his cloth by swearing (as the saying is) "till all is blue.""[18]

Such perjury came in two forms. Sometimes, it was done to cover up other forms of police misconduct. For example, in 1854, Sergeant Henry Amor from A (Whitehall) Division was convicted of perjury and sentenced to 18 months imprisonment. He had been in Hyde Park in plainclothes, and the worse for drink, when he was abusive to a married couple. When they called on a nearby uniformed policeman to intervene, he claimed to have seen them committing an act of gross indecency (sexual intercourse) against park railings. Fortunately, their respectability combined with the honesty of the uniformed constable led to the case against them being dismissed and Amor prosecuted.[19] Similarly, in 1886, four constables and an Inspector, who made malicious allegations against a husband and wife after they complained about another officer for gratuitously slapping their niece, had their prosecution of the couple for being drunk and disorderly thrown out of the Wandsworth Police Court. Even more significantly, the sitting magistrate, Montagu Williams, ordered an enquiry and noted that they had grossly abused their positions. He was convinced that their evidence was "false from beginning to end".[20]

However, more commonly, and perhaps more insidiously, many officers lied to support the prosecutions of people they genuinely thought were guilty. This is sometimes called 'noble cause' perjury in the modern era. Some contemporary observers feared that once policemen charged a man they assumed he must have committed the relevant offence, and

---

17. OBSP, Trial of Rowland Lee et al, 8th April 1872, t18720408-376.
18. 'The Model Policeman', *Punch,* June 17th, 1848.
19. OBSP, Trial of Henry Amor, 2nd January 1854, t18540102-201.
20. 'The Metropolitan Police', *Launceston Examiner,* 26th May 1888, p.6.

would thirst for a conviction, even if it meant stretching the truth.[21] Indeed, it was sometimes claimed that they assumed the guilt of anyone they even suspected, and so were willing to lie in court to secure the 'correct' verdict.[22]

Many London magistrates were concerned that particular officers appeared far too frequently before them as the sole prosecution witness in summary cases, but still felt bound to convict on their evidence rather than publicly stigmatise the men concerned as perjurers. More generally, most such prosecutions were not supported by independent (of the police) testimony. One magistrate estimated that half of all summary cases, and two thirds of those arising out of nocturnal incidents, depended entirely on uncorroborated police evidence. In these circumstances, he felt that the: "...utmost care is required to see that such evidence is not tainted by exaggeration or undue colouring".[23] Some observers also feared that stipendiary magistrates felt bound to commit indictable matters for trial at Quarter Sessions or the Old Bailey, if a policeman had sworn to a charge, without properly scrutinising the merits of the case.[24]

Even then, it was appreciated that the willingness of Metropolitan police officers to bolster each other's evidence, regardless of the truth, was supported by their excellent "esprit de corps".[25] As Ballantine observed, police duties were extremely trying and: "...calculated frequently to cause anger and irritation, feelings which almost invariably induce those possessed by them to exaggerate if not to invent".[26] Similarly, an Edwardian observer, noting the "faulty" conscience that often prevailed in the Metropolitan force, so that it was not possible to feel sure that a constable's sworn evidence was entirely true, attributed it to the "natural outcome of solidarity".[27] Regular appearances in court also meant that the importance that was once attached to an oath often became deadened, while an extremely persuasive "easy manner and composed demeanour" was acquired by officers who were used to the witness box, making unwarranted convictions more likely.[28]

As the extract from *Punch* suggests, many thought that whenever policemen needed witnesses to support their prosecutions, or their own

21. Guest, A., 1891, at p.87.
22. *The Law Journal*, Vol. 8, 1873, at p.659.
23. Anon, 1882, *Metropolitan Police Court Jottings*, at p.52.
24. Smethhurst, James, 1841, at pp.1-28.
25. Guest, A., 1891, at p.87.
26. Ballantine, William, 1890, at p.227 & p.236.
27. Gamon, Hugh, 1907, at p.14.
28. Ballantine, William, 1890, at p.227 & p.236.

defences if they were summonsed by a member of the public, colleagues would readily come forward to testify, whether they had been present at an incident or not. Thus, when P.C. Joseph White, a man with 11 years in the force, was accused of assaulting a respectable married woman on a cross-summons (he appears to have assumed she was a prostitute), he called a P.C. Jackson to support his version of events. The magistrate who convicted White was convinced that: "Jackson's evidence was wilfully false, and had been fabricated for the nefarious purpose of bolstering up the case of the defendant".[29] These problems were often exacerbated by the social status of the policed. As Ballantine astutely observed, the: "...classes against whom they appear are usually without the position that commands consultation, and consequently statements made to their prejudice meet with the more ready belief".[30]

One particularly notorious illustration of police perjury, from the late 1870s, involved a 'cabbie' named Edward Harris who had fallen off his vehicle into the road. As he got up, in a concussed and unsteady condition, he was arrested by a policeman who charged him with being drunk in a public place, then hid his earlier fall from the local Police Court magistrate. Harris was sent to prison for a month. When his injuries came to light, he was released and went home to die from their effects. The Home Secretary, Richard Cross, accepted that the constable was to blame, and asked the Inspector of Police to deal with the matter in private.[31] There were numerous less publicised cases. In 1857, for example, P.C. Albert Dawkins was reported by a Magistrate for illegally arresting a woman at her own house, on a charge of assault. After giving his explanation as to what had occurred to the Commissioners, he was: "...cautioned to be particular both in not overstepping his duty, and in giving clear evidence before a magistrate". The duty Sergeant involved, Alfred Lindsey, who had improperly entered the charge sheet supporting his subordinate, and thus illegally detaining her, was formally reprimanded.[32]

Nevertheless, it was relatively unusual for such misconduct to produce seriously adverse consequences for the officers concerned. This prompted a law journal to insist that the only way to stop the "system of police perjury" was to prosecute all such cases vigorously.[33] However, on the rare occasions when prosecutions were brought, convictions were unusual. All four indictments of Metropolitan policemen for perjury or making false

---

29. *The Law Journal*, Vol. 8, 1873, at p.700.
30. Ballantine, William, 1890, at p.227.
31. Butler, Josephine, 1880, at p.46.
32. MEPOL 17/9, 1857.
33. *The Law Journal*, Vol. 8, 1873, at p.701.

statements in the years from 1849 to 1852 resulted in acquittals, and the officers being retained in the service.[34]

In many cases, no action at all was taken. Indeed, it was often not exposed, even by defendants. One (alleged) victim spoke of the disorientating effect of being in custody and the pressures that could be brought to bear on those detained, even when they were publicly lied about in their own presence: "I was told not to say anything, by some one outside, I don't know his name—we were pushed into the police-court by the constable".[35]

Police Brutality

Police brutality and 'robust' policing were different sides of the same coin. Even in the Edwardian period, it was still thought that the presence of 'rough' areas made it essential that Metropolitan officers should be "big, strong men" who could fight with their fists when necessary.[36] It was often the first question asked of new officers on their arrival at a police station. James Bent, a career officer in Victorian Manchester, freely admitted that he was "too timid to be a policeman" when first appointed. However, he toughened up quickly and became an intrepid officer who would not tolerate "cowardice" in others.[37] A considerable degree of police violence was a constant feature of Victorian London, especially in poorer areas.[38] It became 'brutality' when it was resorted to gratuitously, excessively, or inappropriately. However, according to *The Law Journal*, by 1873, most police violence was unwarranted, and not a response to that from suspects.[39]

Such cases were present from the outset. Thus, in 1829, a mentally disturbed and elderly man in Pimlico, wrongly suspected of being drunk, was arrested and roughly handled by officers, greatly aggravating his psychological condition. A magistrate subsequently discharged him.[40] The following year, in a letter to *The Times*, John Pacey, an apparently 'respectable' individual, claimed that, without giving the slightest provocation, he had had his head "broken" by some police constables when he was on the way home with a friend, at an early hour of the

---

34. pp.13.b.1853, at pp.1-4.
35.Eisner, Manuel, 2003, pp.130-132.
36. Gamon, Hugh, 1907, at p.11.
37. Bent, James, 1891, at p.180.
38. Emsley, Clive, 1985 at pp.126-142.
39. Quoted in Evans, Alan, 1988, at p.15.
40. *The Times*, October 6th, 1829.

evening. He made a complaint to the Commissioners, and was shocked to find that it was summarily dismissed and that one of the constables involved in the incident was later promoted to Inspector.[41] In 1834, according to an East End hatter, many local officers, recruited from the lower type of newly arrived Irishmen, would: "...run out and strike every person they meet".[42] Similarly, and perhaps with rather less risk of bias and exaggeration, William Ballantine's father, a Thames Police Court magistrate, believed that the new police frequently exhibited "unnecessary harshness", when compared to the earlier Bow Street patrols, whom he admired.[43]

This does not appear to have been purely a problem of the heady post-foundation years. A decade after its inception, during Chartist disturbances in Birmingham, a bricklayer, going home one evening was ordered to "move on" by Metropolitan constables drafted into the Midlands city. Perhaps unused to such a request (already routine in London), he responded cheekily, at which point he was struck by the officers: "...knocking out six of his teeth, and felling him to the ground".[44] Such incidents continued to the end of the century. In 1888, for example, Jeremiah O'Leary complained that he had been "cruelly used" by officers who arrested him in Hammersmith for being drunk and disorderly, and showed the cuts and bruises on his back to the court, to support his account.[45] In these situations, as even a police court magistrate noted, the arresting officer would normally say that any injury came from falling to the floor while resisting arrest, and would "call one or two brother constables" to support his account.[46] This was often enough. In 1851, a journal, recording the apparently abortive investigation into the death of an "inoffensive" young labourer, who appeared to have expired as a result of blows from a police truncheon during a street altrcation, noted that if the victim had been a substantial tradesman or a gentleman the case would have been thoroughly examined. However: "...where a poor man is the

---

41. Letter to *The Times*, 13th November, 1830.

42. Quoted in Thurmond Smith, Philip, 1985, at p.54. Unless there was something special to his local constabulary, he appears to have been exaggerating the national provenance of most officers.

43. Ballantine, William, 1890, at p.51.

44. *Hansard's Parliamentary Debates*, Vol. L, 3rd. Series, 7 August-27 August, 1839, at p.362.

45. *Illustrated Police News,* September 22nd, 1888. It was not disputed that he had been "frog marched" to the police station as he had previous convictions for assaulting constables.

46. Anon, 1882, *Metropolitan Police Court Jottings*, at p.49.

sufferer, and a police-officer the offender, there is little hope of justice reaching the latter".[47]

Some officers were quite open about their recourse to the summary 'chastisement' of suspects, rather than risk seeing justice defeated by 'red tape' and legal niceties. Thus, an article in the *Westminster Review* in 1874 recounted how a constable punched a thief to the ground after he had (earlier) beaten up a fellow officer. His attitude was that although the thief would go before a magistrate and get off scot-free, he would not escape without getting some of his deserts. Others freely declared that it was necessary to neutralise potentially dangerous targets in the streets by use of a pre-emptive strike.[48]

Many felt that lower level police brutality in the London area, with suspects being dragged to police stations and abused once in custody, often led to them being "excessively unpopular" with the general public.[49] Some marginal social elements, such as the young, female, and homeless, were especially vulnerable to physically abusive policing, however motivated. For example, in 1844, a constable accosted a 16-year-old girl, who slept in a Spitalfields' privy at night. He allegedly "exposed his person" and tried to touch her, until neighbours intervened.[50] Almost 40 years later, it was claimed, on apparently strong evidence, that an Inspector from Y Division had assaulted a 19-year-old female pauper who was being held at Edmonton Police Station.[51]

Of course, a balanced assessment of levels of Metropolitan police brutality can only be made by contrasting it with its 'rivals', whether continental, colonial or American. Generally speaking, it fares well in such comparisons, albeit that the standard (the low-countries and Scandinavia sometimes excepted) is not usually a very demanding one. Certainly, there was a marked difference between the Metropolitan Police 'model' and the almost paramilitary pattern established for some colonial forces and (often) Ireland, where many thought that too much of the R.I.C.'s time was: "…taken up with military drill, and with matters wholly unconnected with the prevention of crime".[52] Abroad, the Berlin *Schutzmannschaft* was proverbial for its rudeness and use of violence towards the public, and

---

47. 'Police Brutality', *Reynolds's Newspaper*, July 13th, 1851. 'Police Murders Committed With Impunity', *Reynolds's Newspaper*, July 20th, 1851.
48. Emsley, Clive, 1985, at p.131.
49. *The Law Journal*, Vol. 8, 1873, at p.659.
50. Mepol 4/6 'Complaints Against Police', May 14th 1844.
51. *Western Mail,* January 26th, 1883.
52. HANSARD 1803-2005, HL Deb 31 March 1870 vol 200 cc970-82, c970.

compared unfavourably by German newspapers and reformers in the 1880s with the 'typical' English Bobby.[53]

The New York police establishment provides an especially striking contrast. The more democratic nature of American society meant that New Yorkers rejected many of the 'authoritarian' features of the Metropolitan Police as being inimical to their own nation's values of independence. Perhaps as a result, in the late 1850s, a variety of observers, including the New York City Mayor, thought that its policemen were less disciplined than those found in London. Ironically, their very lack of institutional power also resulted in a lack of institutional restraints, so that they ended up with more *de facto* power than their Metropolitan counterparts. The London policeman was well aware that he was a representative of the 'authorities', not a deputy for his fellow citizens, in a city that was not remotely democratic prior to 1884. New York policemen saw themselves as acting for all citizens apart from the latest waves of poor immigrants. As a result, their use of force appears to have been much less restrained and monitored. When New York's locally controlled municipal force was taken over by the State Government, in 1857, a virtual arms race with local criminals ensued, revolvers becoming standard issue for officers. These appear to have been freely, often recklessly, used, so that the *New York Times* could assert that a patrolling officer was an: "...absolute monarch, within his beat, with complete power of life and death over all within his range".[54] The New York police of the later nineteenth century were characterised by endemic brutality, and the regular, almost routine, beating up of detained suspects drawn from amongst the city's 'criminal class'.[55]

By contrast, the only police weapon routinely carried in London, the short truncheon -initially 20 inches but reduced to 17 inches in 1856- was concealed in a pocket until 1863, after which it was carried in a case. (Wrought-iron handcuffs, known as "D" Cuffs because of their shape, were also sometimes carried). Officers were often reluctant even to use truncheons in a mêlée, when their fists would suffice.[56] Some observers felt that this was because they feared being accused of assault.[57] Their use could also aggravate a confrontation. In 1841, P.C. James Carroll was killed with his own truncheon while making an arrest in Church Street, Bethnal Green.[58]

---

53. Johansen, Anja, 2011, at pp.60-61.
54. Miller, Wilbur, 1975, at p.84.
55. Sante, Luc, 1998, at pp.236-250.
56. Greenwood, James, 1902, at p.7.
57. Watts, W.H., 1864, at pp.221.
58. *The Examiner*, October 9th, 1841.

Furthermore, 'aggressive' police behaviour in the London area seems to have declined, rather than increased, after the early post-1829 years, and it has been suggested (perhaps with some exaggeration) that the image of the restrained, imperturbable British 'bobby' was formed in the course of a wholesale retreat from an initial and aggressively pursued authoritarian stance.[59]

As some of the accounts cited above suggest, many observers thought the police were most dangerous when alone on the streets, or in twos and threes, rather than when serving in large, quasi-military, formations.[60] Nevertheless, it was abuses associated with public order policing that gained most publicity.

Public Order Brutality

The Metropolitan police slowly developed a tradition (or at least a reputation) for "containing" industrial disputes and political demonstrations with minimum force, at least when compared to many other western countries.[61] *The Times* felt that Britain was nearly unique in the leniency with which its police treated organised resistance to the executive by political demonstrators. A very different situation allegedly prevailed in France and Spain, where bullets and bayonets were "regularly" used to control politically motivated riots.[62]

However, in reality, problems were manifest from the start of the new force, even if they were markedly less serious than those often found on the Continent. For example, although, as the Parliamentary report into the Coldbath Fields riot of 1833 accepted, the evidence of what had occurred that day was conflicting, the overwhelming majority of the civilian testimony heard by the investigating committee suggested a serious police over-reaction, and their indulgence in wanton violence. Senior officers appear to have lost control of their men in the mêlée. According to one eyewitness, their "ferocious conduct" was motivated by a wanton desire to injure, so that they had pursued and struck down fleeing people. The official report, although something of a 'whitewash', tacitly accepted that serious mistakes had been made, and that the police were not subjected to the type of effective control that, in a: "...moment of excitement and irritation, and after much provocation, could alone prevent individual instances of undue exercise of power". Nevertheless, as the report also

---

59. See for example, Paley, Ruth, 1989, at p.122.
60. *The Law Journal*, Vol. 8, 1873, at p.659.
61. Reiner, Robert, 1992, at p.65.
62. Leading Article, *The Times,* September 15th, 1888, at p.9.

noted, P.C. Culley had been stabbed to death, and two other officers seriously wounded, while no members of the public appeared to have sustained life-threatening injuries.[63]

This 'robustness' in dealing with crowds was manifest in many other incidents. Outside London, in their early decades, the Metropolitan Police were frequently deployed to provincial cities to deal with disturbances, especially those involving Chartists. In 1839, Earl Stanhope alleged in Parliament that a very reliable witness to an incident that occurred in Birmingham on the 4th July, claimed that the Metropolitan force had made a "most wanton and unjustifiable" attack on demonstrators, breaking heads with their truncheons. According to this witness, two of the officers involved had subsequently admitted to being ashamed of what had happened.[64]

Such allegations, and the official response to them, were to become the pattern for subsequent police/public disturbances. Thus, the Hyde Park Sunday Trading riots of 1855 produced accusations and petitions from, *inter alia*, the inhabitants of Grosvenor Square, Mount and Park Streets, who expressed their "horror and disgust at the brutal and violent conduct of the police". It was alleged that constables had struck several women and children. The Report of the Commissioners into the incident also produced a number of apparently reputable witnesses willing to swear that officers were "quite out of temper" and indiscriminate in the beatings they administered (far more so than the Life Guards who provided them with military support). Against this, and as with the 1833 disturbances, there was no evidence of loss of life, or even serious injury, amongst the demonstrators, which led the Commissioners to believe that there had been some exaggeration of police misconduct. Nevertheless, with that qualification, they concluded that Superintendent Hughes, the officer commanding at the scene, had personally had recourse to unwarranted violence, allegedly using a horsewhip on the demonstrators. Their report also stated that he had issued orders that were likely to lead to dangerous and unnecessary confrontations.[65]

However, there had been almost twenty years of relative peace from serious public disorder when Mayne died in office in 1868. This may have

---

63. pp.11.b.1833, at pp.3-4, p.10 & pp.72-73. Eye-witness evidence of William Carpenter.

64. *Hansard's Parliamentary Debates*, Vol.L, 3rd. Series, 7 August-27 August 1839, at p.362.

65. See *Hansards Parliamentary Debates*, 3rd. Series, 139, 1855, cols. 453-4, and Parliamentary Papers, 1856 (2016) xxiii, pp.ix, xi. See also minutes of evidence, reproduced in Taylor, David, 1997, at pp.166-168.

given his successor as Commissioner, Colonel Edmund Henderson, an excessive sense of security. (Lieutenant Colonel Douglas Labalmondiere was acting Commissioner for three months before his appointment). This was punctured by the violence that took place on February 18th 1886 in Trafalgar Square, following a Social Democratic meeting. A crowd stoned clubs and shops in the West End, reviving fears of the 'mob'. The police in the capital had been wrong-footed and badly organized to deal with such a disturbance, something that led to criticism from an investigating parliamentary committee.[66] It also led to Henderson's swift censure, resignation and replacement by Sir Charles Warren, who had been summoned from Egypt.

Mindful of the fate of his predecessor, Warren decided to move vigorously against fresh crowds in Trafalgar Square in October and November 1887, using the foot-guards and mounted lifeguards as well as policemen to do so. *The Times* had warned that the demonstrators, many of whom were drawn from the large number of destitute and unemployed men produced by the recession of the mid-eighties, would need to be dealt with firmly. It felt that Sir Charles Warren's decisive action had defeated an attempt to: "...terrorize London by placing the control of the streets in the hands of the criminal classes". Even so, the paper was alarmed at the results of his action. Events on the 13th November 1887 left some 200 civilians needing hospital treatment for their injuries, after the police, both mounted and on foot: "...charged in among the people, striking indiscriminately in all directions".[67] Even some police officers concurred with this description, and took a much less sanguine view of the case than Warren. One felt that there had been a clear over-reaction, especially by mounted officers. Clearing Trafalgar Square had damaged police and public relations, so that the apparently: "...friendly feeling that had previously existed between the great majority of the poorer section of the public and the police received a rebuff".[68]

Significantly, however, public concern about these incidents, combined with Warren's failure to catch Jack the Ripper and (most importantly) his publishing of an uncleared (by the Home Secretary) article on London policing in *Murray's Magazine,* in October 1888, forced his resignation. In his article, Warren had deplored government weakness in the face of a small but "noisy" section of the public.[69] Already an unpopular Commissioner, when the Home Secretary, Sir Henry Mathews, informed

---

66. Pellew, Jill, 1982, at p.45.
67. Vogler, Richard, 1991, at p.60.
68. Anon, 1888, *The Metropolitan Police and its Management,* at pp. 1-6.
69. Emsley, Clive, 1991, at p.64.

the House of Commons of his resignation, the announcement was greeted with cheers.[70] Despite his departure, problems with public disturbances continued to the end of the century and into the Edwardian period. Metropolitan officers were regularly accused of carrying their wet weather capes rolled loose on their arms as improvised weapons in such situations, and striking out with them too freely.[71]

Concern About Brutality

Police brutality was certainly not sanctioned by higher ranks. Where proved, the consequences were severe for individual officers. For example, P.C. William Kinsman was dismissed from the force for gratuitously truncheoning a spectator at the Coronation in 1830; his victim was also paid 40s. in compensation.[72] Additionally, brutality did not go totally unchallenged by the judiciary, despite their general support for the police. Thus, in 1833, a P.C. Angus was censured and reported by a stipendiary magistrate, who threw out his prosecution of a youth for lewd behaviour. He was subsequently required to leave the police by the Commissioners. Angus had climbed up a tree in Hyde Park, in pursuit of a boy who had exposed himself in public and used indecent words towards some women. The irritated policeman had then struck the boy across the shoulders with a branch.[73] Similarly, one of the 13 P.C.s dismissed in a single week in January 1840 was thrown out after he was: "Complained of by a magistrate for using abusive language to a prisoner".[74] In 1868, it was claimed that some Police Court magistrates were inclined to publicly blame the police for showing "indiscretion" and as a result did not award sufficient punishment for assaults on officers.[75] Such attitudes were manifest in 1886, when the Whitechapel-based P.C. Fooks spoke to Alfred Buckley in a "very cross manner" and hit him twice on the head with his truncheon. When Buckley was prosecuted for disorderly conduct and assault the case was dismissed. However, when he cross-issued a summons against Fooks, the officer was himself convicted by the magistrate. Fooks was sentenced to 14 days' hard labour, something that would necessarily lead to dismissal from the force. Passing sentence, the magistrate observed that: "…constables were often too ready to use their

---

70. *New York Times,* November 13, 1888, 'Sir Charles Warren Resigns'.
71. Jones, Chester, 1912, at p.4.
72. *Poor Man's Guardian,* 24th September, 1831.
73. Thurston, Gavin, 1967, at pp.177-176.
74. HO 61/25, 1840, List of Dismissed P.C.s, 20th-26th January 1840.
75. pp.14.1868, at p.10, note (a).

truncheons".[76] Twenty years later, one P.C. Redman beat another East Ender that he had arrested for assaulting him so severely that the magistrate trying the case dismissed it with the comment: "If you do this to defendants I will not convict".[77]

Despite such cases, magistrates normally supported the police. In 1875, of the 6,988 people taken into custody for assault (i.e. against other civilians), 2,939 were discharged without even being held to bail. By contrast, of the 2,633 detained for assaulting the police, only 44 were totally discharged.[78]

Along with occasional judicial criticism, some more organized public resistance to the existence and abuse of police powers also developed. The short-lived 'Law and Liberty League' was formed in November 1887, under the auspices of the radical socialist, Annie Besant, and with the assistance of the journalist William Thomas Stead. It was aimed at meeting fairly widespread concern about what the *Pall Mall Gazette* called a 'policocracy'. It survived until 1889, and vigorously attacked the Metropolitan force for, *inter alia*, blackmailing prostitutes and mistreating those in police custody. The following decade, the Newcross tailor James Timewell who, with his daughter, had witnessed four officers in Southwark 'frog-marching' a detained man to their station in 1897, was to launch an unsuccessful private prosecution of the officers concerned, and to author numerous tracts against the extent and abuse of police powers.[79] In 1902 he founded the 'Police and Public Vigilance Committee' to combat such abuses.[80]

Nevertheless, the practical risks associated with an excessively robust policing of the bottom quarter of the community were just as important as organized and judicial challenges when it came to moderating police conduct. As Leeson noted, it could be counter-productive, leading to a lack of public co-operation or, even worse, a dangerously violent response by the policed.

Corruption

Police corruption was another perennial problem for the uniformed force, albeit that most of it was quite low level and unsophisticated. As

---

76. *East End News*, November 2nd, 1886.
77. Harding, C., and Wilson, L., 1988, at p.199.
78. PR.11.1875, Table No.6, at p.16.
79. 'The Charge Against Police-Constables', *The Standard,* November 10th, 1897, p.2.
80. Petrow, Stefan, 1994, at p.24.

with brutality and perjury, it often arose directly from their new powers and responsibilities. Again, it is necessary to put this phenomenon into perspective. Throughout the century, the New York police was riddled with corruption at the very highest level, with graft and racketeering on a massive scale, and even the effective sale of police promotion, because of the potential remuneration available from abuse of such positions.[81] For example, according to the notorious forger Austin Bidwell, to be police captain of the Tenderloin precinct meant an extra weekly income (above their pay) of at least $1,000. An equal amount went to Police Headquarters, to be divided between the Chief of Police and other senior officers.[82]

By comparison, Metropolitan policemen were usually a model of probity and restraint. Josiah Flynt, an American who spent eight weeks studying the Metropolitan police at the start of the twentieth century, was struck by the standard of general honesty when compared to urban forces in the United States, and concluded that it was mainly composed of "honest and conscientious men". There was very little corruption, and he could not find any that could be compared to the: "...blackmailing system for which the New York Police have so long been notorious".[83]

Nevertheless, there were still major problems in the London force, if not on an American scale. Despite James Grant's admiring 'surprise' at how few Metropolitan officers had been accused, let alone convicted, of corruption in the first decade of the force, this was probably a reflection of how difficult it was to bring and prove such cases rather than of incidence.[84] The dangers of corruption, along with abuse of position and the 'rubber stamping' of low-level police decisions by senior officers were apparent from the start. Soon after the new force was established, constables were prosecuted for taking bribes in exchange for suppressing warrants that had been issued against those who kept disorderly houses.[85] More seriously, in 1839, P.C. Charles Thresher accosted James Smethurst in the Borough Road and asked him to retire to a more secluded place to discuss a 'delicate' matter. He refused, and was then arrested and taken to a section house, where a shabbily dressed boy and the constable accused him of indecent assault. Smethurst thought the original motivation for this fraudulent claim was blackmail, but that the examining Inspector was "bound to believe the charge". Fortunately, he discovered that Thresher

---

81. Sante, Luc, 1998, at pp.236-250.
82. Bidwell, Austin, 1897, at p.29.
83. Flynt, Josiah, 1903, at pp.447-448.
84. Grant, James, 1838, at p.392.
85. Ballantine, William, 1890, at p.233.

had stolen from an earlier employer, and was acquitted. Smethurst eventually managed to ensure that his accusers were tried for conspiracy.[86]

James Greenwood was also well aware of bribery and abuse of position. He felt that the extensive powers conferred on the police by the Habitual Criminals Act (see above) were excessive for this reason, not being justified: "…by one's experience of the intelligence and integrity of the 'force', satisfactory on the whole as it may be".[87] In 1866, J.M. Ludlow, writing in the *Spectator*, felt that police blackmail of omnibus drivers, prostitutes and publicans was: "…so frequent as to be taken as a matter of course by the victims".[88] Although constables would often go through the motions of proffering money for beer or rides, it was customary in many areas for bus conductors and barmen alike to "wave aside the proffered copper".[89] Many publicans also routinely provided free alcohol to beat officers while they were on duty. P.C. Cavanagh remembered that a colleague, patrolling the Borough during the 1850s, appeared to be a "walking beer barrel" by the end of each night's duty.[90] This was usually done quite discreetly, especially during the day. In the same area of south London, and at about the same time (1859), youths sheltering from the rain watched a constable carefully place his back close to a tavern door, at which a hand slid forth holding a flask, parted his coat-tails, and withdrew without the vessel. The officer then resumed his beat.[91] At night, alcohol might be left on pub windowsills for passing officers, to be consumed outside the premises. Publicans could normally expect some reward for such largesse.[92] For example, breaches of the licensing hours might be overlooked. To combat the problems caused by constables accepting the "perilous gift" of a drink, some police stations in the 1870s considered bringing out coffee and bread to their night patrols.

More seriously, in the late Victorian period, Thomas Holmes (a Police Court 'missionary') regularly witnessed arrangements whereby officers reduced the apparent gravity of a defendant's involvement in a crime, when giving evidence in the summary courts, in exchange for drink.[93] This had been a problem from the very start of the new force. The first Commissioners regularly denounced the practice and, in 1831, required

---

86. Smethhurst, James, 1841, at pp.1-28.
87. Greenwood, James, 1869, at p.193.
88. Smith, Philip Fermond, 1985, at p.54.
89. Rook, Clarence, 1899, at p.255.
90. Cavanagh, Timothy, 1893, at p.24.
91. Bennett, Alfred Rosling, 1924, at p.36.
92. Rook, Clarence, 1899, at p.255.
93. Holmes, Thomas, 1908, at p.4.

senior officers to make unannounced visits to public houses near where courts were sitting to see if any constables were drinking with defendants. Any officer caught doing so was to be deemed "wholly unfit for his situation".[94] Even so, there were cases throughout the century, such as that of P.C. Robert Davies who was dismissed from the force in 1850, after being found drinking with the friends of a defendant in the Rose Public House, near the Old Bailey, during Sessions.[95]

The growing involvement of the police in regulatory matters and the control of vice, pursuant to a variety of directives and statutes, furnished many other opportunities for corruption. For example, during the 1870s, the police were bribed to overlook unlicensed dancing in the Piccadilly Saloon in Haymarket. When they carried out their nightly visit to the establishment, they would knock and wait for three minutes before entering the premises, allowing musicians and alcohol to be hidden and replaced with coffee.[96] Indeed, according to Sir Henry Smith, the whole of C Division was "corrupt to the very core", with many officers receiving bribes from the Haymarket sex industry.[97]

As this suggests, a particularly high proportion of corruption allegations involved the receipt of bribes from prostitutes, whether in cash or 'services in kind'. Thus, in 1834, Richard Swift, a Whitechapel leather-seller, claimed to have seen streetwalkers bribing local officers not to interfere with their work. Perhaps significantly, Swift had not complained about this for fear of the personal consequences, and because his "word would go for nothing" against that of a constable.[98] The 1885 Criminal Law Amendment Act may even have increased such corruption by encouraging interaction between officers and street women.

This type of corruption could become endemic in a Division or area. In July 1887, William Sproston Caine, an M.P., supported by elements of the press, alleged that the police were engaged in the systematic blackmailing of Clapham prostitutes. As a result, there was an inquiry into the local W Division, conducted by Assistant Commissioner James Monro. However, in January 1888, the Home Secretary, Sir Henry Mathews, concluded, in the light of its submissions, that "no evidence has been forthcoming against the police".[99] This apparent 'whitewash' was not accepted by Caine or much of the popular press. *Punch* produced a cartoon, the following

---

94. MEPO 7(2) Police Orders 1829-1833, 22nd April, 1831.
95. MEPO 7(15) Police Orders 1850-52, 23rd December, 1850.
96. Williams, Montagu, 1890, at p.262.
97. White, Jerry, 2008, at p.403.
98. pp.11.d.1834, at p.322.
99. *The Times,* January 6th and February 6th, 1888, at p.7.

month, showing the Home Secretary watching: "Warren's whitening of constables".[100]

To an extent, cases of low-level corruption were not surprising, given the level of officers' salaries, their responsibilities, the boredom inherent in much of their work, and their intimate contact with the streets. Although policemen's pay was "scarcely sufficient for subsistence" they were regularly exposed to the society and bribes of prostitutes when on night duty.[101] As one family-minded constable noted in 1868, how could officers be expected to be: "...honest, independent and scorning bribes-when they are hungry themselves and when the missus and young 'uns are going without".[102] Caine claimed that a Detective Inspector investigating his allegations had freely admitted to him that the temptations for constables operating in areas frequented by prostitutes were almost irresistible, and that it was exceptionally difficult to obtain evidence against corrupt officers from witnesses (prostitutes) whose daily bread depended on the "forbearance of the police" and who could be sent to jail by them.[103]

Clapham was not unique. In the Quadrant, near Regent's Street, similar charges were made against local officers during the 1870s. The streets allegedly became almost impassable for 'decent' people as prostitutes bribed the police to turn a blind eye to their activities. Street women taped money to windowsills, to be picked up later by patrolling officers. Those who refused to pay were arrested and charged, often with unfounded offences. Fortunately, the local police court magistrate began to have grave suspicions about the motives behind many police accusations against streetwalkers. Eventually, it became necessary to transfer large numbers of officers to other Divisions to remedy the situation.[104]

Sometimes, such low-level corruption could extend to quite senior men. 'Walter', the notorious but anonymous Victorian philanderer and pornographer, noticed that one Haymarket prostitute that he regularly visited never got into "police rows", even on nights when dozens of her colleagues were arrested. He asked her about this, and she admitted sleeping with a married Inspector, who would arrive at her premises in plain-clothes.[105]

It was not just prostitution. Other regulatory offences, such as licensing, also provided fertile opportunities for corruption. The police

---

100. *Punch,* February 18th, 1888.
101. Robinson, David, 1831, at p.84.
102. 'Hard Times for Policemen', *Daily News*, October 31st, 1872.
103. *The Times*, February 8th, 1888, p.6.
104. Ballantine, William, 1890, at p.230.
105. 'Walter', 1996, Vol. IV, at p.1683.

power to allocate spaces to costermongers and stall holders in street markets like Petticoat Lane was especially prone to abuse, with regular allegations of bribery to secure favourable locations.[106] Similarly, after the advent of the 1853 Lotteries and Betting Act there were frequent claims that officers took bribes to turn a 'blind eye' to street bookies.

Even worse, corruption could extend to dealings with conventional criminals about serious offences. In the 1870s, for example, an educated prisoner was driven to conclude, after conversations with fellow inmates, that many police officers: "...levy blackmail from thieves, and the number of things that are 'squared' between thieves and police would astonish the British public".[107]

Nevertheless, care must be taken when generalising from the experiences of publicans, stallholders, and prostitutes. Most working people were too poor to afford bribery and had equally little use for it. The financial scale, if not the extent, of police corruption also appears to have been relatively small. Arthur Harding, a prominent Edwardian East End criminal, and certainly no admirer of the police, recalled widespread low level bribery but was firmly of the opinion, when interviewed in the early 1970s, that it: "...wasn't done on the scale it's done today, £20 was a lot of money to give". He also accepted that it was not universal, even among his detective foes in the C.I.D. Cultures of corruption appear to have been localised, sometimes to specific police stations.[108] Throughout the period, on the rare occasions that such matters were proved, dismissal was also the inevitable result, as with P.C. Samuel Munstall, who was fired in 1839 for: "...indecent conduct with a prostitute when on duty".[109]

Occasionally, of course, transgressing police officers would make a 'mistake' in their choice of victims, especially if they strayed outside the underclass. While going to parliament in June 1834, an M.P., H.C. Bulmer, was angered by the "abrupt and rude behaviour" and flagrant misconduct of constables policing the environs of Westminster Abbey. An investigation swiftly ensued.[110] When the lawyer William Ballantine attempted to advise an officer who was being excessively rough with a drunken woman in Piccadilly he was arrested for 'obstructing' the constable. Fortunately, if bizarrely, the Attorney General happened to be passing, and intervened after being informed by other officers that Ballantine was "well known to the police"! The detained woman was

---

106. Gamon, Hugh, 1907, at p.14.
107. Anon., *Five Years' Penal Servitude*, 1877, at p.271.
108. Harding, C., & Wilson, L., 1988, at p.200 & pp.204-205.
109. HO 61/25, 1840, List of dismissed constables 23-29 December 1839.
110. pp.11.e.1834, at pp.1-4.

allowed to escape, to avoid the embarrassment of a court hearing. Ballantine sent an account of the incident, with the numbers of the officers involved, to Richard Mayne, getting a standard reply from a subordinate officer treating his letter "with great coolness". (He received a fuller answer later).[111] Another *cause célèbre* ensued when five military officers, including a Colonel, from the Lifeguards, were arrested at the Argyle (entertainment) Rooms by a group of police officers who alleged that the soldiers were drunk and had assaulted them. The Police Court magistrate swiftly dismissed the charges, and observed that the police had been the aggressors, had fabricated evidence and perjured themselves.[112] However, in an era when clothes and accents provided an immediate indicator of class, the risks of making such mistakes were readily apparent to most constables, keeping their number down.

Generally, members of the judiciary appear to have been relatively open about viewing the Metropolitan police, and their forensic evidence, in a different light to that of their immediate predecessors. In 1834, Judge William Arabin claimed that this even extended to Old Bailey juries.[113] Judges were also unconcerned about some modern procedural niceties. In a pair of cases from the Old Bailey, in 1844, Baron Gurney was sure it was not the business of police-officers to caution those in their custody: "...who are about to make statements, not to do so".[114] (However, there was very strong judicial resistance to the *deliberate* questioning of suspects by officers with a view to securing evidence). Confusion about this issue continued until general cautioning of suspects was enjoined in a letter of 26 October 1906 from Lord Chief Justice Alverstone, and by the Judges' rules of 1912.[115]

Redress Against Police Abuses

It was difficult for ordinary people to secure redress against police abuses, although several avenues were theoretically open to them. From the beginning, aggrieved civilians could complain about police misconduct to both the Commissioner(s) and to a magistrate. The latter option was not easy, and the outcome was likely to favour the police. Throughout the

---

111. Ballantine, William, 1890, at p.227.
112. *The Law Journal*, Vol. 8, 1873, at p.660.
113. pp.11.d.1834, at p.274.
114. *R v Dickinson* March 8th 1844, & *R v Watts and others* August 22nd 1844, Reported in *Cox's Criminal Cases*, Vol. 1 1843-1846, at p.27 & p.75.
115. See discussion on origins by Lord Parker CJ in Practice Note (Judges' Rules) [1964] 1 All ER 237.

century, prosecuting erring officers, via the issue of a police court summons, was made difficult because they were regularly (though not invariably) provided with experienced legal representation, often from Messrs. Wontners, the police solicitors, at Treasury or Police Association expense. The poor men who took action against them were either unaided or represented by cheap but incompetent lawyers.[116]

Perhaps not surprisingly, in these circumstances, of the 65 officers charged with offences in 1849 only 14 were convicted, and many of these were cases of dereliction or absence from duty (police disciplinary matters that also constituted crimes), in prosecutions that were brought by other officers. Only five policemen were accused of offences of dishonesty; all of them were acquitted. From the 26 allegations of assault against civilians, just one officer was found guilty.[117]

Again, all things are relative. It was even harder to bring a case against a member of the Berlin *Schutzmannschaft*. A German police victim could not bring an action himself (as in London) but would have to persuade a public prosecutor to do so, something that was always difficult. Even if a Berlin policeman were found guilty of brutality towards a member of the public, in the course of his duty, he would normally return to the force. In London (and England generally), such a conviction nearly always led to dismissal. Many liberal Germans viewed the English provision for legal redress against police wrongs with envy.[118] It is also clear that Metropolitan Police Court magistrates did not *invariably* 'rubber-stamp' police actions. They might even act of their own volition against erring officers. Thus, in June 1868, P.C.s Clarke and Floyd were dismissed from the force, without back pay, after a Bow Street Police Court magistrate complained about them: "...for giving untruthful evidence when before him on a charge of assault".[119] Such cases acted as a limited form of control on police misconduct.

Additionally, the police force's internal investigations were not without deterrent value. Serious allegations did not *necessarily* have to result in a conviction to lead to an officer being disciplined or even dismissed. In the 1870s, for example, Alfred Cording noted that he had been in the Metropolitan Police, but that a: "...complaint was made against me for assaulting a woman while in the police; I was not fined, but discharged".[120]

116. Guest, A., 1891, at p.88.
117. pp.13.b.1853, at pp.1-4.
118. Johansen, Anja, 2009, at pp.123-126.
119. MEPOL 7/38 Orders for 26/6/1868.
120. OBSP, Trial of Henry Moss and Charles Brooks, 18th September 1876, t18760918-455.

The Force Instruction Book of 1829 provided that all complaints against individual constables should go to the officer's Divisional Inspector, who was enjoined to give them "particular attention". Initially, the Commissioners also dealt with all serious complaints personally, each morning, in their office at Whitehall Place ('Scotland Yard'), complainants being invited to attend with their witnesses. This right was exercised by many ordinary Londoners, such as a shoemaker who thought that a local beat constable was picking on him while having an affair with his wife. He went directly to Mayne, who "took down" his complaint. The matter was subsequently heard by another senior officer, in the presence of the constable in question, but did not result in any action.[121] The public lodged so many complaints that, in March 1830, Peel was persuaded to appoint a special senior officer, with a team of investigators, to carry out preliminary enquiries.[122]

Conclusion

The catalogue of police abuse, though significant, should not be exaggerated. In 1892, looking back on his career (he retired as a Chief Inspector), Timothy Cavanagh, who had been remarkably candid in portraying many of the negative aspects of Metropolitan police life, still felt able to declare that the force was a: "...splendid body of men, intelligent, energetic and trustworthy".[123] Another critic felt that, *generally*, the police were "men of great truthfulness and humanity".[124]

Their confidence in the force was, with many qualifications, probably justified. As well as frequent cases of minor brutality, corruption, and dishonesty, there were numerous well-documented incidents of police 'fair-play' and common decency. Most officers had no *significant* involvement in misconduct. Nevertheless, problems pertaining to abuse of position were never satisfactorily resolved during the Victorian period. Popular concern about this lay behind the 1906 Royal Commission on the Metropolitan Police (albeit that most of its conclusions were either anodyne or laudatory), the public having become concerned about the: "...efficiency and trustworthiness, generally of the men who guard its peace". The remit of its study was to inquire into and report upon the

---

121. OBSP, Trial of John Cronie, 30th June 1831, t18310630-14.
122. Boothman, J.V., 1985, at p.22.
123. Cavanagh, Timothy, 1893, at p.132.
124. Anon, 1882, *Metropolitan Police Court Jottings*, at p.49.

duties and conduct of the force, especially when dealing with cases of drunkenness, disorder, and soliciting in the streets.[125]

Undoubtedly, the incidence of police abuse of power also declined towards the end of the nineteenth century, although this was partly because London's underclass, its 'police property' (those not in a position to object effectively to their treatment) and the chief targets of abusive policing, also fell drastically in size. Nevertheless, the presence of much longer serving, slightly better trained, and far more experienced and 'professional' career officers at the lowest level also played an important role. Arguably, it was the continuation of this phenomenon into the following century that set up the (retrospectively) perceived 'golden era' of mid-twentieth century policing.

---

125. 'The Metropolitan Police', *The Times,* December 24th, 1908.

CHAPTER TEN

ALTERNATIVE PARADIGMS FOR THE DECLINE IN METROPOLITAN CRIME

Introduction

It is easy to find explanations for the decline in Metropolitan crime and disorder that do not rely on the work of the police, whether uniformed or detective. Indeed, it might be a mistake to view change in Metropolitan society as having been legally driven at all. It is possible that, as 'manners' were transformed by other changes, the law began to penalise conduct that was no longer deemed acceptable by respectable people, rather than it being the criminal law that was making them respectable.

A focus on the policing of the slums, rather than on their underlying social and economic problems, was often politically attractive. As an astute American correspondent noted in 1888, some Conservative M.P.s for London seats would vote against the Home Secretary, because their constituents were up in arms about police inefficiency over the Ripper investigation, but would read of landlords: "...turning out into the wintry blasts thousands of helpless tenants without concern".[1] Even then, in a debate resonant with modern concerns, many, like Amelia Lewis, thought that: "It is the 'origin' of 'crime' we must avoid, not the consequences".[2]

When it comes to explaining the post mid-century decline in crime, much significance can be placed on the social and economic improvements of the era. Arguably, crime was widespread in the early part of the era because levels of social disorganisation and poverty were acute. As these fell, so did crime. Perhaps significantly, it was not just crime that showed a marked decline as the century advanced; indices of non-criminal deviance and disorganisation also fell. Thus, the illegitimacy ratio, the proportion of out-of-wedlock births to total births, rose from a little over five per cent at the beginning of the nineteenth century to a peak of seven

---

1. *New York Times*, November 11th, 1888.
2. Lewis, Amelia, 1871, at pp.296-299.

per cent in 1845. It then fell steadily until it was less than four per cent at the turn of the century. In East London, the poorest section of the capital, the figures were even more dramatic; illegitimacy there was consistently well below the average: 4.5 percent in the mid-century and three per cent by its end.[3]

Similarly, illiteracy declined rapidly under the influence of the 1870 Education Act and various charitable initiatives, while the number of those admitted to workhouses also fell steadily as a proportion of the wider population after the 1850s. By the latter decades of the century, the number of newly arrived and impoverished Irishmen, traditionally an important part of London's urban underclass, had also declined, while many of their forbears had become 'Anglicised' and been absorbed into mainstream Metropolitan life, becoming particularly active in the Trade Union Movement.

Decline in Urban 'Crisis'

That urban social conditions, especially those in London, were in crisis in the early Victorian period was a commonplace amongst informed observers, whatever their social provenance and political persuasions. Of course, the 'quality' of life is a variable that depends upon an enormous range of economic and social factors, ranging from levels of real income to standards of housing and sanitation. Only some of these are capable of any form of statistical measurement. However, with that qualification, the period from the 1820s to the end of the 1840s seems to have been particularly harsh. Real increases in working-class living standards do not appear to have occurred until well into the 1850s.[4]

Throughout the 1830s and 1840s, trade levels were poor and food prices relatively high. Swift population growth was not met by a simultaneous expansion in housing or urban infrastructure. Endemic diseases like cholera could still produce epidemics when the right climatic conditions coincided with periods of economic and social distress.[5] During cyclical or seasonal slumps, overcrowding and the 'doubling-up' of families in rooms became common, encouraging disease.[6] As Edwin Chadwick observed, in many areas, the formation of habits of cleanliness

---

3. Himmelfarb, Gertrude, 1994, at p.57.
4. Hobsbaum, E.J., 1969, at pp.154-171, Evans, Eric J., 1983, at p.154.
5. See on this generally Haley, Bruce, 1978.
6. Hardy, Anne, 1988, at pp.401-25.

was "obstructed by defective supplies of water".[7]

The local government of London was ramshackle and woefully ill equipped to deal with these problems in the first half of the century. Before 1855, it was still largely based on the city's parishes, so that the metropolitan area was governed by 172 vestries, along with the City Corporation, seven Sewers Commissions, a hundred paving, lighting and vestries boards, and the boards of guardians set up pursuant to the 1834 Poor Law Act. Limited reforms such as the Municipal Corporations Act of 1835, which provided for the setting up of local health boards, along with the Public Health Act of 1848, and attempts to improve the local government of the vestries in initiatives such as the Sturges Bourne Acts of 1818 and 1819, had proved largely inadequate.[8]

Crime and Demoralisation

The notion that appalling urban conditions were criminogenic was a constant in the nineteenth-century debate on crime. Thus, W.H. Dixon noted that Field Lane in Clerkenwell was a: "...hot-bed of crime and demoralization. Here is one of the great dunghills on which society rears criminals for the gallows".[9] Edwin Chadwick believed that sordid conditions engendered a feckless underclass.[10] Thomas Beggs thought that filthy social habits were an inevitable result of the squalor of lower class life.[11] According to John Mirehouse, "Bad houses, bad air, bad food" always generated crime.[12] Mathew Davenport Hill strongly supported this analysis.[13] In the aftermath of the Ripper murders, even the *Lancet* asserted that poverty, overcrowding, dirt, and bad sanitation made such crimes inherently more likely.[14] For Friedrich Engels, this process had a quasi-scientific basis: "If the demoralisation of the worker passes beyond a certain point then it is just as natural that he will turn into a criminal".[15]

---

7. Anon, 1842, *Report...from the Poor Law Commissioners on an Inquiry into the Sanitary Conditions of the Labouring Population of Great Britain,* at pp.369-372.
8. Roebuck, Janet, 1979, at pp.9-10.
9. Dixon, W.H., 1850, at pp.224-228.
10. Anon, 1842, *Report...from the Poor Law Commissioners on an Inquiry into the Sanitary Conditions of the Labouring Population of Great Britain,* at pp.369-372.
11. Beggs, Thomas, 1849, at p.48.
12. Mirehouse, John, 1840, at p.20 & p.21.
13. 'Charge to the Grand Jury of Birmingham, March 1854', reproduced in Davenport Hill, Mathew, 1857, at p.301.
14. *The Lancet,* October 6th, 1888. Quoted in Haggard, Robert F., 1993, at p.13.
15. Haggard, Robert F., 1993, at p.144.

Soup kitchen in the Victorian East End

THE DISTRESS AT THE EAST-END: A SOUP KITCHEN IN RATCLIFF-HIGHWAY.—SEE PAGE 266.

Unsurprisingly, the potential for the amelioration of such conditions to affect crime rates, and to explain their decline in the second half of the nineteenth century, has continued to have attractions to many modern scholars, because life for the poor clearly did get much better after the mid-century.[16]

London's Social Demoralisation Addressed

From about 1850 onwards, successful action was taken to ameliorate urban living conditions. The survival of typhus in London until the 1870s, and its swift disappearance thereafter, is indicative of a marked decrease in urban 'stress' and the effectiveness of local public health programmes.[17] However, the process had started well before then. Glazed pipes had been introduced in the 1840s, greatly facilitating the provision of clean water and hygienic sewage disposal.[18] The Public Health Act of 1848 empowered a central authority to set up boards to see that new homes had proper

---

16. Roebuck, Janet, 1979, at p.6.
17. See on this Hardy, Anne, 1988, at p.25.
18. Morris, R.J., & Rodger, R., 1993, at p.6.

drainage and water supplies and to supervise the construction of burial grounds.[19] In 1860, the first pure-food Act was passed, being reinforced in 1872.

Urban education spread as a result of voluntary initiatives such as the 'Ragged Schools' of the 1840s, via the Industrial Schools Act of 1866 (29 & 30 Vic. c.118, ss 14-19), which allowed magistrates to send certain classes of potentially deviant children to schools that shared some of the "character" of prisons, to the Elementary Education Act of 1870 (33 & 34 Vic. c.75, s.75), which made basic schooling compulsory for all.[20] By the start of the twentieth century, Walter Besant could note that even in the most crowded parts of East London school attendance was excellent.[21] As already noted, many slums and rookeries were rapidly pulled down from the middle of the nineteenth century.[22] Thus, the infamous slum in the Saffron Hill area of Clerkenwell, where Dickens had set Fagin's den in *Oliver Twist* in 1837, was demolished in the 1860s. Jennings' Buildings in Kensington followed a decade later.[23]

Improvement in Living Standards

Many, like Francis Place, felt that a "rapid increase of wealth and its more general diffusion" were a necessary prerequisite to reducing Metropolitan crime.[24] From the 1850s, this certainly occurred. Although there was not a major change in the proportionate distribution of wealth during the century, the 'cake' got progressively larger.[25] There were high rates of economic growth, including a trebling of national income, between 1850-1914. As a result, there was also a very significant improvement in living standards for most working class people. By 1865, their real incomes were already 20% up from the levels of 1850; by 1875 they had grown by a third. As a consequence, the *per capita* consumption of tea, sugar, coffee and tobacco also increased markedly during this period. General levels of prosperity continued to grow, though not without interruption, until the end of the century, so that the gain in real wages for the average worker was probably about 60% between 1860 and 1900.[26]

19. Roebuck, Janet, 1979, at p.5 & p.6.
20. Stephen, J.F., 1883, at p.264.
21. Besant, Walter, 1908, at p.48.
22. Mayhew, Henry et al, 1862, Vol. 4, at p.226.
23. Mearns, Andrew, 1883, at p.24.
24. Place, Francis, 1972 (1835), at pp.14-15.
25. Armstrong, Alan, 1966, at p.21.
26. Shannon, Richard, 1976, at p.31 & p.202.

Some placed it even higher. In 1909, Charles Wood came to the conclusion that if the wage for skilled workmen in 1850 was taken as 100, in 1875 it was 135 and by 1890 it was 166. Using 1900 prices, it would appear that the net national income per head averaged £18 in 1855, and £42 in 1900.[27]

Food consumption was increasingly aided by cheap imports abroad, such as American wheat and, from the 1880s, frozen meat from South and North America and the Empire. Joseph Rowntree's minimum subsistence budget was 10 to 20 per cent cheaper in 1899 than it had been in 1850. New types of consumer durables also made life a little easier for many working people. For example, by 1891 there were over 5,000 bicycle manufacturers in England alone.[28]

As a result, even stern critics of Victorian industrialism have observed that: "Clearly the last quarter of the nineteenth century was a time when life became very much easier and more varied for the working class".[29] Reflecting this, adult mortality rates declined steadily in the 1880s and 1890s, and life expectancy increased. In the final decades of the Victorian period, the birth rate also started to fall rapidly. In 1870 there had been an average of 6 children per family; by the decade 1890-99 it was 4.3.[30]

The consequences of these developments for crime levels must have been significant, though inherently difficult to assess. Much 'survival' crime in England and London, that is offending prompted by need, would have been reduced as the number of people who felt the sudden press of acute poverty fell. It has even been suggested that the apparently marked improvement in the levels of male/female violence in London between 1840 and 1889 may have been directly linked to the improved economy, something that reduced stress on co-habitant relationships.[31] Additionally, because much of the improvement was in consumable rather than consumer goods, such improvement would not necessarily be expected to produce a major increase in criminal targets (other than the theft of bicycles).

---

27. Rose, Michael E., 1986, at p.9.
28. Shannon, Richard, 1976, at p.202.
29. Hobsbawm, E.J., 1969, at p.164.
30. Bédarida, François, 1991, at p.113.
31. Tomes, Nancy, 1978, at p.341.

CHAPTER ELEVEN

CONCLUSION

At the start of the Victorian period London had a large, increasingly segregated, urban underclass that was radically divorced from the conduct norms that were (ostensibly) held by much of the wider nation. Its existence was closely linked to the widespread poverty, squalor, destitution, and social disorganisation found in the capital at this time. However, its members were no longer imbued with a belief that such social disadvantage was part of the 'natural' order, in the way that they might have been a century or more earlier. Taken together, these factors encouraged the development of localised criminal sub-cultures, public disorder, and high offending rates.

By contrast, over sixty years later, as Queen Victoria's reign drew to a close, many of the concerns of the 1830s were distant ones, while other problems, though remaining, were geographically confined, discreet, and apparently in decline. The urban underclass had dwindled and retreated to the margins of the city. To those who looked it was still readily found, in small clusters of alleys and courts, located amidst greater numbers of poor but in their own terms 'respectable' working-class streets. By then, however, the remnants of the great early Victorian underclass had become an object as much of pity as of fear. At the end of the period, a whole month might pass in quiet areas of London without a police officer arresting anyone, although, in others, it would still be a nightly occurrence.[1] A visiting American could conclude that London was "one of the safest cities in the world".[2] In 1900, it appeared that the city's urban problems had been, or were in the process of being, solved.

Unsurprisingly, Metropolitan crime showed the same fall as the underclass that so often spawned it. However, although these phenomena were intimately connected, the underlying cause for their simultaneous decline was not so obvious to contemporary observers, and continues to be an issue for modern historians. Typically, the *Dark Blue* accepted that the

---

1. Greenwood, James, 1902, at p.6.
2. Flynt, Josiah, 1903, at p.447.

statistics clearly indicated that although the population of the Metropolis: "…has increased there has been a marked diminution of crime". However, it also freely conceded that it was impossible to explain exactly why this had occurred. Some attributed it to 'Philanthropic' Government Acts to: "…educate and Christianise that section of the population from which the criminal classes are recruited". Others, with, the article's author felt, more reason, but much less plausibly to modern observers, ascribed it to the severe powers provided by the Habitual Criminals Act 1869, for: "…crushing out, or at least making highly uncomfortable, those who live by crime alone".[3]

If the crime and disorder of London in the 1840s was linked to defects in early Victorian urban society, changes during the ensuing 60 years had remedied or ameliorated many of them. There had been improvements on all fronts. Certainly, these included the work of the Metropolitan Police and a criminal justice system that was willing to go onto the 'offensive'; but amongst them was the amelioration of pressing poverty by a new, widespread, level of general prosperity and enhanced levels of charitable and public assistance. Alienation had been partially addressed by a process of political incorporation, most obviously indicated by the expanding male franchise, especially in 1867 and 1884. The inculcation, through numerous social agencies other than the police of a (flexible) code of values encompassed in the term 'respectability', stressing restraint, sobriety and self-control had been extended down from the 'political' classes of the 1830s, producing increased cultural and value homogeneity. The demoralising urban crisis occasioned by an archaic city infrastructure had been tackled by enhanced provision for urban planning, slum clearance, social housing, pollution control and sanitation. Many juveniles had been taken out of 'circulation' by compulsory elementary education, something that also provided a forum for transmitting new values. All of these factors encouraged urban stabilisation and the emergence of notions of community. All must have played a part in reducing urban crime.

The transformation in Metropolitan security had been the result of different agencies and factors, working together, in a process that continued to the end of the century and beyond. Thus, it has been observed that the decline in police/public disturbances in the rougher parts of South Islington during the 1920s was largely the result of many of the supports of its long-standing 'street culture' becoming attenuated. This was due to social and economic changes, the greater provision for leisure, and the dispersal of local concentrations of the 'dangerous classes' through

---

3. Anon, 1871, *Our Police System*, at p.693.

demolition and rebuilding. Additionally, there had been a spread through the South Islington working class of new notions of public propriety, something that appears to have started with the skilled workers associated with local rail and print industries. These encouraged a strict avoidance of contact with street cultures.[4]

By then, all of these factors were at *least* 75 years old. It is very difficult to ascribe relative degrees of importance to them, especially as they often overlapped. The new police, for example, deterred crime, but they also acted as 'domestic missionaries' in transmitting, encouraging and upholding many of the values of 'respectability' amongst the lower elements of the urban working class. Simultaneously, they engaged in basic social work that contributed, albeit modestly, towards the improvement of urban conditions: helping the injured, administering non-penal social reforms such as the supervision of lodging-houses and pollution controls, and, very importantly, assisting in the enforcement of universal elementary education after 1870 by supporting school board officials in dealing firmly with truancy and parental non-compliance.

However, the 1834 Police Committee was almost certainly correct in concluding that the police *alone* could not end high levels of Metropolitan crime, even if many would disagree with their view that such a development was contingent on the: "...diffusion of moral and religious education".[5] A purely penal approach to crime and disorder was not sufficient. The numerous new laws of the 1840s failed to deal with the root causes of crime because they were premised on a mistaken belief that: "...men could be awed into virtuous conduct by the mere terrors of punishment".[6] Almost half a century later, even Sir Charles Warren firmly believed that policing, criminal law and the justice system were not *primarily* responsible for the post-1850 decline in Metropolitan crime.[7] Several modern observers have gone further, and suggested that the apparatus of the criminal law changed the behaviour of relatively few.[8]

The 'Araldite' Effect

Nevertheless, such assertions do not mean that the new police were not vitally important to the improvement in urban security. Despite some

---

4. See on this Cohen, Phil, 1981, at pp.116-122.
5. pp.11.d.1834, at p.22.
6. Beggs, Thomas, 1849, at p.19.
7. *East London Advertiser* 10th November 1899, cited in Fishman, William, 1988, at p.178.
8. See, for example, Petrow, Stefan, 1992, at p.74.

attempts to downplay the significance of 1829, they proved to be markedly superior to their predecessors for most of London. By itself, this was not enough, and needed to be combined with the social and economic improvements of the post-1850 period. When these set in, however, the police contribution may well have been a necessary prerequisite for them to become properly effective. This may be termed the 'araldite effect' after the bonding agents, weak on their own, that become extremely strong in combination.

The new police provided a formidable public order force that relegated the fatal viciousness of major riots to history. Additionally, and most importantly, they greatly reduced the incidence of street 'incivility', status, and 'quality of life' crimes, even if their impact was slightly less dramatic and sudden than is sometimes suggested, if only because of their limited numbers and heavy responsibilties. Their extensive powers, albeit often sparingly exercised, produced a gradual and continuous ratchetting up of levels of intervention over the 70 years after 1829. As a result, the police provided the disciplined and relatively secure and stable public environment in which State and private intervention, through a variety of agencies, might operate, and in which the effects of increased general prosperity could take effect. Together, they allowed a sense of community, with its attendant social bonds, to be inculcated, even in a huge modern industrial city.

By the late Victorian period, one observer could seriously claim that, even in the East End, the homeless, with only a few exceptions, were homeless because they: "…cannot or will not work, or because they prefer vice to virtue".[9] This was not entirely, or even largely, true. However, for relatively young, able-bodied, males, a category that covered *most* London criminals, the observation was fairly accurate, at least for much of the time (the troughs of a cyclical or seasonal slump obviously excepted). For the old or infirm and women with dependant children the situation was, of course, very different. Nevertheless, as has been seen, these were not groups that contributed very heavily to the criminal statistics. The social and economic improvements of the era presented a realistic alternative to crime for many of the poor, an avenue that had often been missing in the early part of the century. However, by itself, this may not have been enough, given that the work available was often extremely hard, frequently physically dangerous, nearly always highly monotonous, and usually very poorly paid, while for many the criminal life seemed: "...romantic and

---

9. Barnett, Henrietta, 1888, at p.438.

adventurous, and the profits large".[10] Police pressure probably contributed to making these available, but unattractive, employment opportunities preferable to crime for many fit young Metropolitan men.

The last 60 years in both Britain and America have witnessed the apparent contradiction of ever-greater State intervention to assist the disadvantaged, especially in the inner cities, and unprecedented general prosperity, co-existing with the seeming re-emergence of a large urban underclass, glaringly manifest, for example, in the London riots of August 2011. Inevitably, this has led some to suggest that government 'handouts', encouraging the development of a dependency culture, promote the existence of such a group. However, this is not *necessarily* the lesson of Victorian London. What the experience of that city in the nineteenth century does suggest is that State intervention, like general prosperity, may well be fruitless unless accompanied by social discipline. Increased resources in the inner city, on their own, are not enough. They require both public and personal security to be effective. This security cannot be inculcated purely by moral exhortation.

Other conclusions can be tentatively drawn from the Victorian experience about the nature of police 'pressure'. Nearly all of the major 20th century Metropolitan police historians in the 'Whig' tradition, such as Melville Lee, T. A. Critchley, and Charles Reith, agreed that police effectiveness was contingent on public support, and that their control was more a result of prestige than power.[11] Many nineteenth-century observers reached the same conclusion. This might be termed the "service and consent" model of policing. However, this view does not *always* bear close historical scrutiny. Clearly, such support makes life very much easier for police officers. Nevertheless, the Victorian experience rebuts suggestions that an effective police is necessarily a popular one. Despite claims that 'policing by consent' has been a longstanding British tradition, this was often palpably absent in the nineteenth-century Metropolis.[12] Similarly, the notion that the 'coercive' nature of British policing was concealed because, in the past, they were a widely respected force would have seemed absurd to many Victorian Londoners, particularly in the early decades of the new force's existence.

Although bitterly opposed, and highly vulnerable to being abused, police activity against London's most powerless, least articulate, but also most criminogenic social strata contributed to the advance of manners, social cohesion and discipline in working class communities, and

---

10. Anon, 1883, 'Homes of the Criminal Classes', at p.824.
11. Robinson, Cyril, 1979, at p.41.
12. Waddington, P.A.J., 1991, at p.3.

encouraged an unprecedented degree of public civility in the capital's streets. Officers often imposed their 'law' in a harsh and inflexible but also very effective manner. As a result, the Victorian experience, and its emphasis on a "crime control" model, issues a challenge to some modern community based policing initiatives.

Several other conclusions can be extrapolated from the nineteenth-century experience. By itself, patrolling was not much more effective in *directly* reducing or deterring conventional crime than it has been in the modern period. Despite being faced by a criminal threat that was largely devoid of sophistication, even by present-day standards, and which was often characterised by opportunism and gross ineptitude, beat officers were relatively ineffectual against burglars, robbers, pickpockets and other thieves. It seems that the 'scarecrow' function of uniformed policing has been overrated since its inception. Most London criminals could, and did, eventually adapt to fixed patrols. The 'clear up' rate for Victorian crime was probably little better than it is today. The inexorable expansion of the detectives after the 1830s was a forced and reluctant acknowledgement of these failings and indicative of the limitations on the 'Peelite' model.

However, although the Victorian experience suggests that the simple presence of uniformed officers on the beat is of limited *direct* effectiveness, some aspects of the police work of the period would appear to support the modern 'broken windows' theory of crime control. It suggests that the overt presence of officers, focussing on public order, *can* reduce serious crime, albeit *indirectly*. This is a link that has sometimes been ignored in the modern era. In 1981, for example, Lord Scarman famously reiterated Richard Mayne's definition of the police function as being the protection of life and property and the preservation of public tranquillity. More controversially, he claimed that where the two aims came into conflict, it should be public tranquillity that had priority.[13] It was not a choice, or conclusion, that would have been shared by many Victorian policemen, who felt that the two necessarily went hand in hand. Enhanced public tranquillity and reduced crime levels were inextricably intertwined. Urban discipline promoted social solidarity, prevented the flight of the 'respectable', and broke up criminogenic street cultures. Whatever problems they had with direct crime fighting, the Metropolitan police was very good at promoting discipline in public space.

Less palatable is that the Victorian policing experience suggests that, to be indirectly effective in this manner, street policing needs to go far beyond a mere physical presence, and requires that patrolling officers be

---

13. pp.17.1982, para. 4.57.

pro-active, assertive and equipped with both extensive legal powers and a large measure of personal discretion. They need to be able to stamp their 'authority' on their beats, breaking up and dispersing or (in the parlance of Victorian officers) 'moving on' loitering, unruly or suspicious groups and individuals. To do this, officers sometimes need to be able to enforce apparently minor regulations and act against 'victimless' crimes. It is also helpful if such policing is supported by a swift criminal justice process in which police evidence is given an almost institutionalised preternatural weight, and police malpractice, unless blatant, is often tacitly ignored (as was frequently the case in the nineteenth-century Police Courts).

As a result, and as the Victorian experience clearly shows, any effective 'zero-tolerance' initiatives come with unavoidable and unpleasant risks. It is not a coincidence that New York, which experienced a major reduction in serious crime between 1993 and 1999, something that has been (partly) linked to an aggressive 'incivility' policing initiative, also witnessed a series of allegations of police brutality, often aimed at members of the city's poorest communities.[14] Power leads to its abuse, and police discretion is often the raw material of corruption, while the use of 'extra-legal' sanctions inevitably produces cases of outright brutality. The Metropolitan police of the nineteenth century were, at street level, often a law unto themselves, unless they were foolish enough to become involved with their 'betters'. Many modern notions of 'democratic' policing, based on a sense of legitimacy obtained by responsibility, legality, and even-handedness were attenuated or even palpably absent. The viability of Victorian policing techniques conflicts with a modern desire to encourage popular access to the law and legal redress, and for much greater direct local police accountability.[15]

The Victorian experience also suggests that the only policing alternative to 'aggressive' uniformed patrolling which might seriously affect the incidence of crime is the extensive use of undercover officers and detective work. However, this is, and was, something that also carries unpleasant 'baggage', albeit sometimes of a different type. As with 'zero tolerance' street policing, the more effective the techniques used by detectives, the greater the risk of abuse.

Proponents of nineteenth-century policing reform had overcome intense opposition to the very presence of a large uniformed 'preventative' body on the streets of London, and then, as this proved deficient in some

---

14. 'How to Win the race against crime', Myron Magnet, *The Daily Telegraph*, May 3rd, 2000, at p.16, 'Police Silence on Brutality Broken', *The Times*, May 21st, 1999, at p.11.
15. Reiner, Robert, 1992b, at p.781.

respects, to the increasingly extensive use of detectives. Both battles had been hotly contested. Despite this, nineteenth-century London witnessed a remarkable transformation in attitudes towards government intervention in the lives of its citizens. Such a dramatic change was partly the result of an élitist political system that was not constantly constrained by democratic limitations and opinion, at least until near the end of the period.

The 1834 Police Committee deluded itself (or pretended to do so) when it concluded that its predecessor of 1822 had been mistaken in believing that high levels of liberty and an effective police were often irreconcilable in a city like London, and that the new Metropolitan Police had: "...imposed no restraint, either upon public bodies or individuals, which is not entirely consistent with the fullest practical exercise of every civil privilege, and with the most unrestrained intercourse of private society".[16] From the vantage point of 1900, it was apparent that the 1822 Committee's stark acceptance that enhanced urban security could only be achieved at the expense of contemporary notions of freedom had been proved correct. Those in power in the non-democratic London of the early nineteenth century ultimately preferred improved security to personal liberty. Whether their democratically elected successors in the twenty-first century, returned by constituents with relatively easy access to legal advice, would follow the same route, or be prepared to refight the same battles along the way, is debatable.

Ironically, the Victorian experience also suggests that one of the greatest safeguards against police abuse of power that is not inherently inconsistent with a 'broken windows' strategy of policing is the presence of a highly disciplined and hierarchical force, even if this has to be instilled in a quasi-military fashion. Such a force is much more likely to be responsive to directives from senior ranks and orders from junior commanders. As was noted in 1839, the proper organization of the police was (and is) an: "...important security in the increase of discretion, and the diminution of any motive to the undue exercise of authority". Even then, the worst policing abuses normally occurred amongst "uninstructed" officers, especially those from smaller jurisdictions, rather than trained men in large organisations.[17] With proper training (largely absent in the 1800s) and strict discipline, pro-active street policing can often be conducted with a degree of civility and responsibility, reducing (though not eliminating) popular alienation. Unfortunately, such discipline goes against many modern trends that discourage its accoutrements, whether

---

16. pp.11.d.1834, at p.13.
17. pp.12.b.1839, at p.173.

drill or respect for rank and hierarchy. Interestingly, in the modern era, some retired Metropolitan officers have attributed police rudeness towards the general public to the erosion of formalities, such as the use of first names rather than rank, the abandonment of saluting, insignia and senior officers' regular appearances on the beat to personally inspect operations.[18] Whatever his limitations when it came to handling detectives, Colonel Warren's punctiliousness about discipline in the uniformed branch was not entirely misplaced.

Additionally, and less controversially, late Victorian policing shows the importance of experience and maturity amongst low ranking beat officers when it comes to avoiding abuse of position. Three quarters of former Metropolitan police officers drawing pensions in 1890 had retired after at least 15, and often as much as 25 years service, as ordinary constables.[19] The emergence of a body of career yet 'passed over' officers, with the judgement that came from decades of foot-patrol, who were beyond the stage of potentially misplaced zeal, whether oriented at promotion or reward, or of 'swollen-headedness' from the possession of novel powers, was probably vital in reducing abusive policing during the late 1800s. Significantly, a quite disproportionate number of constables accused of assaulting civilians in (for example) 1849 were in their very first year of service.[20] The presence of experienced men also affected the wider policing 'culture' into which new officers were initiated. The greatly enhanced level of training available to modern police officers, when compared to their Victorian predecessors, might also be expected to reduce abuse of discretionary powers.

Out of the numerous negative aspects of the Victorian Metropolitan policing experience came much good. Although any debate about 'order' invites a discussion about who benefits most from that order, there comes a point at which disorder is dysfunctional for nearly all concerned. In some ways, the nineteenth-century achievement was to create effective new institutions, such as the police, that helped to establish a safer, more ordered, society. This had been a difficult process. It had, however, probably been necessary for the development of 'modern' urban life.

In the late twentieth century, a distinguished professor of criminal law, lamenting that a 'new' disrespect for property rights and a poor level of personal self-discipline was becoming widespread, may have been presenting a slightly utopian view of the early 1900s. Nevertheless, the

---

18. 'Police Officers Incapable of Command', letter to *Daily Telegraph*, June 16th, 1999.
19. Monro, James, 1890, at p.203.
20. pp.13.b.1853, at pp.1-4.

"culturally homogenous" society, with known and shared values, whose departure he regretted, was largely the legacy of the second half of the Victorian period.[21] By 1900, for most working people, the re-distribution of property was the province of political activity rather than criminal initiative. Behaviour norms, at least with regard to potentially criminal conduct, were, in many ways, shared by a very much higher proportion of the population than had been the case at the start of Queen Victoria's reign or is, perhaps, the case today. The Victorian achievement in improving standards of personal conduct was a resounding, if slow, success. It proved that the impact of 'modernity' need not produce increased levels of crime and disorder, and can even co-exist with their decline. In the early twenty-first century, with heightened concern about levels of crime and, even more so, public order in many English cities, sometimes in the very same areas that raised anxiety in the 1840s, it is, perhaps, time to reconsider this nineteenth-century success story.

---

21. Williams, Glanville, 1983, at p.276.

BIBLIOGRAPHY

Contemporary and Pre-1939 Sources

Anon ('A Gentleman'), 1818, *The London Guide, and Strangers Safeguard,* J. Bumpus, London

Anon, 1818, *The Constable's Assistant: Being a compendium of the duties and Powers of constables,* 4th edn., Society for the Suppression of Vice, London

Anon, 1822, *Thoughts on Prison Discipline, And The Present State of the Police of the Metropolis*, Hatchard and Son, London

Anon, 1833, *Old Bailey Experience, Criminal Jurisprudence and the Actual working of Our Penal Code of Law*, James Fraser, London

Anon ('A Metropolitan Rate-Payer'), 1834, *An analysis of the receipts and expenditure of the Metropolitan Police; and a comparative statement of the cost of the old watch and police patrols: compiled from the official returns made to Parliament,* William Strange, London.

Anon (A Vestryman of St. Ann's), 1834, *The Metropolitan Police: its expenses examined, its efficiency questioned and several objections discussed*, London.

Anon, 1842, *Report from the Poor Law Commissioners on an Inquiry into the Sanitary Conditions of the Labouring Population of Great Britain*, London.

Anon ('Stipendiary Magistrate of Liverpool'), 1844, *Juvenile Delinquency*, (Tract reprinted from *The Christian Teacher* for July 1842), Simpkin, Marshall and Co., London.

Anon, 1846, *Cox's Criminal Cases*, Vol.1, *1843-1846*, J. Crockford, London

Anon, 1848, *Sinks of London Laid Open - A Pocket Companion for the Uninitiated, to Which is Added - a Modern Flash Dictionary Containing all the Cant Words*, J. Duncombe, London

Anon, 1851, 'Lost in London', *Household Words,* Vol.III

Anon, 1852, *Confessions of a Detective Policeman,* Elliot, London

Anon, 1853, 'The Dens of London', *Ainsworth's Magazine*, Vol. XXIV

Anon, 1856, 'Crime in England and its Treatment', *The National Review,* Vol. 3.

Anon, 1858, 'Sermon Preached on the 9th June 1858', in *Sermons and Society,* Welsby, Paul (Ed.), 1970, Pelican, London.

Anon, 1862, 'Phases of London Life', *The British Quarterly Review*, No. XXXV,

Anon, 1862, 'Review of Those that Will not Work', *The British Quarterly Review*, No. LXX

Anon, 1871, 'Our Police System', *The Dark Blue,* Vol.II

Anon, 1872, 'How We Make Thieves', *All The Year Round,* New Series, Vol. VII

Anon, 1874, 'London Guardians of the Night', *All the Year Round,* New Series, Vol. XII

Anon, 1877, *Five Years' Penal Servitude by One who has Endured It,* Richard Bentley and Son, London

Anon ('A Ticket-of-Leave Man'), 1879, *Convict Life, or Revelations Concerning Convicts and Convict Prisons*, London

Anon ('A Magistrate'), 1882, *Metropolitan Police Court Jottings,* Horace Cox, London

Anon, 1884, *Police Rule*, Liberty and Property Defence League, London

Anon, 1885, 'The Unseen Poor', *All the Year Round*, New Series, Vol. XXXV.

Anon, 1887, 'Beggars-Sad and Jolly', *All the Year Round*, New Series, Vol. XLI.

Anon, 1887, 'Hospital Life in East London', *All the Year Round*, New Series, Vol. XLI.

Anon, 1888, *Central Criminal Court Sessions Papers, 2nd session 1887-1888*, Stevens and Sons, London

Anon ('A PC'), 1888, *The Metropolitan Police and its Management: A reply to Sir Charles Warren's Article in Murray's Magazine,* E. Dyke, London

Anon, 1896, 'Who will watch the watchmen: a criticism of our police system', *Free Review*, Vol.6, pp.143-150.

Anon, 1897, 'Inadequate Police Protection in South London', *The Justice of the Peace*, October 23rd, 1897, Vol. LXI

Abbot Parry, Edward, 1914, *The Law and the Poor,* Smith Elder & Co., London

Acton, William, 1870, *Prostitution, considered in its Moral, Social, and Sanitary Aspects*, 2nd edition, John Churchill and sons, London.

Adams, John, 1838, *A Letter to Benjamin Hawes, esq. M.P.,* J. Hatchard and Son, London

Adolphus, John, 1824, *Observations on the Vagrant Act: and some other Statutes,* John Major, London

Allen, L.B., 1821, *Brief Considerations on the Present State of the Police of the Metropolis*, John Hatchard, London

'Amigo', 1847, 'Common Lodging Houses and a Model Lodging House for the Poor', *Howitt's Journal of Literature Etc.*, Vol.1, No.2.

Anderson, Robert, 1910, *The Lighter Side of my Official Life*, Hodder & Stoughton, London

Antrobus, Edmund, 1853, *The Prison and the School*, Staunton & Sons, London

Archer, Thomas, 1865, 'The Never Silent Highway', in *The Pauper, the Thief and the Convict*, Groombridge & Sons, London

Ballantine, William, 1890, *Some Experiences of a Barrister's Life*, Richard Berley & Sons, London

Barnardo, Thomas John, 1888, *Saved from a Crime*, J.F. Shaw & Co., London

Barnett, Henrietta Octavia, 1888, 'East London and Crime', *The National Review*, Vol. 12,

Barrington, George, 1809, *The London Spy; or the Frauds of London Described,* Printed by T. Johnston, Falkirk

Bayly, Mary, 1860, *Ragged Homes and How to Mend Them,* James Nisbet and Co., London

Beames, Thomas, 1970 (1852), *The Rookeries of London*, 2nd edn., Frank Cass & Co., London

Beggs, Thomas, 1849, *An Inquiry into the Causes of Juvenile Depravity,* Charles Gilpin, London

Bennett, Alfred Rosling, 1924, *London and Londoners in the Eighteen-Fifties and Sixties*, T. Fisher Unwin, London

Bentham, Jeremy, 1791, *Panoptician; or, the Inspection-House,* Thomas Byrne Publishers, London

Bent, James, 1891, *Superintendent: Criminal Life. Reminiscences of Forty-Two Years as a Police Officer*, John Heywood, Manchester.

Besant, Annie, 1885, *Sin and Crime: Their Nature and Treatment*, Freethought Publishing, London

Besant, Walter et al, 1908, *The fascination of London Shoreditch and the East End*, A. & C. Black, London

Bicknell, P., 1894, *The Police Manual*, 11th edn., London, reproduced in Taylor, David, 1997, *The New Police in Nineteenth-Century England*, Manchester University Press, Manchester

Bidwell, Austin, 1897, *Bidwell's Travels, from Wall Street to London Prison Fifteen Years in Solitude*, Bidwell Publishing Company, Hartford.

Blanc, Louis, 1862, *Letters on England,* Sampson Low, London

Booth, Charles, 1889, *Life and Labour of the People in London*, Vol. 1, Williams and Norgate, London

Booth, William, 1890, *In Darkest England, and the Way Out,* International Headquarters of the Salvation Army, London

Brougham, Henry, 1847, *A Letter to Lord Lyndhurst, From Lord Brougham, on Criminal police and National Education*, 2nd edn., James Ridgway Publishers, London

Burgess, I.G., 1821, *The Trial of Edward Breton (night patrol of St Giles) William Jones (late patrol of Bow Street), William Mason (Constable of St James) for a Conspiracy,* London

Butler, Josephine, 1880, *Government by Police,* 2nd edn., Dyer Brothers, London

—. 1888, *Government by Police,* 3rd edn., T. Fisher Unwin, London

Cairns, J. A. R., 1922, *The Loom of the Law ... The experiences and reflections of a Metropolitan Magistrate,* Hutchinson, London

Canler, Louis, 1862, *Autobiography of a French Detective From 1818 to 1858*, translated by Lascelles Wraxall, Ward and Lock, London

Carlyle, Thomas, 1840, *Chartism*, James Fraser, London

Carpenter, E., 1896, 'Who Will Watch the Watchmen: A Criticism of our Police System', *Free Review*, Vol.6, 1896, pp.144-149.

Carpenter, Mary, 1853, *Juvenile Delinquents: Their Condition and Treatment*, W. & F.G. Cash, London

Cavanagh, Timothy, 1893, *Scotland Yard: Past and Present,* Chatto and Windus, London

Chadwick, Edwin, 1829, Preventive Police, *The London Review*, No.1, Feb. 1829

—. 1868, 'On the Consolidation of Police Force, and the Preventing of Crime', *Fraser's Magazine,* Vol.77, No.472, January 1868

Chatterton, D., 1870, *The Revolution in the Police and the Coming Revolution in the Army and Navy,* London

Close, Francis, 1850, 'The Dangerous Classes', in *Lectures Delivered Before the Church of England Young Men's Society For Aiding Missions at Home and Abroad,* James Nisbet, London

Crompton, Henry, 1905 (written c.1876) *Our Criminal Justice*, T. Fisher Unwin, London

Cubin, J., 1832, *Sketch of a New National Police Bill,* Smith, Elder & Co., London

Colquhoun, Patrick, 1796, *A Treatise on the Police of the Metropolis,* 5th edn., C. Dilly, London

Colquhoun, Patrick, 1806, *A Treatise on Indigence,* Hatchard, London

Danvers, Philip, 1842, *Mendicancy, The Means of Eradicating or Suppressing Mendicancy*, Shaw and Sons, London

Davenport Hill, Mathew, 1857, *Suggestions for the Repression of Crime,* London

Davitt, Michael, 1886, *Leaves from A Prison Diary*, Ford National Library, New York

Dew, Walter, 1938, *I Caught Crippen: Memoirs of ex-Chief Inspector Walter Dew C.I.D.,* Blackie and Sons, London and Glasgow

Dickens, Charles, 1907 (1837), *Oliver Twist,* Everyman, London

—. 1850, 'A Detective Police Party', in *Household Words,* Vol. 1

—. 1850, 'The Modern Science of Thief-taking', in *Household Words,* Vol.1

—. 1996 (1853), *Bleak House,* Penguin, Harmondsworth.

—. 1857, 'Murderous Extremes', *Household Words,* Vol. 15, at p.1

Dickens, Charles, & Wills, W.H. 1851, 'The Metropolitan Protectives', in *Household Words*, Vol. III

Dickens, Charles (Junior), 1888, *Dickens' Dictionary of London*, Macmillan and Co., London

Dilnot, George, 1915, *Scotland Yard: The Methods and Organisation of the Metropolitan Police,* Percival Marshall & Co., London

—. 1928, *The Trial of the Detectives*, Geoffrey Bles Publishers, London

Dixon, W. Hepworth, 1850, *The London Prisons*, Jackson and Welford, London

Dudley, Thomas, 1828, *The Tocsin: or a Review of the London Police Establishments with Hints for their Improvement,* London

Durkeim, Emile, 1933 (1893), *The Division of Labour in Society,* Free Press, New York

Egan, Pierce, 1821, *Life in London,* Sherwood, Neely & Jones, London

Ellis, Havelock, 1890, *The Criminal,* Walter Scot Pubs., London

Ellis, William, 1857, *Where Must We Look for the Further Prevention of Crime?*, Smith Elder and Co., London

Engels, Friedrich, 1958, (1845) *Condition of the Working Class in England*, translated by Henderson, W.O. and Challoner, W.H, Basil Blackwell, Oxford

Ewing Ritchie, J., 1857, *The Night Side of London*, William Tweedie, London

'Fidget', c.1838, *A Letter to the Lord Mayor and Citizens of London, Respecting the Introduction of the New Police,* published by E. Lloyd, London

Fletcher, Joseph, 1850, 'Statistical Account of the Police of the Metropolis', *Journal of the Statistical Society of London*, Vol. 13, No. 3, pp.221-267.

Flynt, Josiah, 1903, 'Police Methods in London', *The North American Review*, Vol. 176, No. 556, pp.436-449.

Fonblanque, Albany, 1832, 'Householders in Danger', *Westminster Review,* Vol.XVI

Fosdick, Raymond B., 1969 (1915), *European Police Systems,* Patterson Smith, New York

Fredur, Thor (J. Rutherford), 1879, *Sketches from Shady Places*, London

Fuller, Robert, 1912, *Recollections of a Detective,* John Lang Ltd., London

Goring, Charles, 1972 (1913), *The English Convict: A Statistical Study*, Patterson Smith Publishing, Montclair

Gamon, Hugh, 1907, *The London Police Court, To-Day & To-Morrow*, J.M. Dent, London

Gissing, George, 1992 (1889), *The Nether World*, O.U.P., Oxford

Glyde, John, 1856, *Suffolk in the 19th Century: physical, social, moral, religious, and industrial,* London

Grant, James, 1837, *The Great Metropolis*, Vol. 1, Saunders and Utley, London

Grant, James, 1838, *Sketches in London,* London

Greenham, G.H., 1904, *Scotland Yard Experiences From the Diary of G.H. Greenham, Late Chief Inspector C.I.D.,* Routledge, London

Greenwood, James, 1869, *The Seven Curses of London*, London

—. 1888, *The Policeman's Lantern: Strange Stories of London Life,* Walter Scott, London

—. 1902, *The Prisoner in the Dock: My Four Years Daily Experiences in the London Police Courts,* Chatto and Windus, London

Greg, W.R., 1856, 'Crime in England and its Treatment', *The National Review*, Vol.3

Gregory, Robert, 1886, 'Is Crime Increasing or Diminishing with the Spread of Education?', *The National Review,* Vol.6,

Griffiths, Arthur, 1898, *Mysteries of Police and Crime,* Vol.1, Cassels and Company, London

Guest, A., 1891, 'The State of the Law Courts', *The Strand Magazine,* No.11

Guy, W.A., 1848, 'The Plague of Beggars', *Frasers Magazine,* Vol.37

Hanway, Jonas, 1785, *The Defects of Police,* London

Hardwicke, John, 1828, 'Police', *The Quarterly Review,* No. 36

Hill, M., and Cornwallis, C.F., 1853, *Two Prize Essays on Juvenile Delinquency,* Smith Elder and Co., London.

Hoare, H.E., 1883, 'Homes of the Criminal Classes', *The National Review*, Vol.1, No.1

Hodder, George, 1845, *Sketches of Life and Character Taken at the Police Court, Bow Street*, Sherwood and Bowyer, London

Holland, E.W., 1870, 'The Vagrancy Laws and the Treatment of the Vagrant Poor', *The Contemporary Review*, Vol. 13

Hollingshead, John, 1861, *Ragged London in 1861*, Smith Elder & Co., London

Holmes, Thomas, 1908, *Known to the Police,* Edward Arnold, London

—. 1912, *London's Underworld*, Aldine House, London

Horsley, John, 1913, *How Criminals are Made and Prevented, A Retrospect of Forty Years,* T. Fisher and Unwin, London

Hunt, J., 1863, *The Policeman's Struggle; Addressed to the Inhabitants of the Metropolitan Police District*, printed for the author, British Library 1414.d.45

'Inspector F', 1862, *Experiences of a Real Detective*, Ward and Lock, London

Jackson, Randle, 1828, *Considerations on the Increase of crime, and the degree of its extent, The principle causes of such increase, And the most likely Means for the Prevention or Mitigation of this Public Calamity*, J. Hatchard, London

Jones, Chester, 1912, *Report by Mr. Chester Jones on Certain disturbances at Rotherhithe,* HMSO, London

Joseph, H.S.,1853, *Memoirs of Convicted Prisoners; Accompanied By Remarks on the Causes and Prevention of Crime*, Wertheim & Co., London

Kingsmill, Joseph, 1854, *Chapters on Prisons and Prisoners and the Prevention of Crime*, Longmans, London

Kirchner, F.J., 1884, *Index to the Police of England, Scotland and Wales*, Manchester

Lansdowne, Andrew, 1893, *A Life's Reminiscences of Scotland Yard,* 2nd edn., Leadenhall Press, London.

Leeson, B., 1934, *Lost London, by former Detective Sergeant B. Leeson,* Stanley Paul & Co., London

Leigh, Samuel, 1819, *Leigh's New Picture of London*. W. Clowes, London

Lewis, Amelia, 1871, 'On Crime', *The Dark Blue,* Vol. ii, pp.296-99

London, Jack, 1977 (1903), *The People of the Abyss*, Journeyman Press, London

Loring Place, Charles, 1872, *The Dangerous Classes of New York, and Twenty Years' Work among Them,* New York

Mackay, Charles, 1850, 'The Devil's Acre', *Household Words*, Vol.1

Madan, Martin, 1785, *Thoughts on Executive Justice, with Respect to Our Criminal Law*, Printed for J. Dodsley, London

Maginn, William, 1830, 'The Desperate System: Poverty, Crime and Emigration', *Frasers Magazine*, Vol. 1, No. VI

Mainwaring, George B., 1821, *Observations on the Present State of the Police of the Metropolis,* John Murray, London

Mayhew, Henry et al,   1862, *Criminal Prisons of London and Scenes from Prison Life*, M.J. Weiner, London

Mayhew, Henry et al, 1862, *London Labour and the London Poor*, Vols 1-4, London

Mayne, Richard, 1863, *Confidential memorandum to Sir George Grey, dated June 1st, 1863,* held at New Scotland Yard Library

Mearns, Andrew, 1883, *The Bitter Cry of Outcast London: An Inquiry into the condition of the Abject Poor*, James Clarke and Co., London

Meason, M. Laing, 1881, 'The French Detective Police', *MacMillan's Magazine*, Vol. 40

—. 1882, 'The London Police', *Macmillan's Magazine,* Vol. 46

—. 1883, 'Detective Police', *The Nineteenth Century,* No. 13

Medland, W. (Ed.), 1803, *A Collection of Remarkable and Interesting Criminal Trials,* John Badcock, London

Melville Lee, W.L., 1901, *A History of Police in England,* Methuen and Co., London

Meredith, Susanna, 1881, *A Book About Criminals,* James Nisbet and Co., London

Miles, W.A., 1836, *Suggestions for the Formation of a General Police*, Printed Privately, London.

Mill, John Stuart, 1996 (1859), *On Liberty*, Wordsworth Classic Editions, London,

Mirehouse, John, 1840, *Crime and its Causes: with Observations on Sir Eardley Wilmots Bill authorizing the Summary Conviction of Juvenile Offenders in Certain Cases of Lacenby and Misdemeanour,* W.J. Cheaver, London

Morrison, Arthur, 1903, *Tales of Mean Streets,* 6th Edition, Methuen & Co., London

Morrison, William Douglas, 1896, *Juvenile Offenders*, T. Fisher Unwin, London

—. 1896, *Crime in England and its Treatment,* T. Fisher Unwin, London,

Monro, James, 1889, *Memorandum on Proposed Increase of Police Rate, October 23rd, 1889,* New Scotland Yard Library, London

—. 1890, 'The Story of Police Pensions', *The New Review*, No. 16, pp.194-207.

Neale, W.B., 1840, *Juvenile Delinquency in Manchester: Its Causes and History, Its Consequences,* Gavin Hamilton, Manchester

Nicoll, David, 1892, *Police Spies and Informers: Anarchy at the Bar, A speech Delivered at the Old Bailey, On Friday, May 5, 1892,* Published Privately, London.

Ormsby, John, 1864, 'A Day's Pleasure with the Criminal Classes', *Cornhill Magazine,* Vol. 9

Owen, Edward, 1906, *Hyde Park, Select Narratives, Annual Event, etc, during twenty years' Police Service in Hyde Park,* Simpkin, Marshall & Co., London,

Pare, William, 1862, *A Plan for the Suppression of the Predatory Classes,* Effingham, London

Parry, Edward Abbot, 1914, *The Law and the Poor, by His Honour Judge Edward Abbot Parry,* Smith Elder & Co., London

Peace, Charles, c.1880, *Charles Peace; or, The adventures of a notorious burglar,* G. Purkess, London

Pearson, John, 1827, *The London Charlies, or Half Past Twelve O'clock and a very cloudy sort of morning,* London

Phillips Day, Samuel, 1858, *Juvenile Crime, Its Causes, Character, and Cure,* J.F. Hope, London

Pike, Luke Owen, 1873-1876, *A History of Crime in England,* 2 Vols, Smith Elder & Co, London

Place, Francis, 1972 (1835), *The Autobiography of Francis Place,* Thale, Mary (Ed.), C.U.P., Cambridge

Plowden, A.C., 1903, *Grain or Chaff: The Autobiography of a Police Magistrate,* Fisher & Unwin, London

Rawson, R.W., 1839, 'An Inquiry into the Statistics of crime in England and Wales', *Journal of the Statistical Society of London,* No.2

Reynolds, S., Woolley, B. & Woolley, T., 1911, *Seems So! A Working-Class View of Politics,* Macmillan, London

Ricardo, Ralph, 1850, *Juvenile Vagrancy; Suggestions for Reform,* London

Ritchie, J. Ewing, 1857, *The Night Side of London,* William Tweedie, London

Robinson, David, 1831, 'The Local Government of the Metropolis', *Blackwood's Edinburgh Magazine,* Vol. XXIX

Robinson, Richard, 1869, 'Anecdotes about the London Poor', *MacMillan's Magazine,* Vol. XX

Rook, Clarence 1899, *The Hooligan Nights: Being the Life and Opinions of a Young and Impenitent Criminal Recounted by Himself and Set Forth by Clarence Rook,* Grant Richards, London

Rowsell, E.P., 1864, 'A Few Chapters on the Working Classes', *Ainsworth's Magazine,* Vol. XXVI, No. 111.

Ryan, Michael, 1839, *Prostitution in London,* H. Bailliere, London

Rylands, L. Gordon, 1889, *Crime Its Causes and Remedy,* Fisher and Unwin, London,

Schlesinger, Max, 1853, *Saunterings in and about London,* Nathaniel Cooke, London.

Sims, George (ed.), 1902, *Living London. Its work and its play,* Vol. 2, Cassell & Co., London.

Sims, George, 1910, *London by Night,* Greening and Co., London

Smethhurst, James, 1841, *Conspiracy: A Petition to Parliament, Containing an Account of the Conduct of two Police Magistrates, the Metropolitan Police Commissioners ... arising out of a wicked conspiracy effected against the author by a Police Constable,* printed by J.C. Kelly, London

Smiles, Samuel, 1859, *Self Help,* J. Murray, London

—. 1870, 'The Police of London', *Quarterly Review,* Vol. 129

Smith, Henry, 1911, *From Constable to Commissioner,* Chatto and Windus, London

Spearman, Edmund R., 1894, 'Known to the Police', *The Nineteenth Century,* Vol. XXXVI

Stallybrass, W.T. 1936, 'The Eclipse of Mens Rea', *Law Quarterly Review,* No. CCV

Stead, W.T., 1885, 'The Maiden Tribute to Modern Babylon', *Pall Mall Gazette,* July 6th.

Stephen, J.F., 1883, *A History of the Criminal Law of England,* Vol. III, Macmillan, London

Sweeney, John, 1905, *Scotland Yard: Being the experiences during twenty-seven years of John Sweeney. Late Detective in C.I.D. London,* Alexander Moring, London

Symons, Jelinger C., 1849, *Tactics for the Times As Regards the Condition and the Treatment of the Dangerous Classes,* Start Publishers, Pall Mall, London

Taylor, W.C., 1839, 'The Moral Economy of Large Towns', *Bentleys Miscellany,* Vol. VI

Thor, Fredur (J. Rutherford), 1879, *Sketches From Shady Places,* Smith Elder, London.

Tempest Clarkson, C. & Hall Richardson, J., 1889, *Police!,* Field and Tuer, London

Thirlwall, Thomas, 1817, *A Vindication of the Magistrates Acting in and for the Tower Division,* London

Thompson, R, 1840, *Berger's Edition of the New Police Act: 'An Act for Improving the Metropolitan Police, with notes,* London

Thurston, Gavin, 1967, *The Clerkenwell Riot: The killing of Constable Culley,* Allen and Unwin, London

Toynbee, Arnold, 1884, *Lectures on the Industrial Revolution in England,* Rivington, London

Toynbee, Paget (Ed.), 1925, *The Letters of Horace Walpole,* Clarendon, Oxford

Trevor, Arthur (Viscount Dungannon), 1842, *Remarks on the Present State of Crime; with a brief enquiry into its probable causes,* Shrewsbury

Trollope, Anthony, 1867, 'The Uncontrolled Ruffianism of London, as Measured by the Rule of Thumb', *Saint Paul's Monthly Magazine,* Vol. 1

Wade, John, 1829, *A Treatise on the Police and Crimes of the Metropolis,* London

Wakefield, Edward Gibbon, 1831, *Facts Relating to the Punishment of Death in the Metropolis,* James Ridgway, London.

Wakefield, Edward Gibbon, 1832, *Householders In Danger from the Populace,* Effingham Wilson, London

Walls, Charles, 1832, 'The Schoolmasters Experience in Newgate', *Frasers Magazine,* Vol. V1, pp.521-537.

'Walter', 1996 (c.1870), *My Secret Life,* Vols. III & IV, Wordsworth Classics, Ware

Warren, Charles, 1888, 'Police of the Metropolis', *Murray's Magazine,* Vol.4

Waters, Thomas, 1853, *The Recollections of a Policeman, by an Inspector of the London Detective Corps,* Cornish Lamport and Co., New York

Watts, W.H., 1864, *London Life at The Police-Courts,* Ward and Lock, London

Wilkinson, George, 1991 (1816), *The Newgate Calendar,* Cardinal, London

Williams, Montagu, 1890, *Leaves Of A Life Being The Reminiscences Of Montagu Williams, Q.C.,* The Riverside Press, Cambridge.

Wills, W.H., 1850, 'The Modern Science of Thief-Taking', *Household Words,* Vol. 1

Wontner, Thomas, 1833, *Old Bailey Experience; criminal jurisprudence and the actual working of our penal code of law: also an essay on prison discipline,* London

Worsley, Henry, 1849, *Juvenile Depravity,* Charles Gilpin, London

Contemporary Newspapers and Journals

Bentleys Miscellany
Blackwood's Edinburgh Magazine
Cobbett's Weekly Political Register
East End News
East London Observer
Hansard's Parliamentary Debates
Household Words
Illustrated Police News
Jackson's Oxford Journal
Justice of the Peace
Lloyd's Weekly London Newspaper
Macmillan's Magazine
Murray's Magazine
Penny Illustrated Paper
Police Quarterly Review
Punch
Reynold's Newspaper
The Dark Blue
The Bristol Mercury and Daily Post
The Penny Illustrated Paper and Illustrated Times

The Leeds Mercury
The Daily News
The Dundee Courier & Argus
The Gentleman's Magazine
The Guardian
The Saturday Review
The Illustrated Police News
The Jurist
The Lancet
Launceston Examiner
The Law Journal
The Link
The Manchester Guardian
The Manchester Times and Gazette
The Morning Post
The Morning Chronicle
The National Review
The New York Times
The Original Half-Penny Journal

The Pall Mall Gazette
The Police Gazette; or Hue and Cry
The Poor Man's Guardian
The Standard
The Times
The Watchman and Police Recorder
Western Mail

Contemporary Parliamentary and Private Papers

The assorted provenance of the papers cited is provided below:

pp.1.1755, A Proposal for Regulating the Nightly Watch within the City and Liberty of Westminster, appended to 'Acts of Parliament' 1755.

pp.2.1773, Abstract of the Proposed Act of Parliament for an Effectual and Uniform Watch ... proposed by Sir Charles Whitworth, Appended to 'Acts of Parliament' 1773.

pp.3.1799, Report of the Select Committee Appointed by the House of Commons, Relative to the Establishment of a New Police in the Metropolis & c. Printed by R. Shaw 1800pp.4.1812, Report on the Nightly Watch and Police of the Metropolis, published March 24, House of Commons, Parliamentary Papers 1812, Vol.2

pp.5.1816, Report from the Select Committee on the State of the Police of the Metropolis, with Minutes of Evidence, Parliamentary Papers 1816, Vol.5

pp.6.1816, Report of the Committee for Investigating the Causes of the Alarming Increase of Juvenile Delinquency in the Metropolis, partially reproduced in Tobias, J.J., 1972, *Nineteenth Century Crime*

pp.7.1816, Report of the Committee for Investigating the Causes of the Alarming Increase of Juvenile Delinquency in the Metropolis, published by J.F. Love, St Johns Square, London.

pp.8.1817, Report from the Committee on the State of the Police, ordered by the House of Commons to be printed 8 July, 1817. Parliamentary Papers 1817, Vol.7

pp.8.a.1819. Evidence given to the Select Committee on the State of the Gaols etc., Parliamentary Papers 1819, Vol. 7

pp.9.1822, Report from the Select Committee on the Police of the Metropolis, Parliamentary Papers 1822, Vol.4

pp.10.1828. Report of the Proceedings of the several police offices, January 19th 1828-No.13, held at National Archives under HO/62/1 pp.10.a.1828. Report of the proceedings of the several Police Offices, 31st January 1828-No. 23, held at National Archives under HO/62/1.

pp.10.b.1828, 11th July, Report of the Select Committee on the Police of the Metropolis, Parliamentary Papers 1828, Vol.6

pp.10.c.1832, Report from the Select Committee on Secondary Punishments, House of Commons, June 1832, published by the Society for the Improvement of Prison Discipline, 1833, London.

pp.11.1833, Report from the Select Committee on the Petition of Frederick Young and Others (Police), Ordered by the House of Commons to be Printed on 6th August 1833, Parliamentary Papers 1833, Vol.xiii

pp.11.b.1833, Report from the Select Committee on Cold Bath Fields Meeting, Ordered by the House of Commons to be Printed on 23rd August 1833, Parliamentary Papers 1833, Vol.xiii

pp.11.c.1833, Report from the Select Committee on Metropolitan Police, Parliamentary Papers 1833, Vol.xiii

pp.11.d.1834, Report from the Select Committee on the Police of the Metropolis, 13th August, 1834, Parliamentary Papers 1834, Vol.xvi

pp.11.e.1834, Accounts and Papers Relating to Crime, Vol.xlvii, Correspondence Relating to the Conduct of the Metropolitan Police, on Tuesday 24th June, 1834 (Lord Howick) Ordered by the House of Commons to be Printed July 24th.

pp.12.1838, Report of the Select Committee on the Metropolis' Police Offices; with the Minutes of evidence, House of Commons, 11 July 1838, Parliamentary Papers 1838-9, Vol.15; also summarised *Justice of the Peace,* Vol.II, Saturday August 11th, 1838

pp.12.b.1839, First Report of the Commissioners appointed to inquire as to the Best Means of Establishing an Efficient Constabulary Force in the Counties of England and Wales, Reports from Commissioners, 1839, Vol.xix

pp.13.1852, Report of the Select Committee on Criminal and Destitute Juveniles, Parliamentary Papers 1852, Vol.7

pp.13.b.1853, Return of Officers of the Metropolitan and City Police Charged with Offences before Magistrates in earch Year from 1849 to 1852 Inclusive. Ordered by the House of Commons to be Printed 31st May, 1853.

pp.14.1868, Report of Departmental Committee on the Police, conducted by Sir. James Fergusson, Mr. Henry Thring and Mr. George Everset, following a reference by Mr. Hardy, Secretary of State at the Home Office, published 6th May

pp.15.1878, Report of the Departmental Committee ... into the...Detective
Force of the Metropolitan Police. Confidential Report printed for
H.M.S.O. London (1878) Held at NA HO 45/9442/66692

pp.15.b.1886, Report of a Commission to Inquire and report as to the
Origin and Character of the disturbances which took place in the
Metropolis on Monday, the 8th Feb. and as to the Conduct of the Police
authorities in relation thereto, Parliamentary Papers 1886, Vol. xxxiv

pp.16.1888, Warren's Report to the Home Office, dated June 11th, New
Scotland Yard Library

pp.17.1982, The Scarman Report, Leslie Scarman.

Police Records and Reports

Extensive use has been made of the MEPO sequence of records at the
National Archives; for example, MEPO 1(30), Correspondence of the
Commissioners, MEPO 7(2) Police Orders 1829-1833, MEPO 4(6)
Complaints against Police, MEPO 7(15), Police Orders 1850-52 and many
others. The Home Office Papers have also been useful, and can be found
under various HO listings, especially HO 61 and 62.

For London, a particularly valuable, source of statistical information
can be found in the annually produced Metropolitan Police returns for
Crime (today kept in the Library of New Scotland Yard, the British Library
and the National Archives). They grew in size from six tables in 1831
(when first drawn up), to 22 in 1848, before declining slightly towards the
end of the century. They must, of course, be used with caution as major
changes in their composition and the extent of the London area policed by
the Metropolitan force have to be 'factored in' and, of course, they do not
include statistics for the small City Force. However, they are extremely
informative. From the beginning, they recorded details of the number of
arrests and the offences for which people were detained, as well as their
subsequent disposals at court. As time progressed, more information was
recorded: sentencing, the defendants' previous characters, the number and
cost of reported felonies, the levels of education of those arrested and
convicted, even the number of suicides prevented. As a result, they have
been described as one of the best and most consistent sources for studying
the history of urban crime: Jones, David, 'Crime in London: The Evidence
of the Metropolitan Police, 1831-92', *in Crime Protest, Community and
Police in Nineteenth-Century Britain*, 1982, at p.117. They are cited
extensively, along with other papers, with the prefix PR.

PR.1.1813, *The Newgate Calendar of Prisoners* for Wednesday September 15th, 1813 [cases coming before the London Grand Jury] held at NA HO 77/20

PR.2.1828, January 31, Report of the proceedings of the several Police Offices, held at NA under HO/62/1

PR.3.1828, *The Police Gazette; or, Hue and Cry*, held at NA HO/75/1 Published 'Under Authority' October 14, 1828

PR.4.1833, *Newgate Calendar of Prisoners,* 11th April, at NA HO 77/40

PR.5.1844, A Police Constabulary List for the Quarter Ending September 1844, Police History Society, Monograph Number 3, 1991

PR.6.1859, Metropolitan Police Returns, Table No.2, Table No.5 Convicted and Sentenced, Acquitted, Bills Not Found, or not Prosecuted, Table No.8.

PR.7. Analysis of the Receipts and Expenditure of the Metropolitan Police from the Year 1829 to 1885.

PR.8.1863 Confidential Memorandum by Richard Mayne to Sir George Grey dated June 1st, 1863, held at New Scotland Yard Library

PR.9.1872, Metropolitan Police Reports, 1869-1876, Report for the Year 1872, Divisional Report, Printed by Eyre and Spottiswoode, 1873, held at the Metropolitan Police History Museum

PR.10.1874, Criminal Returns: Metropolitan Police 1874-table No.19, table No.22

PR.11.1875, Criminal Returns: Metropolitan Police 1875 - Table No.6

PR.12.1875, Metropolitan Police Reports, 1869-1876, Report of the Commissioner of Police of the Metropolis for the Year 1875, Printed by Eyre and Spottiswoode, 1876, held at the Metropolitan Police History Museum

PR.13.1878, Report of the Departmental Committee ... into the ... Detective Force of the Metropolitan Police. Confidential Report printed for H.M.S.O., London, Held at NA HO 45/9442/66692

PR.14.1886, A Report on the history of the Department of the Metropolitan Police known as the Convict Supervision Office: Detailing System, and showing results and effects generally on the Habitual criminal Population. Prepared and issued by James Monro, Assistant Commissioner of metropolitan Police, London, 1886

PR.16.1887-1888, Central Criminal Court Sessions Papers, 2nd session 1887-1888, Sessions beginning December 12th 1887, Stevens and Sons, London

PR.17.1893, Habitual Criminal Register for 1892, printed at Parkhurst Prison 1893; held at NA at MEPO 6/4

PR.18.1996, Metropolitan Police Committee 2nd Annual Report 1996/97, paragraph 6

Modern Secondary Sources

Armstrong, Alan, 1966, The Economic and Social Roots of Poverty, *The Victorian Poor: Fourth Conference Report of the Victorian Society*

Ascoli, David, 1979, *The Queen's Peace: The Origins and Development of the Metropolitan Police 1829-1979,* H. Hamilton, London

Bailey, Victor, 1981, *Policing and Punishment in Nineteenth century Britain*, Croom Helm, London

Barrie, David, 2010, 'A typology of British police: locating the Scottish municipal police model in its British context, 1800-35', Vol. 50, No. 2, *British Journal of Criminology*, pp.259-277.

Barrett, A., and Harrison, C., 1999, *Crime and Punishment in England: A Sourcebook,* UCL Press, London

Ballhatchet, Joan, 1991, The Police and the London Dock Strike, *History Workshop Journal*, Vol. 32, Issue 1, pp.54-68.

Beattie, J.M., 1986, *Crime and the Courts in England, 1660-1800*, Clarendon, Oxford

Bentley, David, 1998, *English Criminal Justice in the Nineteenth Century*, Hambledon Press, London

Bédarida, François, 1991, *A Social History of England, 1851-1990,* Routledge, London

Best, C.F., 1985, *C at St. James: A History of Policing in the West End of London 1839-1984,* Privately Published, Kingston on Thames

Blanc, Louis, 1862, *Letters on England,* Sampson Low & Co., London,

Boothman, John V., 1985, 'Facing the Music: Modern Police Discipline and Primitive Police Discipline 1829-1879 (Part 2)', *Liverpool Law Review* Vol.7, No. 1.

Bratton, William J., 2011, 'Reducing Crime Through Prevention Not Incarceration', *Criminology and Public Policy*. Vol.10 (1), pp.38-63.

Briggs, J., et al., 1996, *Crime and Punishment in England: An Introductory History*, UCL press, London

Brogden, A. & Brogden, M., 1984, 'Henry III to Liverpool 8: The Unity of Police Street Powers', *International Journal of the Sociology of Law*, No. 12,

Brogden, Michael, 1991, *On the Mersey Beat: Policing Liverpool Between the Wars*, C.U.P., Cambridge

Bunker, John, 1988, *From Rattle to Radio: A History of Metropolitan Police Communication,* Brewin Books, Studley

Chesney, Kellow, 1970, *The Victorian Underworld*, Penguin, Harmondsworth

Childs, Horatio, 1903, *"Police Duty" Catechism And Reports By H. Childs*, 5th Edition, London

Clarke, R. & Hough, M., 1984, *Crime and Police Effectiveness: Home Office research Study No.79*, H.M.S.O., London

Cohen, Phil, 1981, 'Policing the Working Class City', reproduced in Fitzgerald M. et al (Eds.), *Crime and Society*, Routledge, London

Coleman, B.I., (Ed.), 1973, *The Idea of the City in Nineteenth Century Britain,* Routledge & Kegan Paul, London

Collins, Philip, 1994, *Dickens and Crime*, 3rd edn., Macmillan, Basingstoke

Cox, D. J., 2010, *A Certain Share of Low Cunning: A History of the Bow Street Runners, 1792-1839*, Willan Publishing, Cullompton.

Cox, David, 2011, 'The Wolves let loose at Wolverhampton': A study of the South Staffordshire Election 'Riots', May 1835', *Law, Crime and History,* Vol. 1, issue 2, pp.1-31,

Davin, Anna, 1996, *Growing Up Poor: Home, School and Street in London 1870-1914,* Rivers Oram Press, London

Davis, Jennifer, 1980, 'London Garotting Panic of 1862', in V.A.C. Gatrell et al., *Crime and the Law*, Europa, London

—. 1984, 'A Poor Man's System of Justice: The London Police Courts in the Second Half of the Nineteenth Century', *Historical Journal*, Vol. 27, No. 2, pp.309-335.

—. 1989, 'Jennings' Buildings and the Royal Borough', in *Metropolis London*, Gareth Stedman Jones et al. (Eds.), Routledge, London

—. 1989b, 'Prosecutions and Their Context: The Use of the Criminal Law in Later Nineteenth Century London', in *Policing and Prosecution in Britain 1750-1850*, Hay, D. et al, Clarendon, Oxford.

Durlauf, S. N. & Nagin, D. S., 2011, 'Imprisonment and crime: Can both be reduced?', in *Crime and Public Policy*, Vol. 10(1), pp.13-54.

Dyos, H. J., 1966, 'The Making and Unmaking of Slums: The Economic and Social Roots of Victorian poverty', in *The Victorian Poor: Fourth Conference Report of the Victorian Society,*

Eisner, Manuel, 2003, 'Long-Term Historical Trends in Violent Crime', *Crime & Justice*, Vol. 30, pp.83-142.

—. 2008, 'Modernity Strikes Back? A Historical Perspective on the Latest Increase in Interpersonal Violence (1960–1990')', *International Journal of Conflict and Violence*, Vol. 2 (2), pp. 288 – 316.

Elliott, Bryn, 2001, *Peelers Progress: Policing Waltham Abbey since 1840*, privately published.

Emmerichs, Mary Beth, 2001, 'Getting Away with Murder? Homicide and the Coroners in Nineteenth-Century London', *Social Science History*, Vol. 25, No. 1, pp.93-100.

Emsley, Clive, 1985, 'The Thump of Wood on a Swede Turnip: Police Violence in Nineteenth Century England', *Criminal Justice History,* Vol. 6, pp.125-149.

—. 1987, 'Policing The Streets Of Early Nineteenth-Century Paris', *French History,* Vol. 1(2), pp.257-282.

—. 1987, *Crime and Society in England 1750-1900*, Longmans, London

—. 1988, 'The Criminal Past, Crime in 19th Century Britain', *History Today,* Vol. 28(4)

—. 1991, *The English Police, A Political and Social History,* Harvester/Wheatsheaf, London

—. 1996, *The English Police: A Political and Social History,* 2nd edn., Longmans, London

—. 1996b, *Crime and Society in England, 1750-1900,* 2nd. edn., Longmans, London

—. 2010, *The Great British Bobby: A History of British Policing from 1829 to the Present,* Quercus, London.

Emsley, Clive and Shpayer-Makov, Haia (eds.), 2006, *Police Detectives in History 1750-1950,* Ashgate, Aldershot.

Englander, D. & O'Day, R., 1995, *Retrieved Riches: Social Investigation in Britain 1840-1914*, Scolar Press, Sussex

Evans, Alan 1988, *Victorian Law and Order,* Batsford, London

Evans, Eric J., 1983, *The Forging of the Modern State, 1783-1870,* Longmans, London

Feeley, Malcolm, 1994, The Decline of Women in the Criminal Process: A Comparative History, *Criminal Justice History*, Vol. 15, p.235.

Feeley, Malcolm, & Little, Deborah, 1991, 'The Vanishing Female: The Decline of Women in the Criminal Process, 1687-1912', *Law and Society Review*, Vol. 25, p.719.

Fido, M. & Skinner, K., 1999, *The Official Encyclopaedia of Scotland Yard,* Virgin Publishing, London

Fisher, Trevor, 1996, 'Josephine Butler: Feminism's Neglected Pioneer', *History Today*, Vol. 46 (6) pp.32-38.

Fishman, William, 1988, *East End 1888,* Duckworth, London

Foucault, Michel, 1979, *Discipline and Punish: The Birth of the Prison*, Penguin, Harmondsworth

Garland, David, 1987, *Punishment and Welfare: A History of Penal Strategies*, Gower, Aldershot

Gash, Norman, 1985, *Mr Secretary Peel: The Life of Sir Robert Peel to 1830,* Longman, London

Gatrell, V.A.C., 1980, Theft and Violence in England 1834-1914, in *Crime and the Law,* Europa, London

—. 1990, 'Crime, authority and the policeman-state', in *Cambridge Social History Britain 1750-1950,* Vol. 3, Thompson, F.M.L. (Ed.), C.U.P., Cambridge

—. 1994, *The Hanging Tree,* Oxford University Press, Oxford

Gatrell, V.A.C. & Haddon, T.B., 1972, 'Criminal Statistics and their Interpretation', in *Nineteenth Century Society,* Rigley, E.A., (Ed.), Cambridge University Press, Cambridge

Gatrell, V.A.C. et al. (Eds), 1980, *Crime and the Law,* Europa, London

Gillis, J.R., 1975, 'The Evolution of Juvenile Delinquency in England 1890-1914', *Past and Present,* No. 67, pp.96-126.

Gilmour, Ian,   1998, *Riot Rising and Revolution: Governance and Violence in Eighteenth Century England,* Pimlico, London

Godfrey, Barry, 2008, 'Changing Prosecution Practices and their Impact on Crime Figures, 1857–1940', *British Journal of Criminology,* Vol. 48 (2), pp.171-189.

Goldkamp, John, 2011, 'Optimistic deterrence theorizing', *Criminology & Public Policy,* Vol. 10, Issue 1, pp.115-122.

Graff, H.J., 1992, 'Crime and Punishment in the Nineteenth Century', *Theory and Methods in Criminal Justice History,* Monkonen E. (ed), Saur, K.G. Verlag Gmbh & Company

Greenstone, J. David, 1991, 'Culture, Rationality, and the Underclass', *The Urban Underclass,* C. Jencks & P. Peterson (eds), Brookings Institution

Gurr, T., 1981, Contemporary Crime in Perspective, *Readings in Comparative Criminology,* Ed. L. Shelley, Southern Illinois University Press, Carbondale

Haggard, Robert F., 1993, 'Jack the Ripper as the Threat of Outcast London, *Essays in History,* University of Virginia, Vol. 35, p.1.

Haley, Bruce, 1978, *The Healthy Body and Victorian Culture,* Harvard University Press, Cambridge, Massachusetts

Hammersley, H., and Atkinson, P., 1995, *Ethnography: Principles in Practice,* 2nd. Edition, Routledge, London

Harding, C. & Wilson, L., 1988, 'The Late Victorian Response to the Problem of Inebriety', *Criminal Justice History,* Vol. 9, pp.196-199.

Hardy, Anne, 1988, 'Urban Famine or Urban Crisis? Typhus in the Victorian City', *Medical History,* No. 32, pp.401-425.

Harris, Andrew T., 2004, Policing the City: Crime and Legal Authority in London, 1780-1840, Ohio State University Press, Columbus.

Harris, Jose, 1993, *Private Lives, Public Spirit: Britain 1870-1914,* Penguin, Harmondsworth

Harrison, Brian, 1994, *Drink and the Victorians: The Temperence Question in England 1852-1872,* 2nd. edn., Keele University Press, Keele

Harrison, J.F.C., 1988, *Early Victorian Britain, 1832-1851*, Fontana Press, London

—. 1998, *Late Victorian Britain, 1875-1901,* Routledge, London

Hay, Douglas, 1980, 'Crime and Justice in Eighteenth and Nineteenth Century England', *Crime and Justice, an Annual Review of Research*, Vol. 2, pp.45-84.

Hay, D., and Snyder, R., (Eds.), 1989, *Policing and Prosecution in Britain 1750-1850,* Clarendon, Oxford

Heidensohn, Frances, 1994, 'Gender and Crime', in *Oxford Handbook of Criminology*, Oxford University Press, Oxford

Himmelfarb, Gertrude, 1984, *The Idea of Poverty: England in the Early Industrial Age,* Faber and Faber, London

—. 1994, 'A De-Moralized Society: The British/American Experience', *The Public Interest,* September 22, No.57

—. 1995, *The De-Moralization of Society: From Victorian Virtues to Modern Values*, Institute of Economic Affairs, London

—. 1995, 'The Value of Victorian Virtues', *Sunday Times,* April 16, 1995

Hobsbaum, E.J., 1969, *Industry and Empire, Economic History of Britain,* Penguin, Harmondsworth

Hostettler, John, 1992, *The Politics of Criminal Law Reform in the Nineteenth century*, Barry Rose Law Publishing, Chichester

Hough, Mike, 1987, 'Thinking about Police Effectiveness', *British Journal of Criminology*, Vol.27, No.1,

Ignatieff, Michael, 1978, *A Just Measure of Pain: The penitentiary in the Industrial Revolution,* MacMillan, London

—. 1979, Police and people: the birth of Mr Peel's 'blue locusts', *New Society*, 30th August 1979, at pp.443-445.

Inwood, Stephen, 1990, 'Policing London's Morals: The Metropolitan Police and Popular Culture 1829-1850', *The London Journal,* Vol.15, pp. 129-146.

James, P.D., and Critchley, T.A., 1971, *The Maul and the Pear Tree,* Constable, London

Johansen, Anja, 2011, 'Keeping up appearances: Police Rhetoric, Public Trust and "Police Scandal" in London and Berlin, 1880-1914', in *Crime, History & Societies*, Vol. 15, No. 2, pp.59-83.

—. 2009, 'Complain in vain? The development of a 'police complaints culture' in Wilhelmine Berlin', in *Crime, History & Societies*, Vol. 13, No. 2, pp.119-142.

Jones, David, 1982, *Crime, Protest, Community and Police in Nineteenth Century Britain,* Routledge Kegan Paul, London

—. 1983, 'The New Police, crime and people in England and Wales, 1829-1888', *Transactions of the Royal Historical Society,* Vol. XXXiii, 5th Series, pp.151-168.

Jones, Gareth Stedman, 1976, *Outcast London: A study in the relationship Between Classes in Victorian Society.* Penguin, Harmondsworth

Kayman, Martin, 1992, *From Bow Street to Baker Street: mystery, detection and narrative*, MacMillan Press, Basingstoke

King, Peter, 1996, "Punishing Assault: The Transformation of Attitudes in the English Courts", *Journal of Interdisciplinary History*, Vol. 27, pp. 43-74.

—. 1998, The Rise of Juvenile Delinquency in England 1780-1840: Changing Patterns of Perception and Prosecution, *Past and Present,* No.160, pp.116-166.

—. 2010, 'The Impact Of Urbanization On Murder Rates And The Geography Of Homicide In England And Wales, 1780–1850', *The Historical Journal*, Vol. 53(3), pp.671-698.

King, P. & Noel, J., 1993, 'The Origins of the 'Problem of Juvenile Delinquency': The Growth of Juvenile Prosecutions in London in the Late Eighteenth and Early Nineteenth Centuries', *Criminal Justice History*, Vol.14

Lea, John & Young, Jock, 1984, *What is to be done about Law and Order?*, Pluto Pubs., London

Lyman, J.L., 1964, 'The Metropolitan Police Act of 1829: An Analysis of Certain Events Influencing the Passage and Character of the Metropolitan Police Act in England', *The Journal of Criminal Law and Criminology,* Vol.55, No.1, pp.141-154.

Linebaugh, Peter, 1998, *The London Hanged: Crime and Civil Society in the 18th Century*, Penguin, Harmondsworth.

Maguire, M. et al (Eds.) 1994, *The Oxford Handbook of Criminology*, Clarendon, Oxford.

Magarey, S., 1978, 'The Invention of Juvenile Delinquency in Early Nineteenth century England', *Labour History* (Australia), Vol.34, pp.11-27.

McKibbin, R., 1979, 'Working Class Gambling in Britain, 1880-1939', *Past and Present*, No.82, pp.147-178.

MacNicol, John, 1987, 'In Pursuit of the Underclass', *Journal of Social Policy*, Vol. 16, No. 3, pp. 293-318.

McWilliams, W, 1988, 'The Mission to the English Police Courts 1876-1936', *Howard Journal,* Vol.XXII, pp.129-147.

Mason, Michael, 1994, *The Making of Victorian Sexual Attitudes,* Oxford University Press, Oxford

—. 1998, *The Making of Victorian Sexuality,* Oxford University Press, Oxford

Mathews, Roger, 1992, Replacing Broken Windows, in *Issues in Realist Criminology*, Mathews, R., and Young J., (Eds.), Sage.

Melling, Michael, 1983, 'Cleaning house in a Suddenly Closed Society: The Genesis, Brief Life and Untimely Death of the Habitual Criminals Act', *Osgoode Hall Law Journal*, Vol. 21, No. 2.

Manchester, A.H., 1984, *Sources of English Legal History*, 1750-1950, Butterworths, London.

Maxim, P.S., 1989, An Ecological Analysis of Crime in Early Victorian England, *Howard Journal,* Vol.28, No.1, Feb. 1989

Miller, William W., 1987, Party Politics, Class Interest and Reform of the Police 1829-56, *Police Studies,* Vol.10

Miller, Wilbur, 1975, 'Police Authority in London and New York City 1830-1870'; *Journal of Social History*, Vol. 8.

—. 1997, *Cops and Bobbies: Police Authority in New York and London,* 2nd edn., Ohio State University Press, Columbus

Mogg, Edward, 1844, *Mogg's New Picture of London and Visitor's Guide to its Sights,* London

Monro, James, 1890, 'The Story of Police Pensions', *The New Review*, No. 16, pp.194-207

Morgan, R. & Newburn, T., 1997, *The Future of Policing*, Clarendon, Oxford

Morris, R. M., 2006, ''Crime does not pay': Thinking again about detectives in the first century of the Metropolitan police', in Emsley, Clive and Shpayer-Makov, Haia (eds.), *Police Detectives in History 1750-1950,* Ashgate, Aldershot, pp.79–102.

Morris, N. & Hawkins, G., 1970, *The Honest Politician's Guide to Crime Control,* University of Chicago Press, Chicago

Morris, R.J. & Rodger, R., 1993, *The Victorian City: A Reader in British Urban History,* Longmans, London

Morris, R. M., 2006, ''Crime does not pay': Thinking again about detectives in the first century of the Metropolitan police', at pp. 79–102, in Emsley, Clive and Shpayer-Makov, Haia (eds.), *Police Detectives in History 1750-1950,* Ashgate, Aldershot,

Paley, Ruth, 1989, 'An Imperfect, Inadequate, and Wretched System? Policing London before Peel', *Criminal Justice History, an International Annual,* Vol. X, pp.95-130.

Parkin, Harold, 1969, *Origins of Modern English Society,* Routledge and Kegan Paul, London

Payne, Christopher, 2011, *The Chieftain: Victorian True Crime through the Eyes of a Scotland Yard Detective,* The History Press, Stroud.

Pearson, Geoffrey, 1983, *Hooligan: A History of Respectable Fears,* Macmillan, London.

Pellew, Jill, 1982, *The Home Office 1848-1914,* Heinneman, London

Petrow, Stefan, 1992, 'The Legal Enforcement of Morality in Late - Victorian and Edwardian England', *University of Tasmania Law Review,* Vol. 11(1), pp.59-74.

—. 1993, 'The Rise of the Detective in London, 1869-1914', *Criminal Justice History,* Vol. 14, pp.91-108.

—. 1994, *Policing Morals, The Metropolitan Police and the Home Office, 1857-1914,* Clarendon, Oxford

Philips, David, 1980, 'A New Engine of Power and Authority: the Institutionalization of Law-enforcement in England 1780-1830', in Gatrell, V.A.C., et al, *Crime and the Law,* Europa, London

—. 1977, *Crime and Authority in Victorian England,* Croom Helm, London

Porter, Bernard, 1988, *The Origins of the Vigilant State,* Weidenfeld & Nicholson, London

Priestley, Philip, 1985, *Victorian Prison Lives: English Prison Biography 1830-1914,* Methuen, London

Radzinowicz, Leon, 1948-56, *A History of English Criminal Law, and Its Administration from 1750,* Vols. 1-4, Stevens, London

—. 1956, 'The Ratcliffe Murders', *The Cambridge Law Journal,* Vol. 14, No.1, pp.39-66.

Radzinowicz, Leon, with Hood, Roger, 1976, *A History of English Criminal Law,* Vol. 5, *The Emergence of Penal Policy,* Stevens, London

Rawlings, Philip, 1992, *Drunks, Whores and Idle Apprentices: Criminal Biography of the Eighteenth-Century,* Routledge, London

—. 1999, *Crime and Power: A History of Criminal Justice 1688-1998,* Longmans, London.

Razzell, P. E. & Wainright, R., (eds.), 1973, *The Victorian Working Class: Selections from the Morning Chronicle,* Frank Cass, London

Reiner, Robert, 1992, *The Politics of the Police,* 2nd edn., Harvester Wheatsheaf, London

—. 1992 b, 'Policing a Postmodern Society', *Modern Law Review,* Vol.55, No. 6, pp.761-781.

—. 1994, 'Policing and the Police', in *The Oxford Handbook of Criminology*, Oxford University Press, Oxford

Reith, Charles, 1948, *A Short History of the British Police*, O.U.P., Oxford.

Reynolds, Elaine, 1989, 'St. Marylebone: Local Government Police Reform in London, 1755-1829', *The Historian,* Vol. 51, No. 3, pp.446-466.

—. 1998, *Before the Bobbies: The Night Watch and Police Reform in Metropolitan London, 1720-1830*, Stanford University Press, Stanford

Richter, Donald C., 1981, *Riotous Victorians*, Ohio University Press, London,

Rigley, E.A., (Ed.) 1972, *Nineteenth Century Society*, Cambridge University Press, Cambridge

Robb, George, 2002, *White-Collar Crime in Modern England: Financial Fraud and Business Morality, 1845-1929*, CUP, Cambridge.

Roberts, M.J.D., 1988, 'Public and Private Charity in Early Nineteenth Century London: the Vagrant Act of 1822 and its Enforcement', *Social History,* Vol.xiii, pp.273-294.

Roberts, R., 1973, *Classic Slum*, Penguin, Harmondsworth

Robinson, Cyril D., 1979, 'Ideology as History: A Look at the Way Some English Police Historians Look at the Police', *Police Studies,* Vol.2, p.35

Roebuck, Janet, 1979, *Urban Development in Nineteenth Century London,* Phillimore Press, Chichester

Rose, Michael E., 1986, 'The Relief of Poverty', *Studies in Economic and Social History,* 2nd edn., Macmillan, London

Rudé, George, 1985, *Criminal and Victim,* Clarendon, Oxford

Samuel, Raphael, 1981, *East End Underworld, Chapters in the Life of Arthur Harding,* Routledge & Kegan Paul, London

Sante, Luc, 1998, *Low Life,* Granta Books, London

Shannon, Richard, 1976, *The Crisis of Imperialism 1865 to 1915,* Paladin, St. Albans

Shand, Alexander Innes, 1886, 'The City of London Police', *Blackwoods Magazine*, pp.594-608.

Sharpe, J.A., 1985, 'The History of Violence in England; Some Observations', in *Past and Present,* Vol.10, No. 108, pp.206-215.

Sheppard, Francis 1971, *London 1808-1870: the Infernel Wen,* Secker and Warburg, London

Sherman, Lawrence W., 1992, 'Attacking Crime: Police and Crime Control', in *Modern Policing: Crime and Justice,* M. Tonry and N. Morris (Eds), University of Chicago Press, Chicago

Shoemaker, Robert, 1991, *Prosecution and Punishment, Petty crime and the law in London and rural Middlesex, c.1660-1725,* C.U.P., Cambridge

Shore, Heather, 1997, "An old offender tho' so young in years': The Criminal Careers of Juvenile Offenders in Middlesex in the 1830s', in *Chronicling Poverty: The Voices And Strategies of the English Poor, 1640-1840,* Hitchcock, T., et al (eds.), Macmillan, Basingstoke

—. 1999, *Artful Dodgers: Youth and Crime in Early Nineteenth-Century London,* Boydell Press, Woodbridge

Shpayer-Makov, Haia, 2002, *The Making Of A Policeman: A Social History Of A Labour Force In Metropolitan London, 1829-1914,* Ashgate, Aldershot.

—. 2004, 'Becoming a Police Detective in Victorian and Edwardian London', *Policing and Society,* Vol. 14, No. 3, pp.250-268.

—. 2009, 'Journalists and Police Detectives in Victorian and Edwardian England: An Uneasy Reciprocal Relationship', *Journal of Social History,* Vol. 42, No. 4, pp.963-987

—. 2011, *The Ascent of the Detective: Police Sleuths in Victorian and Edwardian England,* O.U.P., Oxford.

—. 2011, 'Revisiting The Detective Figure In Late Victorian And Edwardian Fiction: A View From The Perspective Of Police History', *Law Crime And History,* Vol. 1, Issue 2, pp.165-193.

Sindall, Robert S., 1990, *Street Violence in the Nineteenth Century: Media Panic or Real danger?,* Leicester University Press, Leicester

—. 1983, 'Middle-Class Crime in Nineteenth Century England', *Criminal Justice History,* Vol. 4

—. 1987, 'The London Garotting Panics of 1856 and 1862', *Social History,* Vol. 12, No. 3, pp. 351-359.

Smith, Bruce P., 2005, 'The Presumption of Guilt and the English Law of Theft, 1750-1850', *Law and History Review,* Vol. 23, No. 1, pp. 133-171.

Smith, Keith, 2007, *Stumbling towards Professionalism: A post-revisionist overview of the establishment of English policing in the nineteenth century,* Cardiff Law School Research Papers, No: 3, Cardiff University.

Smith, Phillip Thurmond, 1985, *Policing Victorian London,* Greenwood Press, Westport.

Springall, John, 1994, 'Pernicious Reading? The Penny Dreadful as Scapegoat for Late-Victorian Juvenile crime', *Victorian Periodicals Review*, No.27, No.4, pp.326-349.

Stack, John, 1992, 'Children, Urbanisation and The Chances of Imprisonment in Mid-Victorian England', *Criminal Justice History,* Vol.13, pp.113-139.

Stevenson, S. J., 1986, 'The 'habitual criminal' in nineteenth-century England: some observations on the figures', *Urban History Yearbook*, Vol.13, pp.37-60.

Stone, Lawrence, 1983, 'Interpersonal Violence in English Society 1300-1980', *Past and Present,* No.101, pp. 22-33.

Storch, Robert, 1975, 'The Plague of the Blue Locusts: Police Reform and popular Resistance in Northern England, 1840-57', *International Revue of Social History,* Vol. 20, pp.61-90.

—. 1976, 'The Policeman as Domestic Missionary: Urban Discipline and Popular Culture in Northern England 1850-90', *Journal of Social History,* Vol.9, No. 4, pp. 481-509.

Styles, John, 1987, 'The Emergence of the Police: Explaining Police Reform in Eighteenth and Nineteenth Century England', *British Journal of Criminology,* Vol.27, No.1, pp.15-22.

Sugden, Philip, 1995, *The Complete History of Jack the Ripper,* Robinson press, London

Summerscale, Kate, 2008, *The Suspicions of Mr. Whicher: A Shocking Murder and the Undoing of a Great Victorian Detective,* Bloomsbury, London.

Swift, Roger, 1987, 'The Outcast Irish in the British Victorian city: Problems and Perspectives', *Irish Historical Studies*, Vol.XXV, No. 99, pp. 264-276

Taylor, David, 1997, *The New Police in Nineteenth Century England*, Manchester University Press, Manchester

—. 2004, 'Conquering the British Ballarat: The Policing of Victorian Middlesbrough', *Journal of Social History*, Vol. 37 (3), pp. 755-771.

Taylor, Howard, 1999, 'Forging the Job: A Crisis of 'Modernisation' or Redundancy for the Police in England and Wales 1900-1939', *British Journal of Criminology*, Vol.39, No.1, pp.113-135.

Thomas, Donald, 1998, *The Victorian Underworld,* John Murray, London

Thompson, F.M.L., 1988, *The Rise of Respectable Society,* Fontana Press, London

Thompson, E.P., 1973, *The Unknown Mayhew*, Penguin, Harmondsworth

Thompson, P., 1973, 'Voices from Within', in *The Victorian City, Images and Realities*, Vol. 1, H.J . Dyos and M. Wolff (eds.), Routedge and Kegan Paul, London

Smith, Phillip Thurmond, 1988, *Policing Victorian London*, Greenwood Press, Westport

Tobias, J.J., 1966, 'The Criminal Poor: The Making and Unmaking of Slums: The Economic and Social Roots of Victorian Poverty', in *The Victorian Poor: Fourth Conference Report of the Victorian Society*,

—. 1967, *Crime and Industrial society in the Nineteenth Century*, Batsworth, London

—. 1972, *Crime and Industrial Society in the Nineteenth Century*, Penguin, Harmondsworth

—. 1972, *Urban Crime in Victorian England*, Schocken Books, New York (American re-edition of above)

—. 1972, *Nineteenth Century Crime: Prevention and Punishment*, David & Charles, Newton Abbot

—. 1974, *Prince of Fences,* Valentine Mitchell, London

—. 1974, 'A Statistical Study of a Nineteenth-Century Criminal Area', *British Journal of Criminology*, Vol.14(3), pp. 221-235.

Tomes, Nancy, 1978, 'A Torrent of Abuse: Crimes of Violence Between Working-Class Men and Women in London 1840-1875', *Journal of Social History,* Vol.11, No.3, pp. 328-345.

Uglow, Steve, 1988, *Policing Liberal Society,* Oxford University Press, Oxford

Vigar-Harris, Henry, 1885, *London at Midnight,* The General Publishing Company, London

Vogler, Richard, 1991, *Reading the Riot Act: The Magistracy, the Police and the Army in Civil Disorder*, Open University Press, Milton Keynes

—. 1977, 'Vagrancy and the New Poor Law in late-Victorian and Edwardian England', *English Historical Review*, Vol. 59, pp. 59-81.

—. 2000, 'Rational Recreation" and the Law: The Transformation of Popular Urban Leisure in Victorian England', *McGill Law Journal* Vol. 45, at p.910.

Waddington, P.A.J., 1991, *The Strong Arm of the Law: Armed and Public Order Policing,* Clarendon Press, Oxford

Walker, Alan, 1990, Blaming the Victims, Chapter 4, in *The Emerging British Underclass*, Institute of Economic Affairs Health and Welfare Unit, London

Walkovitz, J.R., 1992, *City of Dreadful Delight*, Virago, London

Waller, P.J. 1983, *Town, City and Nation, England 1850-1964,* Clarendon Press, Oxford

Walton, J.K. & Wilcox, A. (Eds.), 1991, *Low Life and Moral Improvement in Mid-Victorian England: Liverpool through the Journalism of Hugh Shimmin*, Leicester University Press, Leicester

Weaver, Michael, 1994, 'Science of Policing: Crime and the Birmingham Police Force, 1839-1842', *Albion: A Quarterly Journal Concerned with British Studies*, Vol. 26, No. 2, pp. 289-308.

Weinberger, Barbara, 1996, *The Best Police in the World: An Oral History of English Policing*, Scolar Press, Aldershot

Wiener, Martin J., 1990, *Reconstructing the Criminal, Culture More and Policy in England 1830-1914,* Cambridge University Press, Cambridge

—. 2004, *Men of Blood: Violence, Manliness and Criminal Justice in Victorian England,* Cambridge University Press, Cambridge

Welsby, Paul (Ed.), 1970, *Sermons and Society*, Penguin, Harmondsworth

White, Jerry, 1980, *Rothschild Buildings*, Routledge & Kegan Paul, London

—. 1986, *Campbell Bunk; Islington Between the wars*, Routledge & Kegan Paul, London

—. 2008, *London in the 19ᵗʰ Century*, Vintage Books, London.

Wohl, A.S., 1977, *The Eternal Slum: Housing and Social Policy in Victorian London*, Edward Arnold Publishers, London

Wilkes, John, 1977, *The London Police in the Nineteenth Century,* Cambridge University Press, Cambridge

Williams, Glanville, 1983, *Textbook of Criminal Law*, 2nd edn., Stevens, London

Wilson, James Q., 1994, 'Penalties and Opportunities', in *A Reader on Punishment*, Duff, A., and Garland, D., (eds.), Oxford University Press, Oxford

Wilson, James Q., & Kelling, George L., 1982, 'Broken Windows: the Police and Neighbourhood Safety', *The Atlantic Monthly,* Vol. 249(3), pp. 29-38.

Young, Jock, 1994, 'Recent Paradigms in Criminology', in Maguire, M. et al, *The Oxford Handbook of Criminology*, Clarendon, Oxford

Zedner, Lucia, 1991, 'Women, Crime, and Penal Responses: A Historical Account', in Tonry, Michael (ed.), *Crime and Justice; A Review of Research,* Vol. 14.

Zedner, Lucia, 1991, *Women, Crime and Custody in Victorian England,* Clarendon, Oxford

INDEX

References to illustrations are shown with the page number in bold. References to footnotes consist of the page number followed by the letter 'n' followed by the number of the footnote, e.g. 69n113 refers to footnote no.113 on page 69.